Struggles for Supremacy

Struggles for Supremacy

Diplomatic Essays by A.J.P. Taylor

Edited and introduced by

CHRIS WRIGLEY

Ashgate

Aldershot • Burlington USA • Singapore • Sydney

Published by
Ashgate Publishing Limited
Gower House
Croft Road
Aldershot
Hants GU11 3HR
England

Ashgate Publishing Company
131 Main Street
Burlington
Vermont 05401–5600
USA

Ashgate website: http://www.ashgate.com

British Library Cataloguing in Publication Data

Taylor, A.J.P. (Alan John Percivale, 1906–90)
    Struggles for Supremacy: Diplomatic Essays by A.J.P. Taylor.
    1. Europe—History—1789–1900.   2. Europe—History—20th
    century.   3. Europe—Politics and government—1789–1900.
    4. Europe—Politics and government—20th century.
    I. Title.   II. Wrigley, Chris.
    940

Library of Congress Cataloging-in-Publication Data

Struggles for supremacy: diplomatic essays by A.J.P. Taylor/edited and
    introduced by Chris Wrigley.
        p.   cm.
    Includes index.
    ISBN 1-84014-661-3 (hc.: alk. paper)
    1. World politics—20th century.   2. World politics—19th century.
    3. Taylor, A.J.P. (Alan John Percivale), 1906–90.   4. Historians—
    Great Britain—Biography.   I. Wrigley, Chris.
    D443.W75   1999
                                                                99–45934

ISBN 1 84014 661 3

This book is printed on acid free paper

Typeset in Sabon by Manton Typesetters, Louth, Lincolnshire, UK
Printed and bound in Great Britain by MPG Books Ltd, Bodmin, Cornwall

Contents

Introduction   1

Part I   Nineteenth Century

1   A World Restored, 1812–22   17
2   The Crimean War: A Triumph of Muddle   20
3   European Mediation and the Agreement of Villafranca,
      1859   23
4   The Struggle for Supremacy in Germany, 1859–66   51
5   International Relations, 1870–98   68
6   The Western Question   94

Part II   Early Twentieth Century

7   Uneasy Splendour: The British Empire at the Start of the
      Twentieth Century   101
8   Joseph Chamberlain   110
9   Entente Cordiale: Great Britain and France, 1898–1904   113
10 Farce before Tragedy: Agadir, 1911   121
11 Admiral Fisher: A Great Man?   124
12 The Last Tsars   126
13 Lament for Imperial Vienna   128
14 War by Time-Table   131
15 War Weariness and Peace Overtures   139
16 Lenin: October and After   151

Part III   Interwar Years

17 The Secrets of Diplomacy   161
18 The Supreme Council, 1919   168
19 The Hole in the Tub   171
20 The Groundwork of History   174
21 German Policy, 1937–38   179
22 Appeasement: German Version   185
23 More Light on Munich   188
24 1938: A German Version   191
25 Dragons' Teeth   198
26 Documents   202

27	The Morning After	203
28	Franco's Friends	205
29	The Moment of Decision	208
30	The Phoney War	211
31	Raw Meat	213
32	After Versailles	216
33	Collapse of Versailles: The Moment of Crisis	218
34	How Hitler Went to War: The German Record	222
35	Feebler and Feebler	225
36	Out of the Diplomatic Bag	227
37	Foreign Relations	230
38	Lloyd George in Action	232
39	Some Awkward Questions	234
40	Conflict at Versailles – and After	235
41	Germany's Breakthrough	237

Part IV   From the Prelude of the Second World War to Cold War

42	American Foreign Policy	243
43	Roosevelt and the War	245
44	The Revision of Treaties: 1830 and 1938	248
45	Munich Examined: Mr Wheeler-Bennett's History	251
46	Munich Again	255
47	How the War Began: An Essay in Diplomatic History	256
48	Diplomatic Supplement	259
49	Old Tunes	261
50	After Appeasement	265
51	Munich Twenty Years After: Appeasement – with the Wrong Man	268
52	Soviet Policy and Czechoslovakia	272
53	The Myths of Munich	276
54	Europe, 1939: The Negotiations with Russia	281
55	The False Alliance	284
56	The Outbreak of War	293
57	1939 Revisited	300
58	Old Foreign Office Tie	314
59	How Germany Lost the War	317
60	Potsdam: The Seeds of Cold War	321
61	Trieste	324
62	Czechoslovakia Today (July 1946)	347
63	German Riddles	356
64	Heartland	360

65 No Sanctity of Contract between Nations?   362
66 How Near is World War III? Dangers of a Power Balance   369
67 War and Peace   372

Index   383

Introduction

Alan John Percivale Taylor (1906–90) was the best-known historian in Britain during the four or five decades after the end of the Second World War. Even with the turn of the century, he remains for many The History Man, much as in the 1950s Sir Mortimer Wheeler (1890–1976) was The Archaeologist. Alan Taylor was a great populariser of history through lectures, the radio, the weekly and the mass-circulation press, yet he remained greatly respected by a high proportion of the history profession. It is sometimes forgotten that his initial research was in diplomatic history and it was in this area of history that his reputation was first established. As he put it in 1976, in one of the essays in this book: 'I, too, have written "pure" diplomatic history in my time.' He also observed, 'In my opinion it remains a fascinating subject, even if an unimportant one.'

At the time, 1928, when Alan Taylor began his research into the diplomatic history of mid-nineteenth century Europe, diplomatic history was experiencing something of a golden era. It was 'relevant' to many of the contemporary concerns. In the aftermath of the First World War there was much debate about the justness or otherwise of the 'war guilt' part of the Treaty of Versailles, 1919. Also the creation of new states after the dissolution of the Habsburg Empire and the subsequent controversies over boundaries ensured continuing public interest in recent diplomatic history. In May 1939, when writing a book review for the *Manchester Guardian*, Alan Taylor observed:

> The details of diplomatic history do indeed seem of irremediable triviality; but in fact, diplomatic history deals with the greatest of themes – with the relation of states, with peace and war, with the existence and destruction of communities and civilisations.[1]

In 1956, when reflecting on the appeal of diplomatic history between the First and Second World Wars, he commented, 'Men wanted to understand the contemporary world; and historians answered them that they could do so if all diplomatic secrets were "revealed".'[2] For all this, Alan Taylor had drifted into this area of diplomatic history when he began his postgraduate research.

Alan Taylor came from a wealthy, middle-class family in Lancashire. The Taylors had made their money from the cotton cloth trade. In 1890 his father, Percy Taylor (1874–1940), had joined the family firm, James Taylor and Sons, founded by Alan's grandfather (1848–1935) in the 1870s. From his early twenties Percy Taylor was earning at least £5,000 a year, then a large income. So Alan Taylor, who was born on 25 March

1906, grew up in comfort. From shortly after his birth until 1913 the Taylor's lived in a large detached house in Birkdale, which was run with the assistance of two live-in maids, a charwoman, another general maid, a gardener and a handyman. Thereafter, the family lived in Buxton and after the First World War in Preston in similar comfort.

Percy Taylor and his wife Connie (1878–1944) were radical Liberals before the First World War. During the war they both moved to the left. Connie vehemently supported the stand of her brother, Harry Thompson, as a conscientious objector. Not only did she become an implacable opponent of the war but she also adopted revolutionary politics. In this she was much influenced by Henry Sara (1886–1953) also a conscientious objector and in the 1920s a leading communist and then later a Trotskyist intellectual. Percy Taylor also moved to the left, joining the Independent Labour Party (ILP), attending the Preston Trades Council and being elected to the borough council for much of the time from 1925 until his death in 1940. As a result Alan Taylor became used to a household in which there was much political discussion and to meeting prominent left-wing political figures.

His mother's vigorous opposition to conscription and the war resulted in Alan Taylor going not to Rugby (where there was an Officer Training Corps) but to the Quaker Bootham School (1919–24). The Taylors were not Quakers but Congregationalists, at least until Connie Taylor walked out of chapel enraged by a preacher sneering at conscientious objectors. Bootham was a major influence on Alan Taylor. Although he did not become a Quaker, his outlook was moulded by the examples of many of the staff and the general values held there. From Bootham he went to Oriel College, Oxford, where he gained a First Class Honours degree in History in 1927. After a brief but unhappy period training to be a solicitor in his uncle Harry Thompson's practice, his parents funded him to return to Oxford and then to go to Vienna in 1928 to embark on postgraduate research.

Alan Taylor's wealthy middle-class background had provided him with a cosmopolitan outlook. His experience of continental Europe by the time he was 20 was vastly greater than most other middle-class people of his age group. He spent the winter of 1913–14 with his mother at Alassio on the Italian Riviera then at Lugano. In 1921 he went to Switzerland with his parents, visiting Geneva. In August and September 1924 he spent six weeks travelling in Germany and France with his mother and Henry Sara. The following summer he went with his mother and Henry Sara to Russia, visiting Leningrad, Moscow and Gorki, returning via Riga and Berlin.[3] His time in Italy and his visits to Germany may well have encouraged him in his early career to study Central European history, though he initially went to Vienna in the hope that Professor Alfred Pribram (1859–1941) would supervise him on the subject of the British Parliamentary Radicals and their relations with the Viennese before the 1848 revolution. When this proved an unsatisfactory topic, Alan Taylor turned to diplomatic history, Pribram's prime interest at that time.

Alan Taylor worked in the Chancellery in Vienna on diplomatic history, starting off on the theme of Anglo-Austrian relations between 1848 and 1866. In his autobiography Alan Taylor was disparaging of Pribram's advice as his supervisor, commenting, 'This sounded dull enough and, if I had stuck to it, would no doubt have proved as dull as Pribram's own book on Anglo-Austrian relations between 1908 and 1914'. Like probably most research students, he found his own topic once working in the archives and this involved 'a problem, not a period': 'The problem was northern Italy in 1848 as seen by the Austrian administration and by the British and French governments, an international crisis that never quite came off.'[4] This resulted in his first book, *The Italian Problem in European Diplomacy 1847–1849* (Manchester, Manchester University Press, 1934) – a detailed narrative study based on archival sources in Vienna, Paris and London.

Alan Taylor left Vienna in 1930 and took up an assistant lectureship in the History department of Manchester University. There he taught European history from 1494 to 1914. Within this he specialised in European diplomatic history 1871–1914, from 1935 teaching as his special subject 'England and the Making of the Ententes 1898–1907'. The following year Lewis Namier (1888–1960) joined the department as Professor of Modern History. Namier was a massive influence on Taylor during the remainder of his Manchester years (1930–38) and possibly beyond. As with Pribram, Alan Taylor later understated his influence. Namier not only stimulated Taylor as a great historian but also fascinated him with his rich experience of continental Europe and its history. It is notable that when Taylor wrote an essay in intellectual biography for the *Journal of Modern History* (March 1977), he began it with a story told him by Namier.[5] Through Namier he came to review books for the *Manchester Guardian* from November 1934 and his second book, *Germany's First Bid for Colonies 1884–1885* (London, Macmillan, 1938), and the edition of Friedjung of 1935 (see the fourth item of this collection) were for a series of books that Namier edited. Alan Taylor also learnt much about style from Namier, among others.

During the 1930s Alan Taylor came increasingly to rely on published editions of documents when writing history. In 1933 he bought a set of the 54 volumes of *Die Grosse Politik der europäischen Kabinette* (1922–26) from a German Jewish refugee. He relied heavily on these, topped up with material from the Public Record Office and the Granville

Papers for *Germany's First Bid for Colonies 1884–1885: A Move in Bismarck's European Policy* (1936). He drew on his Viennese research for his essay, 'European Mediation and the Agreement of Villafranca, 1859' (reprinted in this volume). He drew on British Foreign Office papers as well as the published French documents for his essay 'Prelude to Fashoda' and these plus the published German documents for 'British Policy in Morocco 1886–1902'. After the Morocco essay, published in July 1951, he rarely, if at all, engaged in archival research until he took on writing the life of Beaverbrook, and then he mostly used the Beaverbrook Papers which from 1967 were under his control as Honorary Director of the Beaverbrook Library. His third wife, the historian Eva Haraszti-Taylor, later recalled that he commented to her that primary sources were not necessarily more valid merely because they were primary. All sources needed careful judgement when using them.[6] This heavy reliance on his skills of interpreting published documents worked well with his major international history, *The Struggle for Mastery in Europe 1848–1918* (Oxford, Clarendon Press, 1954), but much less successfully with his *The Origins of the Second World War* (London, Hamish Hamilton, 1961).

From as early as 1931 Alan Taylor tried to return to Oxford University. Although he wrote in his autobiography, 'Most Oxford graduates at a provincial university were exiles, longing to return. I was not'. Nevertheless, while he may well not have set his heart on a career as an Oxbridge academic, his later refusal or lack of interest in chairs elsewhere (the London School of Economics and Political Science [LSE] apart) suggests strongly that if he were an academic it was important to him to be at Oxford. He commented that:

> ... if I had stayed in Manchester I should never have achieved anything except a few academic books. Without the contacts I made in London, which was easily reached from Oxford, I should never have become either a journalist or a television star.[7]

Obviously, however, he cannot have foreseen either the popular journalism or the television opportunities when he applied or departed to Oxford in 1938.

Alan Taylor had established a reputation as a promising scholar of the history of international relations by the time he was elected to a Fellowship at Magdalen College. His application was strengthened by the support of E.L. Woodward (1890–1971), a Fellow of All Souls and a lecturer at New College, who as an external examiner at Manchester had been impressed by Taylor's teaching of diplomatic history as well as by the promise of his early publications. Woodward, always rather sensitive and prone to perceived slight, was to be outraged nine years later when Taylor strongly criticised the editing of the official published foreign policy documents for the interwar years (see Chapter 17 and its successors) and became a vehement opponent rather than a supporter of Alan Taylor.

Before leaving Manchester Alan Taylor had already moved away from the pacifist views of his home. Indeed, by 1931, he had dramatically snapped the apron strings of his mother and broken with his lifestyle of regular weekends at his parents' home in Preston when he married Margaret Adams. The dramatic aspect of this was his failure to tell his doting parents of the wedding until after it had occurred. His public arguments for peace lasted longer – until February 1936. Then fearing German reoccupation of the Rhineland he abandoned his former views and thereafter called for British rearmament.

His change of view was also linked to his understanding of European history. He had not been favourably impressed when he had visited Berlin in 1924 and 1928 and he had been appalled by the growing strength of the Nazis in Upper Bavaria in 1932. By the mid-1930s his work on the pre-1914 published collections of diplomatic documents changed his views on German responsibility for bringing about the Great War. He increasingly saw German policy as expansionist, regardless of who held power in Germany. The most vivid and full statement of this view was his book, *The Course of German History* (London, Hamish Hamilton, 1945). This book, completed in September 1944 and published the following July, caught the public mood. It sold 6,000 copies in six months. In it he concluded of Hitler's invasion of the Soviet Union in June 1941:

> It was the climax, the logical conclusion, of German history ... Germany was at last united ... the single cause ... was the supremacy everywhere of German arms, of German industry, of German culture, of the German people.[8]

Less of a period piece and more intellectually substantial was his work on the history of the Habsburg Monarchy, the first book he wrote after moving to Oxford University. The first version, *The Habsburg Monarchy 1815–1918*, (London, Macmillan, 1941), was mostly written during the summer of 1939. The Second World War helped to change his perspectives on central Europe. He rewrote it during the summer of 1947, removing suggestions that the Habsburg Monarchy might have survived had it not missed opportunities for change and which he now dubbed 'The liberal illusion'. He also responded to his former supervisor's review of the 1941 version. Pribram had commented, 'It can be shown that all the important events in domestic policy from the Vienna Congress till the collapse of the Empire were determined by successes or failures in the field of foreign policy'.[9] Taylor took this point very much to heart in rewriting the book.

Even before revising his Habsburg Monarchy book, Alan Taylor had embarked on what was to be his most substantial diplomatic history. By the autumn of 1946 he had written some 60,000 words on European diplomacy 1878–1919, intended as a book for Hamish Hamilton. However, when Oxford University Press undertook a series, the Oxford History of Modern Europe, Alan Taylor readily switched his planned work to appear in this series, enlarging it to cover 1848–78 as well as 1878–1918. He finished writing *The Struggle for Mastery in Europe 1848–1918* (Oxford, Oxford University Press, 1954) in July 1953. It was a high point, perhaps the high point, of his career as a diplomatic historian. It took the careful and thorough, old-style diplomatic history to a very high level, with Alan Taylor exhibiting his mastery of printed diplomatic documents. Much of it was written during a year's sabbatical leave from Oxford when, strangely, he did not take the opportunity to study unpublished British material in the Public Record Office. He was eager to publish a big book to underline that he was a serious scholar not, as he later put it, a 'playboy' or 'merely a public entertainer'.[10]

By the 1950s Alan Taylor had become both a radio and an early television personality. This had come about not though his expertise as a historian but though his abilities to be 'a controversialist' on current affairs programmes. He had broken into radio broadcasting during the Second World War, when so many regular broadcasters were away, and he had the experience of giving monthly lectures on the development of the war through southern Britain on behalf of the Ministry of Information. He first appeared in seven editions of *The World at War: Your Questions Answered* on the BBC's Forces Network (the precursor of the Light Programme and later Radio 2) between March and June 1942. He appeared on radio as one of a panel in three programmes on 'The Future of Germany' in late 1944 (when his *Course of German History* had been completed but not published). Thereafter, he became a frequent broadcaster either on the progress of the war, on post-war issues or as a lively intellectual for panels. In due course he became an early national television celebrity through being a regular, then a frequent, member of a team of four (with Michael Foot, Robert Boothby and W.J. Brown) on the discussion programme *In The News*. From August 1950 until the end of 1952 he appeared on it 42 times, with a further five appearances in 1953 and 1954. With the coming of commercial television in September 1955 the old team of Taylor, Foot, Boothby and Brown appeared again in the very similar programme entitled *Free Speech*. His emergence as a striking giver of history lectures on radio and, above all, on television followed from his success as a 'controversialist', and not vice versa. Weekly columns in the popular press also followed.

Partly as a result of his media activities and partly because of his great involvement in Magdalen College affairs (as Vice-President at the time of college's quincentenary in 1958), Alan Taylor's major work after *The Struggle for Mastery in Europe 1848–1918* was a study of the succeeding period in European diplomatic history. This was published in 1961 as *The Origins of the Second World War*. Near the end of the book he observed, 'such were the origins of the Second World War, or rather of the war of the three Western Powers over the settlement of Versailles …' and added that when Hitler widened the war to the USA and USSR 'a real world war began'.[11] His was a ground-breaking and highly controversial study, yet was very firmly traditional in that it was Eurocentric and based very heavily on published diplomatic documents.

The Origins of the Second World War and the furore it aroused made him an international name among readers of the 'quality press' as well as among scholars. Many of the points which caused most controversy had been made by Alan Taylor in numerous book reviews from 1947 onwards. A selection of these reviews of the published diplomatic documents and of substantial early diplomatic histories are reprinted for the first time in this collection (in Parts II and III).

Alan Taylor was rightly critical of aspects of the editing of the British series of interwar documents. The British documents had been initiated as a pre-emptive strike in any future war of documents concerning culpability for the outbreak of the Second World War. The Germans had made effective use of their large series of documents *Die Grosse Politik* (54 volumes, 1922–27), which challenged acceptance of German 'war guilt' for the First World War. The German editors, by omitting sections of documents, by the choice of selection, by arranging them out of sequence, presented an unduly favourable version of German policy. E.L. Woodward, in preparing a selection of British documents during the course of the Second World War, argued for the exclusion of the opinions of ministers, Foreign Office officials or British diplomats. When, in the face of the imminent publication of series of documents by the USA and other countries, agreement was given for the British series to be published, Woodward succeeded in securing himself (and his co-editor, Rohan Butler) a free hand. Alan Taylor's criticisms of the first volume issued, *The Secrets of Diplomacy* were to the point, except in questioning the editors' integrity in respect of their freedom of actions (and on this he apologized subsequently in the *Times Literary Supplement*).[12]

In 1961 and 1962 Alan Taylor was pilloried by many as an apologist for Adolf Hitler. This was strange, given his hostility to Germany and, seemingly, to Germans in *The Course of German History*. In this early book he had portrayed Hitler's policy as the conventional German foreign policy – but carried out more ruthlessly. In *The Origins* he suggested, 'With Hitler guilty, every other German could claim innocence'.[13] Robert Birley, in a review of the 1945 book had forewarned the likely misinterpretation: 'In the effort to make the Nazis, not in large measure the result of this anarchy (the economic crises of the late 1920s), but a development quite to be expected of German history, Mr. Taylor nearly succeeds in making them respectable.'[14]

Alan Taylor took up the idea that Hitler did not have detailed plans for a war to start in 1939 in a radio review of Lewis Namier's *Diplomatic Prelude 1938–9* (London, Macmillan, 1948). In a broadcast on the BBC's Third Programme on 13 January 1948, he observed of the period before the outbreak of war,

> ... you can find in Namier the more humdrum truth, discreditable no doubt to both sides in the negotiations – not discreditable from wickedness or sinister intention, discreditable from short-sightedness, vanity and ignorance ... Certainly Hitler aimed at German domination of Europe, but he ... went about this in the most blundering way and, as Namier shows, was quite taken aback at the end when he found that, against all expectations, Britain and France were really going to war.[15]

Alan Taylor's review of Namier's book for the *Manchester Guardian* is reprinted in this collection.

In arguing his case that Hitler did not have clear plans for war he dismissed as of little importance the Hossbach memorandum on Hitler's conference in the Chancellery on 5 November 1937 at which he discussed possible war scenarios with his leading military advisers. In *The Origins* Alan Taylor argued that the 'conference was a manoeuvre in domestic affairs', one to gain increased armaments.[16] Alan Taylor first made this case in a review in 1949, in which he argued of the Hossbach memorandum that it

> ... does not provide the evidence that there was a German, or even a Nazi conspiracy against peace, if by conspiracy is meant a coherent objective plan. It provides the evidence that the Germans, and especially the German governing class, allowed a criminal lunatic to establish himself in supreme power; and that they were abetted by those in England and France who, from feebleness or fear of communism, treated the lunatic as a sane man.[17]

Alan Taylor's interpretation also argued that the other powers were culpable for the outbreak of war in Europe through their failure to combine and to stand up to Hitler. Even before the Second World War had ended, a BBC official warned him of the highly controversial implications of his arguments. He was asked on 2 May 1945 to amend a script for a series of short talks on the war:

> I should say 'made war inevitable' instead of saying that 'the failure of Britain, the USA and the USSR to come together caused the war'. This is mainly in the interests of clarity – in translation that sentence might serve to obscure the predominating war guilt of Germany.[18]

In writing *The Origins* Alan Taylor was explicit that in arguing against Hitler having deep-laid plans he was arguing a case, albeit one which he felt to be plausible,

> Human blunders ... usually do more to shape history than human wickedness. At any rate this is a rival dogma which is worth developing, if only as an academic exercise.[19]

He was also clear that his book would shock some readers. He wrote to Hamish Hamilton, his publisher, 'I'm pleased with it. But I think it will annoy the old boys who thought they had settled everything about the Second World War years ago'.[20]

Alan Taylor was not prepared for the degree of shock and outrage his book provoked. Although he was one of the most anti-German historians, who had been an active opponent of appeasement in the late 1930s, he was accused by many of being an apologist for Hitler. Others felt that what they saw as a taste for controversy had been indulged too far, that his book was deeply offensive. Hugh Trevor-Roper, one of the most notable critics, asked: 'Was Hitler really just a more violent Mr Micawber sitting in Berlin ... ?' Another, Tim Mason, analysed Alan Taylor's failure to deal with ideology – 'National Socialism was perhaps the profoundest cause of the Second World War' – and also argued that the conference recorded in the Hossback memorandum was 'the point at which the expansion of the Third Reich ceased to be latent and became explicit'.[21] Alan Taylor conceded, 'I was quite wrong in suggesting that the meeting presented in the so-called Hossbach Protocol was designed by Hitler as a move against Schacht'; but, characteristically, he added, 'the meeting had no significance'. More substantially, he disagreed with Tim Manson's view (as he put it) 'that without Hitler and the National Socialist party there would have been no German problem – no unrest, no disputed frontiers, no shadow of a new German domination over Europe'.[22] In other words, a major underlying theme of *The Origins* was a further working out of the 'German problem' as in *The Course of German History* (1945).

While *The Struggle for Mastery in Europe 1848–1918* and *The Origins of the Second World War* were Alan Taylor's major diplomatic histories of 1954–61 he did publish two other notable books in these years. *Bismarck* (London, Hamish Hamilton, 1955) was written mostly in the summer of 1954, while he and his family were staying in their holiday home on the Isle of Wight, written quickly and with the aid of few books. In writing the book his view of Bismarck, whom he had earlier deemed to be 'the most unattractive character in nineteenth century history', was transformed with him 'presenting Bismarck as a moderate, pacific statesman and an attractive character'.[23] *The Trouble Makers: Dissent Over Foreign Policy 1792–1939* (London, Hamish Hamilton, 1957) was the book of his Ford Lectures, given in the Examinations Schools, Oxford University in spring 1956. He later called this book his 'favourite brainchild'. It was a return to an earlier interest of his, it was the antithesis of establishment foreign policy studies (whether the official editions of Foreign Office documents or Chatham House) and it dealt with his nonconforming heroes (no heroines). He recalled in his autobiography, 'For me the ideas, the characters and the excitement of presenting them were all mixed up'.[24]

After *The Origins of the Second World War* Alan Taylor's major publications were either on British history or on war. His most substantial books were *English History 1914–1945* (Oxford, Clarendon Press, 1965), his volume in the Oxford History of England, and *Beaverbrook* (London, Hamish Hamilton, 1972), his large biography of his press lord friend. He also wrote well-received brief histories of the world wars: *The First World War: An Illustrated History*, (London, Hamish Hamilton, 1963) and *The Second World War: An Illustrated History* (London, Hamish Hamilton, 1975). In 1982 he commented of war as a theme:

> For fifty years I have been teaching history and writing books about it. All my books and all my lectures have been implicitly about war, from the Napoleonic Wars to the shadow of the final war under which we now live.[25]

Indeed, war was one of his familiar themes he took up again in his later years. Hence his lecture series *How Wars Begin* (BBC, 1977) and *How Wars End* (Channel 4, 1983) as well as a return to his early interests in the French Revolution of 1848 and the Russian Revolutions in the series *Revolution* (BBC, 1978). One of his last essays, 'No Sanctity of Contract Between Nations?' (January 1981, reprinted here), took up concerns he had expressed during the period he mostly concentrated on diplomatic history. In *The Origins of the Second World War* (1961) he had written,

> The old monarchies had valued treaties in so far as these conferred rights; they had never troubled much about treaties which involved obligations. The new attitude corresponded to the 'sanctity of contract' which is the fundamental element in bourgeois civilization.[26]

After the storm over *The Origins of the Second World War* Alan Taylor was more a freelance historian and media personality than a conventional academic tied to much teaching and administration. In 1963 Oxford University had not renewed the fixed-term special lectureship he held, which gave him less teaching and more time for research. He had had the full ten years, with Magdalen College funding replacements for the loss of part of his teaching time. Another university might have promoted him to a Readership or Personal Chair or made a further special arrangement. Taylor declined to go back to the normal conditions of work of a lecturer, so, amidst great media coverage, ended his career as a regular university teacher. However, he did remain a Fellow, then an Honorary Fellow, of Magdalen College until his death. He also gave special series of lectures at University College, London, Bristol University and North London Polytechnic. In the case of Bristol he was given the title of Visiting Professor, something which otherwise eluded him or he avoided. In 1957 Hugh Trevor-Roper, not Taylor, had been appointed to the Regius Chair of Modern History at Oxford and he had not gained other chairs at Oxford or the LSE, but had declined opportunities at other British universities. He was more interested in his public role as a major media figure, a role which apparently brought him more income than his university salary from the early 1950s onwards.

By the time he was 50 Alan Taylor was probably the best known historian in Britain. For the last three or four decades of his life he was 'The History Man' to much of the British public, not only selling large numbers of books but being popular on television either as a lecturer or as a 'personality' who commented on current affairs. Like the major popular historians of the past – Gibbon, Macaulay and Trevelyan – he had crafted a distinctive style and persona for his writings. His is a lucid and sharp prose, marked by a heavy use of paradoxes and epigrams. He came to see himself as the Great Communicator of History to the general public, presenting recent findings on modern history in the press or on radio and television. He also was exceedingly generous in the time he gave to lecture to 'general interest' audiences around the country, mostly under the auspices of the Historical Association. By the 1960s his appearance in a town usually generated audiences of 200 or more, instead of the usual 30 to 50.

Since his death on 7 September 1990 most of Alan Taylor's books have remained in print.[27] His two major Oxford histories – *The Struggle for Mastery in Europe 1848–1918* (1954) and *English History 1914–1945* (1965) – are still read widely, including for many university courses. While the study of *The Origins of the Second World War* has moved on since Alan Taylor's book, it did stimulate what proved to be a fertile debate and is still seen as the beginning of recent reassessments. This new collection of essays, which (with the exception of 'Trieste') have not been reprinted before, provides a reminder that Alan Taylor was first a diplomatic historian before he broadened out his coverage to many aspects of modern British and continental European history.

Acknowledgements

I am grateful for the considerable encouragement I have received in editing these essays from Eva Haraszti Taylor, Maggie Walsh, Bruce Hunter (of David Higham Associates) and Alec McAulay (formerly of Ashgate). I am only sorry that Arthur Wrigley (21 November 1912–26 May 1999) will not be able to enjoy this collection of Alan Taylor's essays.

Notes

1. 'Diplomatic History', a review of two diplomatic histories, in the *Manchester Guardian*, 23 May 1939.
2. 'The Rise and Fall of "Pure" Diplomatic History', *Times Literary Supplement*, 6 January 1956. Reprinted most recently in A.J.P. Taylor, *From the Boer War to the Cold War* (London, Hamish Hamilton, 1995), pp. 1–7.
3. A.J.P. Taylor, *A Personal History* (London, Hamish Hamilton), 1983, pp. 19–20, 41, 64–5 and 76–8.
4. Taylor (1983), pp. 90–91.
5. A.J.P. Taylor, 'Accident Prone, or What Happened Next', *Journal of Modern History*, 49, 1, March 1977, pp. 1–18. Reprinted most recently in A.J.P. Taylor, *From Napoleon to the Second International* (London, Hamish Hamilton), 1993, pp. 1–23.
6. Interview with Eva Haraszti-Taylor, 5 March 1999.
7. Taylor (1983), p. 132.
8. A.J.P. Taylor, *The Course of German History* (London, Hamish Hamilton), 1945, p. 260.
9. A.F. Pribram quoted in C.J. Wrigley, *A.J.P. Taylor: A Complete Bibliography* (Brighton, Harvester Press), 1980, p. 69.
10. Taylor (1983), pp. 198 and 207.
11. A.J.P. Taylor, *The Origins of the Second World War* (Harmondsworth, Penguin, 1964), p. 337.
12. For an excellent recent account of the background to the German and British series see Keith Wilson (ed.), *Forging The Collective Memory*, Providence, Rhode Island, Berghahn, 1996), especially the editor's introduction, Helger H. Herwig, 'Clio Deceived: Patriotic Self-Censorship in Germany after the Great War', pp. 87–127, and Uri Bialer, 'Telling the Truth to the People: Britain's Decision to Publish the Diplomatic Papers of the Interwar Period', pp. 265–88.

13. Taylor (1964), p. 35.
14. *International Affairs*, 22, 1 (January 1946), pp. 136–7.
15. Transcript of 'An Exercise in Contemporary History'; BBC archives, Caversham.
16. Taylor (1964), p. 170.
17. Review of *Documents on German Foreign Policy 1918–1945*, Series D, 1, *1937–8* (London, HMSO, 1949), in the *New Statesman and Nation*, 17 December 1949.
18. BBC archives, Caversham.
19. Taylor (1964), pp. 265–6.
20. Taylor to Hamish Hamilton, 6 August 1960; Hamish Hamilton archives, Bristol University.
21. H.R. Trevor-Roper, 'A.J.P. Taylor, Hitler and the War', *Encounter*, 17 (July 1961), pp. 88–96. T.W. Mason, 'Some Origins of the Second World War', *Past and Present*, 29 (December 1967), pp. 67–87.
22. A.J.P. Taylor, 'War Origins Again', *Past and Present*, 30 (April 1965), pp. 110–13.
23. Book reviews in *Manchester Guardian*, 16 January 1948 and in the *New Statesman and Nation*, 30 November 1957. See also Wrigley (1980), pp. 30–31 and 308.
24. Taylor (1983), p. 210.
25. Diary, *London Review of Books*, 4 March 1982.
26. Taylor (1964), p. 54.
27. In 1998 the Folio Society published a five-volume collection of some of his work in its publishing programme of classic works of history (including Gibbon, Macaulay, and some more recent authors).

Part I

Nineteenth Century

CHAPTER ONE

A World Restored, 1812–22

This essay was first published as 'Kissinger Fireworks' as a review of Henry A. Kissinger, *A World Restored* (London, Gollancz 1979), in the *Observer*, 11 November 1979. Hobbes is Thomas Hobbes (1588–1679), the philosopher, Brock the name of a manufacturer of fireworks.

Clever people are never weary of writing books about Metternich and his foreign policy. There is not all that much to find out about it. The records are abundant and the events well known.

In 1809, when Metternich became Foreign Minister of Austria, she was the subservient ally of Napoleonic France. Four years later Metternich had abstracted her from that alliance and transformed her into the core of the anti-Napoleonic coalition. At the Congress of Vienna he and Castlereagh, the British Foreign Secretary, established the Concert of Europe. Having outwitted France, the revolutionary power, they went on to outwit Russia, the reactionary power, as well. Every student of history knows this, but the temptation to juggle with the fine concepts underlying Metternich's policy or Castlereagh's policy seems irresistible. The resultant books are not works of research or scholarship. They are commentaries on events, variations on the theme of Metternich's cleverness. The authors, of course, are very clever themselves.'

The cleverest undoubtedly was written by a young lecturer at Harvard in the 1950s, and is now republished under strangely changed circumstances. The book has two subtitles. The first stated baldly: 'The Politics of Conservatism in a Revolutionary Era', which is not a satisfactory description. The second is more explicit: 'A Detailed Study of Diplomacy and Political Manoeuvre 1812–22 with Particular Reference to Metternich and Castlereagh'. That too is rather misleading. The study is not all that detailed. Indeed as a contribution to historical knowledge or even understanding the book has few merits. What it has is a ceaseless explosion of ideas, some brilliant, some as banal as Metternich's own, some relevant to the historical period, some with no other purpose than to display the author's virtuosity. Reeling under this Brock's Benefit of intellectual fireworks, the reader appreciates the significance of Hobbes's remark: 'Words are wise men's counters; they are the money of fools'.

The core of truth in the book is that international relations work when the Great Powers have principles in common and run into difficulties when they have not. The French Revolution destroyed the common basis. Hence there was no possibility of agreeing with Napoleon except in terms of force. With his defeat the common basis was rediscovered: legitimacy, which Professor Kissinger defines as 'no more than an international agreement about the nature of workable arrangements and about the permissible aims and methods of foreign policy'. This definition, though plausible, shows that the Professor is not much at home in the history of the period he is supposed to be writing about. But this is really irrelevant. The book is a rhapsody, not a work of history, and the best thing is to gather the plums of Professor Kissinger's utterance.

He is strong on epigram: 'When the fate of empires is at stake, the convictions of their statesmen are the medium for survival.' Does this mean anything? Has it the remotest connection with truth? This is better: 'It is the nature of statesmen conducting a policy of petty advantage to seek in vacillation a substitute for action.' Now back to the profoundly meaningless: 'The memory of State is the test of truth of their policy.' And after that the meaningful but profoundly empty: 'War is the impossibility of peace', and a sentence of practical guidance: 'Perfect flexibility in diplomacy is the illusion of amateurs. To plan policy on the assumption of the equal possibility of all contingencies is to confuse statesmanship with mathematics.' By this time Austria has arrived at the anti-Napoleonic coalition. 'Austria could not join a crusade, for crusades make universal claims and Austria's survival depended on a recognition of limits.'

Now it is Castlereagh's turn. 'An insular power at the periphery of events finds it difficult to admit that war may be produced by intrinsic causes.' But 'war has its own legitimacy and it is victory, not peace'. Castlereagh and Metternich secured a moderate peace with France, and with that the floodgates of epigram are opened:

> The logic of war is power, and power has no inherent limit. The logic of peace is proportion, and proportion implies limitation. The success of war is victory; the success of peace is stability.

Now let us try the Congress of Vienna:

> An international settlement which is accepted and not imposed will always appear *somewhat* unjust to any one of its components. Paradoxically, the generality of this dissatisfaction is a condition of stability, because were any one Power *totally* satisfied, all others would have to be *totally* dissatisfied and a revolutionary situation would ensue.

And on the Congress settlement:

> The issue at Vienna was not reform against reaction – this is the interpretation of posterity. Instead, the problem was to create an

order in which change could be brought about through a sense of obligation, instead of through an assertion of power.

This sounds impressive. In fact, the Congress settlement was never changed by 'a sense of obligation'. It was changed only when someone – Cavour or Bismarck – invoked 'an assertion of power'.

The Concert of Europe lasted for only seven years and broke up when Castlereagh refused to co-operate in a policy of intervention against liberal revolutions. But the peace of Europe lasted for a generation. This leads to generalizations on the nature of statesmanship:

> The test of a statesman is his ability to recognise the real relationship of forces and to make this knowledge serve his ends ... The acid test of a policy, however, is its ability to obtain domestic support.

A wise remark, even more appropriate to the present day than to the time of Castlereagh.

In the next passage, however, the author is again pontificating in the void, composing paradoxes and epigrams for their own sake:

> Most great statesman have been either representatives of essentially conservative social structures or revolutionaries ... A conservative structure produces a notion of *quality*, which provides the framework of great conception; a revoluntionary order produces a notion of *exultation*, which dissolves technical limitations.

Finally, an appeal to history where once more words are rattled around for their own sake:

> History is the memory of States ... Each generation is permitted only one effort of abstraction; it can attempt only one interpretation and a single experiment, for it is its own subject. This is the challenge of history and its tragedy; it is the shape 'destiny' assumes on the earth.

What can be learnt about the author from this bravura display? He appears to be a man more clever than wise, himself intoxicated with words and able to intoxicate others. He has limitless self-confidence, can talk himself out of almost any difficulty and is somewhat lacking in common sense. Yet there is one really sensible idea that he has picked up from his study of history. He knows that the object of international relations is to reach agreement, not to score off the other side. Anyone who writes about Metternich and Castlereagh must prefer peace to war, and these two dead statesman have therefore perhaps been not without their uses to the present secretary of state of the United States.

CHAPTER TWO

The Crimean War:
A Triumph of Muddle

This essay was first published in the *Manchester Guardian*, 27 March 1954, to
mark the centenary of the start of the Crimean War. Lajos Kossuth (1802–94),
a journalist, was the outstanding Hungarian nationalist of the 1848 era.

On 27 March 1854 Great Britain and France declared war on Russia.
This was the technical beginning of a war which no power had wanted
and which they found great difficulty in fighting even when a theoretical state of war existed. Yet its coming had been announced long in
advance; and the powers stumbled into war with a tragic inevitability. It
was a story of bluff and counter-bluff, or – in the contemporary phrase
– of 'brag'. Each power in turn was horrified when its brag was taken
seriously. The conflict began some eighteen months previously, when
Napoleon III backed the claims of the Latin monks at the Holy Places in
order to prop up his imperial prestige. Tsar Nicholas I, though harbour-
ing no aggressive designs against Turkey, would not allow her to fear
some other power more than Russia. He raised the bid. Not only did he
back the Greek monks at Jerusalem. In May 1853, he demanded that
the Turks should recognize his protectorate over all Orthodox Christians throughout the Ottoman Empire.

Bluff

The Turks were tired of being threatened. Moreover ten million Orthodox Christians were a more serious matter than a handful of monks.
The Turks refused the Russian demands. Nicholas I raised his bid again.
He broke off diplomatic relations with Turkey and, in July, sent his
armies into the Danubian principalities which were technically under
Turkish sovereignty. But war still seemed far off. The Great Powers met
in conference at Vienna and devised a compromise which Russia accepted, but which the Turks – to everyone's annoyance – refused. In
spite of this, the Western powers, England and France, declared that
they could not let Russia threaten Turkey. They sent their fleets to
Constantinople, perhaps to frighten the Russians, perhaps to moderate
the Turks, at any rate to bluff somebody.

The bluff did not work. Instead the Turks declared war against Russia on 4 October. By now Nicholas was anxious for a solution. He would have grasped at any way out which would save his face. But when the Turks actually attacked his troops, he answered by sinking some Turkish ships in the Black Sea. This was the famous 'massacre' of Sinope, a legitimate act of war, yet one which did more than anything else to make general war inevitable.

The Western powers raised the bid in their turn. They sent their fleets into the Black Sea and, in January 1854, ordered all Russian ships to remain in port. Even this violent gesture did not provoke Nicholas to war. England and France tried again. On 21 February they sent a delayed ultimatum to Russia, demanding the withdrawal of her troops from the principalities by 1 April. Nicholas ignored this demand and bragged again. On 22 March Russian troops crossed the Danube into Turkey proper.

This at last provoked the Western powers into declaring war. Even now the combatants had no idea where they would fight. The Western allies had a hazy notion that Russia would overrun the Balkans and that they themselves would rescue Turkey in a victorious battle at the gates of Constantinople. The Russians did not prove so obliging. They withdrew beyond the Danube and, in August, from the principalities as well. Instead of defending Turkey the allies had to invade Russia; and they hit on Sebastopol, because they could think of nowhere better to go. It was supposed to be vulnerable to sea power, but in fact it did not fall until September 1855, after a year of miserable suffering and mismanaged 'soldiers' battles'.

This is not to say that the Crimean War was unpopular in England. Public opinion (whatever that may mean) forced war on the government. Some people, such as the poet laureate, Tennyson, wanted war for its own sake, to solve their emotional troubles. The Radicals, who already knew how to shout the loudest, wanted war against Russia as 'the tyrant of Europe'. The Crimean War was the Chartists' delayed revenge for the failure of the revolutions of 1848 – a failure which had been conspicuous in their own case. Those who cheered Kossuth when he came to England in 1851 were the most vociferous for war in 1854.

The Crimean War was fought much more against Russia than in favour of Turkey. It was a war for the balance of power and for 'the liberties of Europe', not a war for the security of the route to India (which in any case did not yet exist). And in a sense it achieved its aim. Before 1854 Russia seemed to dominate Central Europe. After the Crimean War she had little say in European affairs outside the Balkans; and she recovered her control over Berlin and Vienna only in 1945. The unification of Italy and of Germany both followed the Crimean War and were made possible by it. It was the fault of the Italians and of the Germans themselves, not of the Russians, if these brought less liberation than the advocates of nationalism had expected.

England and France claimed to be acting in the name of Europe. But Europe failed to act with them. Their only ally was the little kingdom of Sardinia. If Prussia and Austria, the two German powers, had joined in the war there might have followed a Concert of Europe, which would have made the unity of European civilization a reality. But, they refused to be caught. The endless conferences, which made the Crimean War a story of 'diplomacy interrupted by battles', all proved fruitless. The Congress of Paris, which met at the end of the war in 1856, was supposed to inaugurate a new era of peace. In fact it marked the end of Europe. Germany embarked on the course of playing off east and west – a course which brought her great triumph as well as great ruin and which she is still following.

The liberal alliance

What the Crimean War demonstrated was not the Concert of Europe but 'the liberal alliance' of England and France. Their wars had filled the history of two centuries. Now they were allies for the first time since the days of Cromwell and Mazarin; and, in spite of their future quarrels, were never at war again. The Crimean War seemed to hold out still greater promise. The two most advanced powers seemed to be on the point of leading the destinies of Europe. And they accomplished a good deal. Apart from checking Russian expansion in the Near East, they established an independent Romania and made the Danube an international waterway. A few years later they acted together as godparents when national Italy was born.

But this was the last achievement of the Anglo-French entente during the nineteenth century. Suspicion of Napoleon III mounted in England after his acquisition of Savoy and Nice. Still more, the Free Trade critics of the war won a belated success. Cobden and Bright were the most unpopular men in England while the war was on; and both lost their parliamentary seats in the general election of 1857. They soon had their revenge. The diplomacy of the war had been a muddle; its military conduct even more so. Bright seemed to have been justified when he attributed the war to aristocratic inefficiency and jobbery. English Radicals ceased to regard themselves as the liberators of Europe. They came to believe that war was always unnecessary and usually wicked. The Crimean War taught Englishmen of the Left the doctrine of isolation, after which they still secretly hanker.

CHAPTER THREE

European Mediation and the Agreement of Villafranca, 1859

This essay was the first that Alan Taylor published in a learned journal. It appeared in the *English Historical Review*, 51, 201 (January 1936) and has not been republished until now. It is based on his archival research in Vienna (1928–30), Paris (summer 1930 and subsequently) and London. In his autobiography, *A Personal History* (London, Hamish Hamilton, 1983), Taylor observed that it was 'My last fling with material from the Austrian achives ...'. He added that he had never felt it worth republishing: 'I must have had difficulty in writing it or perhaps I had lost interest in the subject'. I suspect the latter, as he moved away from the 1849–60 period.

The war of 1859 between France and Austria was fought without the intervention of any other great power, but the three neutral states – Great Britain, Prussia, and Russia – played indirectly a considerable part, and their activities, or the guesses at their activities made by the two combatants, were largely responsible for the conclusion of the preliminary peace of Villafranca which brought the war to an end. Of the three, Russia alone had a decided and stable policy. Just before the war Russia had concluded with France the secret treaty of 3 March, and the one object of Russian policy was to assist France by preventing the interference of the neutral powers. The French believed that, if left undisturbed, they could defeat Austria without outside assistance, and all they asked of Russia was to keep the ring for them.

Austria, on the other hand, had always realized the danger of defeat, if the war was limited to a conflict between Austria and France, and fought only in Italy. The Austrian government based its case on international rights and treaty obligations, and appealed on these grounds for the moral support of England as one of the Powers chiefly responsible for the settlement of 1815. From Prussia Austria asked more: she argued that in resisting France she was fighting the battle of all Germany, and that Prussia should in her own interests join in the war in order to prevent the re-establishment of a Napoleonic dictatorship over the whole of central Europe. This argument caused the Prussian government considerable embarrassment. It dared not estrange German feeling by rejecting outright the appeal to German interests, particularly as the prince regent himself had considerable sympathy with German patriotism. On the other hand, it was most unwilling to take the burden of the war off Austria or to assist Austria in any way, unless Austria would surrender part of her supremacy in Germany. Bismarck favoured a policy of holding Austria up to ransom: Prussia should frankly state the price of her assistance, and then it would rest with Austria to accept it or not as she chose. But Bismarck was far away in St Petersburg, had indeed, as he expressed it, been put in cold storage in order to please Austria, and Schleinitz, the foreign minister, did not dare to follow so decided a course. He was certainly unwilling to fight Austria's battles for her, but he knew no means of avoiding this except procrastination; he was forever promising Austria that Prussia would soon be at her side, but always managed to postpone the decision. Schleinitz kept Prussia out of the war, but only because the war was short: he had no alternative policy to keep Prussia out of war in the long run.

The one great interest of the English government was peace, the maintenance of peace before the war and the speedy restoration of peace when once the war had broken out. The Conservative cabinet did indeed profess to support the system of international rights, which had been established in 1815, and Disraeli, in particular, as an avowed disciple of Metternich, attempted to revive the phraseology of the Napoleonic war. Malmesbury, the foreign secretary, was definitely pro-Austrian, and had an intense dislike of Italian nationalism.[1] But the Conservatives were a minority government, existing only because of the disunion among their opponents, and the general enthusiasm in England for Italian nationalism made it impossible for the government to give any practical support to the treaty rights in which it believed. The most that the British government could offer Austria was a mediation pure and simple, and it was to negotiate on this basis that Cowley, the British ambassador at Paris, was sent to Vienna in March 1859. Austria was at this moment anxious to conciliate Great Britain, and the Cowley mission was so nearly successful in removing the points of difference between Austria and France that Napoleon feared the chances of war were becoming remote. He therefore induced Russia to propose, instead of the private mediation of Great Britain, a European congress of the five Great Powers, in the hope that a congress would revive the excuses for war which the Cowley mission had gone far to remove. The British government saw no reason to resist a European congress, although it believed that private mediation was a more promising method,[2] and the Cowley mission was therefore never pursued.

As soon as a congress was proposed, the Austrian government abandoned all attempt at conciliation and adopted an attitude of rigorous legalism, much as a litigate, who has in private negotiations been willing to compromise, will advance his full claims when the case is brought into open court. The Austrians thought that they had done enough to please England by being conciliatory in private. Moreover, they hoped that the open manifestation of the entente between France and Russia would so alarm England as to throw her into the arms of Austria. An anonymous agent reported that Palmerston had said: 'England must strengthen the alliance with Austria ... Whatever may be the sympathies of the English people for the ideas of Nationalism and Italian independence, these desires must be sacrificed to the great political needs of England';[3] and Buol made some attempt to arouse British feeling against the Franco-Russian alliance.[4] On 19 April, the day before the Austrian ultimatum was sent to Austria, Buol informed the council of ministers that 'England and Prussia are coming out more and more openly on the Austrian side'.[5] But in fact the arrogance and ineptitude of Austrian diplomacy from the time the congress was proposed until the outbreak of war had left Austria isolated in Europe, and the French had thus achieved their first object of promoting a war against Austria alone. Loftus, the British ambassador at Vienna, gave Buol a strongly-worded note, in which the entire blame for the war was laid on Austria,[6] and in a speech at the Mansion House Derby, the prime minister, described the ultimatum as hasty, precipitate, and criminal.[7] The effect on Prussia was equally unfavourable. The Archduke Albrecht had been sent to Berlin to attempt to secure Prussian support against France, and the prince regent had been drawn by his old-fashioned German patriotism into an attitude increasingly favourable to Austria. Under his urging, Prussia went so far as to promise that, if the proposed congress failed, and if Austria then sent Sardinia an ultimatum, Prussia would join Austria if France supported Sardinia. This Prussian offer was never considered: the Austrian ultimatum was sent without informing either William or the Archduke Albrecht,[8] and Prussia naturally returned to a position of strict neutrality. Austria was left to face France and Sardinia alone.

Buol had based his whole policy upon Schwarzenberg's theory that the strength of Austria lay in her army, and he had attempted to bully his way through one problem after another. But as soon as Austria became involved in war, the inadequacy of this theory became apparent, and there was a precipitate return to the doctrine of Metternich that the strength of Austria lay in her alliances. Rechberg, Metternich's leading disciple in the Austrian service, succeeded Buol as foreign minister shortly before the battle of Magenta, and it was his aim to recover by a conciliatory diplomacy the moral support of England and the material support of Prussia, which Buol had forfeited. The main consideration for Austria was to get Prussia into the field against France as soon as possible. Rechberg hoped to do this by a combination of blandishments and threats: if Prussia could be persuaded to offer her mediation between Austria and France, then she would probably be drawn into the war by the French rejection of this offer;[9] if Prussia proved adamant, then Austria would threaten to settle directly with France and thus leave Prussia isolated in face of the French menace.[10]

Austria had a valuable ally at the Prussian court in the person of the prince regent himself. As early as 5 June William urged that Prussia could not tolerate the expulsion of Austria from Italy, and that the whole army should be at once mobilized in preparation for armed mediation.[11] It was impossible for the Prussian ministers less favourable to Austria to meet the prince regent with a blank negative, or to argue that the defeat of Austria was no concern of Prussia's, and after lengthy discussions partial mediation was agreed to on 11 June.[12] What Schleinitz set out to do was to transfer the emphasis from Prussia as a *German* power to Prussia as a *European* power by a joint mediation of the three neutral powers. Such a mediation would gain time and, as Schleinitz said to Moustier on 23 June, 'Time is everything for us at this moment'.[13] Moreover, the failure of a joint mediation would not leave Prussia with the unavoidable obligation of entering the war on the side of Austria.[14]

Joint mediation was the last thing Austria wanted. It would destroy any chance of Prussian assistance, and it would revive the idea of submitting to a European congress matters which Austria regarded as her private concern. Rechberg said to Loftus on 30 June:

> If Prussia is prepared to concert and come to an understanding with us as to the basis on which we could accept, and make peace, we shall be very happy to confer upon and to discuss any proposals she may make; but we shall not allow of the intervention of others – to force upon us a Peace. Such a course we should consider to be an infraction of our independent and sovereign rights. We can make our Peace directly with France, when the moment and opportunity arrives, but we shall not permit of the interference of others or submit our affairs to the decision of an European Areopagus.[15]

As a counter-move, Windischgrätz was sent to Berlin to negotiate for Prussian assistance,[16] and Prince Paul Esterhazy was sent to London to urge the English government to refrain from any attempt at mediation.[17]

The French, on the other hand, welcomed the proposal of joint mediation: it would keep Prussia out of mischief, and they would be able to control everything through their steady friend Russia. Some of the French diplomats seem also to have desired joint mediation in order the compel Napoleon to bring the war to an end before it became too much for him.[18] Cavour, in fact, asserted that there was a definite peace party at Paris, working against the aims of Italian nationalism, and supported by both the British and Russian ambassadors;[19] and it is very likely that the sudden anxiety shown by Napoleon after Solferino was largely due to deliberately alarmist reports from Paris. It was, perhaps, fortunate for the Italian cause that the Derby cabinet fell in June for the Palmerston government, which succeeded it, with Lord John Russell as foreign secretary, was far more pro-Italian and far more ready to play an active part in foreign affairs. It was even rumoured that the queen had attempted to secure from Palmerston as a condition of his appointment the maintenance of strict neutrality and of the treaties of 1815, and that Palmerston had refused to make any such promises.[20] Palmerston was notoriously hostile to the Franco-Russian Alliance, and the Russian government, therefore, hastened to show its friendship to France more demonstratively than ever by assuring the French government that it would not participate in any mediation or negotiations without the previous agreement of Napoleon.[21]

The way of joint mediation was thus being made easy for the Prussian government by the conciliatory attitude of France and the increased prospect of English co-operation. On the other side, the prince regent was still pressing for complete mobilization and military action. To stave off this demand, Schleinitz drew up, on 24 June, a dispatch to London and St Petersburg, proposing a joint mediation. The prince regent, however, insisted on laying down in advance that Prussia would only mediate on the basis of the *status quo ante bellum*; the only concession Schleinitz could secure was that there should be a European congress to discuss internal reforms throughout Italy.[22] Schleinitz moved as slowly as he dared: the dispatch to Bismarck was not sent until 26 June,[23] and the London dispatch was not handed to Bernstorff, who had been summoned to Berlin for consultation, until 29 June;[24] it was not until 4 July that Bernstorff read this dispatch to Lord John Russell.[25] Both Austria and France were aware that Prussia proposed a joint mediation, but they were not informed of the pre-condition of the *status quo*, which Prussia had laid down. This clause had been due to the insistence of the prince regent, and Schleinitz, by keeping it secret, hoped no doubt to lessen its force. If, at the outset, Austria had been told that Prussia would only negotiate on the basis of no territorial changes, the mediation would have had a very different character: Prussia would have been acting practically as the ally of Austria. On 7 July the prince regent did, in fact, tell Windischgrätz that he had accepted Austria's state of possession *ante bellum* as the basis of negotiations,[26] but this was a fortnight after the mediation had been first proposed, and in any case the Austrians were made suspicious of the Prussian attitude by a cold and almost anti-Austrian dispatch which Schleinitz had sent to Werther in Vienna only two days before.[27] The French, on the other hand, were at once provided from St Petersburg with full details of the Prussian proposals.[28]

The French government, as soon as it learnt that Prussia was preparing the way for joint mediation, at once drew up proposals of its own for transmission to London and St Petersburg: these terms were to show the conciliatory nature of the French demands – in contrast to the rigorous legalism of Austria – and it was just possible that one or other of the neutral powers might adopt them as its own. On 3 July Walewski, the French foreign minister, telegraphed to Montebello in St Petersburg urging that the Russian government should at once accept the Prussian proposal to negotiate terms of mediation at Berlin, and he formulated seven points, which the Russian government might put forward (as from itself) as the objects of mediation. The most important of these were the surrender of Lombardy by Austria: the creation of an independent state of Venice under an archduke; a confederation of all the Italian states; and a European congress to reorganize Italy on the above basis, and 'taking account of the rights of possession and of the wishes of the populations'. England, Walewski added, is disposed to share our views as to these bases, but she would not impose them on Austria.[29]

The Russian government did not altogether follow the directions of its ally. It was, no doubt, quite ready to support the French terms, but it saw that a greater air of impartiality would be given to the proceedings if Russia adopted the French terms only after having judicially weighed the proposals from both sides. The Russian government, therefore, proposed that the two combatants should be asked to formulate their terms for the consideration of the mediators. This would still, as Gortchakov said, 'keep Prussia out of mischief' and would place Austria in a position of extreme embarrassment: either the Austrian terms would be so uncompromising as completely to alienate Prussia and England, or else Austria would herself have to propose a cession of territory in order to escape isolation.[30]

A very dangerous situation would, however, arise if England did not take part in the mediation: Prussia was committed to supporting the Austrian terms, Russia the French, and the mediators might themselves be drawn into the war unless there was a third party to keep the peace between them. The country least bound to either disputant was England, and the French now strained every nerve to bring England into the mediation, and on the French terms.[31] Walewski had already hinted to Cowley on 26 June that Napoleon might propose to Austria the establishment of an independent kingdom of Lombardo-Venetia, and he had tried to ascertain from Cowley whether England would not use her influence to impose this upon Austria.[32] Walewski also made the most of Schleinitz's notorious unwillingness to support Austria; on 1 July he told Cowley that he had 'reason to know' that Prussia would shape her course according to the policy of the British government,[33] and he did his best to weaken the force of Prussia's condition of the *status quo* by assuring Cowley on 6 July that he 'had reason to know that Prussia would support the surrender of territory by Austria if it were proposed by England and Russia'.[34] England was thus being made to feel, perhaps rather too obviously, that the responsibility of keeping Prussia out of the war rested with her.

Persigny in London was also preparing the way for involving England in the mediation. On 30 June he told Russell that Napoleon might be persuaded to make peace on the basis of the surrender of Lombardy and the establishment of Venetia under an archduke; he hastened to add that these terms were merely a private suggestion of his own, but that it might be worth while for England to suggest them to Austria.[35] This Russell was not willing to do, but he indicated that England would have no objection to these terms. Walewski, therefore, went a step farther. On 4 July he sent Persigny a copy of the seven points which he had telegraphed to St Petersburg, with the information that they were the terms which Russia was going to advance to Prussia and England as the basis of mediation.[36] These terms Persigny communicated to Russell on 6 July with the suggestion that Austria might accept them 'if recommended to Austria by Great Britain'.[37] It is not clear what Persigny wanted. Did he mean that England should recommend the terms directly to Austria? or that she should recommend them by means of the joint mediation? The French were still preoccupied with the danger of Prussian intervention, and Persigny, therefore, presumably meant the latter. But Russell, who was unaware of the French knowledge of the Prussian situation, thought that Persigny desired a direct recommendation to Vienna.

The English government now had two proposals to consider: the French request to support the seven points at Vienna, and the Prussian proposal for a joint mediation, made by Bernstorff to Russell on 4 July; Bernstorff had then emphasized that Prussia 'could not propose to Austria *any* alienation of territory, but could only propose reforms and changes in modes of administration'.[38] The government was also aware from Esterhazy that Austria was most anxious not to have terms proposed to her from London, as she would be bound to reject them. These three points were considered by a cabinet on 6 July, immediately after Russell's interview with Persigny. From the first Russell was wholeheartedly in favour of the French proposals; sympathy with Italy dominated his mind to the exclusion of every other consideration, and he had already on 28 June suggested to Esterhazy 'merely as a speculation' the establishment of Venice under an archduke.[39]

Palmerston was more circumspect. Before the war he had been ready to maintain the settlement of 1815, but now, convinced that there would be a constant danger of war as long as Austria had any Italian territory, he was anxious to get Austria out of Italy altogether. If Napoleon wanted to make peace, he was free to do so; but Palmerston did not wish to be saddled with the responsibility of keeping Austria in Venice, and, as he pointed out to Russell, 'if we were to communicate (to Austria) the details of Persigny's scheme, we should identify ourselves with it, and be committed to an approval of it; but that I should be unwilling to do'.[40] This was a curious reversal of roles from 1848, when Palmerston, as foreign secretary, had advocated the retention of Venice by Austria, and Russell, as prime minister had opposed it. Palmerston's policy always had an element of daring; he probably hoped now, that if England refused to support the French terms, Napoleon might be driven on to expel Austria entirely from Italy and so establish a strong Italian kingdom in northern Italy. Russell, on the other hand, was still dispirited by the Italian defeats of 1848 and 1849, and therefore accepted with enthusiasm a proposal which eleven years earlier he had dismissed as inadequate.

The cabinet as a whole was considerably less pro-Italian than it had been in 1848; apart from Palmerston and Russell, only Gladstone supported the Italian cause. Moreover, the Crimean War had in the interval given England an experience of what interference in continental affairs led to. The bulk of the cabinet would undoubtedly have preferred to have done nothing at all, and in this they were strongly supported by the queen, ably directed by the prince consort. What the queen really wanted was to support Austria – both on grounds of treaty rights and of German sentiment – but, as this was manifestly impossible, she assumed an attitude of strict neutrality and put up the most stubborn resistance to every proposal which Russell advanced.

At the cabinet of 6 July Russell so far got his way as to be allowed to communicate the French terms to Apponyi, the Austrian ambassador, but he was to communicate them privately and without any recommendation. As Palmerston expressed it, 'we wished only to be postmen'.[41] Russell also got part of his way over the answer to the Prussian proposal for mediation. The draft dispatch he produced had been already criticized by the queen, and it was further altered by the cabinet; even so, according to Granville, the Lord President, 'it was sent in a form which was certainly not in accordance with the wishes of the cabinet'.[42] The essential passage of the draft was a rejection of the *status quo* as a possible basis for mediation and an assertion that 'no settlement is possible without some cession of the territory on the part of Austria'; this passage was retained in the dispatch as sent to Bloomfield.[43]

In communicating the French terms to Apponyi, Russell seems somewhat to have exceeded the decision of the cabinet and the wishes of the prime minister. According to his own account:

Count Apponyi said it would be his duty to convey by telegraph the substance of what I had said, but he wished to know exactly in what character the British Government offered these terms to Austria. I said that they merely transmitted them from the French ambassador, offering *no advice* whatever. They believed that if they should be accepted by Austria, the emperor of the French would be willing to treat on these bases. Count Apponyi expressed his opinion that his Government would not be willing to treat on these bases, but he did not know for certain, and he wished to know, supposing they should be willing, what would follow.

I said that in that case Great Britain alone or if Austria should prefer it, two of the neutral Powers, or Great Britain, Russia and Prussia united might propose an armistice.[44]

Reading between the lines, there can be little doubt that Russell made clear to Apponyi his own opinion that, as he wrote to Loftus, 'the terms proposed by the French Ambassador were calculated to lay the foundation of a secure and satisfactory peace'. Apponyi telegraphed the French terms to Vienna on 7 July and added, 'Lord John Russell desires but does not hope for acceptance'.[45] These terms were the first definite proposals which Austria had received from any quarter, and the Austrian government may be pardoned for assuming that they represented the terms which Great Britain would support in case of a joint mediation. Moreover, the Austrians were still uninformed as to the terms on which Prussia proposed to mediate and, with rather less excuse, assumed (or at least suspected) that the terms transmitted from London were the Prussian terms as well as the English.

A further question arises in regard to Russell's actions at this moment: what did he say to Persigny after the cabinet of 6 July? According to his own account, he merely informed Persigny of the cabinet's decision, that is, 'that Great Britain could not recommend in the present state of things any terms to Austria, but that I would communicate them privately to Count Apponyi'. Persigny has not left any record of Russell's attitude at this moment. The account of the negotiations which he gave Malmesbury on 21 July[46] is clearly concerned only with the proposals he made on 10 July,[47] for he expressly says that he went to Lord Palmerston after the armistice, by the emperor's order, whereas the earlier proposal had been made directly to Russell. Malmesbury's account continues: 'Persigny telegraphed the consent of the English Government to his master, who immediately asked for an interview with then emperor of Austria.' This is manifestly impossible, as the meeting at Villafranca was arranged the same day as the armistice; but this contradiction can be safely ascribed to the confusion and mental fog in which Malmesbury always lived. Presumably, therefore, Russell on 7 July merely gave Persigny a non-committal answer. Palmerston, however, told Persigny frankly that he disapproved of the French terms, and refused to be shaken even by the prospect of a prolongation of the war.[48]

The course of the negotiations was entirely changed by the announcement on 8 July of the conclusion of an armistice between Austria and France. The armistice was undoubtedly due to the personal initiative of Napoleon. Various guesses have been made as to his motives for bringing the war to an end, and there is probably an element of truth in most of the guesses. The popular story was that he had been upset by the sight of blood. According to de la Gorce, the determining factor was the movement in the central Italian states in favour of Sardinia, which made Napoleon fear that Sardinia might become so powerful as to escape from French control.[49] More immediate was the uncertainty as to the attitude of Prussia. It is true that the Prussian statesmen were for the most part doing their utmost to keep out of war, but popular feeling was rising and the prince regent would refuse to hold back any longer if German federal territory were violated. Nigra, who visited Napoleon two days after the battle of Solferino, found him very alarmed at the prospect of Prussian mobilization, and suspected that even Russia was advising Napoleon to be moderate.[50] Napoleon later exposed his motive frankly when he said in apology to Victor Emanuel 'that He was much pressed by a Foreign Power who told him that if he crossed the Adige, the war would become general and He would lose His throne'.[51]

Napoleon proposed the armistice in a personal letter to Francis Joseph on 5 July:

> M. mon frère,
>   On me fait savoir de Paris qu'une grande puissance va faire aux belligerents une proposition d'armistice. Si cette proposition était acceptée par Votre Majesté je désirerais le savoir parce qu'alors je ferais donner l'ordre à la flotte qui va attaquer Venise de n'en rien faire, car il est de notre devoir d'éviter de repandre du sang inutilement.[52]

Napoleon evidently wanted to make sure of the armistice: hence the threat of the French fleet, which was in fact by no means ready to attack Venice. The real threat for Francis Joseph lay, however, in the 'Great Power' which was going to propose an armistice, for this revived the danger of European interference in Austrian affairs, which Francis Joseph had gone to war to avoid. There was, of course, no foundation for Napoleon's statement, and Walewski at any rate was well aware that there was no immediate prospect of any of the neutral powers proposing an armistice, for he was still discussing the question with Cowley on 6 July[53] and Moustier made the suggestion for the first time in Berlin on 7 July.[54] Napoleon apparently thought – or chose to think –

that the Prussian proposal for mediation carried with it the proposal of an armistice, and he hoped that the Austrians would make the same confusion.

Napoleon's hopes were well founded. Austrian headquarters had been deplorably ill-informed throughout the war; it is characteristic of their intelligence service that they received the first accounts of the occupation of Milan from a Viennese summary of a Paris newspaper. Richard Metternich, who was the representative of the Foreign Office at headquarters, wrote to Rechberg on 9 June:

> People often say to me, 'Oh, if only we had known! We thought that England would protect our coasts, that the whole of Germany would rise at the first shot from a French gun, that we should succeed in punishing Piedmont before the arrival of the French army, that Tuscany would remain quiet, that the Pope would support us at least with his spiritual arm, and lastly that Napoleon would never dare to make open cause with the revolution &c'.[55]

After the battle of Solferino a number of regiments had become unreliable and had had to be dissolved or moved into the interior.[56] Moreover, Kossuth in Milan was attempting to get into touch with his followers in Hungary, and to organize a landing of Hungarian and Garibaldian legionaries on the Dalmatian coast; indeed it is hardly too much to say that Hungary gave Italy independence. Francis Joseph had thus plenty of reasons for bringing the war to an end, and there were no signs of any improvement in the situation; particularly disquieting was the silence of Windischgrätz, who was in Berlin trying to negotiate an alliance with Prussia.

Napoleon's invitation to negotiate an armistice was therefore accepted by Francis Joseph in a letter of 6 July:[57]

> M. mon frère,
>   Bien que je n'aie pas, de mon côté, reçu la nouvelle qu'un armistice serait proposé par une Puissance tierce, je partage trop le désir exprimé par Votre Majesté d'éviter toute effusion inutile de sang, pour ne pas me prêter volontiers à une négociation directe ayant pour but une suspension d'armes, si telle était l'intention de Votre Majesté. Dans ce cas je Lui proposerais de réunir à Villafranca des commissaires chargés de fixer la durée et les conditions de l'armistice.

Whoever drafted this letter would seem to have been a little sceptical of Napoleon's story, but this scepticism was not long continued. After some further correspondence between the two emperors[58] representatives met at Villafranca, and an armistice was concluded on 8 July. But this was not enough for Napoleon: to remove the danger of Prussian intervention he needed not merely an armistice, but the definite conclusion of a preliminary peace, for he must have been well aware that the prospect of a separate agreement between France and Austria was the thing most calculated to bring Prussia down on the Austrian side.[59] Napoleon, therefore, did not stand aside to allow the joint mediation to mature; he determined to secure peace by direct negotiations with Francis Joseph, and on 8 July, immediately after the conclusion of the armistice, he wrote to Francis Joseph, proposing a personal meeting:

> M. Mon frère,
> Si j'ai saisi le première idée d'une suspension d'armes pour en faire la proposition à Votre Majesté c'est que j'ai espéré qu'elle serait peut-être le prélude d'une entente directe entre nous qui mettrait un terme à un conflit regrettable sous bien de rapports et qui s'il continue fera verser bien de sang.
> Je vais donc loyalement dire à Votre Majesté que si elle croit possible que nous nous entendrons sur les bases générales d'un arrangement ultérieur une entrevue à Villafranca peut tre très advantageux pour la paix du monde; si au contraire elle ne croit pas la chose favourable, alors je tiens à ce que nous ne nous voyons pas, car pour ma part il me serait trop pénible de me battre de nouveau contre Votre Majesté après l'avoir connu et apprécié personnelement.[60]

Francis Joseph had by this time received from Vienna a copy of Apponyi's telegram of 7 July, transmitting the terms communicated by Russell, and these terms were at once accepted by the Austrians as a settled programme upon which France, England, Russia, and Prussia had agreed. The prospect of European mediation on such a basis made Francis Joseph desperately anxious to settle directly with Napoleon. He told Prince Alexander of Hesse, who was to visit Napoleon at Valeggio and prepare for the interview of the two emperors, that he would agree to the surrender of Lombardy (since 'in the course of the next – probably imminent – European war it could be reconquered'), but that he would never agree to the creation of an independent Venetian state under an archduke nor to the sacrifice of the Habsburg agnates in Modena and Tuscany.

Prince Alexander went over to Valeggio on 9 July. Napoleon began the discussion with the words: 'Well here are some suggestions that have reached me from London recently', and he then read out the terms which Persigny had submitted to Russell on 6 July. Napoleon finally wrote down on a sheet of paper his proposed basis of negotiations:

> Italian confederation of all Italian sovereigns.
> Union of Lombardy and Piedmont.
> Venice under an archduke.

With these terms Prince Alexander returned to Austrian headquarters, and Francis Joseph, after some discussion with Rechberg and with the prince, decided to agree to the interview, in the hope of securing further concessions. Prince Alexander thereupon wrote to Napoleon and informed him that Francis Joseph was willing to meet him. The following day the prince received from Napoleon a lengthy letter, in which he emphasized the great superiority of French strength and urged on Austria the wisdom of making peace, particularly as, 'if we dispose of the unhappy Italian question, there is nothing over which we need quarrel with Austria'.[61]

Napoleon could not be aware of the many reasons which were inclining Austrian headquarters to make peace. The Austrian resistance at Solferino had been stubborn and the Austrian army now occupied an almost impregnable position behind the Mincio; there was little outward sign of disorganization and discouragement. Moreover, Napoleon, being much better informed of the situation at Berlin than the Austrians were, was definitely apprehensive of Prussian intervention, and he therefore took great pains to dispel expectations which Francis Joseph had never had. Napoleon rightly appreciated the effect of European pressure on the Austrians and, over-estimating the strength of the Austrian position, he believed that nothing but European pressure would compel Austria to make peace. The terms which Napoleon proposed to offer to Francis Joseph – terms practically identical with those earlier proposed to Russia and England as a basis of mediation with the three minor points abandoned – were at once telegraphed to Moustier in Berlin and Persigny in London, with the instruction to ask for Prussian and British support respectively. The meeting of the two emperors was to take place on 11 July, and there was, therefore, time for Prussia and Great Britain to use their influence in Vienna. It is certain that neither of them did so; what is less certain is the answer they gave to the French representatives.

On 11 July Walewski told Cowley that Prussia had 'informed the Austrian government that, if the terms of France are not accepted, Austria must look neither to moral nor material support from Prussia'.[62] That Prussia had informed the Austrian government of anything we know to be untrue. Moreover, Walewski cannot possibly have received a report from Moustier by the morning of 11 July, and it would therefore appear that he had prepared his version of the Prussian reply well in advance. A few weeks later Walewski modified his story and now alleged that Schleinitz, in an interview with Moustier, had said that 'Austria, if she rejected the mediation of the three Powers, could count neither on the material nor moral support of Prussia'.[63] This may well have been true, and Schleinitz did not deny it. But it obviously refers to a much earlier stage of the negotiations, and presumably was a reply to Moustier's accusation that Prussia intended to take part against France if France rejected mediation, but to do nothing if Austria refused it. Certainly it has nothing at all to do with the French terms.

Moustier's own version of the Prussian attitude is very different. He had requested Schleinitz to support the French terms at Vienna, and on 11 July he reported Schleinitz's reply:

> that His Royal Highness had thought himself compelled to abstain from a step which materially was practically impossible and which he would not dare to make in isolation, after having begun a negotiation with England and Russia. It was, moreover, a pretty serious thing for Prussia to advise Austria to abandon a province which was still in her hands; to give this advice he would have to have a more exact knowledge of her financial and military state and be able to discuss with her the reasons which perhaps could dictate so great a sacrifice.[64]

This account is confirmed by Bloomfield, who wrote to Russell on 11 July that Schleinitz 'had declined advising the prince of Prussia to recommend their adoption by the emperor of Austria or to prejudge the decision to be taken by His Imperial Majesty'.[65] The only variation in the two stories is that to Moustier Schleinitz put the responsibility for refusal on William, while with Bloomfield he accepted it himself. Here Moustier is more likely to be right: the excuses for refusal were no doubt Schleinitz's, but the refusal itself came from William, who, far from wanting to impose terms and a loss of territory on Austria, was increasingly impatient to fight on the Austrian side. In a crown council on 8 July William had argued strongly for an immediate attack upon France, and had only agreed with great unwillingness to postpone the decision for a few days. William, according to his own account, was only waiting for the replies from St Petersburg and London in regard to mediation before coming to an agreement with Windischgrätz,[66] and Windischgrätz himself declared on 12 July that he would have secured a defensive and offensive alliance within twenty-four hours if news of the preliminary peace had not arrived.[67] Windischgrätz may have been over-confident and certainly Koller, the Austrian minister, was more sceptical.[68] But there can be no doubt that, for whatever reason, Prussia did refuse to support the French terms, and that the phrase 'Austria would not be able to count any longer on material or moral support from Prussia', which may well have been used by Schleinitz in reference to the mediation, was unscrupulously distorted by Walewski to refer to the French terms. It is probable, though less certain, that the temporizing measures of Schleinitz were practically exhausted and that, had the war continued, Prussia would have come in on the Austrian side.

The accounts of the English reply are equally contradictory. On 11 July Walewski told Cowley that Russell and Palmerston had declared themselves in favour of the French terms, but that they could not give a final answer until after a meeting of the cabinet, to be held that day.[69] Persigny, in a conversation with Malmesbury on 21 July,[70] also claimed that Russell and Palmerston had agreed to the French terms, but 'that Her Majesty refused her consent, saying the time was not come yet to make these proposals, as the fortresses were not taken. That, however, in the meantime Persigny had telegraphed the consent of the English Government to his master'. Actually, all that Persigny telegraphed on 11 July was that he found Palmerston 'more and more disposed to support the French propositions', and looking forward to an opening for mediation after the meeting at Villafranca, which he did not expect to have any immediate result.[71] This telegram is apparently the only basis of fact for Walewski's assertion that Russell agreed to the French terms in a telegram 'which arrived on the evening before Villafranca';[72] certainly there is no English telegram which could answer this description.

According to Granville, 'Palmerston had never supported the French terms; he had agreed to support them with the consent of the cabinet, but when it met Villafranca had already been signed'.[73] Russell described as '*not true*' an assertion of Rechberg that he 'had openly avowed a wish and desire that Italy should be wholly freed from Austrian domination; and that Austria should cease to hold any portion of Italian territory'.[74] In reply to Rechberg Russell declared that, apart from communicating the French terms to Apponyi without comment, Great Britain 'in the then state of affairs did not contemplate recommending any particular bases of negotiation to Austria', and 'never had in contemplation to propose as bases of negotiation terms to which Austria, from the outset, objected. Still less was she in concert with other neutral Powers to propose terms as mediators. No such concert was ever established, I may say was ever begun. For Prussia maintained that Austria could not be asked to give up any part of the territory she held by Treaty'.[75] This is undoubtedly a correct statement of official policy; Great Britain did not give any official support to the French terms nor did she agree to the Prussian proposal of mediation. Here Russell in his reply to Rechberg was on dangerous ground, for the reason why Great Britain refused to co-operate with Prussia was that she wished to demand the surrender of territory by Austria, exactly the point which Russell had set out to combat earlier in the dispatch. More important, however, is the fact that in this dispatch Russell passes over the actions of Palmerston and himself as distinct from the decisions of the cabinet.

The 10 July was a Sunday, and Russell was out of town at Richmond. it was, therefore, to Palmerston that Persigny made his request for diplomatic support for the terms which Napoleon was to propose at

Villafranca. Palmerston at once rode down to Richmond, and from there Russell wrote a note to the queen (who was at Aldershot):

> Lord Palmerston and he are of opinion that Your Majesty should give to the Emperor of the French the moral support which is asked ... Your Majesty's advisers cannot venture to make themselves responsible for the continuance [of the war] by refusing to counsel Your Majesty to accept the proposal of France.[76]

Shortly after the messenger had left for Aldershot, Apponyi came down to Richmond to tell Russell that he had heard from Vienna that the terms 'transmitted to Count Rechberg by the British government were totally inacceptable'. The same evening a reply came from the queen, strongly objecting to Russell's proposal to support the French terms.[77] At the meeting of the cabinet the following day Russell read the queen's letter, and also informed the cabinet of the Austrian rejection of the terms of 6 July. It was manifestly impossible for Russell to advocate support of the French terms, as they had already been virtually rejected by Vienna. He proposed instead 'that he should write to the Austrian and French governments to urge peace, to propose that the emperors should settle the basis of peace, and that if they failed to agree, England would, with or without Prussia and Russia, propose terms to both belligerents'.[78] This proposal was rejected by the cabinet – 'the third proposal of Lord John's in about as many cabinets which has been so dealt with by his colleagues' – and it was resolved to postpone any decision until after the results of the meeting at Villafranca were known. The only satisfaction Russell got was a declaration of opinion from the cabinet 'that it would be quite consistent with neutrality to employ the influence of the British government to prevent the further effusion of blood and to promote a peace which would be for the interest of all the belligerents'.[79] Even this was too much for the queen, and the prince consort at once wrote to Granville to encourage the organization of further opposition to Russell within the cabinet.[80] The queen, too, prepared further objections for Russell, but postponed sending her letter until 13 July. By this time the news of the agreement of Villafranca had arrived, and the queen was, therefore, able to emphasize to Russell how right she had been; Napoleon, she pointed out, had made England play the part of extortioner against Russia at the end of the Crimean War, while he had consolidated the Franco-Russian entente, and now he had tried to place England in the same position with regard to Austria. She concluded, 'The Queen is doubly glad that we should not now have fallen into the trap to ask from Austria, as friends and neutrals, concessions which he [Napoleon] was ready to waive'.[81] Palmerston and Russell now took up the attitude that they had been throughout in entire agreement with the queen. Palmerston 'rejoiced at the reserve of England' and told d'Azeglio that neither Prussia nor England had supported the four points at Verona;[82] while Russell read the queen's letter to the cabinet with every sign of approval. Granville had been placed in a most difficult position by the direct invitation of the queen to intrigue against the prime minister and the foreign secretary; but the news of Villafranca got him out of his difficulties, and his reply to the prince consort was purely academic.[83]

Russell's eagerness to support the French proposals emerges at every turn. He urged them on the cabinet, he urged them on the queen, he gave Apponyi a clear hint of his approval of them, and it is no unfair assumption that he did not conceal his attitude from Persigny. Palmerston had never been so enthusiastic. On 6 July he had opposed Russell's support of the French terms, and he repeated his objections to d'Azeglio after the cabinet of 11 July;[84] here, however, he was making the best of a bad job, as the cabinet had already decided against supporting them. But in the interval Palmerston had been shaken, partly perhaps by Russell's arguments, but more by the fear that the two emperors were about to make a settlement of Italy without consulting the other powers,[85] and there can be little doubt that on 10 July Palmerston expressed to Persigny his approval of the French terms and his willingness to advocate them at Verona. The French government had, therefore, some excuse for its assertion that its terms would be supported by Great Britain.

There remains a final question in regard to British policy. Who would have been victorious in the long run: Palmerston and Russell, who wanted to pursue an active policy in favour of Italian nationalism and the expulsion of Austria from Italy, or the queen and the majority of the cabinet, who wanted to do nothing, whether from Austrian sympathies or from fear of being involved in foreign complications? The queen put up a strong and continuous resistance at every step, and the cabinet would no doubt have been increasingly difficult to move as Russell's proposals became more concrete. But Russell and Palmerston had a definite idea of what they wanted and of the policy that should be pursued; their opponents had nothing but negations, and would probably have been compelled slowly to retreat. Russell and Palmerston, if they had got their way, might well have committed Great Britain to an attitude openly hostile to Austria in Italy; they would, however, have still been anxious to co-operate with Prussia, and their efforts would probably have been directed towards setting up a joint mediation. Prussia would have been induced to abandon her condition of the *status quo* and in return Great Britain would have agreed not to insist on Austria's being excluded from Italy altogether. Whether Prussia could have been won for such a mediation it is impossible to determine, for it depended on whether the tempering policy of Schleinitz could still maintain itself against the rising tide of German feeling and the increasing restlessness of the prince regent. If it could not, Prussian intervention would have produced a European war of incalculable dimensions and the entire history of Europe would have been changed. In the opposite case, a joint mediation would have produced a settlement very like the settlement of Villafranca, but more permanent, because it would have rested on a European sanction. Austria might never have lost Venice, and in all probability the Austrian dependants would have been restored in central Italy. On the other hand, Austria would have been deprived of Lombardy with as much formality as she had been given it in 1815, and it would, therefore, have been difficult for Austria to embark on a war for the recovery of Lombardy in the name of treaty rights. There can be little doubt that this consideration played a decisive part in the policy of Francis Joseph at the interview of Villafranca.

The two emperors met at Villafranca on 11 July. There is no reason to doubt the general tenor of Persigny's account to Malmesbury that Napoleon showed to Francis Joseph the terms which had been submitted to Great Britain and Prussia by France on 10 July, and said, 'Here are the terms proposed by England and agreed to also by Prussia. Now listen to mine, which, though those of an enemy, are much more favourable. So let us settle everything together, without reference to the neutral Powers, whose conditions are not nearly so advantageous as those I am ready to grant'.[86] It would seem, however, from the letter which Napoleon wrote to Francis Joseph immediately after the interview[87] that the concessions were made only after a certain amount of discussion; but it is very likely that Napoleon had made up his mind beforehand to accept these changes. The two most important modifications of the original French terms were the abandonment of the demand for the establishment of Venice as an independent state under an archduke[88] and the insertion of a new clause that the princes of central Italy should return to their states. But these changes sprang from Napoleon's fear that Sardinia would be so aggrandized as to dispense with French assistance. The first French plan, the seven points, had envisaged Sardinian acquisitions in central Italy; now the process was reversed. Moreover, Venice as an integral part of the Austrian empire and occupied by a large Austrian army would make Sardinia much more dependent on France than would a weak, independent Venetian state.

These concessions alone would probably have been enough to induce Francis Joseph to make peace. Austria was to retain the Quadrilateral, and Lombardy outside the Quadrilateral was defenceless, as the revolutionary wars and the war of 1848 had shown. Austria was thus merely being asked to give up a province which she could never defend, and which she could always reconquer if the European situation changed; that this was in Francis Joseph's mind is shown by his remark to Kempen on his return to Vienna, 'We shall get Lombardy back in a year or two'.[89] But Francis Joseph was always much more sensitive to his ally's or dependants' losses than to his own, as his support of Saxony after the battle of Kôniggrätz was to show; now he was willing to surrender Lombardy in return for a promise (as he thought) that the Habsburg agnates were to be restored.[90] If Francis Joseph had any doubts, they were dispelled by the Austrian view of the European situation. The Austrian statesmen were so blinded by their prejudices that they ignored any factor that was in favour of Austria. Because Prussia had until then kept out of the war, they were convinced that there was nothing to hope for from Prussia or Germany under any circumstances.[91] The last message from Berlin had insisted that, although Prussia was ready to support Austria's territorial bases, she could not bind herself to every detail of the settlement of 1815, and that co-operation would be impossible if Austria demanded from Prussia a pledge that nothing in Italy should be altered in the slightest.[92] Once the Prussians had committed the heinous offence of questioning the Vienna settlement, the Austrians believed they were capable of anything, and Francis Joseph, therefore, accepted without hesitation Napoleon's story that he had Prussian approval for his terms.

In the same way the Austrians ignored any mitigating factors in the English situation. They could not be expected to know of the internal struggle within the cabinet nor of the queen's stubborn resistance to Russell's policy, but they should have realized that English policy was not without hesitation. Even Esterhazy had noticed the queen's sympathy with Austria,[93] and Granville repeatedly hinted to Apponyi that he should take more opportunities of presenting the Austrian case to Russell. These hints were contemptuously rejected by Apponyi: 'I told Lord Granville', he wrote,[94] 'that I had no ambition to convert Lord John Russell to our manner of viewing the Italian Question.' Blinded by their dogmatic adherence to the Vienna settlement, the Austrians had failed to comprehend English policy ever since the time of Canning. They simply would not understand that the English statesmen were equally desirous of securing peace and stability in Europe, although they certainly chose other means than the Austrian. Austria could never have obtained English assistance in 1859; but a capable diplomacy could have made far more of Russell's inexperience and of Palmerston's distrust of the Franco-Russian alliance. The failure was largely due to Apponyi's conservative prejudices; but Rechberg certainly did nothing to correct them until after the war.[95] When on 7 July Apponyi had transmitted the French terms, the Austrians had suspected that they were rather the English terms, and now, on the bare word of Napoleon, this suspicion changed to certainty. Austria seemed to be threatened with a European tribunal sitting in judgement on her claims, and this Francis Joseph was determined never to tolerate; as he wrote to Napoleon the following day, 'Je n'aurais jamais cédé à la pression d'un aréopage européen'.[96] He would, therefore, have had little hesitation in accepting Napoleon's terms even had they been less favourable to Austria.

The conversation between the two monarchs was at once followed by a draft convention, transmitted by Napoleon to Francis Joseph through the agency of Prince Napoleon. The main points of the convention were the cession of Lombardy, excluding the Quadrilateral, to France; the dispossessed princes were to be restored; an Italian confederation, including Venice, was to be set up; and a European congress was to be summoned to settle the affairs of Italy. In matters of detail Francis Joseph, now supported by his advisers, seems to have been a hard bargainer, and Prince Napoleon had a severe struggle before he could bring Francis Joseph to sign the convention.[97] But Napoleon was not troubled by petty details; he was thinking of something much bigger: an intimate entente between Austria and France, similar to the entente between Russia and France which had followed the Crimean War. The signed convention he returned to Francis Joseph with another personal letter:

> M. mon frère,
> Je renvoie à Votre Majesté notre convention signé. Je conçois que certaines conditions avaient paru dures à Votre Majesté mais pour la tranquilliser je lui communique confidentiellement la dépêche que je reçois de Paris. Ayant fait connaître les premières propositions que j'avais addressé à Votre Majesté non seulement les cabinets de Londres et St. Petersburg ont declaré être prêts à les soutenir très vivement, mais le governement Prussien a fait dire que *si l'Autriche refusait elle ne devrait plus compter sur son concours ni matériellement ni moralement.* Votre Majesté vot donc qu'elle a gagné à traiter avec moi.[98]

Napoleon can have had only one object in writing this letter: to complete the estrangement between Austria and Prussia. He must already have told Francis Joseph that England and Russia were prepared to support the French terms; but evidently Walewski's version of the Prussian attitude had reached Napoleon too late to be used at the interview. It was, however, too good to be wasted; and its verisimilitude was enhanced by the fact that it was a distortion of something the Prussian government really had said. As Walewski had already repeated it to Cowley on the morning of 11 July, the distortion was presumably Walewski's, and there is no means of knowing whether Napoleon was aware that it was a distortion. At any rate, it served his purpose of strengthening the Austro-French entente.

In the first days after Villafranca the Austrian government was undoubtedly more bitter against Prussia and England, who had failed to help Austria, than against France, who had defeated her. During the negotiations at Villafranca Francis Joseph was heard to say, 'La seul chose aui me console c'est la figure qui va faire la Prusse'.[99] and in the Laxenburg manifesto, which he issued immediately on his return to Vienna, he told his subjects that he had made peace because the neutral Powers were threatening to impose on Austria terms less favourable than those which Napoleon was offering.[100] This accusation was answered at great length by both Russell and Schleinitz. Russell explained that Great Britain had never supported the terms which he had communicated to Apponyi,[101] and Schleinitz insisted that Prussia would have been willing to mediate only on the basis of the Austrian state of possession in Italy.[102] Neither of these accounts represented the complete truth, though they were at any rate nearer the truth than the accounts given by Napoleon, and they were circumstantial enough to begin to shake the faith of Austria in her new ally.

The arrogant arraignment of Prussia and England, and the entente with France, were the last flickers of the policy inaugurated by Schwarzenberg and so incompetently continued by Buol: that of a complete break with traditional conceptions and the ruthless pursuit of *Realpolitik*, based not upon considerations of tradition or sentiment, but of power and prestige. Such a policy might have suited a strong, consolidated, national state; but it had been disastrous for Austria, and it was fundamentally antipathetic to Rechberg, who desired above all else a revival of the old friendly relations between Prussia and Austria. During the peace negotiations at Zurich in the autumn of 1859, Napoleon did everything to revive Austrian distrust and to strengthen Rechberg's hand in Vienna. For a variety of reasons, but principally from fear of being outbid by England in the competition for Italian sympathy, Napoleon became increasingly pro-Italian as the negotiations proceeded. For Austria the decisive question was the restoration of the Italian princes, in return for which Francis Joseph had surrendered Lombardy. Now Austria discovered that this clause was meaningless, for it did not say how they were to be restored: obviously they could not be restored without armed force, but France refused to restore them by French arms and refused equally to allow Austria to restore them. This example of Napoleon's dishonesty was so glaring that the Austrians began to suspect that Napoleon might have been equally disingenuous on other occasions, and a review of the negotiations of Villafranca led them to the conclusion that they had been greatly misled as to the policy of Prussia, if not of England. By the beginning of 1860 the entente with France had been abandoned and Rechberg was working wholeheartedly for a revival of the Prussian alliance. The friendly relations with Prussia were not to be permanent, but the distrust of Napoleon lasted with certain exceptions until the fall of the second empire.

In view of the internal situation of Austria, it is probable that Napoleon could in any case have made peace with Francis Joseph at Villafranca. Napoleon, ignorant of the weakness of the Austrian position, had resorted to unscrupulous, indeed dishonest, diplomacy in order to make success certain, but at the price of sowing the seeds of future distrust. The Austrians, when they discovered the deception, were the more bitter because their own prejudices and lack of information had made them walk so readily into Napoleon's trap.

Notes

1. On the news of the battle of Magenta, Malmesbury wrote to d'Azeglio: 'I wish you joy of the news you send me and which must give you great pleasure. The said conviction, however, of a party not engaged must be that every victory on whatever side it is gained must prolong the contest and perhaps add to the combantants.' (*Cavour e l'Inghilterra* [1935], ii, 336.) Despite Malmesbury's impartial air it is unlikely that he would have written in similar terms to Apponyi in the event of an Austrian victory.
2. Malmesbury expressed his dislike of the proposed congress after its breakdown: 'Without the Russian proposal of a congress, all would have been settled long ago. The congress has been for me nothing but a source of irritation and anxiety.' (Apponyi to Buol, No. 43D, 23 April 1869. Haus-, Hof- und Staatsarchiv (cited as HHSA), Vienna).
3. Apponyi to Buol, No. 32, 31 March 1859, HHSA. 'According to Mr XXXX Palmerston has entirely abandoned the errors he followed years ago. He has not, it is true, any more sympathy for Austria, but he considers our alliance indispensable for the future. The great danger for Europe is in his opinion Russia and the alliance of this Power with France. A war against England will be in a few years the inevitable result, and it is this danger which England must never lose sight of. To this end she must arm steadily, in order to be ready. Also, she must strengthen the alliance with Austria, the only Power who can give her useful support in the East and assure the support of Germany for England.' The anonymous informant is presumably Klindworth, who was in the pay of both England and Austria, and probably of France as well. His reports are not to be taken too seriously. Palmerston's real attitude to the war is expressed in a note to Granville of 22 April (Granville Papers, PRO, Kew, quoted GD and index number), GD 29, 19: 'The Result will be that they (the Austrians) will be driven out of Italy, and though one must lament the means, one will rejoice at the End'.
4. Buol to Apponyi, No. 1, 30 April 1859, HHSA.

5. These, and other important quotations from the diary of Kempen, the police minister, are most readily accessible to the English reader in Redlich 1929, *Francis Joseph*, p. 260.
6. Loftus to Buol, 26 April 1859, HHSA. 'HM Govt. assign to Austria and fix upon her the responsibility for all the miseries and calamities inevitable consequent upon a conflict, which was on the eve of being averted, but which once begun will infallibly produce a more than ordinary amount of social suffering and political convulsion.'
7. *The Times*, 26 April 1859.
8. This offhand treatment doubtless explains the archduke's disapproval of the ultimatum, which he expressed to Kempen. (Redlich, *Francis Joseph*, p. 261.)
9. This was exactly what the French feared. On 4 June Moustier, the French minister at Berlin, warned Schleinitz that mediation would be admissible only if it 'were preceded by a firm resolution to act towards the belligerent parties in an absolutely equal fashion; I said this to anticipate a generally held opinion, according to which Prussia would put herself on the Austrian side, if France refused mediation, and would limit herself to abstention in the opposite case'. (Moustier to Walewski, No. 69, 4 June 1859. Archives des Affairs Étrangères (cited as AAE), Paris).
10. Werther to Schleinitz, 18 June, *Austwärtige Politik Prussens, 1858–71*, i, 677 (cited as APP); 29 June, p. 710; to Prince Regent, 30 June, p. 711: 'Rather than subordinate herself to mediation and a European congress Austria will settle directly with France and leave Prussia in the air without any influence on negotiations.'
11. *APP*, p. 646.
12. *APP*, pp. 654–6.
13. *APP*, p. 701.
14. Bloomfield to Malmesbury, No. 358, confidential, 18 June 1859. Public Record Office, Foreign Office 64, 478 (cited FO and index number). Schleinitz said that 'From what he now heard there would be but little use in Prussia coming forward alone with propositions to the Belligerents, that they would not listen to her unless an understanding were previously concerted with HMG [Her Mayesty's Government] and that of Russia and that the failure of any such single proposals on the part of Prussia might be attended by the most serious consequences and perhaps lead to an extension of the war'.
15. Loftus to Russell, No. 584, 30 June 1859, FO 7, 572. Cf. Rechberg to Apponyi, telegram, 2 July, HHSA. 'In our interest as in that of Europe we wish the Cabinet of Berlin to decide on an active role. To support its projects of mediation would be at the moment to desire a peace, which would immeasurably increase French supremacy and to which we could never consent.'
16. *APP*, pp. 721–8.
17. Rechberg to Apponyi, private, 12 June 1859. Esterhazy's visit had no official character.
18. So Persigny said to Apponyi on 21 May. Apponyi to Buol, No. 521, 21 May, HHSA. Persigny was so indiscreet that he probably spoke the truth, although he was speaking to the representative of an enemy power. On 2 June Walewski said he wanted mediation in order to bring

pressure to bear on Napoleon to stop at the Mincio. (Reuss to Schleinitz, confidential, 2 June, *APP*, pp. 643–4).

19. Cavour to Nigra, 1 July, *Carteggio Cavour Nigra*, 4 vols (1926–29), ii, 230.
20. Apponyi to Rechberg, No. 59B, 14 June, HHSA.
21. Montebello to Walewski, No. 42, 25 June; Gortchakov to Kissilev, 11/23 June (dispatch communicated to the French government), AAE.
22. Schleinitz to Bismarck and Bernstorff, 24 June, *APP*, p. 696.
23. With another asking that Budberg, in Berlin, be empowered to discuss bases of mediation, *APP*, p. 704.'
24. With a dispatch of 27 June, in answer to a dispatch of Russell to Bloomfield, No. 1, 22 June, FO 64, 472.
25. Russell to Cowley, No. 54, confidential, 4 July, FO 7, 1284.
26. Windischgrätz to Francis Joseph, 7 July, *APP*, p. 728.
27. Schleinitz to Werther, 5 July, *APP*, p. 729.
28. Montebello to Walewski, No. 43, 1 July, AAE. Bismarck to Schleinitz, telegram, 6 July, *APP*, p. 738. The Prussians were very annoyed at this leakage.
29. Walewski to Montebello, telegram, 3 July, AAE. The other three points were no foreign interference in Italy; a lay vice-royalty in the Legations; and certain territorial changes for the benefit of Sardinia in central Italy. These three points were subsequently dropped by the French and their proposals then became the four points. The existence of two sets of proposals later provided the English and Prussian governments with a sort of alibi to use towards Austria. The Prussians declared that they had never seen 'the seven points' and the English were equally surprised at 'the four points'.
30. Gortchakov to Budberg (at Berlin) and to Kissilev (at Paris), 25 June/7 July (dispatches communicated to the French government), AAE. Crampton to Russell, No. 4 and telegram No. 6, 7 July, FO 65, 536. 'Gortchakov begs me to explain that his idea is that the three Powers should come to understanding as soon as possible as to the principle of a mediation, but without defining the bases of it until they have invited France and Austria respectively to express their views as to the conditions which each might think acceptable.'
31. Cavour, too, realized that it was English mediation which would turn the scale. See his letter to Prince Napoleon, 1 July, *Carteggio Cavour Nigra*, ii, 230.
32. Cowley to Russell, No. 53, confidential, 27 June, FO 27, 1298. 'It is felt here that if Austria refused such terms it would be the duty of Europe, and more particuarly of England, to interfere in order to constrain Austria to accept terms of peace.'
33. Cowley to Russell, No. 80, confidential, 1 July, FO 27, 1299.
34. Cowley to Russell, No. 126, 6 July, FO 27, 1299.
35. Russell to Cowley, No. 48, 1 July, FO 27, 1284. Walewski had the same idea, 'as his personal opinion', on 28 June. Reuss to Schleinitz, 29 June, secret, *APP*, p. 709.
36. Walewski to Persigny, private, 4 July, AAE.
37. Russell to Loftus, No. 52, confidential, 27 July, FO 7, 564, in which Russell gives an account of the negotiations as a whole.
38. Russell to Cowley, No. 54, confidential, 4 July, FO 27, 1283.

39. Russell to Loftus, No. 22, 29 June; No. 24, 6 July, FO 7, 564. Both deal with a conversation of 28 June. Russell said in reply to Esterhazy that 'we had no *present* intention of the kind, but that if we saw a favourable occasion, we might perhaps suggest to both parties to put a termination to hostilities'.

40. Ashley, E., *Life of Viscount Palmerston*, 2 vols (1879), ii, 158–60. Palmerston to Russell, 6 July. 'We are asked to propose to the belligerents a parcelling out of the nations of Italy, as if we had any authority to dispose of them. I cannot be a party to Persigny's scheme. If the French Emperor is tired of his war, and finds the job tougher than he expects, let him make what proposals he pleases and to whomsoever he pleases, but let them be made as from himself formally and officially, and let him not ask us to father his suggestions and make ourselves answerable for them.'

41. D'Azeglio to Cavour, 11 July, *Cavour e l'Inghilterra*, ii, 344.

42. Granville to the Prince Consort, 13 July, GD 29, 31. The dispatch was sent without being resubmitted to the queen. The Prince Consort to Granville, 12 July.

43. Russell to Bloomfield, No. 18, 7 July, FO 64, 472.

44. Russell to Loftus, No. 52, 27 July, FO 27, 564. Russell gave a practically identical account in a letter to the queen on 7 July. G.P. Gooch (ed.), *Later Correspondence of Lord John Russell*, 2 vols (London, Longman, 1935), ii, 235.

45. Apponyi to Rechberg, telegram, 7 July, HHSA.

46. Lord Malmesbury, *Memoirs of an Ex-Minister* (London, Longmans, Green and Co., 1882), ii, 200.

47. See p. 39.

48. Persigny to Walewski, very confidential and secret, 7 July, AAE.

49. La Gorce, *Histoire du second Empire*, iii, 102.

50. Nigra, fragment of a memorandum, *Il Carteggio Cavour Nigra*, ii, 290. In fact the Russians gave no such advice, but on the contrary promised Napoleon every support. See above, note 30.

51. Hudson to Russell, No. 34, confidential, 16 July, FO 67, 246.

52. Napoleon to Francis Joseph, 5 July, HHSA. The letter is obviously written in great haste; for instance, it is dated 'le 5 *juin*'.

53. Cowley to Russell, No. 132, confidential, 6 July, FO 7, 1299. Walewski said: 'If time is wanted to discuss the preliminaries of peace and either England, Prussia, or Russia or all three united will propose an armistice, I am certain that the Emperor will accept it.'

54. *APP*, p. 744.

55. Richard Metternich to Rechberg, 9 June, HHSA.

56. H. Friedjung, *Der Kampf um die Vorherrschaft in Deutschland*, 2 vols (1897–98), i, 33.

57. Francis Joseph to Napoleon, 6 July, HHSA.

58. Napoleon to Francis Joseph, 7 July; Francis Joseph to Napoleon, 7 July, HHSA.

59. Cf. Bloomfield to Russell, No. 374, 2 July, FO 64, 479.

60. Napoleon to Francis Joseph, 8 July, HHSA.

61. The account in this and the previous paragraph is derived from the diary of Prince Alexander of Hesse, as summarized by Count Egon Corti in his book, *The Downfall of Three Dynasties* (1934). As the diary is not quoted verbatim, this source must be treated with caution.

62. Cowley to Russell, No. 167, confidential, 11 July, FO 27, 1209.
63. Pourtalès to Schleinitz, 30 July, APP, p. 769.
64. Moustier to Walewski, 11 July, private, AAE. Schleinitz gave a practically identical account of this conversation to Koller, the Austrian minister, a fortnight later (Koller to Rechberg, No. 108B, 26 July, HHSA).
65. Bloomfield to Russell, No. 390, 11 July, FO 64, 478.
66. The Prince Regent to Francis Joseph, 14 July, APP, p. 755.
67. Windischgrätz to Francis Joseph, 12 July, APP, p. 751.
68. Koller to Rechberg, 12 and 14 July, APP, p. 753.
69. Cowley to Russell, No. 160, confidential, 11 July, FO 27, 1299.
70. Malmesbury, Memoirs, ii, 200.
71. Persigny to Walewski, telegram, no. 73, 11 July, AAE.
72. Pourtalès to Schleinitz, 30 July, APP, p. 769.
73. Apponyi to Rechberg, No. 76A, 27 July, HHSA.
74. Loftus to Russell, No. 641, 18 July, FO 7, 573, with Russell's marginal comment.
75. Russell to Loftus, No. 52, confidential, 27 July, FO 7, 564.
76. Russell to the queen. Letters of Queen Victoria, 1837–1861 (1907), iii, 450.
77. The queen to Russell, ibid., iii, 450. The account of the actions of Russell and Palmerston on 10 July is taken from a conversation Palmerston had with d'Azeglio on 11 July. In it Palmerston passed over the letter to the queen with the words: 'It was agreed between them to send an express to the queen at Aldershot to consult Her Majesty', and Palmerston gave d'Azeglio no inkling that he had favoured the French terms. (D'Azeglio to Cavour, 11 July, Cavour e l'Inghilterra, ii, 344).
78. Granville to the prince consort, 13 July, GD 29, 31.
79. Russell to the queen, 11 July. Later Correspondence of Lord John Russell, ii, 235. Palmerston's undated memorandum (Lorne, Palmerston, p. 192), arguing that there was nothing inconsistent with neutrality in giving advice to Austria, presumably accompanied Russell's letter, or was perhaps submitted to the cabinet of 11 July.
80. The prince consort to Granville, 12 July, GD 29, 31.
81. Sir T. Martin, Life of the Prince Consort, 5 vols (1875–80), iv, 465. The prince consort, in his letter to Granville, says, 'the Queen is just writing again to Lord John to draw his attention to these points'. This is presumably the same letter as the one quoted, but there may well have been another letter written on 12 July and not printed by any authority.
82. D'Azeglio to Cavour, 12 July. Cavour e l'Inghilterra, ii, 345.
83. Granville to the prince consort, 13 July, GD 29, 31. The active part played by the prince consort in these negotiations gives an odd air to his comment on Napoleon's letter to Francis Joseph of 11 July (referring to English and Russian support of the French terms): 'Quite untrue, as nobody knew anything of these stipulations', Martin, Life, iv, 460.
84. D'Azeglio to Cavour, 11 July, Cavour e l'Inghilterra, ii, 344. 'It seemed to me that, while desiring not to place obstacles in the way of an arrangement which would bring peace, Lord Palmerston did not conceal from himself its imperfections. Although the Memorandum asserts once more the principle of Italy for the Italians, Lord Palmerston cannot help admitting that, whatever may be the guarantees with which the new creation may be safeguarded, it seems impossible to him not to open the

way by these guarantees for an Austrian invasion of Italy whenever the moment is favourable.'

85. Persigny to Walewski, No. 71, very confidential and secret, 8 July, AAE. 'Lord Palmerston seemed to fear that the two Emperors would be tempted to settle the fate of Italy together and without the assistance of Europe, but he soon rejected this idea himself, relying on the solemn declarations of the emperor and on the impossibility of deciding any territorial change in the map of Italy without the assent of Europe.'

86. Malmesbury, *Memoirs*, ii, 200. Rechberg said on 16 July that Austria had learnt from France that 'Prussia together with England and Russia supproted a mediation project, which gave Lombardy to Sardinia, made Venice independent under an archduke, gave Modena and Verona to Sardinia, set up the Parma family in Tuscany and deposed altogether that Grand Duke of Tuscany and the Duke of Modena.' (Werther to Schleinitz, 16 July, *APP*, p. 759). The information can only have come from Napoleon direct; apparently he communicated all the seven points.

87. Napoleon to Francis Joseph, 11 July, HHSA. 'A peine rentré chez moi j'ai refléchi aux proposition que Votre Majesté m'avait faite et je me suis décidé a les accepter persuadé que l'amitié et l'alliance de Votre Majesté valaient mieux que quelques avantages politiques ... J'espère donc que la paix est faite entre nous et que rien ne viendra plus troubler l'harmonie qui existait entre nos pays et qui doit être s'accoitre par les rapports pleins de franchise qui ont eu lieu entre nous ce matin'.

88. Napoleon did, however, attempt to secure for Venice an autonomous position within the empire. Francis Joseph refused to include this in the written convention, on the grounds that it would be an infringement of his sovereign rights, and, according to Cowley, he added: 'Not all Europe combined will induce me to sacrifice a principle.' (H.R. Wellesley, *The Paris Embassy during the Second Empire*, edited by F.A. Wellesley, London, 1928, p. 186). Napoleon, therefore, had to be content with a personal promise from Francis Joseph that Venice should be given a satisfactory position. This promise was as worthless as the similar promises of liberal institutions for Lombardy which were given by Wessenberg and Schwarzenberg in 1848. Francis Joseph later repudiated his promise on the ground that Napoleon had not fulfilled *his* promise to restore the Habsberg princes (Redlich, *Francis Joseph*, p. 277).

89. Redlich, *Francis Joseph*, p. 277.

90. Instructions for the Austrian delegates to the Peace Conference at Zurich, HHSA.

91. Rechberg said to Werther on 16 July, 'From the discussions at Berlin it was increasingly clear that there would be no help from Prussia or Germany'. (Werther to Schleinitz, 16 July, *APP*, p. 759).

92. Schleinitz toWerther, 5 July, *APP*, p. 729.

93. Esterhazy to Rechberg, private, 2 July, HHSA.

94. Granville to Apponyi, 25 July, GD 29, 18. Apponyi to Rechberg, No. 76A, 27 July, HHSA.

95. Rechberg initiated a new policy of conciliation towards England in a private letter to Apponyi on 2 August, HHSA. Apponyi disliked his new task intensely: 'our opinions and our intentions are too diametrically opposed to make an understanding possible. I will even say that this

complete divergence makes all discussion sterile.' (Apponyi to Rechberg, private, 12 August, HHSA).

96. Francis Joseph to Napoleon, 12 July, HHSA.
97. *Revue des Deux Mondes* (August 1909), lii, 481.
98. Napoleon to Francis Joseph, 11 July, HHSA.
99. Cowley to Russell, No. 223, 16 July, transmitting a report of Claremont, the military attaché, of 13 July, FO 27, 1299.
100. Werther to Schleinitz, 16 July, *APP*, p. 759. Loftus to Russell, 18 July, No. 641, FO 7, 573.
101. Russell to Loftus, No. 52, confidential, 27 July, FO 7, 564.
102. Schleinitz to Werther, 23 July, *APP*, p. 765.

CHAPTER FOUR

The Struggle for Supremacy in Germany, 1859–66

In later life Alan Taylor tended to play down the influence of other scholars on his career. In the case of Friedjung's book he was influenced by both the two most substantial mentors of his early career: A.F. Pribram (1859–1941) and Lewis Namier (1888–1960). Alfred Pribram, Professor of History at the University of Vienna, supervised his research in Vienna, 1928–30, while Lewis Namier arrived at the Department of History at Manchester University as Professor of Modern History (1931–51) one year after Alan Taylor. In taking up Friedjung's work he was emulating Pribram, a friend and successor of Friedjung, who had completed some of Friedjung's work after Friedjung's death in 1920. The abridged translation of the tenth edition (1916–17) of *The Struggle for Supremacy in Germany 1859–1866* (1897) was prepared for a series of books 'Studies in Modern History' edited by Namier for Macmillan. Alan Taylor's own second book, *Germany's First Bid for Colonies 1884–5* (1938) also appeared in the same series.

Alan Taylor later observed that his view of German history had been influenced by the fact that his researches had begun with a Vienna perspective. In his essay written as an introduction to Friedjung's book Alan Taylor commented, 'His account is impartial ... it springs from the fact that Friedjung sympathised with both sides, as he was both an Austrian and a German'. Alan Taylor did acknowledge Friedjung's influence on his writing in his autobiography,

> When I came to write, my model was Friedjung's *Struggle for Supremacy in Germany* and not anything of Pribram's. I do not claim that I came up to my model (A.J.P. Taylor, *A Personal History*, London, Hamish Hamilton, 1983, p. 91)

Alan Taylor dated his introductory essay 3 January 1935, that is after the Nazi assumption of power in Germany in January 1933 (referred to in the essay as 'present uncivilised system of rule') but before the Anschluss of 1938 (the unification of Austria with Germany). The essay was followed six years later by the first version of his history of the Austrian Empire and Austria–Hungary, *The Habsburg Monarchy 1815–1918* (London, Macmillan, 1941), and then by a substantially rewritten volume, *The Habsburg Monarchy 1809–1918* (London, Hamish Hamilton, 1948). In the 1941 version Alan Taylor simply wrote, 'The diplomatic and military history of the war of 1866 has been written once and for all by Heinrich Friedjung and it is unnecessary to repeat his work' (p. 140). In the second version he removed suggestions made in the first version and in his introductory essay to Friedjung (printed here) that there were 'lost opportunities', 'that the Habsburg monarchy might have survived if only this or that statesman or people had been more sensible'.

In this essay Alan Taylor mentions many leading figures in the Habsburg monarchy. The Emperor from 1848–1916 was Francis Joseph. His principal ministers mentioned in the essay were Prince Clemens Metternich (1809–48), Prince Felix zu Schwarzenberg (1848–52), Alexander Bach (1852–59), Anton von Schmerling (1861–65), Baron Frederich von Beust (1867–70), Count Eduard Taaffe (1870–71 and 1879–93) and Count Casimir Badeni (1895– 97). Foreign ministers in the period included Count Karl Ludwig de Ficquelmont (Metternich's successor), Count Karl Buol (1852–59), Johann Bernhard von Rechberg (1859–64), Count Alexander von Mensdorff (1864–66), Frederich von Beust (1865–68), Julius Andrassy (1871–79), and Count Alois von Aehrenthal (1906–12). Maurice Esterhazy, a Hungarian, was an influential conservative Minister without Portfolio in the pre-1865 government. General L. Benedek was the Austrian general defeated at Sadowa in 1866; Helmuth von Moltke was the victorious German general. Hofrat von Biegeleben was a diplomat and assistant to Rechberg. Richard Belcredi was minister of state, 1865–67. Joseph Baernreither was minister of commerce in 1898. Georg von Schonerer, a German Austrian, was a co-author with Victor Adler, the future socialist leader, and Henrich Friedjung of the radical programme drafted at Linz in 1882. Professor Joseph Redlich was a major historian of the Habsburg monarchy who was involved in the politics of its last years.

Henrich Friedjung, the author of *The Struggle for Supremacy in Germany 1859–66* and perhaps the greatest of Austrian historians, was born at Rostchin in Moravia, of Jewish parents, on 18 January 1851, and died in Vienna on 14 July 1920. He was the author of numerous historical works – *The Emperor Charles IV and his Share in the Intellectual Life of his Time* (1876); *The Struggle for Supremacy in Germany* (1897–98); *Benedek's Literary Remains* (1901); *The Crimean War and Austrian Policy* (1907), *Austria from 1848 to 1860* (incomplete: the first volume, 1909; the first part of the second volume, 1912); *Historical Essays* (1919); and *The Age of Imperialism*, which was completed after his death by Professor A.F. Pribram (1920–22).

The *Struggle for Supremacy* is undoubtedly Friedjung's greatest work, for in it he combined the accuracy and the gift of vivid narrative, which stamps all his work, with a deep emotional comprehension of both parties in the struggle. His account is impartial, but the impartiality is not due to aloofness; it springs from the fact that Friedjung sympathized with both combatants – he was on both sides at once. For Friedjung was by conviction a passionate German Austrian, proud of the great traditions of Germany, but equally proud of the great traditions of Austria. The war of 1866 laid the foundation of a united German Empire, such as German patriots had aspired to for years, and Bismarck, its architect, became the national hero of all Germans. Friedjung was no exception – he felt as German as any Prussian or Bavarian – and Bismarck is clearly the hero of *The Struggle for Supremacy*. But Friedjung was also an Austrian and, while he rejoiced that Germany had achieved unification, he could not but grieve that it should be achieved at the expense of Austria. It was impossible for

Friedjung to find an Austrian statesman whom he could set against the titanic figure of Bismarck, for, though he made some attempt to turn Benedek into his hero, he was too clear-sighted to believe that there was anything of a real hero in that conscientious, second-rate officer. What Friedjung sets against the personal greatness of Bismarck is the impersonal greatness of the Austrian tradition and of the cause of the German Austrians.

The essence of the German Austrian position had been the desire to have the best of both worlds – to occupy the leading position in both Germany and the Austrian Empire. This dualism enabled Friedjung to write a great book, but in political life it bound him to a cause without a future. As Friedjung says, the German Austrians were the real losers in the war of 1866. The German Austrian problem was a direct outcome of the rise of nationalism at the beginning of the nineteenth century; until then there had been nothing paradoxical or unusual in the German Austrians being part of Germany (or rather the Holy Roman Empire) and at the same time being connected with other nationalities outside it. But the belief that states ought to have a national basis, that tremendous legacy of the French Revolution, struck at the very root of the German Austrian position. Metternich realised clearly that nationalism would destroy the Austrian Empire, and for this reason he persuaded the Emperor Francis to refuse the crown of Germany when it was offered to him in 1815; quite deliberately Metternich was preparing the way for a non-national Austrian Empire, contrasting with and so preventing the national German state. The liberals who sat in the Austrian Parliament of 1848 were equally realistic: caring for Austria as much as Metternich did, they too recognized that the survival of the Austrian Empire was only possible on a non-national basis, and that basis they found in a free co-operation between the races, a co-operation which produced the Kremsier Constitution of 1849. Nor did on the other hand those German Austrians, who refused to abandon their German nationalism, shirk the conclusion that this and the Austrian Empire were incompatible; the destruction of the Austrian Empire was the price for the achievement of the national ambitions and that price they were prepared to pay.

But after the failure of the revolution of 1848 the German Austrians made their great, their disastrous, mistake. They gave up the struggle against the dynasty and began to co-operate with it. The success of the dynasty had been everywhere so overwhelming that it seemed useless to stand out against it; with short-sighted subtlety the German Austrians now supported the Empire in the hope that they would one day become the heirs of the Habsburgs as completely as the French Revolution had been of the Bourbons. Henceforth they believed that it was in their interests to support the dynastic claims. They allowed their national feeling to be diverted into the dynastic quarrel with Prussia and their liberalism dwindled into an acceptance of the imperial theory that the revolution had destroyed all the traditional rights of the other nationalities. The central Parliament, which Schmerling set up in 1861, was as illegal and as artificial as the absolutism it supplanted; but the Germans participated in it because they believed that the parliamentary game, weighted as it was in their favour, would give them supremacy throughout the Empire. Similarly they supported Francis Joseph's claim to supremacy in Germany in the belief that Habsburg supremacy would mean supremacy for them.

There was a brief moment when Schmerling seemed to be on the point of realizing the German Austrian ambition of a Germany united under Austria and an Austria united under the Germans. But Schmerling's failure was complete even before the war of 1866. The Meeting of the Princes at Frankfurt in 1863 was the end of Austria's attempt to satisfy German national feeling instead of the beginning, and henceforth Austria confined herself to a conservative insistence on her traditional rights. Equally great was Schmerling's failure in Austria: in 1865 Schmerling was dismissed, the central Parliament he had established was 'suspended', and his successor Belcredi planned to remodel Austria on a federal basis. The decline of the German Austrians was confirmed and accentuated by the war of 1866. The leadership of Germany passed irrevocably to Prussia and the German Austrians were excluded for the first time from the national fold. Almost simultaneously they were dethroned from their predominating position in the Austrian Empire – Hungary was entirely removed from their influence and the Germans in the Vienna Parliament were allowed merely to acquiesce in the Compromise, after the negotiations between the emperor and the Magyars had been completed. Under this double shock the German Austrians moderated their ambitions: they no longer hoped to rule all Germany and all Austria, they would be content if they could remain predominant in the western, non-Hungarian, half of the Austrian Empire. But soon their position was challenged even here – at first a German ministry was in power, but in 1879 Francis Joseph broke with the German nationalists and appointed Count Taaffe, a German conservative, as prime minister, with a policy favourable to the Slavs. Francis Joseph disliked the liberalism of the Germans; moreover he believed that they would remain loyal whatever happened, whereas the Slavs needed conciliating if they were to be kept within the Empire.

Friedjung was one of the first victims of the new policy. In 1873 he had been appointed Professor at the School of Commerce in Vienna, and he combined his academic duties with active participation in politics.

In a pamphlet on the Compromise with Hungary, published in 1877, he argued that the Austrian Empire was too much under the domination of the Magyars and that Austrian policy should be directed rather to a close co-operation with the German Empire, and to conciliation of the Germans at home. This pamphlet met with the disapproval of the new ministry, despite the conclusion of the alliance with Germany, and in 1879 Friedjung was dismissed. Thus forced into political life, Friedjung played a leading part in the discussions on future policy which now took place among the German Austrians.

The German Austrians were still shaken and bewildered by their defeat; they could no longer drift on without examining their position, and it was increasingly necessary for them to decide exactly what they desired in the future. They had lost their dominating position in the Austrian Empire, but they still reaped the advantages of being members of a great empire and they were not yet ready to see that empire destroyed in the name of German nationalism; moreover the worst that could befall them within the Empire was the possibility of being put on an equality with the Czechs in Bohemia, whereas in a united German Reich there was the certainty of being subordinated to the Prussians. The German Austrians still wanted to preserve the Empire, but they were not prepared to sacrifice their nationalism in favour of the imperial idea and become Austrians pure and simple, co-operating with other Austrians of whatever race. Centuries of German predominance could not be so easily dismissed and the German Austrians still tried to make the best of both worlds. The crude assertion of cultural superiority to the other races of the Empire was modified; the German Austrians now claimed the task of educating their fellow Austrians in modern ideas of liberalism and freedom. But that education was to be conducted by the method of entrusting the state to German nationalists and securing a permanent German majority in Parliament.

In 1880 Friedjung, in co-operation with Georg von Schönerer, later on the leader of the extreme pan-Germans in Austria, and Viktor Adler, subsequently the founder of the Austrian Social Democratic party, produced the Linz programme as a basis for the future policy of the German Austrians. It is ironical that of these three German nationalists two – Adler and Friedjung – were Jews, particularly ironical in Friedjung's case because he laid such emphasis on his being a German. Friedjung had no desire for the Jews to continue as a separate people; he believed that they should be absorbed into the nationalities among whom they lived. But Friedjung's race did in fact influence and warp his political career, for it made him overrate the ease with which the Germans could dominate and control the other races of the Empire. Friedjung regarded himself as a German, but he was only a German by adoption: he had become a German, because he valued German culture, and the process was no less deliberate for being subconscious. He therefore tended to expect a similar subconscious recognition of German superiority from the other races and he could not understand the reluctance of the Czechs, the Slovaks, or the Croats to follow his example.

The Linz programme set out to revive the primacy of the German Austrians in the Empire by securing for them the backing of Germany. Galicia and Dalmatia, the two extreme provinces of the Empire, were to be given a separate position within the Monarchy; the rest of the Monarchy west of the Leitha (that is excluding Hungary) was to be made more liberal and more centralised, with a suffrage so arranged as to secure a permanent German majority; the entire monarchy was then to be bound to Germany by a tariff union, a common coinage, and a perpetual alliance, voted by the parliaments of both countries. 'The two empires of the German nation are to be united as the firm bulwark of European peace.' The German Austrians would not recover the dominant position in Germany and Austria, to which they had once aspired, but they would be the hyphen, the essential link, between the two empires, and their divided loyalty would be no longer a source of weakness, but the very force which would hold the whole structure together.

The Linz programme, the work of Friedjung more than of any other one man, was in 1882 adopted by the new German Nationalist party as its statement of policy with the addition of the single clause – 'No Jew can be a member of the German Nationalist party'. Despite this, Friedjung co-operated with the party and in 1885 actually became for a short time the editor of the *Deutsche Zeitung*, the party paper. But the new party was very far removed from Friedjung's idealism; it was a nationalist party pure and simple, and it objected to Friedjung not only for being a Jew, but almost as much for being a liberal. It was not long before Friedjung was driven from his editorial post and for the rest of his life he earned his living as a freelance journalist, mostly with contributions to the German press. Friedjung did not cease to be a convinced German Austrian, but he no longer took part in day-to-day politics; the loss of his regular employment gave him more time for historical work and it was in the years immediately after his retirement that *The Struggle for Supremacy* was planned and written.

Friedjung had at first intended to write a history of parliamentary life in Austria since the establishment of the dual monarchy in 1867 – little more in fact than a glorified political pamphlet; but the fortunate chance of access to new sources of information – Benedek's private papers, and the archives of the War Office, thrown open by an exceptionally enlightened minister – diverted Friedjung's attention to the struggle between Austria and Prussia, and he supplemented this written material with interviews with the surviving participants in the period – Bismarck, Moltke, Rechberg, and others. It was another stroke of fortune that Bismarck had just been dismissed from office, and Friedjung therefore found him eager to give the fullest details of his policy before the war of 1866. It is true that certain sources remained closed: no information was forthcoming from Belcredi or from the family of Esterhazy – on the ground that they were unwilling to reveal any secrets so long as Francis Joseph lived – and the archives of the Foreign Office were inaccessible. These archives are now open and it is here that Friedjung's account stands in greatest need of supplement; but research has shown that, while the new material can add much of value to Friedjung's narrative, it does nothing to alter the general outline.

The Struggle for Supremacy was primarily a great piece of historical research, but it was also a continuation of Friedjung's political work in another form. For it was designed partly as a plea for the rehabilitation of the German Austrians and it was published in 1897, just at the crisis of their fate. The Taaffe ministry, which had come into power in 1879, had set out to achieve a parliamentary majority by balancing the nationalities against one another, as Taaffe said, it was his object to keep all the nationalities in a equal state of moderate dissatisfaction. This was a policy of expediency, which made no attempt to provide for a future when the dissatisfaction would cease to be moderate; but it was at any rate a parliamentary policy – it was based on the assumption that Austria was now a constitutional country and that the government of the day must have the support of a parliamentary majority, even though this majority was often created by questionable means. So long as the Taaffe Ministry existed, there was still a hope that the national problems would be fought out within the limits of a parliamentary struggle and that Parliament would represent a central, imperial authority which the nationalities would respect. But the bases of parliamentary life in Austria were becoming increasingly frail – the national parties turned more and more to an attitude of destructive opposition, and in 1893 a coalition of Czech conservatives and German nationalists placed the Taaffe ministry in a permanent minority. Taaffe's resignation could have led to a better system if the coalition had been itself able to form a government; but the Czechs and Germans hated each other even more than they hated Taaffe, and had combined against him only because he had not been prepared to subordinate his policy to either of them.

For thirty years Francis Joseph had ruled Austria as a constitutional monarch; he had never believed in Parliament, but it had given him the control of the army and of foreign policy, which was all he desired. But now the parliamentary system seemed to have broken down and no stable government could be built up. Francis Joseph therefore determined to break with the system of parliamentary government and to appoint a minister who would impose order on the nationalities from above, by imperial, not parliamentary, authority. Such a system of imperial centralism (though on a greater scale, for it had included Hungary) had already been attempted in Francis Joseph's reign by Alexander Bach. Then the Germans had grumbled at the denial of constitutional rights, but their opposition had been half-hearted, since Bach was a German pursuing a German policy. The man chosen now by Francis Joseph was Badeni, a Pole, who had acquired as Governor of Galicia the reputation of a 'strong man'. To be dictated to by a Pole was more than the Germans could stomach, and they would have opposed Badeni whatever his actual measures. But Badeni challenged German nationalism directly by the language ordinance, issued in 1897, by which Czech was placed practically on an equality with German as an official language in Bohemia. The Germans were thus threatened with complete exclusion from the civil services in Bohemia, for, whereas the Czechs were bilingual, few Germans would condescend to learn Czech.

The idea underlying the language ordinance was the same as that which underlay the Taaffe ministry – that the Czechs needed conciliating if they were to remain loyal, whereas the Germans would have to remain loyal in any case for fear something worse befell them. The Germans had indeed often insisted that they were the one race loyal to the Empire as such, as this necessarily implied loyalty even when the Empire acted against their particular interests. Even now the Germans claimed that German was the Austrian 'state language' (a doctrine which Friedjung attempted without much success to defend historically), and that in fighting the ordinance they were fighting for the Austrian 'state idea'. In actual fact, what the Germans meant by 'state idea' was that the Germans were a superior people to whom Austria in some way belonged; the other nationalities were to give up their national claims for the sake of Austria, this supernational entity, but the Germans were to preserve their national privileges intact. The contradictions of the German Austrian position were thus revealed: if Austria was a German state, the other nationalities could not be expected to remain loyal; if it were not a German state, the Germans must stand on an equal footing with the rest.

No doubt the Germans genuinely cared for the Austrian 'state idea', but their struggle against the language ordinance went far to wreck the Austrian state altogether. For the Germans, the founders and upholders of the parliamentary system, broke with the traditions of parliamentary opposition and thus set a most damaging example to the other nationalities. In Parliament the Germans resorted to the most violent obstruction; police had to be called in and there was a wild scene of free fights in the Chamber itself. Great crowds demonstrated in the streets of Vienna and in the other German towns; German Austria as a whole was almost in a state of rebellion. These demonstrations achieved part of their aim – Badeni was dismissed, but the language ordinance was not recalled (though it was later modified); and the Badeni period left to the Empire a most disastrous legacy.

If Badeni had succeeded, parliamentary life would have been destroyed, but the Empire would have been immeasurably strengthened; it would have shown itself to be stronger than the nationalities, the balancing and determining force, which Joseph II and Schwarzenberg had meant it to be. If, on the other hand, Badeni had been defeated by a coalition of convinced constitutionists, then Parliament would have been established once and for all as the vital and central force of the whole Empire. Neither of these things happened. Parliament did indeed remain in existence right up to 1914, but it was an empty form, and, under the guise of emergency decrees, Austria was governed bureaucratically and despotically. Parliamentary government had been destroyed, and destroyed by the Germans, its originators; henceforth there was no chance of a compromise between the nationalities. Nor did the emperor gain what the Parliament lost; Badeni's failure convinced Francis Joseph that any active, constructive policy would arouse opposition and would probably bring the whole imperial edifice to the ground. Francis Joseph was now an old man and his main anxiety was to make the Empire last his time; by pursuing an unobtrusive policy of expedients he did indeed keep the Empire in being, but it was little more than an empty shell, which would fall in the first storm.

The Struggle for Supremacy was concluded just after the fall of Badeni, and it is no detraction from its greatness as a work of history to suggest that much of it was written with the events of the Badeni period in mind. The emphasis which Friedjung lays on the unshakeable loyalty and self-sacrifice of the Germans in 1866 is only to be expected; but Friedjung goes further and places the entire responsibility for the defeat of 1866 on the reactionary policy pursued by the dynasty ever since the time of the Counter-Reformation (with a certain interruption in the eighteenth century). Friedjung shared the German nationalist view that the terms liberal and German were synonymous: when he is criticising the anti-liberal policy of the Austrian government he is thus censuring it for its refusal to depend solely on the Germans, and is implying that a government based on the Germans would have prevented the catastrophe.

Friedjung's convictions appear still more clearly in his judgement on individual statesmen: his appraisal of them is determined by how nearly their policy approximates to the Linz programme. Rechberg comes in for an undue share of praise (perhaps the one grave misjudgement in the book) simply because his timorous avoidance of a conflict with Prussia inclined him towards a co-operation of the two German powers such as Friedjung desired. Schmerling is criticized for his hostility to Prussia, but on the whole he escapes lightly because his domestic policy was based upon a German predominance throughout the Empire. The full weight of Friedjung's censure is reserved for the forerunners of Badeni, who rejected both liberalism and German nationalism – for Belcredi's 'Ministry of Counts', and above all for Esterhazy. The low estimate Friedjung makes of the ability of these statesmen is thoroughly justified – and Badeni was of even poorer quality than Belcredi or Esterhazy. But one has an uneasy feeling that, if they had been abler, Friedjung would have disapproved of them still more. These feudal conservatives were no doubt ruling in the interest of their class; but the best of them recognized (what Friedjung never did) that Austria could not be based upon nationalism, whether German, Magyar, or Czech, and supported a political federalism because they saw in it the only means of holding the Empire together. It is easy to dismiss Metternich and his conservative followers as pure reactionaries, but it is also false. They hated liberalism because it attacked their own position; but they hated it also because it threatened the Austrian Empire, which, they believed, had still important functions to perform. The Empire had lost its original justification – the defence of Europe against the Turk; and the alternative provided by Metternich, the defence of Europe against France and the revolution, was rendered unreal (if it ever had been real) by nineteenth-century political developments. The Empire needed a new function, and enlightened Austrians believed that they had found that function in a policy of economic amelioration. That this policy was not altogether illusory is shown by the support it received: even the German Austrians were attracted, even Friedjung was tempted to become an Austrian pure and simple.

By 1897 the German Austrians had moved far from the dominating position and overweening claims of the Schmerling epoch. Their domination was gone, and they were finding it difficult to resist complete equality with the other races of the Empire. In despair the more extreme Germans, under the leadership of Schönerer, abandoned the idea of Austria altogether and subordinated everything to their nationality. The Habsburgs, the Austrian Empire, and the Roman Catholic Church – everything that stood in the way of complete absorption, cultural and political, into Germany – were to go. The German nationalists evolved the slogan, '*Ein Reich, ein Kaiser, eine Religion*', and Schönerer infuriated the Austrian Parliament by answering the address of loyalty to Francis Joseph with a cry of 'Long live the house of Hohenzollern!'

Such extreme nationalism could have but a limited appeal; it was strong only on the cultural frontiers – in Bohemia and Styria – where everything was overshadowed by the daily contact between German and Slav. In Vienna the differences between Austria and Germany could not be so easily ignored; Vienna was still the capital of a great empire, with all the advantages which that implied, and the inhabitants had no inclination deliberately to depress Vienna to the status of a provincial town. The events of 1897 had shown beyond mistake that insistence on German nationality would wreck the Empire, and that was a price which many Germans were unwilling to pay. Rather late in the day they drew back and some of them began to turn half-heartedly to an imperial policy, which should transcend nationalism.

Clearly such a policy was the only one which might have saved the Empire. The great destructive force was the ambitions of the rival nationalities, whether dominant or subordinate, and everything which cut across the national divisions was, consciously or not, a source of strength to the Empire. The old Austria had been clerical, because the Church provided such an international loyalty, and, in the years before the war, the Socialist party, under the leadership of Viktor Adler, was one of the principal supports of the Empire, again because of its international appeal. The introduction of universal suffrage at the express wish of the Emperor in 1907 was a deliberate attempt to utilise these international forces: Socialism and Clericalism would, it was hoped, become the dominant issues, and the disruptive nationalism of the middle classes would be submerged in the struggle between the two, in the vast game of *rouge et noir*, which would take place throughout the Empire. There was no contradiction in Jews participating in such an international policy, and it is significant that it was a Jew, Joseph Redlich, whom some observers before the war regarded as one of the few men capable of saving the Austrian Empire.

The best Austrians of this school had a dispassionate and conscientious spirit similar to that of a good official of the League of Nations (which closely resembled their ideal for the Austrian Empire), and they believed that the only answer to the increasing danger of nationalism, especially the nationalism of the Southern Slavs, was a bold policy of economic and cultural well-being. They agreed with the government that the first step must be the reassertion of Austrian power, and even the most enlightened of them welcomed the annexation of Bosnia and Herzegovina by Aehrenthal in 1908 as the opening of a new era of energy and reform in Austrian policy. But they were not content with a policy of prestige: the Southern Slavs were first to be cowed, but then they were to be won over by sweeping reforms. Austria was to free the land from the tangled and corrupt legacy of Turkish rule and was to introduce a modern system of education. The condition of the Southern Slavs inside the Austrian Empire would then be so obviously superior to that of the Serbs outside that nationalist propaganda would lose its sting and Serbia herself would welcome inclusion within the Austrian tariff system. This policy of efficient government and positive amelioration had been tried often enough in Austria (and not only in Austria) to resist nationalist movements – particularly of course in Lombardy in the days before 1848. Indeed the programme of reforms, which Baernreither, one of the leaders of this group of Austrian statesmen, outlined for Bosnia in 1910 – settlement of the land, improved communications, education, and more power for the Governor – is almost word for word the programme which Ficquelmont, Metternich's second-in-command, proposed for Lombardy in 1847. Take for instance this passage of Baernreither's memorandum, change Bosnia-Hercegovina to Lombardo-Venetia, Serbia to Piedmont, and the whole thing is applicable to the days before 1848:

> If we can make the material existence of the people of Bosnia and Herzegovina better than that enjoyed by their brothers in Serbia; if we can effectively promote and maintain order, justice, and popular education, while sparing religious feelings, not injuring national idiosyncracies, and, scrupulously avoiding any sort of brandishing of the torch, intervene firmly when there is anything dangerous on foot – then we shall win even the Serbian section of the population over to our side.[1]

It is perhaps doubtful whether an alien government, however efficient and however reforming, can permanently provide any real answer to the appeal of nationalism; that self-government is better than good government is no new discovery. But it is fair to say that neither in Lombardy nor in Bosnia was the reforming policy ever really tried – in Lombardy for sheer inertia and lack of initiative, in Bosnia because the government had no real belief in reform. Aehrenthal was ready to talk about the benefits of Austrian rule in order to please the Austrian liberals; but he was secretly convinced that the Serbs, both within and without the monarchy, would regard any concession as weakness and that they would understand no argument but force. In any case reforms in Bosnia would immediately lead to a demand for reforms from the Croats under Hungarian rule and were therefore bitterly opposed by the Magyars; the Hungarian problem was serious enough, and a quarrel over Croatia might well lead to the break-up of the Empire. It is easy now to see that Austrian statesmen should have braved Hungarian opposition, for the conciliation of the Southern Slavs offered the one chance of preservation for the Empire; but they were perhaps right in fearing Magyar disaffection even more than Croat. The irreparable mistake in this, as in many other problems, was made not in 1908 or in 1909, but by Francis Joseph forty years before, when he had chosen the easy solution of satisfying the Magyars by giving them a free hand with the Croats.

Indeed it is no exaggeration to say that Francis Joseph did more than any other man to bring the Empire to ruin. Throughout his reign he cared only for his military power and his prestige abroad. He is reported to have said to Theodore Roosevelt: 'You see in me the last monarch of the old school', and he was right; he was the last monarch who believed that it was the duty of his peoples to sacrifice themselves for the dynasty, but not the duty of the dynasty to do anything for the peoples, and the last monarch to play fast and loose with his obligations towards his subjects, because he believed that he was above all ordinary standards. Francis II, on hearing someone described as an Austrian patriot, answered, 'But is he a patriot for me?' Francis Joseph never even asked such a question, because it did not occur to him that there could be such a thing as Austrian patriotism distinct from loyalty to him personally. The dynasty did indeed represent an imperial element cutting across the lines of national division; but, as Maria Theresa and Joseph II recognized, it could be a binding force only as long as it brought well-being to its subjects. Francis Joseph, by his concentration on dynastic interests and his short-sighted policy of allying himself with the dominant nationalities in order to safeguard his military power, used up the capital of imperial loyalty which he had inherited from his reforming ancestors. Francis Joseph took from his subjects and gave nothing back; it was therefore inevitable that by the end of his reign his subjects had lost interest in the Empire.

Friedjung was among the most enthusiastic supporters of Aehrenthal's policy and a staunch advocate of reform. But it was not without satisfaction that he received from Aehrenthal documents purporting to prove that the Serbo-Croat leaders were engaged in a treasonable conspiracy against the Empire; for the more disloyal the Croats were, the more the loyalty of the Germans would stand out in contrast. Aehrenthal asked Friedjung to write a series of articles based on these documents, and Friedjung, with the whole weight of his authority as an historian, did all that Aehrenthal could have wished – indeed more than Aehrenthal wished, for the articles were so violent that Aehrenthal had them stopped after the first number. Friedjung not only abandoned all attempt at impartiality, he abandoned too all sense of criticism and vouched for originals in Serbian which he had never seen and which he could not have read if he had seen. The Croat leaders brought an action, and in the ensuing 'Friedjung trial' it was shown that the documents were forgeries of a particularly crude nature.

It was said at the time that the forgeries had been made in the Austrian legation at Belgrade and, although this is probably untrue, the Austro-Hungarian Foreign Office undoubtedly knew that the documents were forged; Aehrenthal himself may not have been so sure of their nature, but he certainly had some doubts of their authenticity and could have had those doubts confirmed if he had bothered to enquire. The main guilt must therefore rest with Aehrenthal and the Foreign Office, but Friedjung too must be condemned for having accepted documents as authentic merely because they were given him by the foreign minister of the Empire. Baernreither, who acted as mediator between Friedjung and the Croat leaders, passed a very fair judgement on the affair: 'Friedjung has been shamefully used by Aehrenthal. But he laid himself open to such abuse by his fantastic loyalty, his credulousness, and his overweening conceit.'[2] The contrast between Friedjung the historian and Friedjung the politician is at first sight overwhelming. Friedjung had chronicled the incapacity and folly of the Austrian Foreign Office under Buol or Mensdorff; now he acted as though a miraculous change had come over it in the interval. Friedjung had castigated severely the blind arrogance of Biegeleben or Esterhazy, when they talked of giving the Prussians a sound thrashing; but he applauded Aehrenthal, when he used exactly similar language about the Serbs. Friedjung had seen the wisdom of compromising, as Rechberg advocated, in 1863; but he was all for bullying and the mailed fist in 1909. It was not so much that Friedjung was incapable of judging contemporary events, although that is a common failing of historians; it was that for the German movement Friedjung had the key, and for the Slav he had not. Friedjung realized what the German movement was, because he was himself by sympathy a German, and his national feeling enabled him to appreciate the strength and, one might say, the sacredness of the German cause. With the Slavs he had no emotional link and therefore their nationalism appeared to him merely as a treasonable conspiracy. The one is indeed the complement of the other. *The Struggle for Supremacy* is shot through and through with emotional appreciation for both sides and it was this very emotion which prevented Friedjung from understanding the elements of the Southern Slav question. He wrote badly and foolishly about the Croats; but that cannot lessen the greatness of what he wrote about the rise of Germany.

What the policy of prestige did not do, its outcome, the Great War, did – it raised the German Austrians once more to the first place in the Empire. The alliance with Germany was made so close by the exigencies of war that the old days of the German Confederation seemed almost to have come again. The idea of *Mittel-Europa* was revived, and there was bound to be revived with it the idea of the predominance of the German

Austrians, for on them the scheme would turn. Such indeed was the basis of a political manifesto in which Friedjung joined in 1915 – Germany and Austria-Hungary were to form a close confederation; Serbia was to be absorbed into the Austrian Empire, at any rate militarily and economically; and the Southern Slavs might later form a third unit within the Habsburg Empire, when they had given sufficient proof of their loyalty. The national cultures were to be tolerated and encouraged, but German was to be the official language throughout the Empire. The plan is very similar to the Linz programme of 1880, and it undoubtedly represents the permanent elements in Friedjung's political programme. There is no longer much talk of reform or of the cultural mission of the German Austrians – they were to predominate, because they had the power of Germany behind them and because they would be the link between the two empires. The old ambition of predominating in both Germany and Austria had indeed gone; but the German Austrians claimed the first place in Austria right down to the fall of the monarchy.

The break-up of the Empire seemed to have solved the old problem of the dual nature of the German Austrians. They could never have brought themselves voluntarily to renounce all that was meant by the Empire – the predominant position and all the advantages Vienna enjoyed as the capital; but with the Empire destroyed there seemed to be nothing now to prevent the German Austrians staking all on their nationality, as the pan-Germans had advocated. Their nationalism was indeed all they had left and it is therefore no wonder that even in the darkest hour of defeat they desired incorporation in the Reich. That unification was denied them by allied dictation; but to all German Austrians after the war it seemed only a matter of time. Almost the last words that Friedjung wrote expressed this belief.[3] 'Now that Austria has fallen, our whole feeling is concentrated in affection for the race which was the kernel of the old Monarchy and so for the German nation as a whole. At present there are obstacles in the way, but in the end we shall return to the mother-country whence one of the best stocks has migrated to the south-east in the pursuance of a historic mission.' It is no injustice to Friedjung to say that he was more at home with German nationalism than with the dispassionate and enlightened ideals of the best Austrians. Friedjung himself is the best illustration of why these Austrians failed: for the Austrian Empire to survive there had to be an abandonment of nationalism, and if Friedjung, a cultured, intelligent man, could not bring himself to this, small wonder that the less cultured, ordinary subjects of the Empire clung to their nationality. On that rock – the refusal of the nationalities to compromise or to abate their claims – the Empire foundered.

It would be a dangerous over-simplification to believe that the break-up of the Austrian empire has in any way solved the Austrian question. Despite the expectations of 1918, the union of German Austria with Germany has not been achieved; but there can be little doubt that, were certain extraneous elements removed – the interference of certain powers and the present uncivilized system of rule in Germany – the Germans of Austria would be as content within a national German state as are the Germans of Bavaria or of Saxony. Yet even the absorption of German Austria into Germany would solve the problems only for the Germans within the present Austrian state and not for the Germans outside it, nor for the other races which once composed the Austrian Empire. It is this, quite as much as the character of the present rulers of Germany, which inclines some German Austrians against unification with Germany, for they hope still to revive the international organisation once secured by the Austrian Empire. In that empire there was never a free co-operation of peoples, but there was at any rate some co-operation on however coercive a basis, and to that extent better than no co-operation at all. Before the war the German Austrians had the opportunity of leading the way to a system of freedom and equality among the nationalities; that opportunity they refused to take, and the events of the last twenty years have made the situation infinitely more difficult. Nevertheless the opportunity is still there, once the German Austrians make it clear that they have abandoned all belief in their cultural superiority over the races of the other states. If, however, the German Austrians try to revive the elements which held the old Empire together – clericalism, the dynasty, and the co-operation of the upper classes against the lower – than the new system will fail as the old system failed, and a revived Habsburg Empire will produce what the old Habsburg Empire produced – a great European war. The lesson of the pre-war years and of the break-down of the Empire is plain – that only a federation based upon equality and free co-operation can be either fruitful or permanent. That lesson was not heeded by Austrian statesmen before the war; it was not heeded by the Allied statesmen in 1919; and there is no sign that it is being heeded today by the politicians in Vienna. Changes there may well be, but there can be little doubt that any new settlement of the Danube valley, however different its protective colouring of professed ideas, will be based like the present settlement and the Austrian Empire upon force, and that it will be as unstable and as productive of European disturbances.

The best thing about the old Empire was that it did produce some men, however few, who saw beyond national rivalries, and who tried to make Austria something more than a machine for building up a large army. It was Friedjung's greatest defect that he had little appreciation for this element in Austria – he saw only the indifference to nationalism, he ignored what was to be substituted for it, and he confused the feudal opponents of nationalism with the military bullies who ruled Austria from 1849 to 1860 and from 1906 to 1914. This is the one great deduction from Friedjung's greatness as an historian, and once this has been said there is little to add of *The Struggle for Supremacy* except unstinted praise. It was said of Burke that he gave up to party what was meant for mankind. Of Friedjung the opposite is true. Driven from politics against his will, he set out to continue his political activity on another field, but he produced instead a great work of history. There was no future in politics for Friedjung's divided loyalty; but it was this divided loyalty, which enabled him to write the best and most impartial account of one of the most decisive and vital struggles in the nineteenth century. The conflict of 1866 marked the beginning of an epoch in which Friedjung was still living when he wrote this book. That epoch was closed in 1918, but the problems with which Friedjung deals were not solved. *The Struggle for Supremacy* is primarily great history; but it is still what Friedjung designed it to be – an introduction to contemporary politics – and such it will remain so long as there is an Austrian question.

Notes

1. J.M. Baernreither, *Fragments of a Political Diary*, p. 81.
2. J.M. Baernreither, *Fragments of a Political Diary*, p. 104.
3. In the preface to his *Historisches Aufsätze*, Stuttgart, Cotta, 1919.

CHAPTER FIVE

International Relations, 1870–98

This essay first appeared as a chapter in *The New Cambridge Modern History*, Vol. XI: *Material Progress and World-Wide Problems*, ed. F.H. Hinsley (Cambridge, Cambridge University Press, 1962).

The last thirty years of the nineteenth century saw the European balance of power at its most perfect: five great powers (with a doubtful sixth), each able to maintain its independence, none strong enough to dominate the others. The irreconcilable antagonism between France and Germany, and the equally irreconcilable, though less persistent, antagonism between Austria-Hungary and Russia in the Balkans, prevented the creation of any preponderant combination. The balance of power took on the appearance of a natural law, self-operating and self-adjusting; Europe enjoyed the longest period of peace known in modern times; and the powers turned their energies outwards to 'imperialist' expansion. All acquired empires; some at their own backdoor, the others overseas.

The Franco-Prussian War, which broke out in July 1870, created this exceptional balance. It began as a French attempt to arrest the progress of German unity; instead it freed Europe from the shadow of French predominance without putting German predominance in its place. It was the last war fought solely in Europe and confined to European great powers. It was indeed confined to two powers. This was unexpected. Great Britain was genuinely neutral once Belgium was secured. But Austria-Hungary prepared to intervene on the French side, though only after French victories. Russia first talked vaguely of threatening Austria-Hungary into neutrality; then, with equal vagueness, planned to compete with her for French favour. These calculations came to an abrupt stop as the campaign developed. The first battles on the frontier went against France. On 3 September the main French army was defeated and compelled to surrender at Sedan. Napoleon III became a prisoner. The French Empire was overthrown, and the Republic proclaimed in Paris.

Sedan ended the war as a struggle for mastery in Europe. The long centuries of French predominance were over. Germany was free to arrange her own destinies. The war was prolonged by the German demand for Alsace and Lorraine. The ostensible reason for this was military security; the deeper cause was a desire to satisfy national feeling. The new Germany should get off to a good start by recovering the lands of the old Reich. The French raised the standard of national defence; and the war which had begun in the cabinets became a war of peoples. Thiers toured Europe, seeking allies. In vain. Neither Austria-Hungary nor Russia feared a German victory. The Austrians hoped for German backing in the Near East; the Russians calculated that a resentful France would keep Germany in check. Only Gladstone, the British prime minister, wished to protest against the transfer of morality, not of power; and he received no support from his cabinet.

Besides, the Russians twisted international relations eastwards by denouncing the neutralisation of the Black Sea, imposed by the Treaty of Paris in 1856. The British threatened war or, at any rate, a revival of 'the Crimean coalition'. Bismarck did not want a situation which might provide France with allies or at least enable her to air her case before an international meeting. He solved the crisis neatly by paying Russia and Great Britain with the same cheque. He proposed a conference, confined to the Black Sea clauses and pledged in advance to their abolition. Thus Russia got freedom from her servitude; the British vindicated the principle that treaties could be changed only by international agreement; and Bismarck was rewarded by a general promise that the conference, which met in London in January 1871, should not mention the war between France and Germany.

The French had therefore to rely on their own strength. This was not enough to reverse the verdict of Sedan. Gambetta sounded the Jacobin appeal of 1793 – the *levée en masse*, and the country in danger. Though he brought new armies into the field, these could not defeat the Germans nor prevent the fall of Paris. At the end of January 1871 the French had to accept the German terms; and these became the definitive peace of Frankfurt on 10 May. France lost Alsace and Lorraine, though retaining Belfort at the last moment; paid an indemnity of five milliard francs (a sum exactly proportioned to the indemnity which Napoleon I had imposed on Prussia in 1807); and had to support a German army of occupation until the indemnity was paid. This was certainly a victor's peace on the Napoleonic model. Yet Bismarck did not attempt to bind the future. France remained a great power. The Treaty of Frankfurt did not limit her armed forces or control her foreign policy. The path of revenge was open if she wished to take it. She could not do so. Sedan and its outcome did not so much change the balance of power in Europe as symbolize that it had changed; and the balance went on turning against France. Germany continued to increase in population and economic resources. France remained almost static.

Few contemporaries appreciated this. They expected an early war of revenge. Though the French, under the leadership of Thiers, followed a policy of 'fulfilment', they also introduced universal military service on the German model, and reorganized their armed forces. Bismarck made isolation of France the mainspring of his foreign policy. In 1873 he brought Austria-Hungary, Germany, and Russia together in the League of the Three Emperors – ostensibly a conservative Holy Alliance against the moribund socialist international which Karl Marx had just shipped off to an early death in New York; in fact no more than mutual abstention from a French alliance. The League carried within itself the germs of a mortal sickness: Austria-Hungary and Russia did not re- nounce their rival ambitions in the Balkans. Instead, their agreement contained the strange provision that, even when they fell into dispute there, they would not allow the conflict 'to overshadow the considera- tions of a higher order which they have at heart'. Like the Holy Alliance, the League of the Three Emperors was a fair-weather system, which would be blown away in the Balkan gale.

The Balkans were, however, still quiet, and France the likely storm- centre. In 1873 Thiers was driven from office; and his monarchist successors wished to restore French prestige by an active foreign policy. Dreaming nostalgically of a Catholic League, they first patronized the pope – prisoner in the Vatican since the Italian occupation of Rome on 20 September 1870. Then, abandoning this course in 1874, they flew at higher game and patronized the German Roman Catholics in the *Kulturkampf*. Bismarck, always ready to perceive widespread conspira- cies against himself, detected – or so he claimed – the hand of international clericalism. At least, this seems to be the most reasonable explanation of the 'war-in-sight' crisis which he unleashed in April 1875. It is unlikely that Bismarck actually planned a preventive war; such a course was against his deepest instincts. But he hoped to frighten the French out of their clericalism and perhaps out of their rearmament. Instead, Decazes, the French foreign minister, exploited the crisis to his own profit. Simulating alarm, he appealed for protection to the other powers; and they responded. Though Austria-Hungary remained silent, both Russia and Great Britain expostulated at Berlin. Bismarck shammed surprise and repudiated all aggressive intention. The crisis died away. It had been a score for France, though of a peculiar kind. Great Britain and Russia had combined to protect France and save the peace, but the peace they saved was the peace of Frankfurt. Neither wished to reverse Sedan, only to ensure that it should not be repeated. Both were satisfied with the existing balance. Both opposed a German attack on France; neither would support a French attack on Germany. Hence the 'war-in- sight' crisis paradoxically determined that there would be no war in Europe for more than a generation.

With relations between France and Germany thus stabilised, only the Balkans remained as a topic of conflict. In July 1875 they burst into flames. The Turkish province of Bosnia broke into revolt. Neither Russia nor Austria-Hungary wished to open the Eastern Question; but once it was opened, Russia could not abandon the Balkan Slavs, Austria-Hungary dared not let them succeed. Both tried to observe the pledge which they had given in the League of the Three Emperors. They sought to avert the crisis by a programme of Balkan reforms. Andrássy, the Austro-Hungarian foreign minister, first proposed that the consuls of the powers should settle the Bosnian revolt on the spot. Then he devised the note of 30 December 1875, containing reforms which the powers should recommend to Turkey. Next, at a meeting with Bismarck and Gorchakov, the Russian chancellor, he produced the Berlin Memorandum of 13 May 1876, which contained not only reforms but a grudging hint of 'sanctions' to enforce them. All these schemes broke on the obstinacy of the Turkish government which held, with some justification, that reform would lead to the disintegration of the Ottoman Empire.

Russia and Austria-Hungary were drifting apart. Andrássy would not go beyond advice, given to Turkey by the three emperors. Gorchakov wished to impose reforms in the name of the Concert of Europe. He brought France into the negotiations; and this inevitably brought in Great Britain also. The British had once been the great proponents of the Concert of Europe; but, since their failure over Schleswig in 1864, they had withdrawn from European affairs. Isolation was the keystone of British policy; and the counterpart of isolation is isolated action. Lacking allies and repudiating diplomacy, the British had only the choice: all or nothing. Either they turned their backs on a problem; or they appealed to force. There was no middle course; and it is no accident that between 1871 and 1904 Great Britain was alone in using the formal threat of war against another great power – in 1878 and 1885 against Russia, in 1898 against France. The British government had swallowed the consular mission and the Andrássy note, though principally in order to guard Turkish interests. The Berlin Memorandum was too much for them – particularly as it reached London at the weekend. They rejected the memorandum and sent the fleet to Besika Bay, thus encouraging the Turks to defy the powers.

This the Turks were always willing to do. The suppression of the revolt was beyond their strength. In June revolt spread to Bulgaria; and the Turks answered with the 'Bulgarian horrors' – the worst atrocities of the nineteenth century, until eclipsed by the Armenian massacres twenty years later. The Russian government, though still shrinking from war, was driven on by the groundswell of Slav sentiment within Russia. At first Gorchakov hoped that the Ottoman Empire would collapse of itself; and at Zakupy (Reichstadt) in July, he reached agreement with

Andrássy that they would allow this to happen. His hope was disappointed. There was deadlock in the Balkans: more revolts, more massacres, but no collapse. Russian intervention drew nearer, Alexander II himself foreshadowing it publicly in November. Gorchakov was desperately anxious to save Russia from repeating the isolation and failure of the Crimean War. He called on Bismarck to repay the supposed Russian service in 1870 by holding Austria-Hungary neutral. Bismarck refused. He claimed later that he would have gone with Russia 'through thick and thin', if the Russians in return had guaranteed Germany's tenure of Alsace and Lorraine. This was a red herring. The survival of Austria-Hungary as a great power was an essential part of Bismarck's system, both at home and abroad; and, while he had no objection to Russia's success in the Balkans, this must be in agreement with Austria-Hungary, not achieved against her. Bismarck's 'great refusal' was a decisive moment in European relations. From refusing to support Russia against Austria-Hungary it was a short step to supporting Austria-Hungary against Russia. In 1879 Bismarck took this step; and so set the pattern for the future.

Failing Germany, Gorchakov tried France. Here, too, he was disappointed. The French pleaded that they had not recovered from the defeats of 1870 – a convenient, though genuine, excuse which enabled them to sidestep the Eastern crisis without offending Russia. The last Russian resort was the Concert of Europe; and this did not altogether fail them. Even Great Britain moved towards the Concert. The Bulgarian horrors had produced a passionate campaign of protest in England under Gladstone's leadership; and the Conservative government had to favour the reform of Turkey. In December 1876 a conference of the great powers met at Constantinople – of all the many gatherings which wrestled with the Eastern Question, the only one to meet on the spot. Once more sweeping reforms were devised; once more the Turks evaded them – this time by the ingenious trick of first proclaiming a constitution and then insisting that all changes must be referred to a constituent assembly which never met. Yet the conference served Russia's purpose. Though the powers would not impose the reforms which the conference had devised, they could not object when Russia set out to do so. The concert, having failed to reform Turkey, would not now protect her.

Even the British were now willing to stand aside. They insisted that nothing must be done to disturb Egypt – a remote speculation where Gorchakov at once met their wishes. They also declared that they would not tolerate a Russian occupation of Constantinople, 'even temporary'. Here, too, Gorchakov replied sympathetically. He had no desire to see Russia saddled with responsibility for Constantinople. But if Turkey collapsed, who could guarantee the outcome? And Gorchakov left it open whether he would then cheat the British or the victorious Russian generals.

From Austria-Hungary Russia needed something more positive than tolerance. She needed a firm promise of neutrality if her armies were to pass safely though the bottleneck of Romania. Andrássy was ready for a bargain. In the last resort, he preferred a limited Russian success against Turkey to a great European war which would shatter the existing set-up in the Habsburg monarchy, almost as much by victory as by defeat; and Gorchakov on his side, cool towards pan-Slav ambitions, was ready to limit Russia's prospective gains. The Budapest conventions, signed on 15 January 1877, laid down that there should be 'no great compact state, Slav or other', if Turkey fell to pieces. In return Austria-Hungary promised to observe benevolent neutrality in a war between Russia and Turkey, and to disregard the triple guarantee of Turkey in which she had joined after the Crimean War. This was a great stroke by Gorchakov despite the restriction. The Crimean coalition was dissolved; and Andrássy in fact kept his promise of neutrality right up to the Congress of Berlin. Besides, who could tell what would happen in the Balkans if Turkey really fell to pieces? Here too Gorchakov could decide whether to cheat Andrássy or the pan-Slavs. The immediate gain was what mattered. Thanks to Gorchakov's diplomacy, Russia was free – as never before in the nineteenth century – to settle the Eastern Question by her own armed strength.

Here was the great surprise. Russian armed strength proved inadequate for the purpose. On 24 April Russia declared war against Turkey, ostensibly to enforce the recommendations of the Constantinople conference. Russian armies advance through Romania and crossed the Danube. There they were arrested by the fortress of Plevna, and battered themselves into exhaustion against it before it fell on 11 December. The prolonged engagement of Plevna – battle rather than siege – foreshadowed the grinding trench-warfare of the First World War. But unlike those battles, it changed the course of history. In June, when the Russians first ran against Plevna, Turkey-in-Europe seemed doomed. By December the Russian armies were worn down; and, equally important, British opinion had swung round. The heroic defence of Plevna obliterated the Bulgarian horrors; and the Conservative government could revert to its original policy of supporting Turkey. The Russian armies staggered to the gates of Constantinople by the end of January 1878; but the Ottoman Empire did not collapse. Though the Turkish armies had almost melted away, the Russians could not give the final push. It only needed first the rumour and then the reality of the British fleet before Constantinople to bring the war to an end.

The Russians had assumed that the Ottoman Empire would fall of itself, once war started. It had not done so; and the Russians were now stuck for peace terms. They first thought of demanding the opening of the Straits; but, since Russia had no Black Sea fleet, this – though a theoretical gain – would be a practical disadvantage. They therefore fell back on inflating the principle proposal of the Constantinople conference and demanded autonomy for a 'Big Bulgaria'. This had no Machiavellian intent. A national state seemed the only alternative to Turkish rule; and the Russian peacemakers drew the frontier according to the best ethnographic knowledge of the time. But the Turks realized that Big Bulgaria would provoke opposition from other powers; and therefore accepted the peace of San Stefano, signed on 3 March, with every confidence that it would soon be overthrown. A general war seemed in the offing. The British kept their fleet at Constantinople, and demonstratively moved Indian troops to Malta. Andrássy, though evading British requests for an alliance, also evaded Russian requests for a promise of neutrality in a further war. No one has divined his real intent, which was probably unknown to himself. But the Russians dared not risk a renewal of war without firm assurance of Austro-Hungarian neutrality, nor perhaps even with it. The British were ready to face war without allies and even in fact without armed forces of any size. It was a contest of nerve; and the British won. On 30 May the Russians agreed to submit the Treaty of San Stefano to an international congress, with the understanding that Big Bulgaria should disappear. Salisbury, who had become British foreign secretary at the beginning of April, rounded off his achievement with two other agreements. He guaranteed Turkey-in-Asia, receiving a lease of Cyprus in exchange; and he secured the belated backing of Austria-Hungary against Big Bulgaria.

The Congress of Berlin which met on 13 June 1878 was a grandiose assembly of European statesmen – the German and Russian chancellors, the prime minister of Great Britain (the first ever to attend an international meeting), and the foreign ministers of the Great Powers. Big Bulgaria dissolved into three; a quasi-independent principality; an autonomous province of eastern Roumelia; and a remnant called 'Macedonia', which was pushed back under Ottoman rule. Austria-Hungary undertook the administration of Bosnia and Hercegovina, where the revolts had started. Unexpectedly, the congress also produced a grave challenge to the rule of the Straits. Salisbury had agreed on 30 May that the Black Sea port of Batum should go to Russia; but British opinion was outraged when this became known. To calm opinion at home, Salisbury announced that henceforth Great Britain would only regard herself as bound to respect 'the independent decisions' of the sultan in regard to the closing of the Straits. In British eyes the sultan was independent only when he was pro-British. Hence they claimed to be free to pass the Straits whenever it suited them. This was a terrifying prospect for Russia, and the spectre of a British fleet in the Black Sea haunted Russian policy for almost twenty years.

The congress claimed to have averted a great war and to have settled the Eastern Question. There was not much in either claim. War had been averted long before the congress met – in fact when the Russian armies could not revive the Ottoman Empire as an independent great power. The events of 1875–78 ended its real strength; and though it tottered on for another thirty-odd years, this was largely because the Great Powers were busy elsewhere and shrank from the turmoil which would follow its overthrow. The practical results of the conference were of little effect. The British fleet never entered the Black Sea until after the collapse of the Russian Empire; and two out of three parts into which Bulgaria had been divided were united within a few years, to the applause of the powers which had insisted on their separation in 1878. The congress did a bad day's work when it put Macedonia back under the Turks, and a worse when it put Bosnia under Austria-Hungary. The first act caused the Balkan war of 1912; the second exploited the world war of 1914.

Such blunders occur at the best-ordered gathering. The deeper puzzle is why the congress made such a fuss about the Balkans at all. Gigantic changes had taken place on the continent of Europe; still more gigantic were to happen outside it. Italy and Germany had been united; France had lost her primacy and two provinces; the pope had lost his temporal power. Soon Africa was to be partitioned; the empire of China was to be disputed between the powers. Here were all the greatest statesmen of the age, assembled in unparalleled number and encompassed by these events. Yet all they could find to discuss was the fate of a few Balkan villages. What is more the Eastern Question continued to dominate international relations for many years after the Congress of Berlin. It shaped the alliances which shot up like mushrooms after summer-rain. Every foreign minister revolved his policy around it. Yet nothing happened. The interminable Eastern crises seemed so many manoeuvres, where great skill was displayed and everyone went home unhurt in the evening.

Why did it all go on? The diplomatists pointed to the deadlock as evidence of their sustained skill. Cynical radicals retorted that nothing happened because nothing serious was at stake and that the Eastern Question was kept going to provide 'outdoor relief' for members of the foreign services. There was something in these explanations. The working of the balance checked any activity; and the Eastern Question had indeed become a question of habit. Men had regarded it as of vital importance for so long that they had forgotten why it was important, if they ever knew. Perhaps the decisive reason, however, is that the

Eastern Question had become essentially a negative affair. When two powers have rival ambitions, a compromise between them is often possible. A deal is more difficult when each merely wants to keep the other out. In the first case, possession is the actual guarantee of the bargain; the second demands reliance on the other's good faith – and in the Eastern Question this was lacking. The Russians, apart from the few pan-Slav hotheads, merely wanted to keep the British navy out of the Black Sea; the British merely wanted to exclude the Russians from Constantinople. But each was convinced of the aggressive designs of the other. Similarly the Austrians merely wished to prevent any hostile power from controlling the route to Salonika; and the French wished to preserve their investments in the Ottoman Empire. All of them in fact wanted an independent Turkey; but each of them interpreted this to mean that Turkey should be subservient to itself. A modicum of mutual trust or even of indifference, and the Eastern Question would vanish from the international agenda. This happened some twenty years later when all the powers turned their backs on the Balkans, much to their own astonishment.

Bismarck, the wisest diplomatic head of the day, always advocated this course. He described the inhabitants of the Balkans as 'sheep-stealers'; and held that the Balkans were not worth the bones of any grenadier, let alone a Pomeranian. This was certainly true so far as material gain was concerned. The Balkans were a miserable prize, compared to almost any other part of the world; and have remained so to the present day. Only prestige and strategy were at stake; but these count for more than profit. Bismarck constantly urged the other powers to ignore the Near East; or, if they would not, to share it out – Constantinople with the east Balkans to Russia, Salonika with the west to Austria-Hungary, and Great Britain in control of Egypt and the Suez Canal. Hence his advice to Salisbury during the congress: 'Take Egypt'. Hence his encouragement to the French that they should find their share of the bargain in Tunis. The powers did not welcome his advice. For one thing, each hoped to acquire its share without yielding anything to others, as the British did four years later in Egypt. More deeply, the negative nature of their aims stood in the way. None of them wanted the trouble which partitioning the Near East would involve.

More deeply still, the powers lacked a common interest or loyalty. This was the age when the anarchy of sovereign states was at its height; and when men believed that in international affairs, as in economic relations between individuals, unchecked liberty for each automatically produced the best results for all. Gladstone alone preached the Concert of Europe. This was a noble aim, but how can there be a concert unless the players follow the same score? No great principle or belief held

Europe together. Monarchical solidarity had ended; the solidarity of peoples had not taken its place. There was not even a common fear – whether of revolution or of some infidel invader. Instead there was only a universal confidence that each power could stand on its own feet without bringing European civilization, or even itself, or disaster. Bismarck himself judged the concert contemptuously: 'Whoever speaks of Europe is wrong. It is merely a geographic expression.' And again: 'I only hear a statesman use the world "Europe" when he wants something for himself.' Bismarck accepted the international anarchy, but was confident that he could control it for his own end. This end was peace. Certainly Germany directed the 'system' so far as there was one; but in Bismarck's time her only object was negative – to prevent war, not to make gains. Since the other powers too had this negative aim, though less consciously, they acquiesced – with some grumbles – in Bismarck's direction.

Before the Congress of Berlin Bismarck had helped Russia and Great Britain towards agreement. In the months after the congress this agreement seemed farther off than ever. The British, invigorated by success, thrust towards new achievements. Salisbury planned to revive the Ottoman Empire under British protection. British military consuls swarmed in Asia Minor; British agents harassed the sultan with advice which he usually disregarded. In the Balkans, Austria-Hungary and France supported what they took to be the winning side. The Crimean coalition which had disappeared during the recent crisis seemed to be resurrected. The Russian Empire was exhausted by the war. Its rulers were exasperated and alarmed by these new threats. They appealed to Bismarck for support; and this time he responded. The Crimean coalition was as unwelcome to him as it had been to the rulers of Prussia during the Crimean War itself. On the other hand the prospect of co-operating with Russia against it was equally unwelcome. Bismarck's solution – though also anticipated by Prussian policy during the Crimean War – was at first sign surprising. Instead of supporting Russia against Great Britain, he concluded on 5 October 1879 a defensive alliance with Austria-Hungary against Russia. He gave a variety of explanations then and thereafter. Sometimes he alleged that Germany was in imminent danger of attack from Russia and needed Austro-Hungarian backing; sometimes he claimed that he was restoring the old greater German union of the Holy Roman Empire. At one time he proposed making the alliance a fundamental law of the German Reich; at another he advised his successors to get rid of it at a convenient opportunity. Historians, both German and foreign, have added theories of their own.

It is fairly easy to solve the problem of why Bismarck acted as he did in October 1879 by asking: what was the alternative? The Crimean coalition would have grown stronger; it would have pressed harder against Russia; and then there would have followed a new war or else – more likely – such a humiliation of Russia as would upset the balance of power. Austria-Hungary and France, the two powers whom Germany had defeated, would have recovered prestige; and after Russia, it would have been Germany's turn. As it was, Austria-Hungary, secured by Germany's support, grew cool towards the British; and affairs in the Balkans drifted towards oblivion. Bismarck made this clear himself when he said to the Russian ambassador concerning Austria-Hungary: 'I wanted to dig a ditch between her and the western powers.' He made it even clearer when he went on from the Austro-German alliance to revive the League of the Three Emperors, which he succeeded in doing some two years later.

There are deeper problems not so easily solved. The Austro-German alliance makes sense as the temporary answer to an immediate difficulty. But why did Bismarck give it such a rigid permanent form? Precise alliances, defined in writing, had gone out with the *ancien régime*, except as the early prelude to war. No great power had a fixed commitment of this kind between the Congress of Vienna and the Congress of Berlin. Now the Austro-German alliance began an era in which every power, except Great Britain, gave formal pledges of action to support some other. Yet Bismarck was himself contemptuous of such attempts to bind the future. Every alliance, he said, had an unwritten clause: *rebus sic stantibus*. Perhaps Bismarck, having now become a conservative statesman, not only wanted things to remain the same, but assumed that he could make them do so. Perhaps, too, he overlooked that alliances by this time were made not between monarchs, but between nations. The alliances of the eighteenth century were family compacts, private bargains between kings and emperors. The new alliances were absorbed by public opinion even though their precise terms were unknown – except for those of the Austro-German Alliance which were published in 1888. Indeed Bismarck's own rule worked against himself. The elaborate clauses, with the reservations and restrictions. were short-lived in their effect. The great names of Triple Alliance and Franco-Russian Alliance shaped men's minds, and determined the pattern of events. Bismarck had meant to preserve his freedom of manoeuvre when he made the Austro-German alliance. Instead every great power, including Germany, was taken prisoner by the system of alliances which he inaugurated.

The contrast between the precise terms of an alliance and its general significance was shown as soon as the Austro-German alliance was signed and throughout its history. Its essential clause was the promise by the two powers to resist any Russian attack. Bismarck meant precisely this, and no more. He would not allow the destruction of Austria-Hungary as a great power, but he would not support her activities in the Balkans. The Austrians never took the reservation seriously: they always assumed that Germany was now committed to them 'through thick and thin'. There began a tug-of-war between Vienna and Berlin which lasted until the Austrians pulled Germany into war in 1914. All Bismarck's diplomacy from October 1879 until his fall was an answering tug: an attempt to escape the inevitable consequences of an alliance which he had himself brought into existence. The simplest way out in his eyes was to reconcile Austria-Hungary and Russia; whenever this broke, as it often did, on Austrian reluctance, he sought to provide other allies for her so that Germany need not be involved. His unrivalled skill enabled him to perform these conjuring tricks with success; but none of them would have been necessary if the Austro-German Alliance had not existed.

The Russians presented no difficulties. They asked only for security in the Near East – the Straits closed to British ships of war, and the Balkan states left in harmless independence. They were eager to revive the League of the Three Emperors; and Bismarck agreed with them once the Austro-German alliance was signed. The Austrians resisted obstinately; their policy was 'the permanent blocking of Russia' with British assistance. In April 1880 the bottom fell out of this policy. The British Liberal party, under Gladstone's leadership, defeated the Conservatives at the general election. Gladstone hoped to inaugurate a new age in internal relations, based on the Concert of Europe instead of individual action. He succeeded only in negation. He abandoned Salisbury's Turkish policy; withdrew the military consuls from Asia Minor; and disregarded the guarantee to Turkey, though he did not return Cyprus, which had been its *quid pro quo*. But the Concert of Europe never came to life. The statesmen of Europe, apart from Gladstone, lacked a common conscience. They relied on the balance of power and thought only of their national interests. Still, Gladstone's acts left the Austrians high and dry. They were driven into the League of the Three Emperors, for lack of anything better.

The new league took another year to come into formal existence. First, the Austrians resisted; then the assassination of Alexander II provoked further delays. The league was finally signed on 18 June 1881. Its predecessor of eight years before had been a declaration of monarchical solidarity; this was a practical bargain with nothing sentimental about it except its name. The three emperors promised each other neutrality; they also asserted 'the European and mutually obligatory character' of the rule of the Straits – a double repudiation, in fact, of the policy of working with Great Britain which Austria-Hungary had previously favoured.

Germany was freed from having to choose between Russia and Austria-Hungary. Russia got security at the Straits, short of an isolated action by Great Britain in defiance of all the continental powers. But where was the gain for Austria-Hungary? The Austrians refused to trust Russia's word and grumbled ceaselessly at the position into which Bismarck had forced them. He found an odd way of satisfying them. Italy had been beating about on the fringe of great-power status ever since her unification in 1861. Her quest for alliances was really a quest of recognition as an equal; and this recognition had been rarely obtained. At the Congress of Berlin Italy had ranked rather below Turkey and slightly above Greece. She had come away empty-handed; and in angry resentment ran after predominance in Tunis. This provoked French competition. The French would have much rather left Tunis alone; but they could not tolerate an Italian outpost on the frontier of Algeria. On 12 May 1881 Tunis became a French protectorate.

The Italians were more humiliated than ever; and the monarchy itself seemed threatened. The house of Savoy, once the ally of revolution, now sought conservative respectability. In October 1881 King Humbert went on a begging mission to Vienna. The Austrians refused his proposal for a mutual guarantee. Early in 1882 the Italians had a stroke of luck. There was a short-lived revival of Pan-Slav feeling in Russia. Bismarck feared that Russia might not remain faithful to the League of the Three Emperors. He took up the negotiations with Italy as a precautionary measure. The outcome was the Triple Alliance, concluded on 20 May 1882. The only clause of practical importance in this was Italy's promise to remain neutral in a war between Russia and Austria-Hungary, hence freeing four Austro-Hungarian army corps for the front in Galicia. The Austrians got this benefit for nothing. Germany paid the price by agreeing to defend Italy against France. This was on paper a considerable liability for Germany, though less – in Bismarck's eyes – than the alternative of supporting Austro-Hungarian expansion in the Balkans. In any case, he always assumed, in true Napoleonic fashion, that whatever he wanted to do he would succeed in doing. He would somehow keep the peace between France and Italy; and thus never be called on to discharge his liability.

Bismarck's calculation proved correct. Triple Alliance and Emperors' League between them so tied up the European powers that none could move without his permission; and this was always withheld. Changes took place only outside Europe, the greatest of them in Egypt. Here Great Britain and France had been wrestling for years, in an uneasy condominium, with the chaotic finances of a spendthrift khedive. In 1882 nationalist disturbances broke out against the Europeans in Egypt. Joint intervention was planned. At the last moment the French government drew back, because of opposition in the Chamber. The British intervened alone; and in September 1882 established a protectorate over Egypt (at first unavowed) which was to last for seventy years. This was a great event; indeed the only real event in international relations between the battle of Sedan and the defeat of Russia in the Russo-Japanese War. All the rest were manoeuvres which left the combatants at the close of day exactly where they had started. The British occupation of Egypt altered the balance of power. It not only gave the British security for their route to India; it made them masters of the Eastern Mediterranean and the Middle East; it made it unnecessary for them to stand in the front line against Russia at the Straits – ultimately indeed unnecessary to stand against her at all. It also, as a more temporary though still important consequence, disrupted the 'liberal alliance' between Great Britain and France; and thus prepared the way for the Franco-Russian alliance ten years later.

This, however, was not the immediate consequence. Instead Bismarck, playing on the French resentment over Egypt, attempted to round off his 'system' by a reconciliation between France and Germany. In the long run the attempt came to nothing; and it is therefore impossible to decide how seriously the attempt was taken by either party – the failures in history have no memorial. Certainly there were reserves on both sides. The French, because of Alsace and Lorraine, could never follow Bismarck's prompting 'to forgive Sedan as after 1815 they came to forgive Waterloo'. Nor would Germany's partners in the Triple Alliance turn wholeheartedly against Great Britain, whose support they might one day need – the Austrians against Russia, the Italians against France. Moreover the colonial disputes which blew up in Africa between France and Germany on the one side, and Great Britain on the other, have led most historians to suppose that the Franco-German co-operation was an accidental product of these disputes, not the other way round. This was probably true so far as France was concerned; but Bismarck, as he himself said, was never 'a man for colonies', and his sudden claim for African colonies seems to fall into place as a move in his European policy – not, of course, that he repudiated the popularity which these claims brought him in Germany.

At any rate, the result is beyond doubt, whatever the cause. Not only was Great Britain isolated – this was her own choice – but her two principal rivals for empire, France and Russia, were for once unhampered by anxieties for their European security; and, more than that, could often count on backing from the other powers. This backing was of a limited kind. No power, except possibly Russia, ever seriously contemplated war against Great Britain. The great disputes which raged from Egypt to the Far East were fought in diplomatic terms, with loans,

notes, and railway concessions as the instruments. Armed power re-
ceded into the background, an ultimate sanction that was almost
forgotten. Egypt illustrates this. The British army controlled Egypt; the
British navy dominated the Mediterranean. The British could have an-
nexed Egypt at a moment's notice; and the French could have done
nothing to stop them. But the British claimed to administer Egypt in the
interests of the bondholders; and the Egyptian question was disputed at
the *caisse de la dette*, not between armies and navies. As a result
international relations ran on two levels. On one were the formal
alliances, which gave promises of support in some hypothetical war
which never happened; on the other were the combinations of bankers
and committees. On the first level Great Britain was the most isolated
of the powers; on the second, the most involved. She had no alliances;
but, as the power with the most world-wide interests, innumerable
ententes and, of course, innumerable quarrels.

Even on this diplomatic plane, Great Britain had a rough time during
1884 and the early part of 1885. French and German colonial advances
against her ran together, for whatever reason. In July 1884 a conference
to settle the Egyptian question broke up without result. Bismarck held
out to the French the prospect of a maritime league directed against
England. To others he boasted that he had revived the continental
system of Napoleon I, though this time with Berlin as centre. The high
point of this continental solidarity came in September 1884 when the
three emperors met at Skierniewice – the last such meeting ever to take
place. Later in the autumn an international conference met at Berlin to
settle the affairs of central Africa, and particularly of the Congo basin.
Again the Franco-German partnership against Great Britain was displayed, in principle if not in achievement. The Berlin Act was a great
stroke in international affairs. It laid down the rules for 'effective occupation' of uncivilized lands; and so ensured that the partition of Africa
should take place without armed conflict between the powers. The
Berlin conference has another incidental point of interest; it was the last
international conference on any concrete subject for more than twenty
years – telling evidence indeed that the Concert of Europe was dissolved. Each power served the common good by pursuing its individual
aims, and peace seemed secure without any conscious effort.

The worst moment of British isolation came in April 1885. On 30
March a Russian force defeated the Afghans at Pendjeh on their norther
frontier; and so seemed to threaten Afghanistan, India's buffer state.
The British, lacking allies, could rely only on force; and on 21 April the
pacific Gladstone secured a vote of credit from the House of Commons
as the preliminary to war. The British planned to operate Salisbury's
doctrine of 1878 and to send an expeditionary force through the Straits.

Bismarck's system worked, as he had intended, for Russia's protection. Every great power – not only Germany and Austria-Hungary but France and Italy also – warned the sultan to keep the Straits closed against the British. It was the most formidable display of continental solidarity on an anti-British basis between Napoleon I's time and Hitler's. Its very success dissolved it. The Russians had felt insecure at the Straits and had therefore sought in Afghanistan a counter-threat against the British. Once convinced that the Straits would remain closed, they lost interest in Penjdeh and agreed to send the dispute to arbitration – quite a score in its way for Gladstone's high principles. Afghanistan remained a buffer-state, as it is to this day: one of the few countries that has always preserved its independence from the competing great powers.

The peaceful outcome of the Penjdeh affair was not the only improvement for the British. The Franco-German entente gradually crumbled during the summer of 1885, rather from a French revulsion against colonial expansion than from a pronounced hostility towards Germany. Moreover the Eastern Question caught fire again in September; and Bismarck had to treat the British with more consideration for the sake of Austria-Hungary. The new Eastern crisis centred, like its predecessor, on Bulgaria. But the positions were now reversed. In 1878 Russia had set up a Big Bulgaria which Great Britain and Austria-Hungary insisted on dismembering. In 1885 two out of the three parts of Bulgaria came together – eastern Roumelia joined the existing principality. Russia sought to dismember Bulgaria or, at the very least, to force it back into subordination. Austria-Hungary and Great Britain defended Bulgaria's unity and independence. The crisis lasted in various forms from September 1885 until March 1888. First, Russia tried to undo the unification that had taken place; next to impose a Russian general as governor; finally to prevent the election of an anti-Russian prince. All these moves failed. The Russians received a barren satisfaction in March 1888 when the sultan, theoretical overlord of Bulgaria, declared the election of Ferdinand of Coburg illegal. But nothing happened. The crisis died away without war.

In retrospect it is tempting to say that nothing vital was at stake. Though it was no doubt humiliating to Russia that Bulgaria had repudiated her patronage, there was no fundamental change in the Near Eastern situation. Was it really worth Russia's while to fight a great war merely for the pleasure of appointing the prince of Bulgaria? In any case, Russia had not the strength to fight a great war even if she wished to do so. All this was less obvious to contemporaries; and the Bulgarian crisis caused an upheaval in international affairs. The League of the Three Emperors was an immediate casualty. The Austrians were determined to resist Russia, despite Bismarck's promptings to the opposite course; and they called for German support. Bismarck referred them to London, where Salisbury, once more in power, was equally reluctant. The two competed in reserves and evasions: both anxious to avoid war or even commitment, both doubtful – in the last resort – whether war was really imminent. Bismarck had a stroke of luck during 1886 when there was a febrile revival of nationalism in France under the nominal leadership of General Boulanger. Bismarck could make out that Germany was too menaced by France to have any forces to spare for the support of Austria-Hungary. This was an adroit and unanswerable excuse. In Bismarck's own words: 'I could not invent Boulanger, but he happened very conveniently for me.' Salisbury, though caring little about Bulgaria, dared not altogether estrange Austria-Hungary and Italy because of the Egyptian question. The result was the first Mediterranean agreement of March 1887 by which Great Britain, Austria-Hungary and Italy promised each other diplomatic support – certainly a gain for Austria-Hungary so far as Bulgaria was concerned, but more immediately an end of the isolation over Egypt with which the British had previously been threatened.

The competition between Bismarck and Salisbury was not yet resolved. The British promise of diplomatic co-operation was almost as non-committal as any promise could be; and Bismarck was himself somewhat compromised by having to agree to the renewal of the Triple Alliance. Both men sought to recover their freedom. Salisbury tried to settle the Egyptian question; and he actually concluded a convention with the sultan (Egypt's nominal overlord) for British withdrawal on conditions. Then Russia and French protests frightened the sultan; and he withdrew his consent. It is easy to understand Russian objections. But the principal French motive was to secure Russian backing in Egypt; yet this would have been unnecessary to them if the British had withdrawn. Such are the confusions of international policy. At all events, the failure of the convention had decisive effects. Salisbury was pushed farther on the path of co-operation with Austria-Hungary and Italy. The French had no alternative to Russia's friendship; and the Franco-Russian alliance was now only a matter of time.

Bismarck did better. He rescued the Russians from isolation in the Near East at little cost to himself. On 18 June, when the League of the Three Emperors technically expired, he concluded with the Russians a new agreement – the Reinsurance Treaty. This renewed the promise of neutrality with two significant exceptions: it would not apply in case of a Russian attack on Austria-Hungary, nor in case of a German attack on France. Neither signatory projected such an attack; and these two reserves had always existed by implication. The other part of the treaty had more practical application: Germany would give Russia diplomatic support in Bulgaria and at the Straits. Russia was still in a minority, but at least she was not alone; and this moral satisfaction perhaps helped to keep her on the peaceful track. The Reinsurance Treaty contained nothing new. It merely formalized policies which Bismarck, and for that matter the Russians, had defined again and again. Its terms would not have surprised or offended the other powers, if they had become known; but they would have outraged German opinion. It was for this reason that Bismarck kept it secret: he was conducting a policy which ran counter to German sentiment. Germany had no conflict of interest with Russia; yet German feeling was more antagonistic towards her than to any other power. Most Germans wished to be 'western' and liberal; while the threat of cheap Russian grain estranged the Junker landowners who had been the one pro-Russian group. Moreover, Russia was the one continental power which remained obstinately independent even at her moments of greatest weakness; and unconsciously the Germans resented this. Bismarck knew how to moderate his mastery; other Germans were less controlled.

Bismarck got his way for the time being. The autumn of 1887 saw the Bulgarian crisis apparently at its height. Bismarck's reserve once more forced Salisbury's hand; and in December Austria-Hungary, Great Britain, and Italy concluded the second Mediterranean agreement. This went beyond diplomatic co-operation and envisaged common action against any 'illegal enterprise' in the Near East. It was more nearly an alliance with other powers than any agreement that Great Britain had made in peacetime, certainly more binding than the ententes made with France and Russia twenty years later. But nothing dramatic happened. The Russians did not attempt any 'illegal enterprise'; and the crisis died away. This peaceful outcome was the greatest success ever achieved by the balance of power; but perhaps it was the general wish for peace which made the balance of power work.

Bismarck would, no doubt, have liked to make his 'system' permanent – Russia checked by the three 'Mediterranean' powers, yet appeased by the Reinsurance Treaty, and France thus safely isolated; and in fact the system ran on until his fall, over domestic issues, in March 1890. Then a general shake-up seemed to follow. Bismarck's successors, the men of 'the new course', were impatient with his complicated pattern of checks and balances. Far from recognizing that German reserve pushed Great Britain forward, they believed that she would become a full member of the Triple Alliance if Germany too backed Austria-Hungary without restrictions. They therefore refused to renew the Reinsurance Treaty, and promised to back Austria-Hungary in the Balkans. They sought British favour by renouncing any German attempt to reach the head-waters of the Nile. In their zest for resolute action, they even promised to back Italian ambitions in Tripoli against the French. Things worked out just as Bismarck had expected. The British, far from being tempted into the Triple Alliance, were delighted to see the Germans shouldering their responsibilities and withdrew towards isolation. The Balkans were fortunately quiet; and the German promises to Austria-Hungary therefore had no practical result. But the Italians boasted of their strong diplomatic position; and this alarmed the French. Reluctantly they turned to Russia for support and alliance.

Reluctance was indeed the keyword of the Franco-Russian alliance on both sides. Not only were republic and despotic monarchy antipathetic; neither had the slightest sympathy with the other's practical concern. Russia had no desire to recover Alsace-Lorraine for France; and France, on her side, was – of all the powers – the most anxious to maintain the independence of Turkey. Their only common interest was security from any German threat, so that each could pursue aims elsewhere. But here again there was no coincidence of policy. Though each was the rival of Great Britain, the rivalries did not overlap. France wanted to get the British out of Egypt; the Russians wanted the Egyptian conflict to continue, so that France and Great Britain should remain estranged. Russia's ambitions centred on north China, where the French had nothing to gain. The Russians had no serious resentment against Germany, despite the failure to renew the Reinsurance Treaty, and thought of the alliance as a general anti-British combination all over the world. The French hoped ultimately to be reconciled with Great Britain, so as to strengthen their position against Germany.

There was conflict even over the military objectives of the two prospective allies. The French wanted to ensure that a considerable part of the Russian army would march against Germany in the event of a general war; the Russians wanted to defeat Austria-Hungary, and were inclined to think that even a German capture of Paris would not be a disaster if they themselves took Budapest and Vienna. Not surprisingly, therefore, the negotiations took long to reach a conclusion: first a general entente in August 1891; then a military convention in August 1892; and finally confirmation of this convention by the political heads in January 1894. The French president was allowed to refer to 'the alliance' only in 1895; and the tsar waited until 1897 before acknowledging it in public. Technically the Franco-Russian alliance was never more than a pledge for common action in case of a war against Germany. This made it impossible for Germany to threaten first one, then the other, and so forced on her the peace which she had kept willingly in Bismarck's time. Ostensibly the alliance was a great defeat for Bismarck's successors. Its practical result was to restore his system in a different form. His overriding object had been to prevent a war between Austria-Hungary and Russia. Now the

French, being committed to support Russia, had the same object. The Balkan conflict was dying away in any case; the influence of both France and Germany accelerated the process. The new balance of power offered only the choice between general war and general peace; and all the continental powers chose peace for many years to come. Triple Alliance and Franco-Russia Alliance alike became defensive combinations; and any power that was tempted towards adventure was restrained as much by its allies as by its opponents.

This restraint applied only in Europe; and the very security there made it easier for the European powers to pursue 'imperialist' aims elsewhere. The European stalemate and the expansion outside Europe were two different aspects of the same situation: each produced the other. The loser was Great Britain with her world-wide interests; and the Franco-Russian alliance began the period of true British 'isolation'. Previously the British had assumed that others were more in need of help than they were. As Salisbury said: 'Great Britain does not solicit alliances; she grants them.' Now, however, a continental power would endanger its security, instead of increasing it, by an alliance with Great Britain. The British had assumed, too, that their overseas rivals – particularly France and Russia – would always be distracted by anxiety for their European frontiers. Now these frontiers were secure. France challenged the British in West Africa and Egypt; Russia moved ruthlessly forward in the Far East; and the Germans too entered the imperialist competition. Yet this competition had an unavowed limit. All the European powers had chosen peace in continental affairs; therefore they would make imperialist gains, too, only so long as these could be achieved peacefully. If the French would not fight for Alsace and Lorraine, how much less would they fight for Egypt or Siam? And similarly with the others. The British were the one exception: having nothing to lose (or gain) in Europe, they were prepared to fight for their imperial position and, with the steady expansion of the British fleet, could fight successfully. Isolation began as an embarrassment; later, freedom from European commitments left the British untrammelled elsewhere.

The new balance of power took some little time to display its effects. It seemed at first that the Near East might again become a centre of conflict, particularly when the Armenian massacres of 1894 and 1895 raised new demands for the reform, or for the partition, of the Turkish empire. The Russians supposed that they had improved their position in the Near East by making an alliance with France. So they had, but only in a negative way. That alliance certainly made it impossible for the British to act on the old assumption of the Mediterranean agreement, that France would remain neutral while the British resisted Russia at Constantinople. Now that France was Russia's ally, the British dared not pass the Straits with a potentially hostile French fleet behind them. The British proposed that Germany should impose neutrality on France. This, in its turn, asked too much; for a German threat to France would bring her Russian ally into action. Germany and Great Britain demanded the impossible of each other. The British threatened to withdraw into isolation; the Germans answered by threatening Great Britain, as Bismarck had done, with a continental league.

The British threat was the more effective of the two. The Straits ceased to be important to them as their control of Egypt hardened; and in November 1895 the British fleet finally withdrew from Aegean waters. A month later, the Germans used the excuse of the Jameson raid to demonstrate their support of the Boer republics by a patronizing telegram to President Kruger; and implied that German, Russian, and French challenges to the British Empire would be knit together. This was empty show. Bismarck had no ambitions outside Europe and no objections to those of France or Russia; his continental league therefore had perhaps some sense. Now the Germans expected support from France and Russia without allowing them much gain in return. Yet the two were not even supporting each other in their imperial enterprises; how much less would they support Germany? Besides, the British navy was now a more formidable force than it had been ten years before; and the British answered the Kruger telegram by setting up a 'flying squadron' to show that they could take on all comers.

Yet just at this moment, when Germany and Great Britain had reached deadlock, the Russian danger at the Straits – so far as it had ever existed – was dispelled; not by Austria-Hungary or Great Britain, but by France. The French had tried to avoid this; but, failing anyone else, they had to act. For, just as Russia offered France security on the basis of the Treaty of Frankfurt, so the French offered Russia security within the framework of the Treaty of Berlin. When the Russians talked in December 1895 of seizing Constantinople, the French replied: 'only if the question of Alsace and Lorraine is opened as well'. This price was too high for the Russians to pay. Moreover, their concern for the Straits was essentially defensive; and, as it gradually became clear to them that the British had abandoned any idea of passing the Straits, the Russians too were prepared to leave well alone. The Austrians would still have liked to follow an anti-Russian course; but, failing support from Germany or Great Britain, they also had no choice. In May 1897 the League of the Three Emperors was renewed in weaker form. Russia and Austria-Hungary agreed to freeze the Near East; and 'on ice' it remained for the next ten years. Every European question had thus reached a temporary stability, so much so that even in the early days of 1914 one good judge held that the existing states and frontiers were fixed 'for ever'.

Every great power behaved as though it enjoyed the geographic security which had enabled the British to build their empire in 'splendid isolation'. This had another curious consequence. The opinion long held by English Radicals, on an isolationist basis, that foreign policy was unnecessary and wars caused by the wickedness of the governing class, spread to continental countries. In earlier times revolutionary socialists, for instance, had condemned the existing international order and had denounced Metternich or Tsar Nicholas I as peace-mongers, upholding an unjust *status quo*. The new socialist international, revived in 1889, taught that the working classes had no country and proposed to organise a general strike against war, assuming that any war could have only a selfish 'governing-class' motive. Even the governing class had twinges of conscience against war; and the first Hague conference, held in 1899, aired projects of international disarmament, though the only practical outcome was the Hague court on a voluntary basis. This court could only settle casual disputes. It could not handle such questions as Poland or the future of the Ottoman or Habsburg empires; and the creation of the Hague court was, in fact, evidence that men had forgotten the existence of such questions.

The delusive stalemate in Europe opened the short-lived era of 'world-policy'. Men supposed that the powers had abandoned their disputes in Europe because the prizes elsewhere were so much greater, whereas the truth was the other way round. The powers had dropped their disputes in Europe because they were too hot to handle. Russia and France had always tried to combine Europe and empire. Germany was the new entrant into the field. Her economic strength now put her in the front rank of the powers, ahead of any except Great Britain and the United States. It seemed reasonable that like them she should become a world power. But there was also a political cause for this development. Bismarck had held that Germany's central position in Europe debarred her from expansion overseas. He said to an enthusiast for expansion in Africa: 'Here is France; and here is Russia. That is my map of Africa.' His successors assumed that the danger from France and Russia had ceased to exist. Indeed, these two powers were regarded as a positive advantage by Germany. For, given their fierce competition with the British, Germany could safely pursue world-aims without arousing British, or for that matter Franco-Russian, hostility. Where Germany had once been the pivot in a system of alliance, she now became the exponent of 'the free hand'; rejoicing at the conflicts of others, and collecting rewards from both sides.

The calculation was correct. Germany never had colonial disputes with France. Her project for a railway to Baghdad was less of a menace to Russia than was the world-wide opposition from Great Britain. Most of all, Germany was a lesser danger to the British Empire than was France or Russia, at any rate until the plans for a great German navy came to fruition – and realisation of that had to wait until 1909. Though there were colonial disputes between Germany and Great Britain – over a hypothetical partition of the Portuguese colonies and over Samoa – these were relatively trivial; and all were easily settled even without the fraudulent hope held out by the Germans that they might, if appeased, become Great Britain's ally.

The decisive centre of conflict in the era of world-policy was the Far East. Here too, as in the Near East, a decrepit empire was breaking up under European penetration. Unlike the Near East, however, there was no question of security – no Russian fear for the Black Sea or British anxiety for the route to India. The sole prize was trade, or rather the expectations of trade with a vast hypothetical China market which, in fact, never became real. The British had long held a near-monopoly of what trade there was; but they had no grave objection to sharing this trade with others so long as these others maintained the open door. Hence they did not complain seriously when the Germans entered the Far East by seizing Kiao-Chow in 1897. British antagonism was against Russia; for the Russians, being weaker economically, used their military power to close the Chinese door, not to open it.

The Far East was a tougher problem for the British than the Near East had been. Sea-power was less effective, and allies harder to find. The Russians could approach northern China by land; and, with the French in Indo-China, the British could risk their fleet in the China seas even less than at Constantinople. Even worse, there seemed no Far Eastern equivalent of Austria-Hungary: no power whose need to resist Russia was as great as the British. In the early days of 1898 there was an alarm that the partition of China had begun; and the Russians indeed acquired a long lease of Port Arthur, dominating the Yellow Sea. The British beat about for allies. They tried Japan, who had herself staked out an abortive claim to Port Arthur in 1895; they tried the United States. Both evaded entanglement. Most of all the British tried Germany, the proposal was plausible from the British point of view. Great Britain and Germany were modern industrial powers. Both wanted to preserve the Chinese empire and the open door. The scheme broke on the fact, so easily ignored, that Germany – unlike Great Britain – was still in Europe. A Far Eastern war would be for the British a war in the Far East; for the Germans it would be a continental war for survival. This price was too high to pay for the China market. The Germans had to stand aside, and consoled themselves that they were bound to gain from the inevitable war between Great Britain and Russia.

The British were forced back on their own resources. Since they could not resist Russia, they played for time; and of this the Russians were always generous. As usual, the Russians planned more ambitiously than they performed. They were short of money; their railway across Siberia was not completed; their energy was exhausted once they had acquired Port Arthur. Meanwhile, the British improved their position elsewhere. In 1896 they had begun the reconquest of the Sudan. In September 1898 they destroyed the dervish army at Omdurman. At almost the same moment a French expedition under Marchand arrived at Fashoda, farther up the Nile. It arrived two years late. The expedition had been designed as a move in diplomacy. Its object was to reopen the Egyptian question and to bring the British to the conference table. Once the British army advanced up the Nile, diplomacy ended; armed strength took its place. The British refused to negotiate. They demanded Marchand's unconditional withdrawal. The French had no choice but surrender. The British army could destroy Marchand's tiny force; the British navy controlled the Mediterranean. Neither Germany nor Russia would aid France. Fashoda was a triumph for 'splendid isolation'. The British established their domination of the Nile valley entirely by their own strength – indeed with allies they would have had to share. Moreover Fashoda made British isolation still more secure. The British no longer needed the votes of associates now that their hold over Egypt rested on military strength; and the British navy at Alexandria could forget about the Straits.

British self-confidence was at its height, and overreached itself. The British, having routed the French on the Nile without war, thought that they could do the same with the Boers in South Africa; and the triumph of Fashoda led straight to the outbreak of the Boer War a year later. This turned out to be a tougher affair than the British had expected; and the war absorbed all their resources for three years instead of finding them in Pretoria by Christmas. Yet the Boer War too displayed the virtues of splendid isolation. All the continental powers sympathized with a small nation struggling rightly to be free, as powers usually do when the small nation is not struggling against themselves. All of them would have liked to humiliate Great Britain, and to exploit her embarrassment. Yet the talk of a continental league came to nothing. The underlying European conflicts reasserted themselves. The Russians proposed mediation in the Boer War by the powers. The French tactfully replied that they would agree to anything which the Germans agreed to. The Germans, however, could co-operate only if the powers 'mutually guaranteed their European possessions for a long period of years' – in other words, a French renunciation of Alsace and Lorraine, but (given the restriction to Europe) no backing for Russia in the Far East. The negotiations collapsed. In any case, they were futile. The British navy dominated the seas – so much so that the entire army could be sent to South Africa without any fear that the British Isles could be invaded. If all the armies of Europe had mobilized, not a single soldier would have reached the Boers.

The Far East continued to be Great Britain's one weak spot; and the Boer War offered Russia the chance of easy success. The British were saved unexpectedly by the Chinese themselves. The Boxer rising of June 1900 was the greatest repudiation of the West by a non-European civilization since the Indian Mutiny. The legations at Peking were besieged, the German minister killed. This humiliation forced Germany into the lead. An international force was sent out under the German field-marshal Waldersee: the only time in history when troops of all the great European powers served under a single commander. Intelligent observers had some excuse when they expected that European unity would be achieved in a 'consortium' for the exploitation of China. Of more practical importance, the Germans concluded with Great Britain an agreement (16 October 1900) to maintain the integrity of the Chinese empire. The Germans were only concerned to prevent the British grabbing a 'sphere' for themselves; the British, however, thought that the agreement could be turned against Russia. For a few months, the British seemed to have turned the corner and to have manufactured a Far Eastern equivalent for the Mediterranean Agreements.

The Anglo-German agreement was, however, a bluff against Russia and the bluff was soon called. The Japanese were eager to resist further Russian expansion; but, if they were to fight a war overseas, they must be secure from the French navy. In March 1901 they asked the British to keep France neutral. The British were still at war in South Africa; they had no ships to spare for the Far East, and passed the Japanese inquiry to Germany. The Germans equivocated. They offered 'benevolent neutrality'; then explained that this meant 'strict and correct neutrality', no more. The myth of Anglo-German co-operation in the Far East was exploded. The British tried to resurrect it by offering to Germany a formal alliance; but no offer could be high enough to involve Germany in a great European war. There was no formal estrangement between Great Britain and Germany. Politicians in both countries continued to talk of the 'natural alliance', but after March 1901 it was clear that this alliance could not be translated into effective action so long as France and Russia remained independent powers.

The British continued to rely on time. The Japanese were less patient. They resolved to clear their position one way or the other: either a pact with Russia to share the Far East and exclude all others, or an alliance with Great Britain to keep France neutral. They opened both negotiations in November 1901. The Russians were generous of words; they offered nothing. Their only serious proposal was that Japan should be excluded from the Far East like everyone else. The British were more forthcoming, particularly when threatened with the alternative of a Russo-Japanese combination. The war in South Africa was ending. The British now had ships to spare for the Far East. On 30 January 1902 Japan and Great Britain reached agreement on mutual aid if either were attacked in the Far East by two powers. In practical terms, this meant that Japan could stand up to Russia without fear of being taken in the rear by the French navy. The alliance did not necessarily imply war with Russia. Indeed both parties to it hoped that it would make compromise with Russia easier, now that they could not be played off against each other.

Nor did the Anglo-Japanese agreement imply any British estrangement from Germany. On the contrary, the British assumed relations would be more cordial now that they did not have to plague the Germans with requests for help. Indeed the alliance strengthened British isolation from a European point of view. Previously they had often sought the help of one member or other of the Triple Alliance against the Franco-Russian alliance, though always in vain. Now they could rejoice, like every other power, that the two alliances cancelled out. Yet, against all expectations, the Anglo-Japanese agreement ultimately turned international relations upside down. Not only did it eliminate the inevitable war between Great Britain and Russia on which the Germans had counted. Assisted by fantastic Russian blunders, it led to a great war in the Far East which shook the balance of power in Europe and so ended the deadlock which had given Europe a peace of unparalleled duration.

CHAPTER SIX

The Western Question

This essay was first published as a review of F.V. Parsons, *The Origins of the Morocco Question 1880–1900* (London, Duckworth, 1976), in the *Times Literary Supplement*, 3898, 26 November 1976. Alan Taylor clearly enjoyed a major study on a subject he had written about 25 years earlier.

Diplomatic history is out of favour. The Foreign Office archives which historians once ransacked in order to discover the causes of war are dismissed as containing merely, in Bismarck's phrase, 'what one clerk said to another clerk'. Now the causes of war are sought in economic rivalries, competitive armaments, public opinion or the aggressive plans of totalitarian rulers. Diplomatic history is left to the writers of theses. In my opinion it remains a fascinating subject, even if an unimportant one. I must declare an interest. I, too, have written 'pure' diplomatic history in my time. I even wrote an academic article on British policy in the early days of the Morocco question. F.V. Parsons, who has laboured in the archives for twenty years where I laboured for one, convicts me of many small errors. But he adds disarmingly that these 'do not affect the author's perverse talent for coming to an effective conclusion despite misuse of evidence'.

In return for this compliment I congratulate Mr Parsons on producing the most scholarly and thorough work of diplomatic history I have ever read. His book is excessively long – over 600 pages. It is excessively detailed, its pages festooned with quotations from the archives of five states. It is also devoted to a relatively unimportant subject. In 1905 and again in 1911 Morocco provoked an international crisis which on each occasion brought Europe to the brink of war. In the past twenty years of the nineteenth century, though there was much diplomatic activity over Morocco and many alarms, nothing happened. There could be no more perfect case of Sherlock Holmes's dog in the night: 'the dog did nothing in the night'.

Morocco was often described as the 'Western Question' to set off against the Eastern Question of the Ottoman Empire at the other end of the Mediterranean. Here, too, was a derelict Islamic state with a turbulent population and chaotic finances. Here, too, were rival powers, suspicious of each other and convinced that a crisis was approaching. But there were differences which prevented the Morocco question from becoming acute.

Only two great powers were vitally involved. Great Britain feared that Tangier in the hands of a European power would endanger Gibraltar. France did not want any such power on the frontiers of Algeria. The concern of both was essentially negative. Their aim was to keep others out rather than to get in themselves. Salisbury defined British policy as 'Do not awaken the sleeping dog'. The French usually agreed with this though they were occasionally pushed on by colonialist enthusiasts both at home and in Algeria.

Complications came from other powers. Spain, once a great power and still possessing some scraps of Moroccan territory, wished to demonstrate that she could become a great power again. Italy, not yet an acknowledged great power, tried to behave like one in Morocco, once Italian statesman declaring that Morocco was for Italy 'a matter of life and death'. Germany, with no interests of her own at stake, used Morocco to provoke discord or occasionally co-operation between the other powers. There was an interminable quadrille. Sometimes Spain worked with France against alleged British designs. Sometimes she worked with Italy against France and tried to enlist Great Britain as well. Sometimes Germany stirred up French suspicions of Great Britain and sometimes the reverse. Every combination broke down or proved unnecessary. Nothing happened in Morocco except great activity among the diplomats at Tangier.

Mulai Hassan, ruler of Morocco until his death in 1894, was determined that nothing should happen. He remarked that 'the Sultan of Turkey had ruined his Empire by cultivating relations with foreign Powers' and 'he preferred to keep his people ignorant, poor and weak, so he could then govern them easier'. He gave a patient and apparently sympathetic hearing to the European diplomats who sought out him and his itinerant court at Morocco City or Fez. He dutifully paid compensation whenever a European was killed by unruly tribesmen. He even accepted military missions though he took care to isolate them from his native forces. But he did nothing. He staved off all plans of reform. He discouraged the building of railways. Morocco remained unchanged until Mulai Hassan's death.

Apart from Morocco's strategical position, there was really nothing to fight over. Foreign trade, mostly in British hands, was trivial. There were no great resources waiting to be exploited. There were of course financial adventurers, the most remarkable of them an Austrian crook named Geyling who peddled arms in Morocco and was then installed at Mogador as Hajj el-Kerim Bey, Minister Plenipotentiary and chargé d'affaires of Orelie-Antoine, King of Aranconia-Patagonia. Obsolete arms were sold to Mulai Hassan. The Italians even managed to saddle him with a warship. Later Krupps became involved in the sale of arms and the construction of fortifications. Perhaps the close links between Krupps and Wilhelm II led German statesmen to believe that there was something to be gained in Morocco after all. But there was not much in it. Morocco came to be regarded as an economic prize only after the turmoil was over.

What kept the Morocco question going was the activity of the diplomatic corps at Tangier. Like all diplomats they regarded their place of assignment as the most important in the world. Moreover, they had to create a stir if they were to win promotion. Each diplomat attributed sinister designs to his colleagues. When the diplomats proved sluggish, they were prodded into activity by alarms from their interpreters and other native agents. Not content with suspicions, each diplomat in turn resolved to solve the Morocco question all on his own. In 1880 Sir John Drummond Hay, the British minister who had been in Tangier for some forty years, produced a detailed programme of reforms. A conference actually met at Madrid. The French, seconded by the Germans, ensured that it came to nothing.

Thereafter the pattern was always the same. A diplomat pursued Mulai Hassan with a programme of reforms. Mulai Hassan was receptive and evasive. Meanwhile he alarmed the remaining diplomats at Tangier who one and all assured him that the visiting emissary was not authorized to speak for the other powers and should be disregarded.

In 1885 the French minister Ordega announced that he proposed to turn Morocco into a French protectorate. After some turmoil he was recalled and departed for another post where he could do no harm. Sir William Kirby Green, who succeeded Drummond Hay in 1886, believed that the right method was to bully Mulai Hassan and did this so successfully that he fell dead from an apoplectic fit during the attempt. In 1890 the German minister Tattenbach had a go and returned with concessions which proved meaningless. The greatest show came in 1892 with Sir Charles Euan-Smith, the next British minister, who had established a British protectorate over Zanzibar and now intended to do the same with Morocco. He, too, pursued Mulai Hassan. He, too, received a friendly welcome. He, too, achieved nothing and left in a rage. The vizier came after him with an agreement allegedly containing all that he had demanded. When translated, the document proved to contain nothing of the kind and Euan-Smith tore it into small pieces. With this his career in Morocco ended.

Troubles would have been less if the foreign ministers had disavowed their over-zealous representatives at Tangier. Instead they sought an easy success with the public opinion of their country by claiming that the programmes were part of a grand design, and the other foreign ministers of course believed them. Elaborate precautions were taken.

The Royal Navy demonstrated its might by including Tangier in its annual cruise. French troops were mobilized in Algeria. Italy and Spain talked menacingly of their Mediterranean entente. It all proved unnecessary. There were no grand designs for seizing Morocco, merely yet another diplomat who had taken leave of his senses.

Mr Parsons's book really ends with the death of Mulai Hassan in 1894, thus covering fourteen entertaining, though futile, years. What follows is epilogue, which Mr Parsons proposes to cover fully in his next book. With Abd el-Aziz, the new weak ruler, Morocco threatened to break up and by 1902 was on the verge of doing so. After the Fashoda crisis in 1898, when the French lost all chance of recovering any share of power or influence in Egypt, they began to look to Morocco as a possible compensation.

The Germans welcomed the Morocco question as a cause of conflict between Great Britain and France. Instead there came the Anglo-French entente of 1904 and thereafter the German attempts to disrupt it. In 1911 most of Morocco became a French protectorate, with a small cut going to Spain in recognition of her former greatness. The Morocco question of the early twentieth century was also 'pure' dipolomacy, though in this case considerations of prestige almost led to a European war. Even the French achievement was of little significance. The protectorate, established after so much diplomatic activity and such grave alarms, lasted little more than thirty years. Now all European diplomacy over Morocco is as though it had never been. Only the lovers of diplomatic history treasure the vanished Morocco question. I hope that Mr Parsons's next book on the question will be just as long and just as detailed as the present one, though I also hope that he will not take twenty years to write it.

Part II

Early Twentieth Century

Uneasy Splendour:
The British Empire at the Start
of the Twentieth Century

This essay was first published in Purnell's *History of the Twentieth Century*, published in magazine-size parts (1968–70). Alan Taylor was the editor-in-chief and J.M. Roberts the general editor.

Queen Victoria outlived the nineteenth century by three weeks. It was fitting that the nineteenth century and the Victorian age should end virtually at the same moment. That century had been very much Great Britain's. She had risen to the pinnacle of her glory and had set her mark on the world. Much of the globe was coloured red, and many, or even most, of the features which seem characteristic of the century had originated in Great Britain, from steam power to a belief in progress and evolution. Her industrial pioneers were secular missionaries, helping to transform societies to the British model. For example, every European country, except Spain and Russia, adopted for its railway the gauge which Robert Stephenson had casually inherited from the Durham coal-mines, and in some countries, including France and Italy, trains kept to the left, as they still do, thanks to the British engineers who laid the tracks.

Since 1884 time throughout the world was determined by Greenwich, and every map in the world was based on the Greenwich meridian. Virtually every European country went over to a gold standard for money which was operated by the Bank of England. The games which modern Europeans played, such as tennis, golf, and football, were all devised in Great Britain. The predominance of towns over countryside which was becoming general in Western Europe had started in Great Britain, and the tendency for both upper and lower classes to become bourgeois in their social and moral outlook was of British origin, even though the name was French.

Great Britain was also the political model which most European countries followed. During the earlier part of the nineteenth century democracy had been regarded with alarm, and it was expected to bring political and social revolution in its train. Even Queen Victoria had declared: 'She will never be Queen of a democratic monarchy.' Despite these alarms, the British ruling class held firm to a policy of concession, at any rate to the extent of household suffrage. The industrial working classes could exert a decisive influence if they wished to do so.

It seemed that they did not. In 1900 only two Labour members were returned to the House of Commons, and the two traditional parties Conservatives (or as they were called in reference to Ireland, Unionists) and Liberals, were confident that they could play the game of Ins-and-Outs for ever. The ruling class still ruled. The Marquis of Salisbury was prime minister, with an aristocratic lineage going back to the sixteenth century, and the government was so full of his Cecil relatives that it was known as the Hotel Cecil. The great families rivalled in wealth and power those of Hungary or Russia. The servants employed by a magnate, such as the Duke of Westminster or the Earl of Derby, for his private comfort were as numerous as the entire staff of a London general hospital, and five dukes spent on themselves more than was spent on university education throughout Great Britain. The old Whig doctrine had again proved true: concessions could be made without harm to those who made them, usually indeed much to their benefit. Not surprisingly, many European countries adopted the liberal constitutionalism which worked so happily in its home of origin.

Nevertheless, British complacency was crumbling when the nineteenth century ended; it had been crumbling for some time. Great Britain had once been the workshop of the world. She was ceasing to be so. The Great Exhibition of 1851, which had been intended to celebrate her superiority, marked instead the beginning of her decline. Though she held her own in the old staples, coal and cotton, she slipped behind in newer industries, such as chemicals, electrical engineering, and even in steel. Germany, in particular, first rivalled and then out-stripped her as an exporting nation. Many English people lost their faith in free trade and began to clamour for protective tariffs. As things turned out, the alarm was excessive. An Indian summer was approaching for free trade, though this could not be foreseen in 1901. Coal and cotton would boom once more, and the Liberals, as advocates of free trade, would win their last and greatest electoral victory. Even this, when it happened, did not restore British self-confidence in its old form. The doubts and fears were too deep-rooted.

When the British lost their old predominance as exporters of goods, they found a new source of strength and wealth in the export of capital. They became foreign investors instead of exporters, or rather they added one role to the other. The yield from their foreign investments went far beyond covering the deficit on their trading account and provided a surplus each year for fresh investment. The typical British capitalist of the early nineteenth century was a factory-owner or a railway king. The typical capitalist of 1901 was a financier, floating limited companies in the City. Radical observers announced the coming of economic, or finance, imperialism, and declared that the British Empire had become a vast investment trust, purchasing riches for the sake of a few rich men. At all events, the Empire was seen as the key to Great Britain's future.

Great Britain's empire

For much of the nineteenth century, the British empire was the only one in the world. In earlier times, the British had had to contend with others: at first with the Spaniards and the Dutch, then with the French. Their rivals had all gradually dropped out of the race. The Dutch empire was of little account. The Spanish empire dissolved into anarchic republics. France had been exhausted by trying to establish an empire in Europe during the Napoleonic wars and hesitated to resume her overseas ambitions. The British Empire survived alone in glory.

It had three facets. The original colonies of settlement had all become self-governing communities of white men, mostly British in origin, and, though still theoretically subordinate to the mother country, were in reality held to her by ties of affection and sentiment, not of law. In 1897, during Queen Victoria's Diamond Jubilee, Joseph Chamberlain, the colonial secretary, tried to win the colonies for a supreme Imperial Council and an Imperial *Zollverein*. He failed. Nevertheless, when the Boer War broke out, the colonies voluntarily decided to send military aid to Great Britain, and this aid was repeated on a larger scale during the First World War. With the self-governing colonies, empire was changing into co-operation or, as it was later called, commonwealth.

India was at the opposite extreme. The British raj was the most stupendous example of rule by one people over others since the great days of the Roman empire. The British, from the viceroy downwards, ran India with an autocracy tempered only by remote control from the government and Parliament in London. India provided profitable employment for the high-minded products of the English public schools. Half the British army was stationed in India – of course at Indian expense; and, in addition, a large Indian army was maintained under British officers. Moreover, despite lip-service to free trade, India was in practice a secure market for British goods. The raj had originated as a by-product of the East India Company's trading activities, and its British servants naturally placed their orders with British firms. India was indeed the brightest jewel in the British crown and, what was more important, the greatest source of British strength and profit.

Imperial strategy revolved almost entirely round the security of India and of the route to it. The scattered colonies in Africa and the Indian Ocean were coaling stations and naval bases. With no serious imperial rival, the British rarely bothered about open annexations, except actually on India's borders. They assumed that all the world was already theirs without having to take the trouble of making it so. Outside Europe or on its fringes were a number of derelict empires in decline – Morocco, the Ottoman Empire, Persia, and China. The British were more concerned to keep others out than to get themselves in, and these empires tended to become unacknowledged spheres of British influence. Thus, the British created the system of maritime customs in China and ran it for more than a generation. They pressed unwelcome reforms on the Ottoman sultan, fought the Crimean War in his defence, and were prepared to fight again in 1878. They preserved the independence of Morocco and Persia with less exertion. This was empire on the cheap.

The great security for the British Empire was absence of rivals. The Royal Navy dominated the seas and oceans, and no European power attempted to compete with it. There was a short alarm in the 1860's when the coming of steam made sailing ships obsolete and it was feared that Napoleon III might repeat his uncle's challenge to British seapower. The alarm soon passed, and the Royal Navy resumed its supremacy. Trafalgar seemed to have brought a victory which would last for ever.

The British had a further reason for security. They were completely detached from European affairs. In earlier centuries, from the Glorious Revolution of 1688 until the battle of Waterloo, the British constantly intervened in order to maintain the European balance of power, that is to prevent any single country, usually France, from dominating the Continent. The defeat of Napoleon seemed to have achieved this aim. France was held in check by the three conservative monarchies – Russia, Prussia (later Germany), and Austria (later Austria-Hungary), and they were held in check by France. When Russia appeared to exercise too great an influence, Great Britain joined with France against her in the Crimean War, and the allied victory, though indecisive, was adequate. The maintenance of the balance of power, once a reason for intervention, now became the reason for non-intervention. It was assumed to be self-operating, a law of nature evolved by a kindly providence for Great Britain's benefit. Even the defeat of France by Germany in 1870 did not over-alarm the British. If anything, it was regarded as an improvement. The danger of a new Napoleon became more remote than ever. The Europeans could look after their own balance, and the British could exploit the rest of the world.

Powers break into British preserves

In the last two decades of the nineteenth century this comfortable situation came to an end. The balance of power worked only too well. Germany and Austria-Hungary formed a defensive alliance in 1879 and added Italy as a somewhat doubtful third partner in 1882. Russia and France, after much havering, answered with a similar defensive alliance in 1894. Triple Alliance and Dual Alliance held each other in check, and there could be no new conflicts in Europe short of a general war. All the powers except Austria-Hungary looked outside Europe for glory and gains, and the very precision of the balance left them free to do so. Inevitably they broke into what had been Great Britain's exclusive preserves. All the coasts of Africa were on one or other of the British routes to India. Russian expansion in central Asia threatened the north-west frontier of India. French expansion in Indo-China was a similar threat to the south-east. Perhaps worst of all, the European powers broke into the derelict empires and were not impressed by Great Britain's assurances that she was maintaining a benevolent watch over these empires in the general interest.

The British had one particularly vulnerable spot, Egypt. They had worried about this as a possible back door into the Indian Ocean long before the Suez Canal was built. Hence their eagerness to eject Bonaparte in 1798. The opening of the Suez Canal made their problem much more acute. They were not so much anxious to control it themselves as to ensure that no one else did so and, pursuing this negative aim, established themselves, more or less accidentally, in Egypt in 1882. They shrank from open annexation and therefore claimed to be acting as the mandatory for the great powers – a claim hard to justify when at least two of the powers, Russia and France were anxious to get them out. The British needed friends to vote on their side at the international committees, if only to make a good show, and the need became greater when similar committees proliferated in the other derelict empires, such as Turkey and China. British isolation seemed to have become a source of danger instead of strength. This was in part a misleading impression. The British needed friends only as long as they, and others, stuck to negotiation. If it came to war, they were still secure – or so they thought.

The supremacy of the Royal Navy remained unchallenged. In 1884 Bismarck, the German chancellor, during a momentary irritation, talked of a continental league which would combine all the European navies against Great Britain. He soon abandoned this idea, and a little later, in 1889, the British began a reconstruction of their navy, which put it safely ahead of all rivals. A new danger appeared only in 1900. Then the second German Navy Law projected a great navy which could challenge the British in their home waters. This threat was to transform international relations in subsequent years. At the opening of the twentieth century, the German navy existed only as an idea, and by then the British had settled many of their overseas problems.

Of course the British would have liked simply to have forbidden overseas expansion by others. As an Australian premier said in 1885, when the Germans were laying hands on part of New Guinea: 'We are told that the Germans make good neighbours, but we prefer to have no neighbours at all.' It would have involved the British in an endless round of conflicts and would have overtaxed the strength even of the Royal Navy. Hence the British had to resort to a series of partitions. They took the areas which they regarded as vital, indeed they took more than anyone else, and let the others go. The entire continent of Africa, and much of Asia also, was shared out in this way.

The British had, as well as their naval preponderance, one diplomatic advantage. They assumed that, while an individual power might compete with them, the powers as a whole would not team up against them. If only because of their dislike of each other. As Charles II said to his brother James, Duke of York: 'They will never kill me to make you king.' They went further. They tended to assume that Germany was still their 'natural ally' who would obediently turn out for the defence of the British Empire if it were necessary. This assumption was fallacious. The European balance of power worked here also against British interests. The Franco-Russian alliance made the price of aiding Great Britain too high for Germany, even if she had wanted to do so. Moreover it was no longer clear that she did want to.

The Germans, too, developed overseas ambitions, though on a moderate scale. They, too, had to be appeased by partitions of colonial territory. This could be tolerated. The situation worsened when, in moments of dispute, the Germans threatened to co-operate with other rivals of Great Britain, particularly with France. Bismarck did this first in 1884, though he soon reverted to his older policy of detached friendship. In 1894 there was a more serious threat, when both Germany and France opposed a British attempt to smuggle the upper Nile into the Congo Free State. Worst of all, in 1896 the German kaiser openly patronized the Boer republics in South Africa, the independence of which Great Britain was attempting to subvert. In the end nothing came of this interference, and in 1898 the Germans were mollified by a plan for partitioning the Portuguese colonies – a plan which also came to nothing.

Despite British efforts, the old confident relations between Great Britain and Germany were not restored. In a paradoxical way, the British resented German activities outside Europe more than they did those of Russia and France, even though the German activities were more modest and less threatening. The British had, as it were, got used to troubles from Russia and France. They accepted that this was how these tiresome powers behaved. They were angered when Germany took the same line, much as an individual might be more angered by a challenge from a friend than from a rival. The Germans were accused of acting out of sheer contrariness. One school of thought in Great Britain began to regard them as the greatest danger for the future. This school was still small. Most British statesmen believed that Germany could be won over at some price or another. In 1898 Joseph Chamberlain, the colonial secretary, tried to secure a precise alliance. The attempt failed, and this helped to increase the British sense of isolation.

Isolated but still proud

Nevertheless the British were far from despair. Indeed they reached their greatest imperial triumph at their moment of greatest isolation. Queen Victoria's Diamond Jubilee in 1897 was deliberately celebrated as an exclusively imperial affair. In 1887 representatives of the continental monarchs were invited to her first Jubilee. Only representatives of the empire were invited to the second.

Lord Salisbury, the prime minister, achieved a more practical success. He had been exasperated by the ceaseless diplomatic harassments of the French in Egypt. He had watched with peculiar suspicion the French designs to improve their bargaining position by breaking into the valley of the upper Nile, which was then under the control of the Dervishes.

In 1896 Salisbury began to plan the reconquest of the upper Nile or Sudan. In 1898 these plans matured. The Dervish army was destroyed at the battle of Omdurman. Lord Kitchener, the British commander, learned that a small party of Frenchmen had established themselves at Fashoda, further up the Nile. He arrived there with a greatly superior force. The Royal Navy dominated the Mediterranean and controlled all access to Egypt by sea. Salisbury refused to bargain. He insisted on unconditional withdrawal. The French were helpless. They abandoned Fashoda and therewith all chances of embarrassing the British in Egypt. The Fashoda affair was the nearest that the British came to war between the conflict with Russia over Constantinople in 1878 and the Agadir crisis with Germany in 1911. They won without allies and practically without effort. The extra cost to the navy was only £13,000. British pride reached its height.

New dangers accumulated. In October 1899 the British, after mutual provocation, went to war with the Boer republics. They expected the war to be over by Christmas. Instead, it dragged on for nearly three years. The British had to mobilize over 500,000 men. Their military resources were absorbed by the Boer War. All the European powers sympathized with the Boers, mainly no doubt from jealousy of the British, and perhaps for worthier motives also. There was talk of European mediation or even intervention. Nothing came of it. The European powers were still suspicious of each other. In any case, there was nothing they could do. The war was being fought in South Africa, and the Royal Navy stood unchallengeably in the way. The Royal Navy could even give a firm guarantee against invasion of Great Britain, so that the entire home garrison could be sent to the war. The British went on with the war until they achieved unconditional surrender or the next thing to it. Isolation had once more proved to be splendid.

The falling shadows

All the same, it was an uneasy situation. The British could no doubt get over not having a friend in the world and did not worry much about moral disapproval from the Continent. But there were practical grounds for anxiety for even alarm. The British had always assumed that the derelict empires would not actually totter over the brink of collapse. They had even assumed that these empires had got some fight left in them. By the time of the Boer War, these assumptions were proving ill-founded. Salisbury had already written off the Ottoman Empire in 1896. This was one reason why he had moved into the Sudan: once securely in control of Egypt, he did not mind even if the Russians laid hands on Constantinople; in fact they did not. At the other end of the Mediterranean Morocco looked as if it might fall to pieces at any moment, and Salisbury was already foreseeing that there would have to be a partition with France.

The really disturbing case was China. This empire was much the biggest of the undistributed prizes, or so many imagined at this time. The British had tried persistently to hold China together, at any rate from the moment when others threatened to break in. Their efforts were proving increasingly unsuccessful. In 1898 there had already been a first sketch of partition, when Germany, Russia, and Great Britain all laid their hands on bits of Chinese territory. Worse things followed. In 1900 the Boxers raised a wild rebellion against all foreigners. The Great Powers united to rescue the beleaguered legations in Peking. Their international force was the only one on record to which all the great European powers contributed. It was unlikely to be the harbinger of international co-operation in the re-ordering of China. Rather there seemed imminent a new scramble, this time for the Celestial Empire – a scramble with far greater prizes than ever before, and in which Great Britain faced formidable rivals.

The Boer War had only seemed to show the dangers of British isolation. On a more detached examination, it showed that Great Britain was still secure. The troubles in China gave a more real demonstration of danger, particularly since they happened to coincide with the Boer War. Great Britain began a serious search for allies. She turned to Germany, this time on an official level. A formal treaty of alliance was actually drafted in the Foreign Office. But the Germans would not jeopardize their position in Europe for the sake of British interests in China, and they certainly would have jeopardized it if they had joined Great Britain against Russia and France. In any case, the Germans were by no means sure that their interests coincided with the British in the Far East. On the contrary they hoped to make gains of their own.

Then the shadow lifted. The British discovered a reliable ally who was actually prepared to stand in the front line. This was Japan, the only non-European country which had successfully re-made itself on the European model. The Japanese were eager to resist Russia. They only asked the British to hold the ring while they did so. This was a wonderful bargain for the British. They made an alliance with Japan in January 1902. The Boer War ended victoriously a few months later. When British statesmen now surveyed the world, they could see some trouble spots – with the French in Morocco, with the Russians in Persia. These difficulties could be faced without an ally. Isolation was still possible.

It was also possible in a deeper sense. The British were still confident that the European balance was secure without any action on their part. They still assumed that the rival alliances cancelled out. British strategy remained exclusively imperial. It occurred to hardly anyone that Great Britain might need a European policy, let alone that she might be compelled to intervene in a European war. Isolation might be a little tarnished. There might be uneasy moments. It remained splendid all the same.

CHAPTER EIGHT

Joseph Chamberlain

This essay was first published in Purnell's *History of the Twentieth Century*, published in parts (1968–70). Alan Taylor was the editor-in-chief and J.M. Roberts the general editor.

Joseph Chamberlain (1836–1914) was the major force behind imperial policies in 1895–1903. Lord Salisbury, the prime minister, once referred to the Boer War (1899–1902) as 'Joe's War'. Alan Taylor did not care for Chamberlain. In a 1977 book review he gave the view that Chamberlain was 'a democrat who was also a tyrant, a champion of the poor who lived in a lavish style'. Of his tariff reform campaign, launched in 1903, Taylor went so far as to comment, 'This campaign was not Radical; it was a precursor of Fascism. Chamberlain used every Fascist impulse, including anti-semitism'. (*Observer*, 15 May 1977.)

Great causes sometimes find their leaders in unexpected places, and Joseph Chamberlain was certainly a surprising leader for British imperialism. Imperialism was a movement for overseas expansion. Chamberlain represented Birmingham, the most inland city in England, and often showed a parochial spirit. Imperialism evoked traditional British glories. Chamberlain rejected many of those traditions, including the predominance of the aristocracy and the Established Church, imperialism was aggressive and nationalistic. Chamberlain was at first a Radical opponent of wars. Perhaps he stumbled on his true nature by surprise. Or perhaps his imperialism was more altruistic than it appeared.

Chamberlain began life as a Birmingham manufacturer. He had great energy and a dominating spirit. He found an outlet for these in local government, making Birmingham for some time a model city in England. He was a practical reformer, creating tramways, libraries, and savings-banks, where others turned out fine phrases. As a Unitarian, he led the fight for secular education, freed from the control of the Established Church. During this fight, he set up a political machine, modelled on the American caucus, and was thus the initiator of modern mass parties in Great Britain. He entered Parliament when already middle-aged and was given office by Gladstone in 1880. Chamberlain was impatient with Gladstone's delays. In 1885 he attempted to capture the Liberal Party by announcing the 'unauthorized programme' of Radical measures.

Gladstone answered by advocating Home Rule for Ireland. Chamberlain resisted Home Rule, and his resistance split the Liberal Party. He claimed to be defending the greatness and power of the United Kingdom. If so, he succeeded. He was also trying to oust Gladstone. In this he failed. Chamberlain was suspended between the parties, in name a Radical Unionist. In practice more and more an enemy of his old friends. In 1895 he found at last a new resting place. He joined the Conservative or Unionist government under Lord Salisbury.

He chose, to general surprise, the colonial office, and announced that the colonies were a great undeveloped estate, held in trust for the British people. His imperialism was not clear-cut. In Chamberlain's opinion, the British Empire should provide a richer life for the British people, just as the Roman empire had once provided free bread for the inhabitants of Rome. He believed that the Anglo-Saxons were the highest race of the day and that the future lay in their hands. Other races, particularly the Latin, were doomed to decay. The Americans, of course, would share British greatness in some modest way, and the Germans, too, according to the ethnographical twaddle of the time, were accepted as Teutonic cousins. Together these three would run the world.

As colonial secretary, Chamberlain tried to bring the self-governing colonies under his direction. They were not attracted. To stave off his proposal of an imperial customs union, they demanded British taxes on foreign wheat and free import only for their own. This was the policy of imperial preference which Chamberlain was ready to espouse. He was delivered from it by disputes with the Boer republics. Determined to impose imperial sovereignty on them, he pressed ruthless demands and so brought on the Boer War. For a time, he was a national hero. The war dragged on too long, and Chamberlain lost his glory.

Devious and destructive

In 1902, when Salisbury retired, Chamberlain was passed over as prime minister in favour of Balfour. He fought back by advocating Tariff Reform – protective duties on all foreign goods including food. Balfour was evasive. Chamberlain left the government and split the Unionist Party. He also brought it to ruin. At the general election of 1906, the British people rejected stomach-taxes and gave the Liberals their greatest majority since the Reform Bill. Only 150 Unionists were returned. Shortly after the election Chamberlain suffered a paralytic stroke. His active life was at an end, though he lingered on until 1914.

Chamberlain's great energies and great fights were successful only in destruction. He ruined first the Liberal and then the Unionist Party. He defeated Irish Home Rule and left Ireland as an almost insoluble problem for the future. He estranged the Boers and ultimately lost South Africa for the British Empire. He was unscrupulous in his means. He is said to have lured Dike, a Radical rival, into a disastrous divorce case which similarly ruined the Irish leader, Parnell. He was almost certainly privy to Jameson's raid on Johannesburg in 1895, which outraged the Boers. Chamberlain brought a new bitterness into British politics. He was unsparing in victory and savage in defeat. Joseph Chamberlain was not a good advertisement for the imperial cause.

CHAPTER NINE

Entente Cordiale: Great Britain and France, 1898–1904

This essay was first published in Purnell's *History of the Twentieth Century*, published in magazine-size parts (1968–70).

Great Britain and France had been often enemies and often friends. Their love–hate relationship, to use a fancy term, dominated European history for centuries. They worked closely together as early as the time of Sir Robert Walpole in the eighteenth century. After the Napoleonic wars, they set up an unofficial 'liberal alliance', and the phrase 'entente cordiale', was actually invented to describe their relations in the 1840s, not the reconciliation of 1904. The British made a formal alliance with Napoleon III in order to wage the Crimean War and an informal alliance in order to aid the liberation of Italy. The Third Republic, which followed the Franco-German War, for long had Great Britain as its only friend.

The English knew France better than they knew any other country except perhaps Italy. English writers and artists found their models in Paris. George Moore and Arnold Bennett, for example, both thought of themselves as writing French novels in English. The upper classes, from the Prince of Wales downwards, had intimate links with Parisian society. Politically the two countries had much in common, even though France was a republic and a democracy.

The French Declaration of the Rights of Man (1789) and the British constitution were two different ways of securing the liberty of the individual.

This happy friendship was spoiled by a muddle. Great Britain and France took over a joint responsibility for Egypt, as agents of the international bondholders and guardians of the Suez Canal. When the Egyptians resisted, the British intervened by force. The French held back at the last minute. The British found themselves in sole control of Egypt and, after some havering, preferred it that way. The French tried to get the British out of Egypt by diplomatic means, and this became the principal obsession of French policy from 1882 until 1898. Other disputes broke out in various spots of Africa and on the borders of Siam during the general scramble for imperial expansion. France seemed to have become Great Britain's main antagonist all over the world.

There were repeated attempts at reconciliation even when the disputes were at their height. The colonial disputes were settled without war. Siam was settled in 1893, by mutual hands-off agreement, though after an alarm of war. Late in 1894 the two countries almost reached a general settlement, which broke down when the French would not promise to keep out of the Nile valley. By the 1890s there was another cause of estrangement. In 1894 the French made an alliance with Russia. They wanted this solely as a defensive combination against Germany. The Russians, who had no particular anxiety about Germany, proposed to turn it into an alliance against Great Britain's imperial interests, and since Germany posed no threats, this is what the alliance tended to become.

Reluctant allies

In 1896 the Russians contemplated laying hands on Constantinople. The French answered by demanding that the Russians should help them to recover Alsace–Lorraine from Germany and to eject the British from Egypt. This price was too high for the Russians, and they forgot about Constantinople. Instead they insisted that the French should support them against Great Britain in the Far East. This was an alarming prospect for the French. They were unwilling to estrange Russia and still more unwilling to aid her, particularly when the Russians gave no compensating aid elsewhere. In 1898 the French conflict with Great Britain over Egypt reached its climax in the Fashoda crisis. The French were helpless on their own. The Russians displayed indifference. The French had to withdraw from the Nile unconditionally.

Théophile Delcassé became French foreign minister during the Fashoda crisis. As his first act, he had to set his name to an instrument of national humiliation. He was determined not to suffer another. He claimed later that reconciliation with Great Britain had been his aim from the beginning. This was probably wisdom after the event. It seems rather that his first idea was to make the Franco-Russian Alliance an effective combination against Great Britain. He widened its terms so that they did not point solely against Germany. He offered French money with which Russia could build strategic railways towards the frontier of India. During the Boer War, he seconded various futile gestures which the Russians made against the British. In 1902, when the British made an alliance with Japan, Delcassé agreed to a counter-declaration with the Russians that their two countries intended to dominate the Far East.

This was a dangerous line to take. If Russia and Japan went to war, Great Britain was pledged to hold the ring, and the French might thus find themselves challenging the British navy for no purpose of their own. The menacing crisis in the Far East was the first factor which drove Delcassé to seek reconciliation with Great Britain. Once France and Great Britain were on good terms, Great Britain might restrain Japan, or at least France could make out that she was persuading Great Britain to do so. Delcassé even fancied that he might reconcile Great Britain and Russia. In any case, he could not allow the existing bad relations to drift on.

There were other reasons for action. The colonial party in France wanted to be done with the Egyptian quarrel and to co-operate with Great Britain against German expansion in Africa. The French Radical government which was now in power wished to get back to the liberal alliance. The most practical consideration was Morocco. The British had propped up this decaying empire as a neutral buffer between Gibraltar and French North Africa. Now the authority of the Moorish ruler was breaking down. The French might find themselves driven to intervene, if only for the sake of Algeria. It would be dangerous if this intervention were resisted by the British.

The British also had reason for wanting a reconciliation. Though isolated in Europe, they had managed to win the Boer War. They had acquired a Far Eastern ally in Japan. All the same, they had many anxieties. A great German navy was beginning to take shape, and it would be a considerable relief for the British if they did not have to send battleships to the Far East as a barrier against the French. Moreover, they still did not have a free hand in Egypt. After Fashoda they were safe from any military threat; but the plans of their representative, Lord Cromer, for reforming Egyptian finances could not be carried out without the consent of the bondholders' committee, and this could not be obtained in the face of French opposition.

Friendship – but at what price?

The difficulty was to find a price big enough for the French to give up the last shreds of their Egyptian dream. The British would not pay this price in Egypt itself. Where else could it be found? The answer was provided by events, not by British ingenuity. Morocco was nearing a break-down and would obviously become a topic of international discussion. The British did not at first contemplate a bargain with France. Instead they tried to build up a combination against her. In 1901 the British were seeking an alliance with Germany, primarily for the sake of the Far East. The Germans refused. The British then suggested that, if the Far East were too dangerous a field for co-operation, perhaps

Morocco would do instead. Great Britain and Germany would appear as the two pacific upholders of the *status quo*. Once more the Germans refused. They replied that they had no interest in Morocco. In reality, they were rubbing their hands at the prospect of yet another Anglo-French quarrel. They saw the British in trouble all over the world, from Morocco to China, and imagined that they would some day collect a high price for their friendship. The Germans never defined this price, even to themselves, and indeed it is difficult to see what British concession could ever have made it worth Germany's while to take on France or Russia for the sake of Great Britain's imperial interests. Alliance between Great Britain and Germany was conceivable only if Germany first dominated Europe – an aim which the Germans did not then consciously harbour and one in which the British would never have acquiesced. The Anglo-German alliance was thus never seriously on offer.

The British at this time had little reason to quarrel with Germany, but they saw the advantage of being less dependent on her fickle goodwill. Nevertheless they still went on hoping that Morocco would somehow struggle along. As late as the autumn of 1902 they assured the Sultan of Morocco that they would stand by him. However, he failed to stand by them. At the end of the year the wild tribes revolted. The sultan's authority was clearly breaking down. The British imagined that collapse might follow at any moment. They had to negotiate with the French, whether they wanted to or not. The French also were anxious to talk. Delcassé, as a patriotic Frenchman, did not welcome the idea of German support. Negotiations with the British were the obvious alternative.

The ice was broken in a dramatic way. Edward VII, who had come to the throne in 1901, prided himself on his diplomatic gifts. He wanted to restore the international prestige of the British monarchy, after its long obscurity in the later years of Queen Victoria. On a more practical level, he liked foreign travel. He was eager for a round of foreign visits – Portugal, Spain, Italy. He proposed to throw in a stay in Paris on his way back. The British ministers welcomed the idea, though with some qualms. Edward VII's visit to Paris in May 1903 was a great success, thanks partly, no doubt, to careful preparation in the French press. Though hostile at first, the Parisian crowds were won over by Edward's persistent cheerfulness. The reconciliation was accomplished as far as sentiment was concerned.

Edward VII had not been accompanied by any British minister. There were no practical discussions during his visit. In July President Loubet paid a return visit to London. There was a little initial difficulty. Edward VII insisted on knee-breeches. President Loubet replied that he represented the republic of *sans-culottes*, and that he would wear trousers as the American representatives in London had always done. Edward VII reluctantly gave way – a bigger concession no doubt for him than if he had handed over Morocco and Egypt, and China into the bargain. President Loubet did not come alone. Delcassé accompanied him and began serious negotiations with Lord Lansdowne, the foreign secretary. Lansdowne was by nature a man of gloom, who always expected things to go wrong. As secretary for war, he had been largely responsible for the early catastrophes in the Boer War, and he had no faith that the French could be resisted in Morocco. Like Delcassé, he was anxious for a deal.

This was not easy. Delcassé intended to propose for Morocco a mutual hands-off, such as the British had proposed long before for the valley of the upper Nile. But Lansdowne had firm prompting from Lord Cromer in Cairo that a deal with the French would be useless unless they dropped their opposition on the bondholders' committee. Lansdowne had to insist that the French should openly abandon their traditional claims to a voice in Egyptian affairs. Delcassé answered that France must receive something solid in exchange, if only for the sake of French public opinion. That something could only be a free hand in Morocco. Delcassé was prepared to make some concessions. The coastline of Morocco opposite Gibraltar should be allotted to Spain in any future partition. Moreover there should be an agreement between the three powers that this coast remain unfortified.

Altogether it was a good bargain. Of course both sides complained. The British, led by Cromer, remarked that they were already in control of Egypt and were abandoning Morocco merely for the sake of France's technical acquiescence, which she ought to give in any case. The French answered that they were surrendering solid legal rights in Egypt and were receiving nothing in exchange except a vague future possibility of making gains in Morocco. They even wanted to make their acquiescence over Egypt conditional on their acquiring Morocco – a condition which Cromer sternly refused. In the end both sides agreed that they had not done badly. The British certainly made their gain at once when the agreement was signed. On the other hand, they had accepted a heavy moral responsibility. On paper they were only bound not to hamper France in Morocco. Actually, having collected their reward, they were under an unmistakable obligation to help her get what she wanted. The British got their Egyptian bird in the hand. They had to ensure that the French got their two birds in the Moorish bush.

The deal over Egypt and Morocco was settled in principle by the end of July 1903. The details were worked out in October. But difficulties were only beginning. The British cabinet took a lot of persuading. The

War Office refused to admit that they were unable to defend Morocco. The Admiralty would not tolerate any European power opposite Gibraltar. The colonial office raised difficulties over all the minor colonial disputes which were also being tidied up. All these objections were gradually overborne by the weight of the evidence which Lansdowne produced.

The secret articles

There was a larger difficulty when it came to preparing the agreement for publication. It was harmless to announce that the French would drop their opposition in Egypt. Nobody would be shocked except old-fashioned French imperialists. But Great Britain and France could not announce their plans for dividing Morocco between France and Spain when they were both officially on friendly terms with the sultan. This deal had to be put in secret articles, and there was considerable fuss when these articles were revealed some years later. The two wicked imperial powers, it was said, had deliberately partitioned Morocco. This was not quite true. They had merely laid down how it should be partitioned in case the sultan's rule broke down. The distinction was real, even if somewhat fine, and there was, of course, a temptation for France to ensure that the sultan's rule did break down.

A further criticism was made later. The two countries, it was alleged, had provocatively excluded others from any share in Morocco. This also was not quite true. Spain was to receive a cut. Italy, the other interested power, had been bought off by a French promise that she could grab Tripoli from Turkey when the French got Morocco. Germany was the really aggrieved party. The Germans had repeatedly insisted that they had no interests in Morocco, but perhaps they had not expected to be taken at their word. Delcassé gave them assurances in regard to the 'open door' for trade, and at first they professed to be content. Only later did they become champions of Moorish independence, and this was done as an attempt to wreck the Anglo-French entente.

In the early days of 1904, when negotiations were still going on, neither party worried about Germany. The real trouble was Russia. Delcassé had moved towards reconciliation with Great Britain largely in the hope of making her more friendly to Russia in the Far East – or at any rate less friendly towards Japan. The British refused to change their line. In January 1904, when relations between Japan and Russia were moving towards a crisis, Delcassé threatened to break off the entente negotiations altogether. The threat failed to move the British. A month later, the Japanese attacked the Russian fleet at Port Arthur, and the Russo-Japanese War began. Delcassé was now as much in a hurry to reach agreement as he had been earlier slow to do so. Good relations with Great Britain were essential if France were to avoid being drawn into the Far Eastern war on Russia's side. In the last analysis, the Russo-Japanese War precipitated the Anglo-French entente and ensured that it was made largely on British terms.

The agreement was signed and published, except for the secret articles, on 8 April 1904. It was popular in both countries. Nearly everyone was glad that the interminable disputes were over. Some of them, such as the rights of French fishermen on the coast of Newfoundland, went back as far as the treaty of Utrecht in 1713. All of them had dragged on for many years. Now the slate was wiped clean. The two enlightened liberal countries were friends again. It seemed a wonderful triumph for the civilization of Western Europe. There would be no more Fashodas, certainly no more Trafalgars. Some Frenchmen went further. French Radicals particularly had never liked the alliance with autocratic Russia, and they liked it still less when Russia was locked in the Far Eastern war. She had lost all value as a counterpoise against Germany. Many Frenchmen would have been glad to get Great Britain as an ally in exchange.

This alliance was not on offer. The British had not the slightest intention of becoming involved in European affairs. Even those who were anxious about the German navy assumed that they could deal with it unaided. Of course the entente had some anti-German purpose. It meant that the British would not have to go begging for German support against France and, now that Japan was defeating Russia in the Far East, the British also did not need German support against Russia. The Anglo-French entente in fact marked a last assertion of British isolation, not its abandonment. All the threats to the British Empire had, it seemed, been removed. This was indeed the case. Three years later, when Russia had been defeated by Japan, the British were able to tidy up Anglo-Russian relations in Persia, the one remaining area in dispute. The British never again had a serious colonial conflict with a European power, at any rate until after 1918.

Yet the Anglo-French entente did not bring peace and security for Great Britain. In retrospect, it appeared as her first step towards the Great War of 1914. This was the doing of the Germans. At first they regarded the Anglo-French entente with complacency and pleasure. They imagined that a conflict between Great Britain and Russia was bound to come. Then France would have to choose between her old ally and her new friend. If she chose her new friend, Russia would turn to Germany for support. The Franco-Russian Alliance would be broken.

These expectations nearly worked out. In October 1904 the Russian Baltic fleet, bound for the Far East, fired on some harmless British fishing boats off the Dogger Bank, thinking that they were Japanese destroyers. The British threatened war. The Russians were too weak to fight. They paid compensation.

The Germans now saw another chance. Russia was in revolution and collapse thanks to the war with Japan. She could not aid France even if she would. The Germans therefore discovered an interest in Morocco. The kaiser went to Tangier and announced his friendship for the sultan. When Delcassé wished to resist German pressure, the French government refused to support him, and he resigned. He seemed to have been driven from office on German orders. The kaiser was delighted. Bülow, the German chancellor, was made a prince. The Germans calculated that the British would do nothing to help France and that the entente would be destroyed.

The British, it is true, had promised only diplomatic support to France in the entente. But there comes a time when diplomatic support is meaningless without military backing. Reluctantly, the British were drawn into military conversations with the French. In 1906, for the first time since 1864, they envisaged sending an expeditionary force to the Continent. The crisis passed over without a war. There was a conference at Algeciras, which temporarily put a brake on French designs on Morocco, though without admitting Germany's claim to a share. But the essential change had taken place. Henceforth many British people were convinced that Germany was seeking to destroy the independence of France and was aiming to dominate Europe.

Thus the Anglo-French entente was more than a simple settlement of differences between two colonial powers. Russian actions in the Far East did much to start it off and hastened its conclusion. German actions in Morocco turned it into an unofficial alliance.

CHAPTER TEN

Farce before Tragedy: Agadir, 1911

This essay was first published as a review of Geoffrey Barraclough, *From Agadir to Armageddon: Anatomy of a Crisis* (London, Weidenfeld and Nicolson, 1982) in the *Observer*, 31 October 1982. Alan Taylor's attitude towards Geoffrey Barraclough (1908–84) was ambivalent, being often irritated by him yet also supporting him on occasion as a lifelong acquaintance. Alan Taylor had preceded Barraclough as a pupil at Bootham School, York, as an undergraduate at Merton College, Oxford and as a Fellow of the British Academy. In his autobiography, *A Personal History* (London, Hamish Hamilton, 1983), Taylor wrote of Barraclough that he 'often bit the hand that fed him' but he did write a book for a series that Barraclough was editing, *From Sarejevo to Potsdam* (London, Thames and Hudson, 1966).

In May 1911 some ingenious members of the French government launched a plan to transform Morocco into a French protectorate. Kiderlen, the German secretary of state, answered by sending a gunboat, the Panther, to Agadir. His object was to acquire some compensation for Germany in Morocco or elsewhere. The British government imagined that France and perhaps Great Britain were threatened in their vital interests. The answer was a bellicose speech at the Mansion House by Lloyd George and the dispatch of the Home Fleet to its war stations. Such was the crisis of Agadir which is presented by Geoffrey Barraclough as the harbinger of the First World War.

Professor Barraclough, who has a lifetime of experience in writing historical narrative, provides a vivid account of the political manoeuvres accompanying the Agadir crisis. The story inclines to the dramatic side. The leading actors – Kiderlen in Germany and Caillaux, the premier, in France – were not building up a situation leading to a war ultimatum; they were conducting skilful though unscrupulous negotiations which achieved a bargain as they had expected from the first. France duly got its protectorate over Morocco. Germany got some rather trivial slices of the French Congo which Kiderlen imagined would open the way to the larger prize of the Belgian Congo as well. The crisis of Agadir was not, in my opinion, the first stage to world war but rather a last episode in an age of European rivalries in Africa which had been running for the previous forty years. None of the participants, not even Lloyd George, projected a war: they were showing off, as they had done for years past.

In so far as the Agadir crisis had any sense, it was as a struggle, not between France and Germany, but between Schneider-Creusot, the

Franco-German combine, which already had a monopoly of Morocco's iron ore, and German interlopers, Mannesmann Brothers, who tried to stir German national passions. The combine won after a certain amount of uproar. Barraclough passes over one point of relevance. At the opening of the crisis, the French High Command informed its government that the army was not fit to fight Germany. On top of this the Russians refused to support their French ally and the British lacked an army equipped to support France however much they might want to do so. Everything military and financial points to a sham crisis, designed to rouse the Reichstag and the French Chambers.

Karl Marx once said that history repeats itself – the first time it is tragedy, the second time farce. The reverse is true about the Agadir crisis: the first time it was farce, what followed was tragedy. Few people except the English Radicals expected the Agadir crisis to turn into war. But a great European war broke out three years later. This is Barraclough's main theme. Even before the Panther arrived in Agadir the leading European countries were in a state of economic crisis: increasing unemployment, trade union activity, and social violence. In Great Britain the suffragettes were active; there was political conflict over Ireland and the House of Lords; in Liverpool soldiers opened fire on mobs of striking workers. Stable European civilization was breaking down.

Barraclough lays down a clear thread of events from Agadir to the outbreak of war in August 1914. Once the French acquired Morocco, the Italians decided they must occupy Libya, then part of the Ottoman Empire. The Turks were not co-operative; the Italians invaded Libya and, when the Turks proved obstinate, threatened the Aegean islands as well. The Balkan states believed that with Turkey already in difficulties their chance had come to overthrow Turkey-in-Europe, which they duly proceeded to do. This success went to the heads of the Serbs who tried to overthrow Austria-Hungary as well. Here is Barraclough's analogy with the present day. For the Aegean, read the Persian Gulf; for the Triple Entente and the Triple Alliance, read the Soviet Union and the United States and here we are: world war in three years, nuclear this time.

I distrust these analogies. The relations between the Great Powers were exceptionally friendly between 1911 and 1914. The future of the Baghdad Railway was amicably settled. Germany and Great Britain arranged a partition of the Portuguese colonies. Throughout 1913 a conference of ambassadors meeting in London kept the peace more successfully than the Council of the United Nations has ever done. The Great War of 1914 did not begin as a conflict between the Great Powers but as a conflict between Austria-Hungary and Serbia, the one a declining power, the other a small power which had just arrived. Foreign offices and foreign ministers did not provoke the war of 1914. It was the offspring of the rival general staffs.

I have long held that great wars are first designed by military commanders and then launched by them. This will happen next time except that it will happen more quickly.

CHAPTER ELEVEN

Admiral Fisher: A Great Man?

This essay was first published as a review of *Fear God and Dread Nought. The Correspondence of Admiral of the Fleet Lord Fisher of Kilverstone. Vol. 2: The Years of Power 1904–1914*, edited by Arthur Marder (London, Cape, 1956). John Arbuthnot Fisher (1841–1920) joined the Royal Navy in 1854. He was instrumental in bringing about major naval reform from 1902. He was First Sea Lord from 1904 until 1910 and was created Baron Fisher of Kilverstone in 1908. After the resignation of Prince Louis of Battenberg in October 1914, Fisher returned as First Sea Lord and served until spring 1915, when he resigned because of his dissatisfaction with the government's continued support for naval involvement at Gallipoli. He did hear shots fired in anger during the bombardment of Alexandria, July 1882.

The correspondence of generals and admirals has a peculiar fascination. No one expects these men of action to possess much in the way of literary gifts; but they often develop a spluttering explosiveness as they wrestle with this unaccustomed and, to them, distasteful medium of words. The fighting men before 1914 were particularly choice – perhaps because they had so little real conception of the Armageddon which they were always prophesying. Sir Henry Wilson comes out top of the bunch. Every sentence of his reveals an arrogant fatuity and a political frivolity such as one would find only in an Irishman. It now appears from the letters which Professor Marder has so laboriously and devotedly edited that 'Jackie' Fisher can give Wilson a close run. Every letter is a peach. There are rather too many of them; and he was too fond of repeating himself, in accordance with one of his favourite tags: 'Reiteration is the Secret of Conviction!!' Reading them straight through is almost as shattering as a broadside from one of Fisher's beloved Dreadnoughts. Exclamation marks, whole sentences in capital letters, inarticulate bellows, bestrew the pages. Add to this a glance at the Herkomer portrait of Fisher; and it is difficult to believe that he was altogether sane.

Still, perhaps it would have been a good thing if he had bitten some of the others. The serious theme of the book is Fisher's remaking of the British navy which ensured its adequacy in the First World War. He scrapped old ships; made the fleet an effective fighting force; ran after every invention from wireless telegraphy to oil-firing. Most remarkable of all, these reforms, though they improved the navy enormously, actually saved money. On occasion, the government had even to put forward reduced estimates, much to its embarrassment. All this is now old stuff.

The long lines of Dreadnoughts are as obsolete as the Spanish armada. Tested by later events, Fisher made many good guesses and a few wrong ones. He foresaw the submarine, though not the answer to it: indeed he advocated a Channel tunnel as the only way of breaking a submarine-blockade. He imagined that the Germans would oblige him by sallying forth to undertake a great naval engagement, and was much at a loss when they stayed in port. His one really foolish idea was that it would be possible to land an expeditionary force on some sandy beach in north Germany – even the generals knew this was wrong. But, by and large, he was more farsighted and certainly more creative than his service contemporaries. Who can blame him for being wrong now and then, seeing that, like all the other fire-eaters, he had never heard a shot fired in anger?

The topic of more lasting interest is how he did it – how he put his ideas over on the politicians and on the ruling circles of the day. Fisher knew how to flatter: he won the hearts of every First Lord, and Asquith's into the bargain. It is particularly curious how he landed the politicians in a mess, through his over-confidence, during the 'acceleration' crisis of 1909; and then compelled them to get out of it, himself looking as innocent as could be all the while. His dealings with the Court merit special notice. He charmed Edward VII and played royal backing hard to secure his success. George V was a different matter – a sailor with many friends among the stuffier admirals whom Fisher detested. So Fisher turned round and became a democrat, insisting that the navy was a parliamentary force and even applauding John Ward's attack on the army officers after the Curragh mutiny. Fisher, in short, was convinced that he was always right, others always wrong; and he was not troubled with scruples in carrying his view through. He was supposed, perhaps correctly, to be the greatest admiral since Nelson. But it did not add up to much. Nelson's domination of the seas lasted a hundred years; Fisher's about ten. Now he has only the wistful charm of yesterday's music-hall comedian.

CHAPTER TWELVE

The Last Tsars

This essay was first published as a review of Hugh Seton-Watson, *The Decline of Imperial Russia* (London, Methuen, 1952), in the *New Statesman and Nation*, 44, 1133 (22 November 1952).

Alexis de Tocqueville (1805–59) was of a French aristocratic family. He was a magistrate, an active politician (1839–52) including being briefly in 1849 Minister for Foreign Affairs, and a historian. His major work on the French Revolution was *L'Ancien Régime et la Revolution* (1856).

Revolutions claim to break with the past; but, in a longer perspective, they are seen to continue it. De Tocqueville demonstrated long ago the continuity of French history despite the revolution. Hugh Seton-Watson does not aspire to be the de Tocqueville of the Russian revolution; but his history of Imperial Russia in decline points in the same direction. His book was badly needed. Plenty of books, hagiographical or otherwise, trace the rise of Bolshevism; nowhere is there a competent analysis of the old empire which fell into Lenin's hands. Professor Seton-Watson starts with the accession of Alexander II in 1855 and carries his account to the outbreak of the First World War. His work is not straight narrative, but a survey divided into three parts – the first age of reform, the period of reaction, and the years of the 'last chances'. The first means Alexander II, the second Alexander III; the third means the revolution of 1905 and its consequences rather than the feeble despotism of Nicholas II. In each section there is an analysis of the economic and social forces; then an account of political development; and finally a summary of foreign policy. This last subject is not effectively co-ordinated with the rest of the book. Foreign policy was not something detached from the country and the people even in the days of Imperial Russia; and it is an unsatisfactory device to tuck it away almost in an appendix. Moreover, in these sections, Mr Seton-Watson has been content to rely on the work of others; and he gives the impression of looking at Russian foreign policy from the angle of Vienna, which was indeed his starting-point.

In the rest of the book, it is an advantage to have Russian history examined by one who was originally a Balkan expert and who still perhaps regards Russia as in essence the greatest of Balkan countries. Mr Seton-Watson can put many things into proportion. He can find parallels elsewhere for Russia's agrarian problems; he can emphasize that Russia, too, is a multinational state, with the Russians themselves in the minority; and he can recognize that, if things had gone a little differently between 1858 and 1861 or even in 1905, Russia would have become embedded in Western civilization instead of, as now, drifting away from it. Having wearied of the 'Czech soul' and the 'Romanian soul' and the 'Serb soul' he is not now anxious to discover a Russian soul; this is a great relief. Of course, there are things that pull Russia away from Europe – not the Byzantine tradition, manufactured by Professor Toynbee, but the simple geographic fact that Russia's back-door opens on to Asia. European pressure, from the wars of intervention to Hitler's invasion, compelled Russia to turn her back on Europe; and the inevitable result is to make her appear as a sort of Byzantine monster. But in the period before 1914 Russia was being pulled more and more into the European world; and here Professor Seton-Watson might have stressed more the economic developments that were tying Russia to the world-market. When Turkey closed the Straits to Russia in 1914, this cut her off from world trade and drove her, whether she would or no, to the policy of 'Socialism in a single country'. In the perspective of history, Bolshevism may well appear as nothing more than the economic consequence of the closing of the Straits.

But old Russia had one characteristic which distinguished her from the rest of Europe; she was a true autocracy. The Tsars ruled, and they ruled alone. There were influential ministers, but no ministry: no co-ordination of policy, no system of government. The Bolshevik revolution changed nothing of this: Stalin is Tsar of medium competence, neither more nor less. Mr Seton-Watson does well to emphasize this point. The Russian people are sensible and civilized; their economic system admirable. All is made barren by the disease of despotism, chronic in Russian history; and until the Russians discover the secret of political liberty they will be a great nuisance to the rest of us.

CHAPTER THIRTEEN

Lament for Imperial Vienna

This essay was first published as a review of Edward Crankshaw, *The Fall of The House of Habsburg* (London, Longman, 1963), in the *Observer*, 15 September 1963.

The Empress Elizabeth was assassinated by an Italian anarchist at Geneva in 1898. Archduke Rudolf committed suicide with his mistress at Mayerling in 1889. Archduke Franz Ferdinard was assassinated with his wife at Sarajevo on 28 June 1914 – the event which set off the decisions leading to the outbreak of the First World War.

They say that men become attached even to Widnes. It is not surprising therefore when they fall in love with Vienna and grow wistful for its imperial past. Some admire the cultured life and the aristocracy: some praise its rich art and music. Others claim that the peoples of central Europe were happier and more peaceful under the beneficent sway of a Habsburg monarch. Mr Crankshaw is a lover on all counts. His book is a lament for the Habsburg monarchy and, at the same time, an attempt to explain historically why it fell.

I am temperamentally out of tune with writers who wish that the past had been otherwise than what it was. In my opinion, we have quite enough to do narrating and explaining what happened without wishing that something else had happened. Even Mr Crankshaw, with his gentle tolerance, often sounds like a sensible Englishman of the nineteenth century demonstrating to an Irish peasant the advantages of remaining a citizen of the United Kingdom.

It is difficult moreover to defend a past institution without being unfair to its opponents. Mr Crankshaw has not escaped this weakness. For instance, he writes, at the time of the liberation of Italy:

> The wolves were gathering round, all of them, including the best of them (Cavour), impelled by no other purpose than the aggrandizement of nation states, none of them remotely concerned, as Franz Josef was concerned, however wrongheadedly, with the reasonable and peaceful administration of a supra-national State, none of them, alas, deeply interested in radical social reform.

This is unjust to Cavour, one of the few nineteenth-century statesmen who was deeply interested in social reform; and misleading, too, in its implication that Franz Joseph (so, incidentally, he spelled his name not 'Franz Josef', as Mr Crankshaw writes) was ever interested in social reform, even superficially. Again, Mr Crankshaw asserts on a later page that no ruler has ever relinquished an empire voluntarily:

> To ask a statesman to contemplate clear-headedly the dissolution of the complex it is his first duty to uphold, and to devote himself to ensuring that in its passing the way is smoothed for its successors and that the smallest number will be hurt, is to ask too much.

Mr Crankshaw should know better. He is himself a citizen of the country which has given up empire during his lifetime, in exactly this enlightened way. Mr Crankshaw also manages to blame the peoples for the First World War.

> Why, in 1914, when the current of civilization was moving with such majesty and speed, did the whole process suddenly have to break down? And if the answer is the deterministic answer that the masses had been held back too long, that the improvement of their condition, while swift, was not swift enough – what then did this cataclysm achieve for them?

I thought, in my simple way, that the rulers of Europe, including Franz Joseph, went to war in 1914 and dragged the peoples along with them. I do not believe I am wrong: and even believe that we are all better off without those glittering figures of empire.

Fortunately, this is not only a book of 'might have beens'. Mr Crankshaw is concerned, most of the time, with the task of a historian, to find out what happened. He has disentangled very well the problems and conflicting forces which proved too much for the Habsburg monarchy in its last years. He is at his best with individuals, He admires the Empress Elizabeth, without being blind to her faults. He grasps clearly the tragic fates which overcame Crown Prince Rudolf and the Archduke Franz Ferdinand. He shows that Franz Joseph was a man of ordinary abilities, with an extraordinary devotion to duty. Many people said that only the emperor held the monarchy together. Franz Joseph believed them. Franz Joseph regarded himself as the servant of his monarchy, and served it doggedly for more than sixty years. Mr Crankshaw implies that Franz Joseph was therefore the servant of his people. Surely this is using modern democratic terms, alien to Franz Joseph, and which Mr Crankshaw also condemns. Franz Joseph served an institution, and expected his peoples to serve it also. He did not seek to justify either the monarchy or himself. This was his strength, and also his undoing.

It would be as foolish to make Franz Joseph solely responsible for the dissolution of the Habsburg monarchy as it is, say, to make another Austrian, Hitler, solely responsible for the Second World War. The forces of nationalism and economics counted for more than the acts and decisions of any single man. All the same, responsibility was not simply thrust upon Franz Joseph. He fought for it, and insisted on keeping it. The peoples were denied all responsibility, and naturally behaved irresponsibly.

Mr Crankshaw is entirely right in claiming that only a few nationalist fanatics, mostly German, wanted the monarchy to break up. The popular grievances, though many, were all concerned with changes inside the existing frame. The Habsburg monarchy was not evil or oppressive. It was merely feeble, and those who determined its policy, including Franz Joseph, were always in a muddle. Mr Crankshaw gives striking figures which show how Austria-Hungary lagged behind her neighbours in arms expenditure and preparations for war. Yet this feeble power and her despairing emperor gave the signal for war in 1914.

This was a last display of the imperial illusion: the belief that Austria-Hungary would still prove herself great when really challenged. Franz Joseph had this illusion a little. Others had it more strongly. Mr Crankshaw quotes Joseph Redlich, supposedly an advanced liberal, who was delighted at the coming of war in 1914. Redlich looked on war as a sort of cold bath which would stimulate the monarchy's decaying limbs. It was difficult to appreciate the monarchy's weakness when Vienna still displayed imperial grandeur. Strains from the 'Merry Widow' (not mentioned, alas, by Mr Crankshaw) mingled with the works of Mahler and Webern. Mr Crankshaw's book recalls a Mahler symphony – powerfully constructed, rather too long, and loaded with more romantic feeling than the subject deserves.

CHAPTER FOURTEEN

War by Time-Table

This essay was first published in Purnell's *History of the Twentieth Century*, published in parts (1968–70). This essay itself follows a theme that Alan Taylor was developing in lectures for a short, pictorial book of the same name: *War by Time-Table: How The First World War Began* (London, MacDonald, 1969), in a series which like the Purnell volumes had John Roberts as its general editor. In the 1969 book Alan Taylor commented of 1914, 'The deterrent failed to deter … There is a contemporary moral here for those who like to find one'.

It was often said before 1914 that one day the weapons of war would go off by themselves. In 1914 this happened. Though there were no doubt deep-seated reasons for disputes between the great powers, the actual outbreak of the First World War was provoked almost entirely by the rival plans for mobilization. Events moved so fast that there was no time for diplomatic negotiations or political decisions. On 28 July the great powers were at peace. On 4 August all except Italy were at war. They were dragged into war by their armies, instead of using the armies to further their policies.

The Great Powers had been elaborating plans for mobilizing mass armies ever since the Franco-German war of 1870–71. As usual, men prepared for the last war instead of for the next one. The general staffs all assumed that the coming war would be decided by the first engagements on the frontiers, as had happened in 1870, and each general staff aimed to get its blow in first. Yet they were all terrified that the other side might beat them to it. Each one of them attributed to others a speed and flexibility which they knew they did not possess themselves. The deterrent of the overwhelming blow put the generals in a panic instead of giving them security. Such is the usual way with deterrents.

The plans for mobilization were all based on elaborate railway time-tables, precisely calculated over the years. The moment the signal was given, millions of men would report at their barracks. Thousands of trains would be assembled and would proceed day after day to their allotted places. The time-tables were rigid and could not be altered without months of preparation. Germany and France both had only one plan for mobilization – each directed, of course, against the other. Russia and Austria-Hungary had alternative plans: the Russian either for general mobilization against both Germany and Austria-Hungary or for partial mobilization against Austria-Hungary alone; the Austrian against Serbia, Italy, or Russia. If one of these plans began to operate, it would make the switch to an alternative plan impossible. The time-tables could not be changed overnight.

None of the plans had been rehearsed. No great power had mobilized since the Congress of Berlin in 1878, except for Russia during the Russo-Japanese war, and that was irrelevant to European conditions. The plans existed only on paper and were the more rigid on that account. No general staff had the experience of extemporizing plans as it went along. Moreover the plans had been worked out in academic secrecy. The generals did not tell the statesmen what they were doing or, if they did, the statesmen did not take it in. Count Leopold von Berchtold, the Austrian-Hungarian foreign minister, thought he could threaten Serbia without losing his freedom of action against Russia. Sergei Sazonov, the Russian foreign minister, thought he could threaten Austria-Hungary without losing his freedom of action against Germany. Bethmann Hollweg, the German chancellor, thought he could threaten Russia without losing his freedom of action against France. Sir Edward Grey, the British foreign secretary, thought that he could protect Belgium without becoming necessarily committed to France. They were all wrong. When they learned their respective mistakes, they surrendered helplessly to the dictates of the military time-tables.

The statesmen had not been unduly alarmed by the assassination of Archduke Franz Ferdinand at Sarajevo. They were used to troubles in the Balkans and assumed that this trouble would end as earlier ones had done – with alarms, threats, and ultimately negotiations. They recognized that Austria-Hungary had grievances against Serbia and believed in any case that, as a great power, she was entitled to get most of her own way. Even Sir Edward Grey held that Serbia, being a small country, must pay the price for peace, however unjust that might be. But there was nothing Europe could do until Austria-Hungary formulated her demands. These demands, when they came, were excessive. For this very reason, they seemed to offer all the more opening for negotiation and compromise.

The Austrians, however, were determined not to be dragged before a European conference. They wished to keep their dispute with Serbia as a private quarrel. Hence they first broke off relations and then on 28 July declared war. Even now the other European statesmen were not dismayed. Bethmann Hollweg, Sazonov, and Grey all arrived independently at the same solution. This was the Halt in Belgrade. The Austrians would occupy Belgrade and thus vindicate their military prowess. Then they would declare their willingness to halt and would hold Belgrade as a pledge during negotiations. There would be a compromise, very much at Serbia's expense, but she would remain an independent country, and hence the prestige of Russia, Serbia's patron, would be vindicated also.

This ingenious proposal broke down for an unexpected and most extraordinary reason. Though Austria-Hungary claimed to be a great power, her army was in no condition to occupy Belgrade and so could not halt there. Mobilization, even against Serbia, would take some weeks. In any case, the Austrian general staff dared not mobilize against Serbia unless it were first assured of Russian neutrality, for, it if did so, it could not switch over to the alternative plan for mobilizing against Russia. Hence the Austrian general staff preferred to do nothing. As a little extra twist of irony, the Serbs had decided not to defend Belgrade, which could therefore have been occupied by a single Austro-Hungarian company, and the Halt in Belgrade would really have been possible after all.

Just as the Austrians knew nothing of the Serbian plans, so the Russians knew nothing of the Austrian plans, or lack of them. The tsar and his ministers assumed that Austria-Hungary would attack Serbia almost at once. The Russians were resolved that they would not leave Serbia in the lurch as they had done during the Bosnian crisis of 1908–09. Somehow they had to assert Russia's interest in the Austria–Serbian conflict. They could no longer claim to be included in negotiations. These, as between Austria-Hungary and Serbia, were over. Direct negotiations between Russia and Austria-Hungary could be initiated only if Russia answered the Austria-Hungarian gesture of declaring war against Serbia by some corresponding gesture of her own. Sazonov, the Russian foreign minister, thought he knew the answer. The Russian army should begin a partial mobilization directed solely against Austria-Hungary. In this way, he imagined, there would be no Russian challenge to Germany. Now the time-tables interfered again. The Russian generals were horrified at Sazonov's proposal. A partial mobilization, they insisted, would rule out any general mobilization against Germany for months to come. Russia would be helpless, at Germany's mercy.

Sazonov might have persisted if he had been confident of German neutrality. Exactly the opposite was the case. Bethmann Hollweg and Kaiser Wilhelm had promised to support Austria-Hungary against Russia and believed that threats were the best way of doing this. Moreover the German generals took alarm at the rumour of even a partial Russian mobilization. Far from recognizing that this would cripple Russia in any activity against Germany, they believed that it was a preliminary to general mobilization and thus a sinister device for stealing a march on the German time-table. On 29 July therefore the German ambassador warned Sazonov that any Russian mobilization, however partial, would provoke German mobilization – and war. Sazonov believed the first part of the warning. He still could not believe that any power would proceed from threatening gestures to the real thing.

Decision lay with Nicholas II, the Russian tsar. By nature, he was a retiring family man, who preferred tennis and sea-bathing to the affairs of state. But he had inherited a unique position as an absolute monarch, and he dutifully discharged his trust. Now he had to show that Imperial Russia was a power of the first rank. Throughout 29 and 30 July he debated with Sazonov and with the minister of war. Or rather he sat lackadaisically by while the two ministers argued. The orders for partial and for general mobilization both lay on his desk. Really there was little to discuss. The only object of partial mobilization had been to appease Germany, and, now that the Germans had refused to be appeased, there was no sense left in it. The only alternatives were general mobilization or nothing, and to do nothing would be to abdicate as a great power.

In the evening of 29 July the tsar agreed to general mobilization. Half an hour later he changed his mind. The order was cancelled. The next day the discussion began again. One of the generals said: 'It is hard to decide.' Nicholas II was provoked. He answered roughly: 'I will decide', and signed the order for general mobilization. This time there was no going back. The red notices of call-up were soon displayed all over Russia. The troop trains began to gather. Nicholas wrote in his diary: 'I went for a walk by myself. The weather was hot. Had a delightful bathe in the sea.' The decision had been made without consulting either France, Russia's ally, or Great Britain, Russia's friend. Later on, British and French statesmen were criticized and condemned for failing to warn Russia against this grave step. What held them back was fear that, if they did so, Russia might break with them and go over to the German side. As well, the British and French statesmen, just like the Russian, did not realize exactly how grave the consequences would be. They appreciated that a general Russian mobilization would increase the tension, but they also supposed that for this very reason it would speed up the opening of negotiations between the Great Powers. They still envisaged some sort of European conference and had no idea that in German eyes Russia's mobilization made war inevitable.

Here was the strongest factor in 1914, and one which proved catastrophic. All the Great Powers had carefully-prepared plans for general mobilization which would put them in a better position for fighting a great war. These plans would take some time to mature, and even then the mobilized armies could be held on the frontiers in suspense. For all of them there was a margin, though a thin one, between mobilization and war. For all of them, that is, except Germany. The Germans had no plans for general mobilization as such. The German general staff had wrestled for twenty years with the problem of how they were to win a two-front war against France and Russia with one army. Their answer was to defeat France before the Russian army was ready. The French frontier itself was too strongly fortified for a successful attack to be possible. Hence Count von Schlieffen, who had been chief of the German general staff from 1891 to 1908, devised a plan for encircling the French armies by marching through Belgium.

This was a difficult operation. There were only eighty miles between the supposedly impassable Ardennes and the Dutch frontier. Through this gap four armies, 840,000 men, had to be pumped. All of them had to go through the single railway junction of Aachen. The troop trains could not pile up at Aachen, however much its marshalling yards were extended. They had to go on so as to clear the lines for more trains behind. Hence, in the German plans for mobilization, there was no stopping at the frontier. The advance into Belgium was an integral part of the mobilization. Schlieffen never reflected that Germany might want to make a show of strength without actually starting a war. He was a technician pure and simple. Helmuth von Moltke, his successor, had no gift for strategy. He accepted the plan just as Schlieffen had left it. Or rather he gave no thought to the question until the news of Russia's mobilization. Then he opened the drawer of his desk and followed Schlieffen's instructions.

Kaiser Wilhelm and Bethmann Hollweg, with whom the political decisions rested, had no idea how restricted they were by the military plans. They never asked, and the general staff never told them. They went on dreaming that they could rattle the sword, as other European rulers did, without actually drawing it. Now on the morning of 31 July, Moltke appeared with the news that Russia was mobilizing. He insisted that the German armies must mobilize at once and invade Belgium. Bethmann Hollweg asked whether there were no lesser alternative. There was none. Bethmann Hollweg bowed to the dictates of strategy. The preliminary orders for mobilization were sent out. An ultimatum was dispatched to St Petersburg, demanding that Russia should arrest her mobilization within twenty-four hours.

The demand was of course refused. On 1 August the German ambassador handed to Sazonov Germany's declaration of war. The kaiser, wearing full Guards uniform, drove in an open carriage from Potsdam to his palace in Berlin. Surrounded by glittering generals, he was keyed up to sign the order for general mobilization. Bethmann Hollweg appeared with startling news from London, Sir Edward Grey had stated that Great Britain would remain neutral, if Germany would refrain from attacking France. The kaiser was delighted: 'This calls for champagne. We must halt the march to the west.' Moltke changed colour. Eleven thousand trains would have to be stopped in their tracks. He said in a trembling voice: 'It is impossible. The whole army would be thrown into confusion.' Once more the time-table dictated policy. Wilhelm acquiesced and signed the mobilization orders.

The streets were crowded with cheering people. It appeared to simple Germans that they were threatened with attack by Russia's Mongol hordes. Until this moment the German Socialists had been contemplating, somewhat glumly, their pledge to declare a general strike against war. Now they rallied to the defence of European civilization against the barbaric East. The Reichstag passed the war-credits unanimously. The parties declared a policy truce for the duration of the war. Inspired by this unity, Wilhelm declared: 'I see no parties any more. I see only Germans.'

War had started between Russia and Germany, though neither power was in a condition to fight it. All Germany's offensive power was directed against France, with whom as yet she had no ostensible cause of quarrel. A pretext had to be found. On 1 August the German ambassador called on René Viviani, the French premier and foreign minister, and demanded a promise of French neutrality. If Viviani had agreed, the ambassador would have gone on to demand the surrender of Toul and Verdun as a pledge. Viviani cut the discussion short: 'France will act according to her interests.' The Germans did not renew their demand. It occurred to them that France might agree and then their offensive plans would be ruined. Instead German aeroplanes dropped a few bombs on Nuremberg. The Germans announced that these aeroplanes were French, and with this pretext declared war on 3 August. The French statesmen had been somewhat worried how they were to explain their secret obligations under the Franco-Russian alliance. Now they did not need to do so. France, too, was fighting a war of national defence. The French troops' trains also began to roll towards the frontiers.

Thus Germany, Russia, and France were brought to war by Schlieffen's time-table. Two great powers, Great Britain and Italy were not included in the schedule. Italy, though allied to Germany and Austria-Hungary, was determined not to fight on their side. She badgered her allies for approval that she should remain neutral. At the same time, she badgered them for the rewards she would have received if she had not stayed neutral. This complicated double-play ended by missing on both counts.

The British government was technically uncommitted. It had friends, but no allies. Some Englishmen, mainly Conservatives, believed that Great Britain should at once rush to the aid of Russia and France. Others, mainly Radicals and Labour, thought that Great Britain should remain strictly aloof. As one Radical paper said 'We care as little for Belgrade as Belgrade does for Manchester'. Grey, the foreign secretary, felt that he was committed to France, but tried to avoid saying so. He waited for his hand to be forced. As he wrote later: 'Circumstances and events were compelling decision.' On 30 July he refused to give Russia any promise of support. On 1 August he even suggested that Great Britain would stay neutral if France were not attacked – though it is uncertain whether he meant what he said. On 2 August the leaders of the Conservative opposition delivered a letter to Asquith, the prime minister, urging support for France and Russia. The Liberal cabinet took no notice. Instead they resolved that they would not allow the German fleet to enter the Channel and attack the French ports. This was not a decision for war. It was a decision for armed neutrality, and the Germans were delighted with it: keeping out of the Channel was a cheap price for keeping Great Britain out of the war.

The crux – Belgian neutrality

The British government had one little worry. It was determined to protect the neutrality of Belgium, as its great predecessor Gladstone had done in 1870. Then a request that both France and Germany respect Belgian neutrality had kept Great Britain out of war. So why not now? On Sunday, 2 August, the cabinet resolved that 'any substantial viola-tion of Belgian neutrality would compel us to take action'. The neutralists in the cabinet regarded this as a victory. Like everyone else, they did not grasp that Germany's strategy revolved on the invasion of Belgium. The Belgian people also did not grasp this. They spent that Sunday enjoying a sunny neutral afternoon. The same evening the German ambassador presented the demand that German troops should be allowed to pass through Belgium. The Belgian government deliberated until the early morning and resolved that the German demand should be refused. It still hoped that resolute opposition would deter the Germans and there-fore appealed to the British government only for 'diplomatic intervention'.

Monday, 3 August, was a Bank Holiday in England. There were cheering crowds in the streets of London, as there had been in Paris and Berlin. Lloyd George, the chancellor of the the exchequer, who had previously been against the war, was much affected by the display of wartime enthusiasm. In the afternoon, Grey explained to the House of Commons the equivocal entanglements with France and Russia into which he had drifted. Fortunately, he was able to take on the news about Belgium, and this united practically all the members of the House of Commons. Later in the evening, the cabinet decided that a polite message should be sent to the Germans, requesting them to leave Bel-gium alone. Grey apparently did not think there was any urgency. At any rate he did not send the message until the next morning, when German troops were already in Belgium.

About midday, the news reached London, though there was as yet no Belgian appeal for help. However, the news stirred Grey into firmer action. Without consulting the cabinet, he sent off an ultimatum to Germany, demanding by midnight a promise to respect Belgian neutrality. At 7 p.m. Bethmann Hollweg refused to make any such promise. He complained that Great Britain was going to war 'just for a scrap of paper'. Did he use these very words? Did he speak in English or German? We shall never know. But a fortnight earlier there had been amateur theatricals at the British Embassy in Berlin. The piece by Sardou was entitled *A Scrap of Paper*. No message from Berlin reached London. Asquith and other cabinet ministers sat around, perhaps still half-hoping for a favourable reply. Someone unknown ingeniously pointed out that midnight in Berlin was 11 p.m. in London. Hence they could declare war an hour earlier and get off to bed. The declaration of war was in fact handed to the German ambassador at 11.50 p.m. The time-tables had won another triumph.

There was a final twist. The British had gone to war in order to protect Belgian neutrality. But when Asquith met his generals on 5 August, he learned that time-tables dictated even to the small British army. There was a prepared plan for placing this army on the left flank of the French. There was no plan for sending it to the aid of Belgium. Thus Great Britain found herself a full ally of France after all.

The British declaration of war committed the entire British Empire also, including the Dominions and India. Only the Canadian Parliament subsequently expressed independent approval. The one country still trailing behind was the one which had started the race: Austria-Hungary. On 6 August Austria-Hungary declared war on Russia. On 12 August, after complaints from Russia, Great Britain and France declared war on Austria-Hungary. Every country claimed to be fighting a war of self-defence, and so in a sense they were. But all of them believed that attack was the only form of defence. Hence, in order to defend themselves, they attacked each other. The general staffs, who had given the signal for war, proved wrong on every count. The war was not short; there were no quick victories; defence turned out to be the best form of defence.

CHAPTER FIFTEEN

War Weariness and Peace Overtures

This essay was first published in Purnell's *History of the Twentieth Century*, produced in parts (1968–70). Alan Taylor was the editor-in-chief and J.M. Roberts the general editor.

The First World War affected the lives of ordinary men and women to a far greater degree than any war between supposedly civilized powers had ever done before. In the autumn of 1914 the hopes of a quick victory for either side faded, and from that moment the war machine clamoured for more men and more resources, a clamour which continued for almost four years. Millions of men were drafted into the armed forces. More millions, and women also, were directed into work on munitions or other industries essential for war. In most countries, profits and wages were regulated, more or less ineffectively. Prices rose as the government poured out paper money, and supplies ran short. The free market which had brought prosperity in normal times now broke down. There was rationing of essential goods, particularly of foodstuffs. Very often there was a sharp reduction of the pre-war standard of life, and even so the rations were not supplied in full. Quite apart from the countless dead on the battlefields, the war brought hardship and sometimes starvation to the living.

There was social discontent and political unrest. The surprising thing is how slowly and how late this was translated into war weariness. For much of the period, men were demanding instead that the war should be waged more fiercely and more completely. The demagogues who called for aerial reprisals or the internment of enemy aliens evoked more response than did the few enlightened men who sought a way out. Equally surprising, the rulers of most countries, though usually of a conservative cast, showed little anxiety that the war would shake the fabric of society. On the contrary, they believed that failure to achieve a decisive victory would open the door to revolution. In the last year of the war, the prospect of revolution came to haunt Europe in the shape of Bolshevism, but even this only spurred the governments of the various belligerents to more violent efforts.

In the first two years of the war, peace overtures came from Woodrow Wilson, President of the one great neutral power, and not from any of the countries at war. Wilson strove to be 'neutral in thought and deed'. He refused to judge between the combatants, though his private sympathies were on the Allied side. His sole aim was to bring the belligerent countries to the conference table, and he therefore shrank from propounding terms of peace himself. His overtures were rebuffed by both sides. The Allies and the Central powers remained equally confident of victory, though they did not know how to achieve it. Even the few who advocated compromise were fundamentally in disagreement. Compromise, it was agreed, meant an acceptance of the *status quo*, but each side had a different *status quo* in mind. On the Allied side, the *status quo* meant a return to the frontiers of 1914 with reparation for the devastated areas particularly in Belgium and northern France. For the Germans, the *status quo* meant the actual situation as established after their first victories. Germany would retain all she had conquered or at the very least be generously compensated for any territory from which she withdrew.

A question of territory

Thus there were few peace overtures during this earlier period, because any common ground was lacking. The Germans made some cautious soundings of Russia in the hope of detaching her from the Allied side. Even here they were trapped by their own victories after the campaign of 1915. They would not surrender all the Russian territory they had overrun, and the Tsar, Nicholas II, was equally determined to liberate the soil of Holy Russia. In the autumn of 1916 the reactionary Russian ministers at last took alarm. They began to fear that war weariness was really beginning in Russia and were ready to respond when the Germans made overtures through Stockholm. At exactly this moment the German high command insisted on a declaration in favour of Polish independence. General Erich Ludendorff, the real director of the German high command, imagined, wrongly, that thousands of Poles would then join the German army. The Poland he proposed to recognize was entirely drawn from Russia's share of the partition. The negotiations with Russia naturally broke down. The Germans lost their chance of ending the war on the Eastern Front.

The topic of peace was first publicly aired in December 1916, though there was no serious intention behind it of ending the war. The impulse came from the renewed demand in German governing circles for unrestricted submarine warfare. The Germans had tried this earlier in 1915 and had then given it up when faced by American protests. Also they did not possess at that time enough submarines to make their threat effective. Now Ludendorff insisted once more. The German attack on Verdun had failed to produce a French collapse. The German armies had been heavily strained by the prolonged engagements on the Somme, and Ludendorff did not believe that his armies could achieve a decisive victory in 1917. On the contrary he confessed that the Germans would have to stand on the defensive when he prepared a withdrawal to the Hindenburg Line. Ludendorff accepted, however, the claim of the German naval leaders that unrestricted submarine warfare would bring about the collapse of Great Britain. It might also provoke the United States into entering the war against Germany. Ludendorff did not care. He did not imagine that the Americans could develop any effective military strength, still less that this could be deployed on the European battlefield.

Bethmann's Peace Note

Theobald Bethmann Hollweg, the German chancellor, was less confident. He had seen the brave hopes of German generals and admirals dashed time and again. He was anxious to stave off unrestricted submarine warfare, but this could be done only if he offered a firm prospect of ending the war on Germany's terms. On 12 December 1916 Bethmann therefore issued a Peace Note. This merely announced Germany's willingness to negotiate. There was no indication of the terms Germany would propose. Privately Bethmann intended that they should be those of victory: control of Belgium and north-east France for Germany. Even so, he imagined that war weariness in the Allied countries would produce some sort of favourable response. There had in fact been some discussion behind the scenes in Great Britain whether victory was possible. The people had not been consulted and were still not disillusioned. David Lloyd George, who had just become British prime minister, rejected Bethmann's Peace Note out of hand and answered by demanding the complete defeat of Germany, or, as it was called, the 'Knock Out Blow'.

President Wilson, like Bethmann, wanted to avoid a breach between Germany and the USA. He, too, recognized that negotiations for peace were the only way of achieving this. Despite the failure of Bethmann's Note. Wilson tried much the same tack. On 20 December he invited the contending powers to formulate their war aims: perhaps these 'would not prove irreconcilable'. The Germans failed to answer. They knew that their aims, if openly stated, would outrage Wilson and be the more likely to provoke him into war. The Allies, though offended at being put on the same moral level as the Germans, devised idealistic war aims which could not be denied Wilson's approval. The interchange had not much reality. Both sides were bidding for Wilson's favour, not trying to clear the way for negotiations. The Germans did not bid at all seriously.

Even Bethmann had despaired of preventing the renewal of unrestricted submarine warfare and merely kept Wilson in play until the submarines were ready. The Allies picked out the more respectable bits of their aims, but there was a great deal more which they intended to demand and which they did not reveal to Wilson.

Obstacles to peace

These first manoeuvres brought out the obstacles to a negotiated peace then or thereafter. Governments had to display a confidence of future victory in order to keep up the spirits of their peoples. If any country stated the terms which it expected would follow its victory, the opposing side was indignant and spurred to new efforts. If, on the other hand, the country tried to be moderate, the enemy regarded this as a confession that it foresaw defeat. More than this, negotiations were not needed to demonstrate that Belgium was the insuperable obstacle to a negotiated peace. The Germans were in possession and would insist on remaining there more or less openly. They even perversely used their own invasion of Belgium as proof that her neutrality was no protection for the Ruhr. They argued that what they had done in 1914, the British and French would do next time. The British, on their side, were equally adamant that Belgium must be evacuated and fully restored by the Germans. This was the ostensible reason why Great Britain had entered the war, and the British never wavered from it. The fumbling negotiations, far from making victory unnecessary, showed that nothing could be achieved without it.

Social unrest

Even so, the idea of a compromise peace, however impractical, had been aired for the first time, and this was not without effect on the warring peoples. The early months of 1917 brought the first open signs of war weariness, though rarely in the clear form of a demand to end the war. Living conditions were at their worst during the hard winter of 1916–17. Food, clothes, and fuel ran short. There were strikes everywhere in factories and coal-mines. In Germany there was a mutiny among the bored sailors who never left harbour. But there was still a margin for concession. Wages were increased. The trade unions were brought into partnership with government departments and the armed forces. Rationing did something to ensure that the reduced supplies went round more fairly.

In two great countries, the social unrest had political results. In Austria-Hungary, the Emperor Karl, who had succeeded to the throne in November 1916, tried to conciliate the nationalities of his nondescript empire. In Russia, the tsar, Nicholas II, abdicated and a republic was proclaimed, in the belief that this would provide a government more worthy of the national confidence. It is sometimes said that the first Russian revolution of 1917 was made by the army and was against the war. On the contrary, the army was never in better spirits or better equipped. The revolution came after bread riots in Petrograd and took the army by surprise. The generals and the politicians who most favoured the war at first welcomed the overthrow of the tsar as a preliminary to waging the war more effectively. Nevertheless, the people of Russia were not given a voice, at least in theory, and this voice was soon raised for peace.

The Emperor Karl and the democratic politicians in Russia both recognized that their countries would be ruined unless peace was made in the near future. Both made overtures for peace though they used different ways of doing it. Emperor Karl's way was by secret negotiations, a last splutter of old-style diplomacy. His brother-in-law, Prince Sixte of Bourbon-Parma, approached President Raymond Poincaré of France with terms which he thought the French might accept. Poincaré did not object to them, and Prince Sixte then showed them to Karl as official French demands. The most solid point in them was that France should recover Alsace and Lorraine. To this, Karl on his side made no objection. The British and French governments were now highly excited. They imagined that they were in sight of a separate peace with Austria-Hungary which would deprive Germany of a valuable ally and perhaps even open a backdoor for the invasion of Germany.

In fact the whole affair was a muddle, as usually happens when amateurs dabble in diplomacy. Karl only meant to invite terms which he could show to his German ally. The British and French supposed that he was deserting his ally. There was a further difficulty. Great Britain and France were at war with Austria-Hungary only in theory. Their forces never clashed except for an occasional naval encounter in the Adriatic. Italy was the only Allied power seriously engaged against Austria-Hungary, and the Italian statesmen had no particular interest in securing Alsace and Lorraine for France. The Italians wanted South Tyrol and Trieste. In 1915 the Austrians had accepted war rather than surrender these territories, and their resolve was still unshaken.

However, Lloyd George and Alexandre Ribot, the French premier, dangled peace with Austria-Hungary before the Italian foreign minister, Baron Sonnino, though they did not reveal Emperor Karl's so-called peace offer. Sonnino was unmoved. No peace without victory was his policy as it was that of his allies, except that in his case it was victory over Austria-Hungary, not over Germany, that he wanted. The Austrian peace offer, never very seriously made, ran into the sands. Soon in any case the French decided that they would not welcome a peace which merely benefited Italy, while they went on fighting Germany. Only Lloyd George continued to pursue the dream of a separate peace with Austria-Hungary. General Smuts, for the British war cabinet, and Count Mensdorff, the Austrian diplomat, had long meetings in Switzerland. Their discussions always broke on the same point. Lloyd George wanted to be able to attack Germany through Austrian territory. The Austrians would only abandon their German ally after a general peace had been made. The Habsburg monarchy remained shackled to the war.

Socialist efforts

The Russian search for peace was more open and created more stir in the world. Russia was now theoretically a democracy, and the Provisional government sought to satisfy the wishes of the Russian people. They abandoned the imperialist aims of tsardom which had been enshrined in the secret treaties and announced a programme of peace without annexations or indemnities. At the same time they remained loyal to their Western allies and desired a general peace, not merely Russia's withdrawal from the war. There were many in the West, particularly among the socialist parties, who desired the same thing. For the first time, public opinion in the West took the talk of peace seriously. Even in Germany there was a pull in the same direction. The moderate Russian socialists thought that peace without annexations or indemnities would prove irresistible, if socialists from all the warring countries combined to support it. They proposed a meeting of European socialists at Stockholm. The German socialists agreed to come. British and French socialists also wished to come, though their object was to show that Germany would not agree to the programme and thus to keep Russia in the war, not to secure a real peace. The French government refused to allow their socialists to go. The British government reluctantly gave their socialists permission to attend the Stockholm conference. However, the British seamen, who were furiously anti-Germany because of the U-boat warfare, refused to convey the socialist delegates. The Stockholm conference was never held.

With this, the hope for a general peace without annexations or indemnities was dead. However, its influence went on rumbling. In Germany, Matthias Erzberger, a leader of the Centre Party, began to doubt whether Germany would win the war. He put forward a peace resolution in the Reichstag, and the Social Democrats supported him. Bethmann also welcomed the peace resolution as a means of restraining the high command. Instead, the high command secured his dismissal. When the peace resolution was passed by the Reichstag, George Michaelis, the new chancellor, endorsed it 'as I understand it'. What he understood was that it would not count as annexation for Germany to keep her present conquests nor would it count as indemnities if she were paid to leave them. When later Germany made peace with Russia and Romania, it turned out that the Centre and the Social Democrats understood the peace resolution in the same sense. The peace resolution of the Reichstag had no effect in Allied countries. In Germany it helped to stem war weariness. Many Germans believed that the Reichstag had proposed idealistic peace terms and that the Allies had rejected them.

There was another remarkable overture for peace in 1917. The pope – Benedict XV – wanted to save the old order in Europe. Especially he wanted to save the Habsburg monarchy, the last surviving Roman Catholic power. Also he felt the socialist competition for peace. On 12 August 1917 the pope proposed peace to the warring powers in much the same vague terms as Woodrow Wilson had used earlier. The papal peace note envisaged a return to the *status quo* of 1914 and even mentioned the restoration of Belgian independence – not terms likely to please the Germans. The Western powers had promised Italy that they would not accept the help of the Vatican in peace negotiations. Arthur Balfour, the British foreign secretary, rashly asked for more precision in regard to Belgium. When France and Italy protested, he withdraw his enquiry. Nevertheless, the Vatican passed the enquiry on to the German government. The Germans, who meant to hang on to Belgium, gave an empty answer. The pope had failed to break the deadlock, like the socialists before him.

The German government was not wholly inactive. Richard von Kühlmann, who became secretary of state on 6 August, doubted whether Germany could win the war and was proud enough of his diplomatic skill to believe that he could end it. His aim was to divide the allies by negotiating separately with one of them. There had already been some unofficial approaches from French politicians in the same direction. Joseph Caillaux, who had been prime minister before the war, gave repeated hints that he was ready for a separate peace with Germany, though it is uncertain whether he actually attempted to negotiate with German representatives in Rome, while Germany and Italy were still not at war with each other. Aristide Briand, another former prime minister, also fancied that he could make a separate peace and perhaps recover Alsace, or part of it, at the same time. None of this was more than empty talk by out-of-work politicians. The French people, after all their sacrifices, would not accept peace without regaining Alsace and Lorraine. The Germans would not surrender the two provinces unless they were defeated.

Kühlmann thought in any case that it was a waste of time to negotiate with any French politician. In his opinion, it was British resolve which kept the war going. If the British were satisfied, the war would come to an end. Kühlmann therefore approached the British government through the King of Spain. He hinted, quite without authority, that the Germans might withdraw from Belgium if the British made a separate peace. The British, far from wanting to desert their allies, were afraid that France and Italy, both in a shaky position, might desert them. The British answered Kühlmann that they were prepared to discuss peace terms only if their allies were included. Kühlmann announced that Germany would never surrender Alsace and Lorraine. Lloyd George in return pledged that Great Britain would fight by the side of France until Alsace and Lorraine were recovered. The mere attempt to start discussions over peace terms thus, far from bringing understanding, drove the belligerents farther apart.

Pressure from below

The fumblings towards negotiations, which had always been pretty futile, now came to an end and were not seriously resumed until the end of the war. There was, however, considerable pressure from below for some sort of action. Indeed 1917 was the great year of war weariness and even of revolt against war. This went farthest in Russia. Once the Provisional government had failed to secure a peace without annexations or indemnities, its hold over the Russian people crumbled. It sought permission from its Western allies to make a separate peace. This was refused, for fear of the effect it would have on public opinion in France and Italy. For in these countries war weariness reached the level of action and resistance to war. In both countries discipline was breaking down in the armies, and order was breaking down behind the lines. In France, after the military failures under General Robert Nivelle in April 1917, most of the army refused to obey orders for any new offensive. At one time fifty-four divisions were in a state of mutiny. The more rebellious soldiers talked of marching on Paris and overthrowing the government. In Italy there was less open mutiny, but soldiers deserted their units and went home, where the police dared not arrest them and often did not want to. Thus, by the summer of 1917, the French army was incapable of fighting, and the Italian army was at little more than half its paper strength. The spirit in the factories was little better. In Turin and Milan, the workers were already planning to take over the factories for themselves as they did after the war.

Yet this discontent did not last. The war weariness gradually faded away, and there was a revival of national enthusiasm, though on a more cautious scale. General Henri-Philippe Pétain, who took command of the French armies in May 1917, assured the French soldiers that they would not be flung into more futile offensives and declared his intention of waiting for the Americans. When there was a governmental crisis in November, President Poincaré recognized that he must decide between Caillaux, the man of compromise peace, and Clemenceau, the man of more ruthless war. He chose Clemenceau as premier. From this moment, France was committed to the bitter end. Clemenceau arrested a few so-called pacifist agitators and arraigned Caillaux before the high court for correspondence with the enemy. These gestures were hardly necessary. There was still enough national enthusiasm to sustain Clemenceau, particularly with the Americans just over the horizon.

In Italy the national spirit was actually revived by a catastrophe – the great defeat of Caporetto. As the shattered Italian armies fell back behind the Piave, politicians of all parties rallied to the national cause. Disputes stopped in the factories. Soldiers went back to their units. The war actually became popular in Italy for the first time.

Russian overtures

The Russian army, it seemed, was beyond saving. It began to break up after an unsuccessful offensive in July. The Russian people had become indifferent to the war. There was no mass movement to stop the war, but still less was there any mass support behind the Provisional government. There was merely indifference, and this indifference enabled the Bolsheviks to seize power in November. Peace was the most urgent point in the Bolshevik programme. Lenin, the Bolshevik leader, believed that the people of every warring country would immediately respond to an appeal for peace it if were made firmly enough. The imperialist governments, as he called them, would have to conform, or they would be swept away by their angry proletariats.

On 8 November 1917 Lenin read the Decree on Peace to the All-Russian Soviet. It proposed immediate negotiations for 'a just and democratic peace' – with no annexations, no indemnities, and self-determination for every people, however long they had been ruled by another. An armistice of three months should be at once concluded on every front, so that negotiations should proceed. Here was certainly an overture for peace, the most practical and urgent made throughout the war. The German government responded. They welcomed an armistice on the Eastern Front, though they were not moved by the idealistic phrases.

The Western powers were more embarrassed. They wanted the Russians to go on fighting, not to make an armistice. They did not believe that the Germans would ever make peace on Lenin's principles, nor did they intend to do so themselves. Lloyd George and Clemenceau were both symbols of war to the end. If they now compromised, they would be replaced by more sincere peacemakers – Caillaux in France, Lord Lansdowne in England. The old theme was repeated that the only way of saving society and beating off socialist revolution was to carry the war to a victorious resolution. On 29 November the Allied supreme council gave a sharp and final negative to Lenin's Decree on Peace. From this moment the Bolsheviks were denounced as treacherous and disloyal, and their withdrawal was blamed for the continuance of the war. At the same time, anyone who proposed a compromise peace or even idealistic terms could be branded as a Bolshevik. This was a convenient arrangement, with rewarding results. War weariness became a symptom of Bolshevism. Most people disapproved of Bolshevism, which was supposed to maintain itself by Chinese methods of torture and to practise among other things the nationalization of women. Most people therefore did their best not to be war weary.

Peace at Brest Litovsk

Peace negotiations between Germany and Soviet Russia were duly held. The Germans interpreted no annexations in the peculiar form that they should keep what they possessed. They also interpreted self-determination to mean that the inhabitants of the Russian territories occupied by German armies did not wish to be put under Bolshevik rule. Trotsky, who led the Soviet delegation, resolved to appeal from the German rulers to the German people. On 10 February 1918 he announced to the astonished conference: 'No war – no peace' and departed. The German and Austrian workers were now supposed to come to the aid of their Russian comrades. So at first they did. There was a renewed outbreak of strikes in both countries. Once more the strikers were mollified by increased wages and more food, itself looted from the Russian land. The strikes died away. On 3 March 1918 the Soviet government reluctantly concluded with Germany and her allies the Peace of Brest Litovsk. This peace was not based on the principles which Lenin had laid down. The confident hope that idealistic terms would automatically end the war was dispelled.

With this, overtures for peace virtually came to an end. Some vague chat drifted on between British and German spokesmen at The Hague and between British and Austrian in Switzerland. An American, George Heron, also talked interminably to well-meaning Austrian professors who had no influence on their government. In July 1918 Kühlmann said in the Reichstag that the war would ultimately have to be ended by negotiations. For this he was dismissed from office by order of the high command. No one in the Allied countries went even as far as Kühlmann, though Lord Milner and perhaps others had the bright idea of buying Germany out of Western Europe by allowing her a free hand to dominate Russia. All such ideas were mere whimsy, another aspect of the anti-Bolshevism with which many Western statesmen were driving themselves demented.

War weariness, strangely enough, also declined. Food supplies improved in both Germany and Austria-Hungary, as the occupied Russian lands were more systematically looted. In many parts of Austria-Hungary there was a collapse of public order, or something near it. Deserters formed 'Green bands' and lived by terrorizing the countryside. These disturbances did not reach the industrial areas and had little effect on the Austro-Hungarian armies. In any case, with Russia out of the war, it did not much matter what happened in Austria-Hungary. Her armies in Italy could stand against the Italian forces which were in equally bad shape.

Both Germans and allied peoples were shored up by the prospect of decisive victory. The Germans were inspired first by Ludendorff's offensives from March to July. During this period there was no war weariness in Germany – a clear indication that it sprang far more from boredom and discouragement than from hardship. During the same period the British and French people were actually stimulated by defeat. From the middle of July onwards they were inspired by victory. After 8 August the allied armies rolled forwards. War weariness, though still there, was replaced by a confidence that the war would soon be over.

There were now peace overtures of a different kind. The earlier overtures had been political devices with which to embarrass the enemy or sometimes to placate a powerful neutral. At the end of September 1918 both Germany and Austria-Hungary made peace overtures with a genuine intention of ending the war. The two governments imagined that they were still free to choose: if the allied terms were unsatisfactory, Germany and Austria-Hungary would go on with the war. This was an illusion. The two governments were making peace overtures only because they had lost the war. Moreover, as soon as the peace overtures became known, war weariness burst out. Later it was alleged that the German armies had been stabbed in the back. This was the reverse of the truth. Ludendorff confessed that the war was lost when he insisted on an immediate request for an armistice. Only then did political discontent blaze at home. Similarly, in Austria-Hungary the nationalities staked out their claim to independence only when the imperial government had begged for peace terms from President Wilson.

An ignorant, though rational, observer might assume that war weariness would provoke peace overtures. But, in the First World War, peace overtures, themselves usually a political manoeuvre, provoked war weariness, and when these overtures were rejected, enthusiasm for the war was revived. No doubt the people ought to have demanded an end to the war. In fact fiercer war was from first to last the popular cause.

CHAPTER SIXTEEN

Lenin: October and After

This essay was first published in Purnell's *History of the Twentieth Century*, produced in parts (1968–70). In this essay Alan Taylor gives the judgement on Lenin, 'He was a very great man and even, despite his faults, a very good man'. Later in his autobiography, *A Personal History* (London, Hamish Hamilton, 1983), Alan Taylor recalled visiting Lenin's mausoleum in Red Square in 1925, commenting, 'Lenin looked very attractive with his reddish beard and a quizzical smile. I decided then that he was a really good man, an opinion I have not changed'.

Lenin was the prophet and idealistic leader of the revolution. But civil war and famine demanded harsh realism from those in power. Lenin's response laid the foundations of a system whose dangers he saw – and tried too late to correct.

The outbreak of the First World War found Lenin in Galicia, close to the Russian border. With industrial unrest sweeping Russia, he had expected a revolution at any moment and was preparing to direct it. Instead the war ended unrest and Socialist discontent in every country. The Socialist International collapsed. Revolutionary Socialists, including even some of Lenin's followers, became patriots overnight. Lenin himself was briefly interned by the Austrian authorities and transferred, a solitary and disregarded figure, to Switzerland.

Lenin and his wife Krupskaya settled in Zurich, where they lived on exiguous remittances from his family. Lenin worked in the public library, researching into the economic causes for the war. The result was a highly-charged book on *Imperialism, The Highest Stage of Capitalism*, which blamed the war on foreign investments. Alternate days Lenin did the housework, while Krupskaya read in the library, less productively. Occasionally they went for short holidays in the mountains. They had no Swiss friends and few friends even among the Russian exiles. In 1915, opponents of the war from many European countries gathered at Zimmerwald. Lenin attended, to small effect. Most of the Socialists at Zimmerwald were pacifists and wished to end the war for humanitarian reasons. Only Lenin proposed the slogan: 'Turn the imperialist war into a civil war.' Lenin called himself 'the Zimmerwald Left', by which he meant that he stood alone.

In Russia, Lenin's followers, the Bolsheviks, had dwindled to a handful. The more prominent were in exile like Lenin himself – in France, in the United States, or elsewhere. The second-rank leaders, such as Stalin, were in Siberia. Only the unknown remained, and Lenin had little contact with them. He sent only brief messages that they should prepare for a revolution. But he had little hope for it. In January 1917 he told a gathering of Zurich students: 'We older men (he was then 46) will not live to see the international Socialist revolution. But you youngsters, you will see it.'

In March 1917, out of the blue, there was revolution in Russia. The tsar abdicated. A provisional government was set up. In Petrograd the Soviet of Workers' and Soldiers' Deputies really exercised such authority as existed. The revolution had not been made by the Bolsheviks nor indeed by any other Socialists. It has been a spontaneous uprising by the masses. Far from ending the war, the revolution produced the cry that the war should be run better and more energetically. Even the first Bolsheviks who returned from exile took up this slogan. Lenin was in impotent frenzy: it seemed that the opportunity for upheaval and civil war was being thrown away. Somehow he must get back to Russia and bring his followers to their senses.

Lenin returns to Russia

The French government would not allow Lenin to travel through France. A Swiss Socialist, negotiating on his behalf, secured approval from the German High Command that he could go through Germany. Some thirty Russians, not all of them Bolsheviks, had a slow and uncomfortable train journey. There was little food, and smoking was possible only when locked in the lavatory. Finally Lenin arrived in Petrograd at the Finland Station. He expected to be arrested. Instead there was an official deputation from the Soviet waiting with flowers and greetings. Lenin brushed the deputation aside and pushed out of the station. He climbed on to an armoured car and shouted to the crowd: 'The revolution is being betrayed by its leaders.'

Lenin at once met the Bolshevik Central Committee and told them they must prepare for a new revolution. All, including Stalin, thought he was crazy, and it was resolved to destroy all records of his speech – one survived by chance. Lenin was undismayed. He said: 'The masses are a hundred times more revolutionary than we are', and he went on preaching revolution.

In July there was another outbreak of mass demonstrations. Lenin, worn out by the unaccustomed strain of practical activity, was away in the country. The Bolsheviks could not decide whether to encourage the demonstrations or to damp them down. *Pravda*, their organ, came out with a blank front page. By the time Lenin returned, the demonstrations were dying down. The Provisional government now arrested many Bolsheviks. They accused Lenin of being a German agent. Lenin was sure that, if he fell into their hands, they would kill him without trial. He went into hiding and escaped over the border into Finland, disguised as an engine driver. There he took refuge in the house of the Helsinki chief of police, himself a Bolshevik. From afar he still urged his followers to prepare the revolution. Meanwhile he occupied his leisure writing an academic tract entitled *The State and Revolution*.

The Provisional government was threatened by a military counterattack. It turned to the Bolsheviks for aid. Their leaders were released from prison. Trotsky became chairman of the Petrograd Soviet. Under his authority, the Soviet set up a Military Revolutionary Committee for the defence of the revolution. The Bolsheviks ordered Lenin to remain in Helsinki. He ignored their ban and returned to a suburb of Petrograd, where his hiding place was known only to Stalin. From there he instructed his followers to seize power. They trembled and failed to obey him. A secret meeting of the Bolshevik Central Committee was called. Lenin appeared, clean-shaven and disguised. The argument lasted all night. Its conclusion: the seizure of power would take place on 15 October. That day came and went with no seizure of power. Lenin summoned another meeting. Again the seizure of power was determined. Again the fixed day passed without action.

The action came instead from Kerensky, head of the Provisional government. He closed down the presses of *Pravda*. Trotsky gave the order that they should be reopened. Thus, casually, the Bolshevik revolution began.

Revolution and peace with Germany

The Provisional government was overthrown virtually without combat. On 25 October (7 November by our calendar), six Red Guards were killed – four by stray shots from their own side. The seizure of power was not planned by Lenin. It was not directed by him. He arrived at Smolny, the Soviet headquarters, only when everything was on the move. Trotsky, not Lenin, made the Bolshevik Revolution.

The All-Russian Congress of Soviets was about to meet. Theoretically power had been seized in its name. When the delegates met, they were told that a Soviet government had been formed. They duly approved without being given the chance to do anything else. Lenin had proposed that Trotsky should head the new government. Trotsky replied: 'First, I am a Jew. Second, you will stay outside and criticize.' Reluctantly Lenin became chairman of the Council of People's Commissars. He held this post until his death.

Lenin had no experience of administration and tired easily. He laid down broad principles and left others to apply them. He was older than the other Bolsheviks, who called him always 'the old 'un'. They respected and feared him, but he often had to fight to get his own way. He was always far from being the unquestioned dictator. Within twenty-four hours Lenin announced his programme: the land for the peasants, Socialism for industry, and immediate peace. The Soviet Congress applauded. The old officials refused to conform. Chaos spread across Russia.

Lenin believed that if one of the warring powers made peace, all the others would follow. If not, revolution would sweep across Europe. At his behest, Trotsky invited all the countries at war to attend a peace conference. The Entente powers refused. Germany agreed to an armistice, and the Bolsheviks negotiated with them at Brest Litovsk. The Bolshevik proposal was a peace with no annexations and no indemnities. The Germans answered by demanding the surrender of a third of Russia's territory. Many of the Bolsheviks wished to proclaim a revolutionary patriotic war. Lenin replied: 'The soldiers have voted against the war. They have voted with their feet by running away.'

Trotsky proposed a compromise. He would refuse to sign the German terms and would merely declare that the war was over. The Germans, he argued, would not dare to resume hostilities. Lenin was unconvinced. He waited in vain for any signs of revolution in Germany or Austria-Hungary. Trotsky made his declaration. The Germans broke off the armistice and advanced farther into Russia. The great problem was posed: should the Bolsheviks perish heroically or should they sacrifice Russian territory in order to survive? Lenin had no doubt: the Bolshevik regime must survive at all costs. After bitter debate he carried the day. In sullen silence Bolshevik delegates signed the Treaty of Brest Litovsk.

Communism in practice

This was the turning point in Lenin's life. Until this moment he had been an idealist, believing that a perfect Socialist society could be established without delay by those who had sufficient faith. Now he realized that faith was not enough. He transformed himself into a practical statesman, who postponed Utopia to a distant future. His original object in October 1917 had been immediate peace and immediate Socialism. In March 1918 he aimed only to hang on: somehow Bolshevik rule must survive until international revolution broke out – and that would take much longer than he had originally expected. Lenin not only made sacrifices of territory. He was equally ready to sacrifice principles or human beings, so long as the Bolsheviks, now called Communists, remained in power.

In March 1918 the Soviet government moved to Moscow. Lenin took up residence in the Kremlin. He lived humbly and shared a bathroom with the Trotsky children, who delighted in him as a welcome playmate. He also acquired a country cottage where he spent much time duck-shooting. No one could be less like the conventional dictator. Lenin dressed simply, with a cloth-cap stuck at an angle. He refused to exceed the normal, and very inadequate, food rations until ordered to do so by the Central Committee. He went around a good deal in streets and factories, addressing meetings in a rather academic way. He always welcomed visitors and had an engaging twinkle in his eye, which some people found sinister.

Lenin had never supposed that Socialism could be established in a single country, particularly one so backward as Russia. He agreed with Trotsky that either revolution would become universal or the capitalists would unite against the one Socialist state. Hence the aim of Soviet foreign policy, so far as it existed, was to keep the capitalist powers divided. Once the Treaty of Brest Litovsk had been signed, Lenin gave every appearance of co-operating with the German imperialists and was even ready to enlist their aid when the Allies, in answer, began to intervene in Russia against the Bolsheviks.

Intervention hardened the Bolshevik dictatorship and also provoked terror. Lenin was not sorry. After being harassed ineffectively himself by the tsarist police, he was glad to turn the tables and got particular pleasure from the protests of more moderate Socialists, who were shocked at this departure from democracy. Lenin maintained that proletarian democracy still existed so long as there was freedom of discussion within the Communist Party, and this he still tolerated. Though violent in speech, he was not yet violent in acts against his own comrades. On 30 August Lenin addressed a factory meeting. As he was leaving, a woman called Dora Kaplan fired a revolver at him. Two bullets were lodged in his body and not removed. Lenin had never been strong and from this time became frailer than before.

Lenin, though clearly the most powerful man in the Soviet government, did little of the practical work himself. He remained in Moscow, while Trotsky, Stalin, and others directed the war of defence against the Whites and the Allies. Lenin had time on his hands. He listened to individual grievances and sometimes redressed them. He read all the foreign newspapers and sought to establish contact with revolutionaries in other countries. His most considerable activity in 1919 was the writing of a pedantic tract, which instructed British Communists to support the Labour leaders 'as a rope supports a hanged man'.

Civil war

After the defeat of Germany, Lenin feared Allied intervention more than ever. He offered to leave most of Russia in White hands if only the Bolsheviks were allowed to survive in Moscow. When the peace conferences assembled in Paris, Lenin answered by founding the Third or Communist International, as the general staff of the coming revolution. He knew that the few foreign delegates represented nobody but themselves and yet insisted on the pretence of large-scale support. Angelica Balabanoff, an idealistic Italian Socialist, expostulated with Lenin against the crookedness of his agents, such as Zinovyev. As she talked, she realized that Lenin knew this already. When she finished, Lenin screwed up his eyes and said to her: 'Comrade Balabanoff, what use can life make of you?' Then characteristically he gave her a passport and smuggled her out of Russia despite the protests of the secret police. There was nothing Lenin liked better than conspiring against his own associates.

Gradually the Red Army, under Trotsky's leadership, won the Civil War. By 1920 the White generals had been defeated. The Poles attempted to invade Russia. They were defeated, and the Red Army invaded Poland. Trotsky opposed this. He declared that the revolution could not be extended by bayonets and that the Polish workers would respond to the call of patriotism. Lenin could not resist the temptation of success. He claimed that the Red Army would be welcomed in Poland and that when it reached the German frontier, the German Communists would rise also. Instead the Red Army was defeated at the gates of Warsaw. Lenin swung round and was now as insistent on peace as he had been on war. With his approval, the Treaty of Riga surrendered to Poland great areas of ethnic Russian territory.

Lenin had justified the Communist dictatorship by the needs of civil war. Now the war was over, but Lenin had no intention of weakening Communist control. On the other hand, he recognized the exhaustion and poverty of Russia. In his new crisis he showed once more the ruthless realism with which he had promoted the peace of Brest Litovsk. The New Economic Policy which he introduced in 1921 abandoned most of the Socialist measures which were now dismissed as 'war Communism'. Private trading was restored. The peasants were encouraged to produce food for profit. The merchant, previously persecuted, became an honoured citizen. If Lenin had had his way, the industries and resources of Russia would have been distributed as concessions to foreign investors. Only the refusal of the foreign capitalists spared Russia from becoming an imperialist colony.

Lenin was still waiting for the international revolution, and began to think that he would have to wait for a long time. He saw also a tiny chink of hope even if the international revolution did not come. Perhaps in time Russia would become an advanced industrial country, and then Socialism would be a workable system. He announced over and over again: 'Communism equals Soviet power plus electrification.' Being entirely ignorant in scientific matters, he imagined that with electricity everything would work itself. Lenin had now stood Marxism on its head. According to orthodox Marxism, the political order grew out of the economic system. In Soviet Russia, a political dictatorship was preparing to force Socialism on an almost pre-capitalist country. Implicit in Lenin's policy was 'Socialism in one country' and the long period of Stalin's dictatorship.

Lenin was becoming physically weaker. He spent long stretches at his country cottage. When he presided over the Council of People's Commissairs, smoking was forbidden and each item limited to ten minutes. The growth of bureaucracy exasperated him. His correspondence was full of complaints against red tape. For Lenin still had a fantasy that, since he was supreme in Russia, the workers ruled. He did not appreciate that the Communist dictatorship had lost whatever working-class character it once possessed. Even within the party, democracy was finishing, and Lenin helped to finish it. In his enfeebled state, he could no longer tolerate disagreement.

In May 1922 he had a stroke. He recovered somewhat during the summer and began to prepare his succession. He nominated Stalin as general secretary, then rebelled against Stalin's control and almost in his last act urged the party to throw Stalin out. Lenin had another stroke in December 1922 and a third, even more severe, in March 1923. He still tried to take a political line. Despite Stalin's supervision, he managed to slip out to Trotsky a plan of rebellion by which the two of them should overthrow the party dictatorship and restore democracy. Thus at the end Lenin sensed that somehow everything had gone wrong and stretched out his hand to Trotsky as his only personal friend and near equal among the Bolshevik leaders.

Lenin fought against death. With his wife's help, he re-learned to speak a few words and to walk a few steps. One day in October he insisted on being driven to the Kremlin. He went into his old office and leafed through the papers on his desk. On 20 January 1924 he complained of his eyes. A specialist came out to see him. Lenin's main anxiety was that the doctor should not have to return to Moscow late at night. This little kindness was his last recorded act. Lenin died on the evening of 21 January 1924.

Lenin did more than any other political leader to change the face of the twentieth-century world. The creation of Soviet Russia and its survival were due to him. He was a very great man and even, despite his faults, a very good man.

Part III

Interwar Years

CHAPTER SEVENTEEN

The Secrets of Diplomacy

This essay was first published as the front-page review in the *Times Literary Supplement* (12 April 1947). It reviewed the first volume to be published of *Documents on British Foreign Policy, 1919–1939*, Second Series, Vol. 1 (London, HMSO, 1947), edited by E.L. Woodward and Rohan Butler. In it Alan Taylor makes high claims for published diplomatic documents, not least in deeming, 'The *Grosse Politik der Europäischen Cabinette* was as good as a military victory for Germany, for it was a decisive weapon in shaking the moral foundations of Versailles'.

The review also created much bitterness on the part of Llewellyn Woodward (1890–1971), who had earlier been supportive of Alan Taylor's career – being a major supporter of his successful application to be a Fellow of Magdalen College, Oxford in 1938. Woodward took great exception to the suggestion that Rohan Butler and he had failed to assert their independence as scholars as effectively as the editors of the 1898–1914 series had done earlier. He demanded that Alan Taylor withdraw such assertions, which the latter did. Even so when Alan Taylor published his major diplomatic history, *The Struggle for Mastery in Europe, 1848–1918* (Oxford, Clarendon Press, 1954), Woodward further demanded that his name be taken from the list of acknowledgements even though he (Woodward) had read an early draft of some 40 per cent of the book. This episode revealed that at least occasionally some of 'the great and good' could find out who were the reviewers for the *Times Literary Supplement* during the period when reviewers were assured anonymity – and then wage vendettas thereafter.

The conflict between secrecy and publicity is the trickiest question in foreign policy. Once, absolute monarchs, with dumb armies at their disposal, could conduct a diplomacy that was really secret and could make war or peace without explanation. In a day of mass armies and of total war public opinion, now, has to be mobilized: the issues of foreign policy need to be expounded, in however perverted a form. For constitutional countries the need goes deeper. There the elected representatives of the people claim the right to know what is being done in their name and often, indeed, try to prescribe policy.

Foreign policy was a cause of dispute between Crown and Parliament in this country as early as the reign of James I, when the Puritans resented James's abandonment of the Protestant interest in Bohemia; and since then there has rarely been a time when at least some members of Parliament did not suspect the motives of those who were conducting foreign affairs. The diplomatists, on their side, know that a policy, however innocent, cannot be pursued in full publicity; and their justifiable resentment at interrogation adds to the suspicion of their critics. Negotiations can only be flexible if they are secret; they will be barren unless they secure popular consent. These are the contradictory propositions which have to be reconciled in modern times by democratic governments.

The nineteenth-century solution in Great Britain was the system of publishing Blue Books with extracts from diplomatic correspondence. These were sometimes forced from an unwilling government by demands in Parliament; but foreign secretaries, especially Canning and Palmerston, also used them as engines of propaganda, to whip up popular support for their policies, or for themselves. These Blue Books, however carefully edited, often provoked the resentment of foreign governments, to whom publicity in foreign affairs was in itself an offence. In the earlier part of the nineteenth century, British governments certainly cared less about the feelings of foreign statesmen than about the criticism of Parliament. As this country became more deeply committed in European affairs, obstacles to such publicity increased: foreign governments would not negotiate unless they had an assurance of secrecy; and, besides, most of them could now retaliate by threatening an appeal in the same form to their own public opinion. In the twentieth century, frank Blue Books only accompany a declaration of war. The United States of America alone can still afford to disregard the feelings of other countries, and therefore publishes its current transactions. The Americans, in fact, reveal their diplomacy because they have none.

For others, the problem of publicity has demanded new solutions. Publication has to be postponed; therefore, when it comes, it is an appeal to the historian rather than to the working politician. The struggle is transferred from Parliament to the universities. Oddly enough, this struggle originated with Bismarck. As one of the last practitioners of the made, or cabinet war, Bismarck wanted to win German admiration for his secret diplomacy and thus strengthen his position as chancellor of the German Empire. He commissioned Sybel, the historian, to write the story of the unification of Germany, and gave him access (though not without restrictions) to the archives of the Prussian Foreign Office. Sybel published many documents, often in a garbled form. The French were provoked to respond. They could be franker than Sybel, for the regime which brought on the Franco-Prussian War had fallen and the French Republic did not mind discrediting its predecessor: their answer, therefore, was a great collection of documents (only completed after the First World War) – the first genuine appeal to the judgement of independent historians. The pace became quicker after the Russian Revolution; for the Bolshevists were anxious to discredit the tsarist governments and, perhaps even more, the former allies of Russia. One of their first acts was to publish the secret treaties of Russia with her allies, and they divulged other recent documents, the publication of which undoubtedly had a considerable effect on the discussion of foreign affairs in England and France.

The next advance came again from the Germans. They set out to answer the 'war-guilt lie' of the Treaty of Versailles by the publication of documents from their archives which would reveal not German policy only but the policy of all the great powers. Their publication, in fifty-four volumes, bore the arrogant title *The Foreign Policy of the European Cabinets, 1871–1914*. This undertaking, in spite of its learned appearance and gigantic dimensions, was a work of propaganda. For this reason the editors did not arrange the documents chronologically, as the French had done, but presented them in chapters according to subject. As Thimme, the chief editor, wrote later, this arrangement of the documents was devised 'so that they should be quickly understood and have their effect'. And this effect they certainly had. The *Grosse Politik der Europäischen Cabinette* was as good as a military victory for Germany, for it was a decisive weapon in shaking the moral foundations of Versailles.

In this country, of the two books still chiefly used in schools and universities for the study of the period before the First World War, one by a German, Professor Erich Brandenberg, is avowedly based upon the *Grosse Politik*; the other by an American, Professor Sidney Bradshaw Fay, follows the *Grosse Politik* almost as closely, and Professor Fay has recently, too late, regretted the conclusions to which he came. For the *Grosse Politik*, by its selection of documents and still more by the arrangement of them, gave a false impression of the harmlessness of German policy and of the malignancy of Germany's opponents. For instance, the documents relating to the Moroccan crisis of 1905 are in one volume; the documents concerning the abortive Russo-German alliance of 1905 (the Treaty of Björko) are in another. Thus it remains obscure that the object of Germany's Moroccan policy was to force France into a continental *bloc* under German leadership. Or again, the German attempt to extract from Great Britain during the negotiations over naval limitation some promise of neutrality appears relatively harmless until the reader discovers, at some volumes' distance, that this promise was being sought in order to discredit the British in Russian eyes and that a similar promise was being sought from the Russians for a similar purpose.

The British and French publications were both evoked by the *Grosse Politik*. The British started first, and their series, covering the period from 1898 to 1914, was completed just before the outbreak of the recent war; the French collection, starting in 1871, 1901, and 1911, has still large gaps. The British editors were scholars of integrity, and they included in every volume from Volume III a statement 'that they would feel compelled to resign if any attempt were made to insist on the omission of any document which is in their view vital or essential'. This was a valuable declaration, if only as evidence of the spirit in which the editors had approached their task. No department of state likes to reveal its secrets and its methods of work; and it is essential, if these collections are to be of full value, that their editors should possess a critical, scientific, freedom. They must regard themselves as watchdogs of the public, not as employees of the Foreign Office. The British editors had this spirit, but they had not otherwise thought deeply about the scholarly purpose of their task. They took over, apparently without question, the German method of arrangement by subject; only by the time Volume VII was reached did they defend this method, by describing it as 'the British way'. The French, however, broke with this obviously pernicious method. Their collection, equally honest, surpasses the scientific value of the British in being chronological; the objection that it is difficult to follow any single subject is met by conveniently cataloguing the documents, according to subject, at the beginning of each volume.

Clearly, the problem of arrangement is fundamental to the value of the book as a serious contribution to the history of diplomacy. The decision regarding arrangement lies in the answer to the question: 'For whom are these collections intended?' The German documents, provocatively presented, with the personal interest of marginal notes by Bismarck and William II, doubtless caught the attention of the general reader for a month or two; the British and French documents can never have had a wide sale. In any case, except for the German need to shake the 'war-guilt lie' all these collections make an appeal to the verdict of the future, not of the immediate, public. They supply material necessary for the historian, and they should therefore aim to facilitate his critical use of it. A printed collection does not render unnecessary the historian's ultimate resort to the archives; but it should enable him to follow the same transaction (often even to read accounts of the same conversation) in the words of a number of different witnesses. But this advantage is gained only if the collections are chronological. The historian of the period before 1914 finds himself driven to the laborious task of rearranging in order of date 15,000 German and 8,000 British documents. No wonder that even Thimme, the German editor, wrote towards the end of his life: 'I regret now that all the pre-war publications were not arranged on the same chronological pattern'. By then the mistaken method which Thimme had chosen had done all the mischief of a first-class bad example. The Germans had won the battle against the 'war-guilt

lie' and Thimme was, perhaps, beginning to look forward with apprehension to the longer struggle for the verdict in future generations.

In the publication of documents regarding the war of 1939–45 the
British government determined not to be forestalled. Their resolve to
publish documents from the Foreign Office archives was announced on
29 March 1944; to avoid delay work was begun in two parts; and the
first volume of the second series, dealing with certain topics in 1930
and 1931, has now appeared. The editors have again followed the
method of arrangement by subjects. Their explanation of this choice is
lamer even than that given by Dr Gooch and Dr Temperley: 'The
disadvantages of a chronological method without any "sorting out"
into subjects are too obvious to need mention.' The decision is peculiarly unfortunate for the period between the wars. Besides the
inconvenience to the historian, arrangement by subjects conceals gaps
in diplomatic activity. For instance, if in a chronological collection
covering the year 1930 no correspondence to or from the British Embassy in Moscow is included its absence may give a hint that the British
Foreign Office at that time was disregarding the Soviet Union in its
calculations. But since the present documents are arranged in chapters
on the London Naval Conference, &c., no such conclusion can be
drawn.

The question once more arises – for whom is this collection intended?
The leaflet accompanying the volume says that the purpose of the
collection is not only to provide students of recent history with the first-
hand material necessary for their studies, but also to enable the people
of Great Britain to read for themselves a documentary record of the
conduct of foreign policy, under the direction and control of Parliament, in the years between the two great wars.

The editors do not define their position as precisely as did their
predecessors. The accompanying leaflet of explanation states that: 'they
(the editors) have had complete freedom in the choice of documents for
publication'; but in their preface they describe themselves as 'carrying
out the instructions of the Secretary of State'. German historians may
welcome an official position; it was not hitherto 'the British way' for
historians to subordinate their independence to a government department. Part of the present volume, for instance, seems to have the
deliberate purpose of vindicating the British foreign service; for the
documents in the chapter on Anglo-German relations can only have
been chosen to show that the British Embassy in Berlin was more fully
aware of political conditions in Germany than its critics asserted.

There is another and graver departure from the previous practice.
The new volume is a collection limited to official dispatches and telegrams; there are no private letters and no minutes, either by the foreign

secretary or by members of his office. But the historian is not content only with what was done; he must seek to know why it was done. Can anyone deny that much of the value of the earlier collection lies in the minutes of Sir Eyre Crowe, Sir Arthur Nicholson, and Sir Edward Grey? The present editors claim that the inclusion of minutes would have made their collection too bulky. No doubt; but a more powerful reason might be that the secretary of state would find it intolerable to reveal the confidential minutes of civil servants while they are still in active service. This is an objection that can be disregarded in countries where a revolution has intervened, as in Russia after 1917, in Germany after 1918, and in France after 1870. It remains valid in this country; and therefore the historian, and the public, must do without the full evidence until a longer period has passed. In that case the Foreign Office might well have been content with a shorter collection, and not sought to conceal that the present collection is no more than a glorified Blue Book.

It is, however, not too much to ask that even the present editors should have given the minutes of foreign secretaries; since such records are the only evidence of the importance attached to a document by the responsible minister, evidence the more essential now that the amount of correspondence has so much increased. Besides giving these, Dr Gooch and Dr Temperley performed a further service to the historian when they indicated to what other ministers (such as the prime minister or the secretary for war) documents were shown, and which of them were submitted to the cabinet. Between the wars the independence, and the importance, of the Foreign Office declined, and the influence of the prime minister increased. The student of foreign affairs cannot be satisfied, therefore, until he sees the cabinet papers and the papers of the Committee of Imperial Defence. What concerns him is the policy and motives of the British government, not the official proceedings of the Foreign Office, recorded in documents many of which were manifestly written for publication from the beginning. That dispatches were 'written for the Blue Book' was an old complaint in the nineteenth century. With the decline of the Blue Book official correspondence resumed its value, though some foreign secretaries, Lord Salisbury, for example, still conducted most of their diplomacy by private letter. But when the Bolshevists transmitted the text of the secret treaties from their wireless station and so provoked the battle of the publications between the wars, they killed the goose that laid the golden eggs. The secrets of the archives no doubt still exist, but not in the archives where they would most naturally be sought.

Just as the British government engaged a staff of historians to write the history of the Second World War almost before it had begun, so foreign offices everywhere are already writing the dispatches by which their conduct can be justified after the conclusion of the next war. After the First World War two circumstances were in combination: complete freedom of publication, and unawareness by the writers of the documents concerned that they would ever be published. These circumstances can never be repeated.

Thus *Documents on British Foreign Policy 1919–1939* is unlikely to repeat the political success of the *Grosse Politik*. Still, the verdict of independent historians is a verdict worth winning. If the British government attaches importance to this verdict, they will not rest content with the present publication; it will open to unrestricted examination the archives (at present closed after the year 1885) up to 1914, or even up to 1919.

No doubt the departments concerned will be reluctant to reveal their records; Lord Palmerston, in the 1860s, objected to the revelation of correspondence relating to 'so recent a period' as the wars with revolutionary France seventy years before. But these departments are the servants of the public; and the British government can have nothing to hide either from the British public or from the rest of the world after the individuals concerned have left their service.

CHAPTER EIGHTEEN

The Supreme Council, 1919

This essay was first published as a review of *Documents on British Foreign Policy 1919–1939*, First Series, Vol. 1: *1919*, edited by E.L. Woodward and Rohan Butler (London, HMSO, 1948), in the *Times Literary Supplement*, 2405 (6 March 1948).

The publication of the documents on British foreign policy between the wars is proceeding in two parts. The first volume of the second series, which dealt principally with 1930, was noticed in these columns on 12 April last year. The present volume is the first of the first series. Though bearing the title *1919*, it covers a narrow field; it records, almost without omission, the proceedings of the Supreme Council from the signature of the peace treaty with Germany until 15 October 1919. The great topics had been settled, and the great men had departed: even Clemenceau appeared only casually and with some irritation. The general effect is that of a party after the principal guests have left: stale cigarette-smoke hangs in the air, and half-consumed glasses of wine are mixed together to compose a nondescript alcoholic drink, which – it is mistakenly hoped – will continue to maintain the gaiety of the evening. There is a certain livening of interest when Lloyd George reappears at the conference table on 15 September; but as he had come only to propose that the conference should be wound up, and as he failed in this purpose, the reader is not spared further hundreds of pages, and the threat of a second volume also entirely given over to the proceedings of the Supreme Council hangs over him.

The Supreme Council had certainly plenty on its hands. Though peace had been made with Germany, the treaty had not been ratified; and the terms of the treaty could not be enforced so long as the armistice remained in operation. Still, the allies had forces on the Rhine which could take action if the need arose. Elsewhere their strength was running away to nothing. As Clemenceau remarked on August 11 in answer to an appeal to send forces to save two million Armenians from massacre: 'France could do nothing: Italy could no nothing: Great Britain could do nothing and, for the present, America could do nothing. It remains to be seen whether, as the result of this, any Armenians would remain.' There were German troops in the Baltic provinces; the allies had no force with which to expel them. The Bolshevist government in Hungary challenged the frontiers of the succession States; the

THE SUPREME COUNCIL, 1919

allies had no force with which to meet this challenge. The Rumanians defeated Bela Kun and occupied Budapest without the authorization of the Supreme Council; the allies had no force with which to compel their withdrawal. The allies were helpless in Asia Minor and feared that they were becoming helpless even in Bulgaria. The Supreme Council tried to restore the economic life of Europe by exhortation and, in particular, strove to get the coal-trains running again. In its few spare moments it returned to its real function of drafting the peace treaties with Austria, Hungary, and Bulgaria; or rather, have hasty, improvised decisions on the points referred to it by the various drafting committees.

Former allies were even more troublesome than former enemies. Italy and Greece quarrelled in Asia Minor; Italy and Yugoslavia quarrelled over Fiume; Czechoslovakia and Poland disputed over Teschen. In the background loomed the gigantic shadow of the Russian problem. The Supreme Council discussed the question how the allies, though not at war with Russia, could impose a blockade on her; they reached no conclusion. The Poles offered to march on Moscow if they were paid one million sterling a day; the Supreme Council wisely declined this offer and decided to use the Poles, if at all, against the Germans in the Baltic provinces. The approaching conflict between France and England over the Near East raised its head only once: when British troops were withdrawn from Syria, Clemenceau insisted that the substitution of French troops did not imply his acceptance of the rest of the arrangement for Turkey-in-Asia that Lloyd George was offering.

Apart from this preliminary breeze the unity of the great allies on the Supreme Council is remarkable. To be more precise, the unity was that of France and Britain. The Japanese representative did not concern himself with European affairs; the American representative inserted an occasional negative in any cause which he supposed President Wilson to have at heart; the Italian representative was concerned to make mischief, and especially to sap the French position whenever a plausible opportunity occurred. The British and French representatives were all the more patient and conscientious. The result of their actions was occasionally discreditable, as in Hungary; still, even in regard to Hungary, the detailed record of their proceedings shows an honest effort to give Hungary a liberal system of government. It was the fault of Romania, and also of the Hungarians, that these efforts failed. The Supreme Council was an experiment, short-lived and rudimentary, in world government; so far as it succeeded it owed its success to Britain and France. Any attempt of this sort demands two things: some concern with the general interest of Europe (or of the world) and some readiness to make sacrifices for these interests. Only Britain and France showed any trace of either of these; if they had seen the position more clearly they would have held together against the purely selfish powers, Italy and Japan and without the isolationist power, America. Clemenceau sensed this reality; hence he towers above the others in this record. The British representatives preferred to keep up the pretence of allied solidarity. Balfour probably had no grasp of general policy, though he possessed a gift of exquisite draftsmanship with which he could evade any dangerous subject; Lloyd George can hardly be judged from his brief inclusion, but he seems to have been impatient with the great issues which were vaguely present in Clemenceau's mind. Still, it would be rash to base any firm conclusions on these bare minutes, as dry and abstract as the record of a board meeting.

It was, no doubt, inevitable and desirable that the formal record of the proceedings of the Supreme Council should be made available to historians; all the same, it may be questioned whether their right place is in a series designed to serve the general interest in British foreign policy. The entire proceedings have already been published by the United States government; and it should not have been beyond the editors to inquire about American plans before they made their own. Apart from this, the editors were so much pressed for space that they decided to exclude all Foreign Office minutes, although these are essential for understanding how foreign policy is made, and the historian would certainly choose these even if the price were the loss of the proceedings of the Supreme Council. On the other hand, if it is held (and rightly held) that British foreign policy after 1919 cannot be fully described or understood solely on the basis of Foreign Office dispatches, then this argument – though it justifies the printing of the proceedings of the Supreme Council – demands still more the publication of the minutes of the British cabinet, of cabinet papers, of the proceedings of the Committee of Imperial Defence, and of the intelligence summaries prepared by the various service departments. This, however, is not projected; the series is to be confined to Foreign Office documents. It is an attempt to assert the independence of a department of state which had, in reality, lost its independence. Between the wars British foreign policy was largely made elsewhere, and the role of the Foreign Office, when it was not formal, was to restrict and modify these impulses from outside. Even in the present volume, for instance, it is clear that British foreign policy during the later meetings of the Supreme Council was being shaped by Lloyd George, who hardly appears. The editors are technically competent and conscientious; it is all the more regrettable that they agreed to exercise their gifts within departmental limits.

CHAPTER NINETEEN

The Hole in the Tub

This essay was first published as a review of *Documents on British Foreign Policy 1919–1939*, Second Series, Vol. 2: *1931* (London, HMSO, 1948), in the *Times Literary Supplement* (19 June 1948). In this essay Alan Taylor was more restrained in his criticism of the principles of the editing, if not of Ramsay MacDonald (1866–1937), the British Prime Minister, and Arthur Henderson (1863–1935), his foreign secretary.

The year 1931 was that of the great financial crisis; this ended the brief attempt to restore the liberal world-order which had existed before 1914. Diplomacy toiled after events, accumulating reports and statistical tables, without discovering in them a solution to Europe's troubles. As Mr Stimson said at one of the many futile conferences held in that year of futilities: 'When there was a tub with a hole in it out of which all the water was running, it was no use pouring in more water until the hole was stopped up.' The hole, however, was never found. Instead of diplomacy, there were 'exchange of views' at interminable conferences, where statesmen repeated mechanically the same arguments and issued empty phrases of high-sounding good will. With rare and unwelcome honesty, Snowden said, during the London Conference in July 1931: 'I suppose, in a sort of sentimental way, they (the governments) are ready to do what they can, but, so far as the discussions at this Conference have proceeded, I do not think they have given very much evidence of either a knowledge of what should be done or a willingness to do what it is necessary to do.' This verdict need not be confined to the London Conference.

As the crisis deepened, statesmen travelled the more: a solution which defied discovery in Paris might be run to earth in London or in Basle. British statesmen visited Berlin in order to strengthen the position of the Brüning government; and the reader finds relief from the waste of technicalities in a description of Mr MacDonald getting into his flying-suit. Later Brüning visited London. Not to be outdone, M. Laval visited Berlin also, and then Washington. This bustle achieved little except to give statesmen a sense of activity and importance. The German economic situation continued to deteriorate; Great Britain abandoned the gold standard; Germany made ever more methodical preparations to repudiate first reparations and later the treaty-settlement of 1919.

It would not be possible, on the basis of the documents here published, to credit the British government with a policy. It exuded goodwill and hoped that everyone would behave sensibly if it displayed enough belief in their so doing. Thus, it urged the German government to be moderate in order to strengthen the position of Briand in France; and it urged the French government to be moderate in order to help Brüning. It sought to persuade the German government to drop the plan for a customs union with Austria (the objections to which were purely political) by assuring it that 'we fully accepted Germany's assurances that her motives and purposes are not political but economic'. Yet at the same time the British listened sympathetically to the German refusal to renounce frontier revision in return for financial aid; they were impatient only with the French claim that the Germans should cut down their military expenditure. For the British, and still more for the Americans, the crisis was solely a crisis of 'confidence'; it was to be solved by others, and especially the French, giving to the Germans the 'confidence' which the British banks had already shown to their exceeding cost. Political questions were relevant only in so far as they would strengthen confidence in Germany. Thus, in October, 1931, President Hoover and Mr Stimson

> urged M. Laval to do something about the frontiers of Central Europe. While making it clear that the United States government was not departing from its traditional attitude of aloofness, they maintained that political unrest in those regions was at the root of all political and financial difficulties of the moment. No serious body of Germans called the Western frontier in question and none acquiesced in the Eastern frontier. The latter was indefensible.

The British and American governments lived from hand to mouth. They dealt helter-skelter with problems as they arose, discussing though not solving them; they did not consider the remote consequences of their actions. They believed that stable exchanges and settled frontiers were 'normal'; and expected to find a prosperous and contented Germany round one of the corners that they tried to turn.

They were aware, in an abstract way, of what Lord Tyrrell called 'the inevitable fact of German economic predominance in Europe'. But since the danger from Germany was remote, they acted as though it did not exist. The military report printed in this volume shows, fairly enough, that Germany was not rearming on any serious scale in 1931; the British government assumed that this would remain true. The British were certainly well informed of the rise of the Nazi Party. This increased their desire to strengthen the position of Brüning by concessions. Moreover they were not free from the illusion, shared by many Germans, that the Nazis would be tamed by office. Thus, one diplomatist wrote of Goering: 'He is relied upon to look after discipline in the party, and particularly to keep a watchful eye on unsafe young men like Goebbels, the Berlin leader.'

Where the British sought appeasement, the French demanded security: they were equally at a loss concerning the means by which it could be obtained. They clung to their treaty rights from failure to devise anything better, yet saw them whittled away in one episode after another. The French had no European order to set against the coming German order in Europe; therefore their negations were as futile as the Anglo-Saxon assertions of 'confidence'. Only the Italians had vision of a sort. Grandi and Mussolini talked in high terms of the balance of power: they looked forward with artistic delight to the coming turmoil, in which they would first play off England against France, then Germany against both. Thus the volume ends, appropriately enough, with the failure of the naval negotiations between France and Italy. Trivial in comparison with the great economic dangers, this failure was a further warning that the period of French supremacy was coming to an end.

The documents in the present volume do not add much to our knowledge, though it is useful to have the record of negotiations in systematic form. The most valuable material is the verbatim record of the London financial conference, an admirable object-lesson in the helplessness of statesmen. Again one looks in vain for anything that can be dignified with the name of British foreign policy. In this sense, the exclusion of minutes from the collection, though designed to protect the permanent members of the Foreign Office, may leave some of the story untold. It would be asking too much to expect thought from MacDonald or Henderson; but there may have been some thinking among members of the Foreign Office and the Treasury.

CHAPTER TWENTY

The Groundwork of History

This essay was first published as a review of Documents on British Foreign Policy 1919–1939, *First Series, Vol. 2:* 1919 *(London, HMSO, 1948), in the* Times Literary Supplement *(4 September 1948). In the review Alan Taylor was again critical of the principles behind the editing and concludes with a riposte to E.L. Woodward's insistence that the editors were not constrained by Whitehall in what they chose to publish.*

The publication by the Foreign Office of the collection of official documents for the period between the two wars is now proceeding with commendable regularity and dispatch. The present volume, which is the second of the first section (1919–29) of the documents, covers the period from October 1919, to January 1920, and is drawn entirely from the records of inter-allied conferences. Of its 970 pages more than 700 are devoted to documents of the last stage of the Paris peace conference then in the doldrums. Clemenceau continued to preside at the meetings of 'heads of delegations', still by courtesy called the 'Supreme Council'; but the other delegates were officials or diplomats and Jules Cambon sometimes deputized for Clemenceau. Lloyd George had left Paris after the signature of the Versailles treaty at the end of June, Balfour after the signature of the Austrian treaty in September: it was Eyre Crowe who represented the 'British Empire' at these meetings. Most of them were concerned no longer with the process of peace-making (though the treaty with Bulgaria was signed at Neuilly in November), but with the more humdrum problems and embarrassment of the post-war world.

The peace conference was formally wound up when the Versailles treaty came into force on 10 January 1920. Its work was taken over by no fewer than three organizations. The first was the periodical meeting of heads of governments which inherited the designation of the 'Supreme Council'; the second was the League of Nations, which was constituted as soon as the Versailles treaty came into force; the third was the Conference of Ambassadors in Paris, which was entrusted with the task of handling all minor current questions of the execution of the peace treaties. The concluding section of this volume covers the initial meetings of the new 'Supreme Council': the first of these had taken place in London in December 1919, before the formal end of the conference in Paris.

The three months covered were a time of waiting – a relatively colourless and uneventful interval after the turbulent period of upheaval and peace-making in the first part of 1919 and before the shape of things to come in the post-war world began to reveal itself in 1920. The power of the victorious allies was ebbing as demobilization proceeded more and more rapidly in response to popular demand. It became difficult to fulfil the commitments light-heartedly entered into earlier in the year for garrisoning the plebiscite areas and certain other trans-ferred territories, notably Danzig and Memel, in Eastern Europe. Ominous references occur in the minutes of these conferences to the inability of the allies to make their decisions effective if they are defied locally – for instance, in East Galicia and in the Caucasus; Lloyd George at one of his rare and fleeting appearances speaks of 'serious labour troubles' in Great Britain. It was a sort of interregnum. Power was slipping from the grasp of those who had ruled without challenge at the moment of the armistice. It had not yet become clear who, in different parts of the world, were to become the legatees of that power.

In retrospect the most significant phenomenon of these months was the mounting wave of opposition to the treaty in the United States leading up to the 'great refusal' to ratify it. It is a sobering comment on contemporary sense of proportion in estimating the weight of events that this process seems to have attracted a quite modest amount of attention and was hardly discussed by the allied statesmen. This volume contains one semi-official memorandum prepared by Berthelot for Clemenceau and communicated to Lloyd George in December, 1919. (It is an informal document, and it is not quite clear from the text whether it was addressed to Clemenceau or to Lloyd George.) The gist of it is a proposal that the allies should appease the Senate by declaring in favour of the majority of its reservations in the hope that the two or three really obnoxious ones would then be dropped. It is an able argument – if logic had been what was required – but displays a depressing degree of political naivety. No action was taken, or could usefully have been taken, on it.

In Eastern Europe important events also occurred which revealed the growing impotence of Paris and London. The policy of supporting the 'White' Russian generals in an anti-Bolshevik crusade was fizzling out, partly because British opinion was now less than half-hearted about the value or propriety of such a crusade, partly because the generals them-selves had proved weak, inefficient and unpopular. Yudenich's offensive against Petrograd had failed in October 1919, leaving the allies with an awkward situation to mop up in the Baltic provinces. Kolchak in Sibe-ria finally collapsed in December; and by that time Denikin's days in south Russia were also numbered. The defeat of Denikin raised the question of the fate of Transcaucasia. Curzon, committed to the hope-less policy of a Middle Eastern settlement which would be equally distasteful to Soviet Russia and to Turkey, pressed for the recognition by the Supreme Council of independent republics of Georgia and Azerbaidjan; and this was granted in January 1920 – obviously against the better judgement of Lloyd George and Balfour.

Curzon's miscalculation on the confines of Asia was repeated in Eastern Europe by Clemenceau, who nourished the similar illusion that Poland could be built up as a balwark against both Soviet Russia and Germany ('to keep Russia in check and to contain Germany') and as a dividing line between them. Poland was the keystone of the policy of the *cordon sanitaire*. The whole policy was endorsed at an Anglo-French conference in London in December 1919, which decided to abandon the bankrupt plan of supporting 'White' Russians, to 'leave Bolshevik Russia, as it were, within a ring fence', and to strengthen Poland and the other border states. Since the conception of building a barrier of small states to hold Russia and Germany apart provided in the long run the most fatal political mistake of the peace conference, it is depressing to record that, in spite once more of the frank scepticism of Lloyd George and Balfour, it was adopted without opposition and almost without discussion.

Since the German issue did not arise in an acute form till after the period covered by this volume, most of the other questions with which it deals seem rather small beer. The endless discussions about the intractable dispute over Fiume and the Italo-Yugoslav frontier produced one illuminating exchange between Lloyd George and Clemenceau:

> *Mr. Lloyd George* ... did not believe that this matter could ever be settled by notes. It was no use for the Powers to sling documents at each other's heads. The question would never be settled until people who had authority to sign a document could meet together. Personally he was so anxious for a settlement of the question of Fiume that he would go anywhere and at all risks, and there were risks at a time when strikes were threatening. A point that strongly impressed him had been that the question would go from bad to worse if it were not settled soon.

Lloyd George ended by proposing a meeting at San Remo.

> *M. Clemenceau* said it was easier to find a place than to settle the question. It was important that everyone present should have full powers. There would be no difficulty about this in the case of Mr. Lloyd George and himself. He did not feel so sure, however, in regard to Signor Nitti ... Italy was now suffering from the worst kind of revolution, a military revolution. The danger was that the Italian representatives might come and say that they were in agreement with their Allies, and were ready to give the necessary orders, but they knew that the army and fleet would not obey them.

Nothing could illustrate more vividly the clash of temperaments and convictions between the British liberal with his inherent belief that all that is required for the solution of a difficulty is to bring men of good will together to discuss it, and the hard-headed French radical who understands revolutions by experience and knows that in the end it is the guns that talk. But it must be added that only a few such accretions of flesh and blood clothe the dry, very dry, bones of these official minutes.

It remains to offer a few general comments. The editor – Mr Butler for these early volumes – has discharged himself accurately of the task of collecting the records of the relevant conferences of the period and of omitting a few of the least important routine items: the pruning knife should have been applied here more, rather than less, freely. References to other documents in the volume continue to be made not by page but by number of the document; this is an ancient and presumably sacrosanct tradition which does not add to the convenience of the reader. Nor can Mr Butler be blamed for following the odd Foreign Office habit of prefixing the name of any foreigner with the letter M. (understood to be short for 'Monsieur') even at the risk of leading the unwary to regard it as just another initial. But it seems hardly necessary to confer this indignity, in addition to a mis-spelling of his name, on the Ukrainian brigand-anarchist Nestor Makhno, coyly disguised in a footnote as 'M. Maknov'.

More seriously this volume raises again the question asked on the appearance of the three previous volumes about the scope of the series. Its purposes as originally announced were 'to provide students of recent history with the first-hand material necessary for their studies' and 'to enable the people of Great Britain to read for themselves a documentary record of the direction and control of foreign policy'. It cannot fairly be said that the present volume helps very much to fulfil either of these purposes. We learn much that was said, but hardly anything of why it was said. Can one suppose that the Foreign Office addressed no memoranda of instructions or guidance to the British delegates at these conferences? Or that it received no report of what transpired at the conferences, or behind the scenes, other than the discreet official minutes? No trace can be found of any such documents in these pages. Comparison with the series of documents published after the First World War is no doubt in some respects unfair, but it is unavoidable. The reader of that series had the impression, which time has confirmed, that everything important that could be found in the archives was revealed to him. The reader of the present series has frequent cause to suspect that he is getting all the crumbs from the cake, and hardly any of the plums.

The point may be illustrated from the present volume. On 11 December 1919, Berthelot handed to Curzon a memorandum which 'contained a review of the question of oil as a whole' and 'showed the importance of the two governments standing together on this'. On 12 December it was agreed that the matter should be referred to British and French oil experts. On 13 December it was agreed that the meeting between them should take place on the following Wednesday (which was, as a foot-note adds, 17 December). The student would gladly have bartered these particulars for a sign of the Berthelot memorandum or of the British comments on it or for some account of what passed between the experts on Wednesday, 17 December, or afterwards. Perhaps all this is reserved for the next volume. But, if so, one might have expected some note to that effect; as it is, a footnote explaining that the negotiations led to the San Remo oil agreement already published as a White Paper reads uncommonly like a 'sign-off'. The reviewer cannot guess whether to attribute such gaps to an absence of really confidential documents from the archives at the disposal of the editors or to restrictions which the editors may have been moved to impose on themselves.

CHAPTER TWENTY-ONE

German Policy, 1937–38

This was first published as a two-part review of *Documents on German Foreign Policy*, Series D, Vol. 1: *From Neurath to Ribbentrop, September 1937–September 1939* (Washington, Government Printing Office, 1949), in the *Manchester Guardian*, 19 and 22 August 1949. Part 1 was entitled 'The Last Days of Neurath' and Part 2, 'Austria and After'.

1. The Last Days of Neurath

The German Foreign Office documents which came out recently in Washington are more interesting, though less sensational, than earlier messages suggested. The German Foreign Office under Hitler was a subordinate department, performing technical duties rather than deciding policy; and the State Department and the British Foreign Office are perhaps flattering their own independence as well as that of their German colleagues when they bring out these papers. Hitler hardly appears in this volume: he provides the noises off as in a Greek tragedy.

Thus the German Foreign Office aimed to be neutral between China and Japan: and this policy was confirmed by Hitler on 17 August 1937. But this policy was never accepted by the Propaganda Ministry, which always followed a line favourable to Japan. Then, on 19 October, the Foreign Office learnt accidentally from the War Ministry that Goering had just stopped all supplies to China on Hitler's instructions; and official policy had to be hastily revised. In fact the German diplomatists had to guess at Hitler's intentions as though he were a foreign power. Neurath, as foreign minister, was never on confidential terms with Hitler. Ribbentrop was in a stronger position and always tried to tell Hitler what he wanted to hear; for this very reason, he was less regarded in the Foreign Office.

Warnings

There is not much evidence that the Foreign Office deliberately 'rigged' the diplomatic reports, so as to have a particular effect on Hitler (in any case he probably did not read them). The only instance in this volume seems to be the reports from the German Ambassador in Washington. He states again and again that the United States would back Great

Britain in the event of a war. Weizsäcker, the state secretary, wrote to him:

> Your warnings that we should have no illusions as to the American stand in the event of a world conflict are by all means valuable; it can do no harm if you point this out again and again.

Hitler meanwhile had got hold of a nonsensical pamphlet on America by a Baron von Rechenberg and instructed the Foreign Office to read it; they replied, ineffectually, by discrediting the Baron's character. Again, the Foreign Office regarded the German-American Bund as a pure embarrassment in relations with America; and supplied Hitler with arguments against it. Hitler agreed to repudiate it; but could never resist its racial appeal and continued to patronize Kuhn, its leader.

The difficulty of making sense of this volume is increased by the policy of the editors. Instead of presenting the documents chronologically, they have sorted them arbitrarily into topics with flashy, misleading headings. Although the volume purports to cover German foreign policy from September 1937 to September 1938, Czechoslovakia is reserved for Volume II and Spain for Volume III. This is Hamlet not only without the Prince of Denmark but without Lady Macbeth as well. What remains are the miscellaneous dealings with the Great Powers, the Austrian question, and the Far East. There is as well a long section on German dealings with the Vatican. Though this provides striking evidence of the conflict between Foreign Office conciliation and Nazi intransigence towards the Roman Church, it has little relevance to international affairs: perhaps its was put in to demonstrate the clericalist sympathies of one of the sponsoring bodies.

In spite of the muddle a pattern emerges, a pattern shown in the title – from Neurath to Ribbentrop. Neurath continued the policy of Stresemann and seemed to be carrying it to success. This policy assumed that Germany could not fight a general war. Thus Weizsäcker, in November 1937: 'For a long time to come we cannot consider engaging in a war with England as an opponent. What we want from England we cannot obtain by force but must obtain by negotiation.' Again in December: 'We ourselves are not yet strong enough to engage in European conflicts and shall therefore not seek any.' Even Hitler at this time thought that Germany could act against Austria or Czechoslovakia only if England and France were involved in war with Italy. German policy therefore aimed to undo the settlement of Versailles without a general war. France had to be isolated or at least exposed to the friendly pressure of England and Italy. For this reason Germany had left the League of Nations and emphasized the Bolshevik danger, which made Russia impossible as a great power. (It is clear from these documents that the Germans believed their own story.) This German aim suited British policy, which had no objection to changes in Europe so long as they were not accompanied by general war.

The appeasers

In November 1937, Lord Halifax visited Hitler. He 'recognised that the Chancellor (Hitler) had not only performed great services to Germany but also, as he would no doubt feel, had been able, by preventing the entry of Communism into his own country, to bar its passage farther west'. Farther on:

> Halifax admitted of his own accord that certain changes in the European system could probably not be avoided in the long run. The British did not believe that the status quo had to be maintained under all circumstances. Among the questions in which changes would probably be made sooner or later were Danzig, Austria, and Czechoslovakia. England was only interested in seeing that such changes were brought about by peaceful development.

After Halifax's visit, appeasement got into its stride. Chamberlain talked of colonial concessions and emphasized that he did not wish to isolate Germany. 'Nothing was further from his thoughts than an intention to weaken the Axis. It was a pillar of European peace.' The pillar metaphor seems to have appealed to Chamberlain. He repeated Hitler's comparison of England and Germany 'to two pillars upon which the European social order could rest', and said this comparison 'particularly pleased' him. Lesser appeasers took up the running. Mr R.A. Butler is reported as saying: 'The generation which had come up in the foreign service in recent years ... was free from any pro-French leaning. But this group in the Foreign Office had never really made much headway, and the first real break in the French line had come with Sir Nevile Henderson.' Henderson wrote off Austrian independence to Papen and added: 'I am convinced that my view will prevail in London, only you must not rush the solution of the problem.' Of Sir Horace Wilson it was reported:

> The impression that would be created in the economic field by an understanding between Germany, England, and Italy (he did not mention France – probably un-intentionally) could scarcely be over-estimated. Russia ought to be left out entirely at the present time. In his opinion, the system there was bound to 'melt away' some day.

Even on 11 March 1938, Inskip offered Austria to Ribbentrop:

> He could definitely state that the British Cabinet would not decide in favour of military intervention by England if the Austrian question was solved in the German sense. However, it would be a different matter if Germany settled this question by force.

There was the rub; and the Austrian affair turned out to be the first blow against appeasement, instead of its first success.

2. Austria and After

The demonstration of German force against Austria was not intentional. Quite the reverse. The German Foreign Office documents, show that on 1 October 1937, Neurath noted: 'The Führer did not approve of Goering's previous policy, which was too severe, and stated that Germany should cause no explosion of the Austrian problem in the foreseeable future, but that we should continue to seek an evolutionary solution.' Even on 26 February 1938, Hitler

> wanted the evolutionary course to be taken, whether or not the possibility of success could today be foreseen ... He did not now desire a solution by violent means, if it could at all be avoided, since the danger to us in the field of foreign policy became less each year and our military power greater each year.

It is true that Ribbentrop, writing on 2 January 1938, had questioned the sincerity of appeasement.

> The visit of Halifax is to be considered as a manoeuvre to obtain information and as a camouflage ... England and her Prime Minister, after the Halifax visit, in my opinion, see no possible basis for an agreement with Germany ... England is at all events preparing by military and political measures for a conflict with Germany.

This dispatch has already won exaggerated attention from the nonsense it contains, the climax of which is: 'National Socialism, however, is thought capable of anything. Baldwin already apprehended this, and Edward VIII had to abdicate, since it was not certain whether, because of his views, he could co-operate in an anti-German policy.' As to Chamberlain, so little did he believe in appeasement that he said of Garvin's articles: 'They were too long for him and therefore he did not read them.' The dispatch (like most of Ribbentrop's) was designed to defend the writer, not to give an accurate report; he was leaving London, and merely wished to excuse himself for not carrying out all the boasts which he had made on arrival.

Enforced blackmail

Once back in Germany he found the wind still blowing in favour of appeasement, and was soon boasting again of what he would accomplish. The dispatch of 2 January had one firm recommendation – to strengthen the links with Italy and Japan. This was the basic difference between Neurath and Ribbentrop. Neurath had hoped that British difficulties with Italy and Japan would point the contrast with a friendly Germany; Ribbentrop intended to use the Axis and the Anti-Comintern Pact in order to blackmail the British. Whatever his policy, the outcome in Austria compelled a strengthening of the Axis and thus committed Germany to the blackmailing alternative.

The Austrian affair was a striking illustration of violence brought on by muddle. The Austrian Nazis, despite Papen, despite the Foreign Office, even despite Hitler, would not take 'the evolutionary course'. This drove Schuschnigg to reprisals in self-defence and, even more alarming for Germany, to an attempt at co-operation with Czechoslovakia. Schuschnigg had therefore to be summoned to Berchtesgaden and compelled to retreat. Even now the Germans thought they had merely restored the previous position, by which Austria was imperceptibly Nazified. But Schuschnigg was no longer prepared to slither helplessly downhill. His proposed plebiscite was a challenge to Hitler. If Hitler had acquiesced, German expansion in Europe would have been stopped at the outset; he accepted the challenge and, by so doing, took the decisive step on the road to war. Far from being long planned, it was a step resolved on overnight and executed in hurry and blunder. Hitler's letter to Mussolini of 11 March 1938, emphasized that he had been driven to act by Schuschnigg's approach to Czechoslovakia; these passages were suppressed when the letter was published in Italy.

Ribbentrop was in England on 11 March on his farewell visit. At lunch Chamberlain said of Austria: 'Once we had all got past this unpleasant affair and a reasonable solution had been found it was to be hoped that we could begin working in earnest toward a German–British understanding.' During lunch news of the German ultimatum and demand for a withdrawal of the plebiscite arrived. Lord Halifax was 'somewhat excited'; Chamberlain 'personally thought it would be better if the plebiscite were not held now'. Ribbentrop reported further:

> Lord Halifax said he considered it exceedingly serious that Schuschnigg had been threatened with invasion. I replied that the telegrams which were read here did not say that at all. Chamberlain immediately admitted this. However, Lord Halifax expressed the opinion that the exertion of pressure implied such a threat. Chamberlain again stated that personally he understood the situation.

'The intelligent class'

Even after the Austrian affair Chamberlain and his associates still hoped for appeasement. Thus Woerman, German chargé d'affaires, reported on 22 April:

> Mr. Butler said that he knew from close association with Chamber-
> lain and Lord Halifax that both, now as in the past, held fast to the
> idea of a real understanding with Germany and that the events in
> Austria had not altered this in any way. He made himself the
> spokesman, as it were, of the younger generation in England – that
> is, not the intellectual class. In contrast with the actual intellectu-
> als, among whom there was now as in the past a strong antipathy
> to the authoritarian States, the circles close to him fully understood
> that Germany had to pursue her national aims in her own way. The
> German and British people, were of the same blood – which in
> itself meant a bond of unity. To the circle close to him it was
> inconceivable that Germany and England should meet again on the
> battlefield.

There are times when it is an advantage to be an intellectual and not
merely intelligent.

Still, the British government was not content with appeasement. It
also tried to win Italy away from Germany and concluded with Italy the
agreement of 16 April. This would have made sense only before the loss
of Austria. Once the Germans were on the Brenner Mussolini had no
further freedom of action. Nor, for that matter, had Hitler. Unless he
was prepared for a breach with Italy he had to renounce South Tirol,
and he did this in his speech of 7 May. South Tirol cemented the Axis;
in Ribbentrop's phrase, 'it made the fronts rigid' – that is, Italy and
Germany could no longer squeeze concessions from the British by offering to abandon each other. Mussolini had to make out that war would
be easy: 'The British were undoubtedly splendid sailors, but it was
something else again to fight in the desert at 50 degrees centigrade. His
Italians were accustomed to it.' The British, on their side, answered by
drawing closer to France, as shown by the royal visit to Paris in July.
On 18 July Dirksen, the new Ambassador in London, reported:

> The British Cabinet is showing growing understanding for the
> demands of Germany in the Sudeten question. It would be willing
> to make great sacrifices to satisfy Germany's other legitimate de-
> mands – on the one condition that these objectives are sought by
> peaceful means. If Germany should resort to military means to
> reach these objectives, then England would without doubt resort to
> war at the side of France.

Before the Austrian affair and the appointment of Ribbentrop appeasement had had some plausibility; at least, it was as plausible as the policy
of Locarno. After March 1938 it had no chance of success. Not for the
first nor for the last time in history a policy was adopted just when it
ceased to be appropriate.

CHAPTER TWENTY-TWO

Appeasement: German Version

This essay is another review of *Documents on German Foreign Policy*, Series D, Vol. 1 (see previous essay). It was published in the *New Statesman and Nation* (17 December 1949). It is notable for a discussion of the Hossbach memorandum. His scepticism about the use of this memorandum as evidence of Hitler having clear, long-term plans for war was to be a controversial aspect of *The Origins of the Second World War* (London, Hamish Hamilton, 1961).

The revelations of secret diplomacy provided many sensations after the first German war; by now they have become a habit. The victorious powers captured most of the German Foreign Office archives, and a team of historians (nine Americans, nine Englishmen, four Frenchmen) have been rummaging in them ever since. The present volume is the first large-scale result of their labours. It is nothing like so startling or entertaining as the fifty-four volumes on diplomacy before the first German war which the Germans published in the interwar years. Thimme, the editor of those volumes, was a publicist of genius; even though he occasionally rigged the effects for the sake of Germany's good name, he deserved to produce a best-seller. Those volumes, too, had the great attraction of reproducing the marginal notes of Bismarck, Bülow, and William II – a trio who tumbled their way through diplomacy like inspired clowns in a circus. Most of all, these pre-1914 documents gave the impression, well-founded or not, that they revealed genuine decisions: they seemed to determine the fate of nations.

The new series is going to be much duller. The editors, are, no doubt, more impartial than Thimme. Their only whim is to treat the Vatican as a great power, evidence of Papistical, not of national, bias. But they lack the art of presentation. This ponderous volume of twelve hundred pages will never qualify as a bedside book; it is too heavy to hold even when wide awake. German diplomats between the wars were more commonplace in mind and clumsier in expression than their predecessors. Perhaps they appreciated that their actions were no longer decisive; at any rate this is obvious to the reader. The German foreign ministry went plodding on its routine way, only to have the wheel wrenched from its hand at the moment of crisis. Neurath and his staff had no more idea than foreign statesmen what Hitler was up to. Nor, for that matter, had Hitler himself. The Austrian crisis and the Far Eastern question, the two main topics of this volume, both illustrate this. Hitler intervened only on a sudden impulse, without plan or preparation. The editors reprint the Hossbach memorandum of 5 November 1937, in which Hitler expounded his aggressive designs. This is evidence that he was a violent and unscrupulous man; it is not evidence that he had any concrete projects, and his prophecy of events bears no relation to what actually happened. For instance Hitler talks of war in the period 1943–45, though he does not say against whom; rambles about separating France and England, immediately after calling them 'hate-inspired antagonists'; lists unlikely possibilities and builds further speculations upon them, altogether a farrago of nonsense.

Nevertheless the volume is of great value for the general picture which can be drawn from it. It confirms the impression from other sources that the first months of 1938 saw the real crisis in the history of Nazi Germany. Until the beginning of 1938 Hitler was still something of a figurehead. Fritsch and Blomberg were in control of the army; Neurath was in control of the foreign ministry; Hitler provided occasional explosions – the noises off which were to win concessions from the entente powers. The German foreign ministry had a consistent policy: this was to improve Germany's position by all means short of war. The German diplomats encouraged the gradual sapping of Austria's independence; they welcomed British, and still more Russian, difficulties in the Far East; they encouraged Italian ambitions in the Mediterranean. On the other hand, they shrank from committing themselves and were sharply conscious of German weakness against a European coalition. They kept up good relations with China, partly to prolong the Far Eastern war, partly to be able to switch over to the British side against Japan, in exchange for British concessions in Europe. Similarly they kept clear of Italy and perhaps intended to sell Italy out to France at the right moment. In fact Germany with no interests in the Mediterranean and few in the Far East, was in an extremely favourable diplomatic position. It is difficult to see how she could have missed the peaceful establishment of a hegemony over Eastern Europe, if she had continued to follow the Neurath line.

Three things tipped the balance in favour of lunacy and so postponed German domination of Europe for a decade or two – Ribbentrop, the belated Austrian resistance, and the efforts of the appeasers. Ribbentrop had a single talent: he could present in diplomatic terms exactly what Hitler wanted to hear. Previously Hitler had been in the position of a lunatic who thinks he is Jesus Christ: no one believes him and therefore he even doubts it himself. The German diplomatic service and foreign ministry returned a unanimous and continuous verdict against Hitler's intuitions; Ribbentrop confirmed these intuitions. Neurath had tried to explain to Hitler what was going on in the world; Ribbentrop, as foreign minister, listened for Hitler's whims and then produced evidence in their favour. Still, Ribbentrop would not have had such a catastrophic effect if his rise to power had not coincided with Schuschnigg's attempt to arrest Nazi penetration into Austria. The Austrian crisis of March 1939 went against all German plans, even Hitler's: these had assumed an imperceptible crumbling of Austria or, as it was called, 'an evolutionary solution'. Schuschnigg called Hitler's bluff and compelled him to show that it was not bluff after all. The ease with which Austria fell first gave Hitler the conviction that his ravings were sound reality. As a result, when the Czechs challenged him in May he at once set to work to bring down a crisis upon them.

Most of all, Hitler's confidence was reinforced by the assiduous pilgrimage of the appeasers. The foreign ministry gave warning of the danger of war; Ribbentrop could silence them with the evidence of British and French timidity. As so often in history, appeasement was adopted just when it ceased to be appropriate. There was something to be said for concessions to the Weimar republic, even for concessions to the conservative coalition of Neurath and Fritsch. Perhaps concessions to these would have made Germany satisfied, though powerful. When appeasement got under way, it merely provided Ribbentrop and Hitler with the evidence that violence and aggression were the profitable course. After the annexation of Austria, appeasement had missed the bus, though it is doubtful whether there was ever one to catch. Moreover, since Hitler himself did not know what he wanted, even the most hardened appeasers could never discover what they were expected to concede. Later this was attributed to Hitler's Machiavellian diplomacy; in reality he had no firm intention except to humiliate the leading statesmen of the Great Powers. All allowed themselves to be humiliated. The exceptions in this volume make a curious pair: they are Lord Londonderry and M. Blum. Both refused to grovel before Hitler, and both foretold what would be the consequences of his actions.

Thus the present volume does not provide the evidence that there was a German, or even a Nazi, conspiracy against peace, if by conspiracy is meant a coherent, objective plan. It provides the evidence that the Germans, and especially the German governing class, allowed a criminal lunatic to establish himself in supreme power; and that they were abetted by those in England and France who, from feebleness or fear of Communism, treated the lunatic as a sane man.

CHAPTER TWENTY-THREE

More Light on Munich

This essay was first published as a review of E.L. Woodward and Rohan Butler (eds), *Documents on British Foreign Policy 1919–1939*, Third Series, Vol. 2: *1938* (London, HMSO, 1949), in the *New Statesman and Nation* (15 October 1949). Alan Taylor also reviewed the volume in the *Manchester Guardian*, 13, 14 and 15 September 1949, the resulting essay being reprinted as 'Full Speed to Munich' in his collections of essays, *Rumour of Wars* (London, Hamish Hamilton, 1952) and *Europe: Grandeur and Decline* (Harmondsworth, Penguin, 1967).

This volume, together with its predecessor published earlier in the year, presents the record of British diplomacy in the Czech question from March to October 1938: twelve hundred documents in total to be added to our knowledge of 'Munich'. It is a strictly Foreign Office record, confined to the telegrams and dispatches to and from British diplomats abroad. Without knowledge from other sources it would be difficult to guess that Munich was Chamberlain's personal work, which the Foreign Office sometimes assisted, sometimes regretted, but never originated. In a tantalising footnote, Professor Woodward, the editor, writes: 'Mr. Chamberlain had considered the possibility of a visit by himself to Herr Hitler as early as August 30. He had discussed the plan with one or two of his colleagues, and had mentioned it to Sir N. Henderson during the latter's visit to London.' What is the evidence for this? We are not told; and at the end we still grope after Chamberlain's actions and motives as much, perhaps, as the members of the Foreign Office did at the time.

Still, though Chamberlain sometimes conducted a private diplomacy, the Foreign Office was the main executant of policy; and Professor Woodward's two volumes give us some, though not all, the truth about British policy at the time of Munich. They give us enough at any rate to arrive at this conclusion – a conclusion which was to be expected: that the humdrum explanations were on the whole right and the melodramatic explanations on the whole wrong. For instance, Munich was not part of a deep-seated plan to launch Hitler into war against the Soviet Union. This plan, so far as it existed, was conceived only after Munich. The British government erred in ignoring the Soviet Union, not in plotting against it. They were, no doubt, much to blame; but the Russians were also much to blame for their impenetrable secrecy. If Hitler was to be stopped without war, it was essential that Russian strength should be feared by him and counted on by the Western Powers. This was impossible without knowledge; and the Russian refusal to allow this knowledge makes one suspect that they were not strong or that they had no great objection to a war.

The graver fault of the Chamberlain government was the deliberate exclusion of the United States from the Czech question: if an American representative had sat in at Munich, Hitler would not have succeeded as he did. This is the core of the story: the British government wished Hitler to succeed, i.e., they wished him to achieve without war a settlement of the Sudeten question which would be entirely satisfactory both to the Sudetens and, more important, to himself. Their motives were not ignoble. Certainly they were anxious to avoid war, though not so anxious as, say, M. Bonnet, the French foreign minister, for whom this was the sole consideration. Stronger than this was the feeling that in the Sudeten question they had a weak moral case. They were the survivors of a generation which had been brought up to believe that all the troubles of Europe would be ended if frontiers were redrawn on national lines. The Congress of Vienna had sinned against the national principle (this is one of the few pieces of historical twaddle universally known); they were not going to do the same. The Sudetens were indisputably Germans; therefore they should be included in Germany and German unity thus 'completed'. The Czechs themselves had contributed unconsciously to this frame of mind by insisting that Czechoslovakia was a national state; they would have been wiser to argue that east-central Europe could not be reordered on purely national lines without an upheaval of millions of people, such as has since taken place.

British statesmen and diplomats were affected by another historical legend – that appeasement had worked with France in the generation after Waterloo. Most of all, they wished to give in to Germany because they could think of no alternative; as Nevile Henderson repeatedly insisted, Germany would still be the greatest European country even after defeat in war (as indeed she is). This is very different from their fearing defeat. Complacent and old-fashioned, any such disaster as the fall of France, or even of Poland, never occurred to them; it is as though they had come under the sway of Professor Namier's historical generalization (much preached by him in the 1930s) that world-upheavals take place at the turn of each century, not in the middle of one. When Chamberlain or Halifax talked of British weakness, they meant only that they would not be able to defend Czechoslovakia, or even to restore her, by means of war; they did not see that to admit this was to abdicate as a European power. Or rather they saw it, and tried to make the best of things by hoping that they were abdicating in favour of a Germany which would then become civilized and peaceful. This hope was indeed the only alternative to calling on Russia and America to offset German preponderance.

Thus high principles and realism, sloth and conviction, were all mixed together in the six months' campaign of British diplomacy: a campaign to compel the Czechs to put themselves at Hitler's mercy and a campaign to compel the French to desert the Czechs. There was plausibility in every step, even in the final threat to condone a German attack on Czechoslovakia, unless the Czechs committed suicide. Yet, despite all argument, everything was wrong from beginning to end: wrong not merely in its estimate of Hitler or of the Russians or of the Czechs; wrong, because it was degrading. In the last resort, policy is a matter of feeling, not of calculation. Munich had a bad taste; and anyone of real character must have felt it so. In this sense the Bolsheviks and others were right when they accused the Western statesmen of being rotted with materialism; they had lost the sense of right and wrong. Lord Halifax had not lost this sense: hence his elaborate explanations, arguing with himself rather than with his interlocutor, and hence, too, his tendency to bolt which appears again and again in these volumes. No other Englishman comes well out of this record; though, as one would expect, Chamberlain's associates come out worse than he does. Strangely enough, there is one honest man, his judgements always right, and his moral sense acute – M. Daladier. Puzzled and reluctant, badgered by the sophistications of Bonnet on one side and by the barren cross-examination of Sir John Simon on the other, Daladier never made a reasoned convincing case: he knew only that Munich was wrong. In the deepest sense, Daladier had the real victory. The British got their way: they achieved the dismemberment of Czechoslovakia without war, as they had always intended. But, owing to Daladier's stubbornness, they had to pay a price which they had always intended to refuse: they had to guarantee rump-Czechoslovakia, and the breach of this guarantee was the undoing both of Hitler and of the men of Munich. Thus there is something to be learnt even from this record of crookedness and folly: when a policy tastes wrong, one should spit it out.

CHAPTER TWENTY-FOUR

1938: A German Version

These two essays – Part 1: The German Appeasers and Part 2: The Triumph of Hitler – were published in reviews of *Documents on German Foreign Policy 1918–1945*, Series D (1937–45), Vol. 2: *Germany and Czechoslovakia 1937–1938* (Washington, Government Printing Office, 1949), in the *Manchester Guardian*, 15 and 16 December 1949.

Alan Taylor also reviewed the British publication of the volume in the *New Statesman and Nation*, 39, 997 (15 April 1950), in the course of which he observed that the old-style diplomats 'meant to establish Germany as the dominant power of Europe; and they would have done it except for Hitler's pursuit of theatrical violence. We should therefore be very grateful that Hitler broke loose in 1938'.

1. The German Appeasers

The second volume of German Foreign Office documents published in America, and soon to be published in England, covers German relations with Czechoslovakia from November 1937 until the Munich conference in September 1938. To be more exact, it covers relations as known to the German Foreign Office; and this was often remote from the point of decision. In Germany, as in England, the professional diplomatists went on their way, imagining that they were in charge of policy, only to have the wheel wrenched from their hands at every critical moment. The German collection at least gives some documents on Hitler's interventions, whereas the reader of the British collection has to guess at Chamberlain's activities. Apart from this, it would be difficult to decide which collection is more misleading as a full picture of policy.

The German 'professionals' had their own Czech policy – a long-term policy by which Czechoslovakia was to be detached from France, and still more from Russia, and to be brought by peaceful means under German control and protection. Thus Eisenlohr, the German minister in Prague, wrote in January, 1938:

> German policy should be directed towards isolating Czechoslova-kia in any future potential negotiations, but then to handle her so considerately that her French alliance gradually loses its intrinsic value, in the same and even greater measure than is the case with the Franco-Polish alliance ... It would be a great and tempting goal for German policy, by the exercise of moderate force and patience, to guide this problem along peaceful lines to ultimate solution.

In February 1938 Eisenlohr told Henlein:

> As long as Reich policy could achieve its vital objectives by peaceful means and so far there was no reason to doubt this, he might reckon only with a peaceful policy on Germany's part.

This policy met with a response from the Czech side. In November 1937 Eisenlohr reported a conversation with President Beneš:

> We must understand that Czechoslovakia wanted 'assurances' – it remained uncertain whether by this word he meant German promises or his country's alliances with France and Russia, probably the latter – but Czechoslovakia would never allow herself to be used as an instrument of policy directed against Germany or to be made to serve Russian, French, or British policy to such an end ...

and Eisenlohr concluded cynically: 'Beneš would be willing to come to an agreement with Germany five minutes before a Franco-German rapprochement'. Hodza, the Prime Minister, and Beran, the leader of the Agrarians, were even more emphatic in their wish to bring Czechoslovakia within the German sphere.

A peace party

Eisenlohr therefore insisted that Henlein and his party should negotiate seriously with the Czech Government. When, in March 1938, K.H. Frank, Henlein's assistant, attempted to raise unacceptable demands, in order to 'hinder settlement and bring about eventual armed conflict with the Reich', Eisenlohr had him rebuked in Berlin. On 16 March Eisenlohr telegraphed: 'Party leadership is abandoning former intransigent course and will adopt policy of gradual furthering of Sudeten German interests.' Thus the assurances given to Czechoslovakia at the time of the German seizure of Austria were sincere so far as the Foreign Ministry was concerned. Henlein, however, had appealed from the diplomatists to Hitler. On 28 March Henlein appeared in Berlin and reported triumphantly: 'The purport of the instructions which the Führer has given to Henlein is that demands should be made by the Sudeten German party which are unacceptable to the Czech Government.' And again: 'We must always demand so much that we can never be satisfied.' Henlein was to visit London again 'and to continue to use his influence with a view to assuring non-intervention by Britain'.

On 29 March Ribbentrop, who had just become foreign minister, held a conference at the Ministry, where he stressed the same view: 'The final object of the negotiations ... would be to avoid entry into the (Czech) Government'. Yet on 2 April Weizsäcker, the state secretary (equivalent to our permanent under secretary), could say to the Czechoslovak minister: 'If this country made the necessary moves in favour of the Sudeten Germans, it would then have no need to be anxious about German–Czech relations.' Were Weizsäcker and the professionals henceforth merely lying in order to provide cover for Hitler's aggressive plans? This is part of the explanation; but men's motives are never simple, and it is reasonable, though charitable, to suppose that they were also hoping to anticipate aggression by achieving a peaceful success.

This hope was encouraged by the eagerness with which British and French spokesmen offered 'appeasement'; and the German documents supply additions for an anthology of appeasement already too long. Thus Nevile Henderson said in May: 'France was acting for the Czechs and Germany for the Sudeten Germans. Britain was supporting Germany.' And Mr (now Sir) I. Kirkpatrick is reported as having said to Prince Bismarck on 10 May:

> The whole question could only be satisfactorily settled by the German and British Governments arriving at a direct understanding with regard to the objective to be attained ... If the German Government would advise the British Government confidentially what solution of the Sudeten German question they were striving after, he believed that he could assure us that the British Government would bring such pressure to bear in Prague that the Czechoslovak Government would be compelled to accede to the German wishes.

Bonnet, not to be outdone, told the German Ambassador on 26 May: 'If the Czechoslovak Government continued unyielding, the French Government would inform them that under these circumstances they would be obliged to submit their obligation under the alliance to revision.'

Persevering

The appeasing chorus was briefly silenced during the alarm of 21 May, when the Czechs took precautionary measures against a German surprise. The present collection supplies no evidence whether the Czechs did well to be alarmed. The German officials denied all stories of mobilisation or of unusual troop movements – Ribbentrop denied it even to the Italians; but, as later events showed, he was not honest even to Germany's close ally.

Perhaps Hitler staged a deliberate false alarm in order to discredit the Czechs and to push the Western powers farther along the road of appeasement, as though that were necessary. His military directive of 28 May, reproduced here, declares: 'It is my unalterable decision to smash Czechoslovakia by military action in the near future'; and it has been argued that he was provoked to this by the Czech action on 21 May.

Hitler's mind does not seem to have worked in this logical way; it is much more likely that he was reacting, like a mischievous boy, to a Supreme Command memorandum of 20 May which repudiated aggression in the near future.

At all events, Weizsäcker still counted on a peaceful outcome. He wrote to Dirksen, Ambassador in London, on 1 June: 'We do not seek a new crisis, nor, indeed, a complete break between Henlein and Prague. We have no intention of allowing Henlein to dictate to us the terms of reference, or, indeed, the date of the negotiations.' The British responded in kind. Wohltat, of the Ministry of Economics, visited London in June and spoke to Sir Horace Wilson, Mr R.A. Butler, Sir Campbell Stuart, and a number of leading bankers. He summed up his impressions on 4 July:

> The British Government were prepared to recognise Germany's position in central Europe, and also the inclusion of the Sudeten Germans within the German frontiers, if the German Government would state what are the limits to the expansion of German sovereignty. The British are also prepared, in my opinion, to accept German economic supremacy in the markets of North, East, and South-east Europe.

2. The Triumph of Hitler

In July and August, 1939, while the Runciman mission wore down Czech resistance in Prague, Weizsäcker carried on a private struggle to keep German policy on peaceful lines. On 9 July he urged Ribbentrop to make it clear to Hitler that 'the surprise factor had been gambled away'. On 21 July he told Ribbentrop that 'Even if it was our business to fool foreign countries, it was nevertheless our duty not to dupe one another, I did not believe we should win this war'. Therefore, they should evade war and instead 'accelerate the process of the chemical dissolution of the Czech State by means of economic pressure'. Weizsäcker evidently shared the view of Chamberlain and Lord Halifax that Hitler had more sense than Ribbentrop, for on 31 July he argued again with Ribbentrop and said: 'The Führer will not undertake the proposed coup against Czechoslovakia at a politically active juncture such as the present.'

British apologies

Ribbentrop, however, knew better, and on 19 August brought Weizsäcker to heel. Weizsäcker recorded the conversation for his own satisfaction and kept it in a sealed envelope:

Ribbentrop explained to me that the Führer was firmly resolved to settle the Czech affair by force of arms ... The other Powers would certainly not make any move, and even if they did, we should accept their challenge and defeat them also ... Herr von Ribbentrop declared that the Führer had never yet made a mistake; his most difficult decisions and acts (occupation of the Rhineland) already lay behind him. It was necessary to believe in his genius, just as he, R, did from long years of experience. If I had not yet reached the stage of blind belief, then he desired of me, in a friendly manner, and urgently, too, that I should do so.

On 30 August Weizsäcker made a last attempt. He submitted to Ribbentrop a report on the political situation in which he wrote: 'If Germany invades Czechoslovakia she will have the Western Powers as her enemies. The war would develop into a European one. This war would end sooner or later in a German capitulation.' This was the end of Weizsäcker's attempt to moderate Hitler's policy, so far as the official record goes; there is naturally no hint here of the irregular methods which he may have employed during September.

Since the German Foreign Ministry had been brushed aside by Ribbentrop and Hitler its archives reveal little of the crisis in September. The German professionals took seriously the British and French warnings that there would be war if Czechoslovakia was attacked; Hitler dismissed these warnings, and every repetition of them made him more confident. For the warnings were given in timid, imploring form – the bleating of frightened sheep rather than the roar of awakening lions. Thus Nevile Henderson said on 6 August: 'Great Britain would not think of risking even one sailor or airman for Czechoslovakia and any reasonable solution would be agreed to so long as it were not attempted by force.' And Bonnet on 2 September: 'The Führer's work would find its logical culmination not in war, which would mean final destruction of European culture and economy, but in continued peaceful development by revision of the peace treaties and understanding with France and Britain.'

Even when the crisis arrived warnings were still accompanied by supplications. On 26 September, after the breakdown of negotiations at Godesberg, Chamberlain sent a message to Hitler: 'Reports to be expected in immediate future on final Czech rejection of German memorandum are not last word'; and again: 'The Führer should take no notice of any reports on the course of the present negotiations with the French and the Czechs unless they came directly from the Prime Minister'.

The German record adds a few details to the story of Sir Horace Wilson's mission to Berlin on 27 September, when he delivered to Hitler the final warning that Great Britain would support France in the event of war. Wilson accompanied this warning with so many apologies that finally even Sir Nevile Henderson revolted; and 'advised him against continuing the conversation'. When Henderson had left the room Wilson had a brief chance alone with Hitler. His last words were: 'I will still try to make those Czechs sensible.' No wonder Hitler was confident of success.

The neutral allies

There is more of interest in the record of German dealings with her allies and dependants. So long as the crisis was remote, Mussolini ran over with declarations that he would march at Hitler's side. Hitler evaded all Mussolini's efforts to pin him down to a defined plan or to a date for action. All the greater was Mussolini's alarm when war seemed to be approaching; by the middle of September he was explaining that Italy would be more useful to Germany if she remained neutral.

Franco, however, beat Mussolini in the race of neutrality. On 16 September he complained that he had been ignored: 'Germany did not appear to take into consideration the cause of Nationalist Spain.' On 26 September he told the Germans: 'Spain appreciated that it was materially impossible for Germany to give Spain any effective help in the event of a European war'; therefore he would have to negotiate a neutrality agreement with England and France. News of this Spanish move roused Ciano to 'intense indignation': 'Franco's ideas are a direct betrayal of the common cause.' All the later history of Mussolini and of Franco was implicit in this episode.

Hungary played a more active role. Originally the Hungarians had hoped to co-operate with Germany in a war against Czechoslovakia. They were warned off by the German Foreign Office and were themselves rather frightened by the magnitude of events. Hitler stirred them up again after his first meeting with Chamberlain. On 21 September Hitler told Imredy, the Hungarian prime minister: 'This was Hungary's last chance to join in ... In his opinion, the best thing would be to destroy Czechoslovakia.' The Hungarians promised to send Hitler a note of their claims. This seems to have been the moment when Hitler realized that, whatever temporary concession he might make, he could always destroy rump-Czechoslovakia by stirring up Hungary and the Slovaks.

Finally, there is the question of Poland and Russia. Beck's policy was clear, to make gains at the expense of Czechoslovakia and to bar the way against Russia, but without becoming the associate of Germany. Information about Russia was scanty even for the Germans: they inclined to suppose that the Russians would give the Czechs air support

– hence the need to overrun Bohemia immediately on the outbreak of war. Very curious is Litvinov's remark on 22 August: 'If the old democratic Germany still existed, the Czech question would have had quite a different aspect for the Soviet Union. We have always espoused the cause of self-determination of peoples.' On 29 September Potemkin, acting foreign minister, passed this verdict on Munich: 'What was happening now was the rebirth of the "notorious Four-Power Pact" … The Powers now taking part in the destruction of Czechoslovakia would bitterly regret their submission to a militant nationalism.'

CHAPTER TWENTY-FIVE

Dragons' Teeth

This essay was first published as a review of *Documents on British Foreign Policy 1919–1939*, First Series, Vol. 3: *1919* (London, HMSO, 1950), edited by E.L. Woodward and Rohan Butler, in the *New Statesman and Nation*, 39, 984 (14 January 1950). The essay ends with a characteristic comment by Alan Taylor.

Four great empires were shattered by the first German war. The victorious allies found some sort of policy for three of them; they failed to find a policy for the fourth, Russia. This failure is the theme of the most recent volume of Foreign Office papers. The allies had originally intervened in Russia in order to get the Germans out; and their most pressing concern was still to expel German troops from the Baltic States. Even this was beyond their means. The allies had no troops to spare of their own; Lloyd George objected to using Polish troops, since this would commit him to a pro-Polish policy elsewhere; and the Americans even objected to a blockade of the Baltic, since this would retard the recovery of Silesia and the establishment of 'normalcy'. The White Russians, to whom the allies were committed, hated Bolshevism; they hated the independence of the Baltic States still more and were willing to use German troops against it. In November 1919 a Foreign Office memorandum pointed out, that if there were a combination of Baltic States, 'it will be a *cordon sanitaire* not against Bolshevik Russia, but against anti-Bolshevik Russia'. As the allies could not effectively threaten von der Goltz and his legionaries in the Baltic, they had to threaten the German government in Berlin; and Noske, after a good deal of evasion, finally supplied the authority which the allies lacked. This was hardly a victory for the so-called Supreme Council.

By the autumn of 1919 the Baltic States had made peace with Soviet Russia and had been recognized by the allies; elsewhere policy was still lacking. British representatives and the remnants of British forces sprawled across Russia from Archangel to the Caucasus. None had any strength, and none could persuade the local White leaders to adopt 'not necessarily a full democratic government in the Western sense, but a modern government'. The Foreign Office remained obstinately ignorant of conditions in Soviet Russia. Though the readers of the *Manchester Guardian* or the *Daily News* could form a clear and fairly accurate picture, the Foreign Office preferred to rely on the gossip of Poles and

émigrés, patiently recording that Bolshevism was on the verge of collapse or that 'Lenin (who represents the moderate element) is losing
influence'. One of the curiosities of modern times is the unshakeable
conviction of the Foreign Office that no journalist (except of course *The
Times* correspondent at Riga) ever had information of value about
Soviet Russia. In July 1919, it is fair to say, Mr Harvey, a member of the
Foreign Office, jibbed at the assumptions of British policy. He wrote: 'It
is impossible to account for the stability of the Bolshevik Government
by terrorism alone.' Support should be withdrawn from the White
armies. 'The Russians would then be left to themselves and the Government of Lenin would have to justify itself in the light of its works.' This
memorandum met with the disapproval of Mr Harvey's superior and
did not reach Lord Curzon, let alone the War Cabinet. Mr R.H. Hoare
had no better luck in December. His argument in favour of recognizing
the Soviet government was minuted by Lord Curzon: 'Mr. Hoare not
unfairly says that our policy has been attended with much grief and
with lack of success. But I am not clear that his would be free from
either of these vices.'

The policy of the War Cabinet, so far as it had one, was to continue
to send inadequate aid to the White Russian forces: it would be dishonourable to desert those who had once received British encouragement. It
was, however, equally dishonourable to fail to follow this policy to its
logical conclusion by intervening in Russia in a massive way; yet everyone knew that this was out of the question. The War Cabinet fell back
on the device of appealing to the allies to formulate a general policy
towards Russia. Curzon minuted appropriately: 'If any one is sanguine
enough to believe that this moribund (Peace) Conference is capable in
its death throes of producing a Russian policy, I am not that man.' As
expected, the peace conference never managed to devise a Russian
policy. The Americans complained at the British withdrawal from the
Caucasus, but refused to go there themselves or even to contribute
towards the cost of the British expedition; the French complained that
the British, by helping Denikin, were encroaching on the French sphere
of interest. Curzon, who had wanted an independent British policy,
watched the failure of allied co-operation with sour delight but he was
equally at a loss when it came to his turn. In December 1919 he
dispatched Sir H. Mackinder on a special mission to southern Russia.
Mackinder came back with the recommendation to back Denikin with
military and financial means. His report, which does little credit to the
judgement of the founder of geopolitics, was firmly rejected by Lloyd
George; and therewith British policy in Russia fell to pieces. The British
agents with the Whites were withdrawn; and Curzon minuted: 'So ends
a highly discreditable enterprise.'

Though relations with the Whites ended, relations with the Bolsheviks were not established. In autumn, 1919, the British government were forced into unofficial contact with the Soviet government in order to discuss the exchange of prisoners. Chicherin and Curzon corresponded by long-distance wireless, a correspondence in which Curzon was first winded and then outwitted. O'Grady, a respectable Labour MP, was sent to negotiate with Litvinov at Copenhagen; there followed the first experience of that Russian tenacity and ingenuity now familiar to all. In 1919 it was surprising and disconcerting. Litvinov was inexhaustibly patient in luring O'Grady from the technical question of the exchange of prisoners to more general topics; and his plausible charm finally tempted O'Grady into signing an agreement about prisoners which was, in some points, directly contrary to his instructions. This was a nonsensical situation. The Bolshevik government existed; it was being treated as a government; and Curzon tried to invoke common standards of behaviour. Yet O'Grady was forbidden to discuss political questions even in the most general terms. The British government was not only ignorant of everything that went on in Soviet Russia, it was determined to remain so. Since the Soviet government had been so ill-mannered as to refuse to succumb before the feeble British intervention, it should be taught a lesson – and ignored. In fact, the British government had already arrived, by simple intuition, at the Russian policy which it still maintains.

The other aspect of East Europe which affected British policy in 1919 was Poland, and especially the Polish claims to Ukrainian territory. Lloyd George fought strenuously against the Polish demand for east Galicia. For instance he said to Paderewski on 5 June 1919: 'You have got twenty millions of Poles free, you have got an absolutely united Poland. It is a thing which no Pole could have conceived as possible five years ago; and in addition to that, they are claiming even populations which are not their own ... They are more imperialist, believe me, than either England and France, than certainly the United States.' (The peculiar grammar is usual in the protocols of international meetings.) The British first advocated autonomy for east Galicia; then accepted a Polish mandate with a plebiscite after ten years; were pushed into extending this to twenty-five years; and finally saw the limit disappear before their eyes. Lloyd George talked sound sense when in January 1920 he advised the Poles to limit their ambitions:

> If the Poles made a sincere attempt to make an equitable peace and the Bolsheviks either refused peace or, having made peace, proceeded to repudiate it, Great Britain would feel bound to assist Poland to the best of her power ... If, on the other hand, Poland insisted on retaining within Poland areas which were indisputably

Russian according to the principles generally applied by the Peace Conference, and if the Bolshevik Government refused the peace on this ground and attacked Poland in order to recover Russian districts for Russia, it would be very difficult, if not impossible, for the British Government to get public opinion to support military or financial outlay in these circumstances.

Here again, the British made the worst of both worlds. They would not support Pilsudski's ambition of incorporating all the Ukraine and so making Poland the Great Power of Eastern Europe; on the other hand they could not compel the Poles to be satisfied with their ethnic territory. British policy was muddled and contradictory: with the Poles, as with the Bolsheviks, the British tried to behave as a great power when the means of power were no longer theirs. It is not surprising that those at the receiving end had a less charitable explanation; and Bolshevik suspicions of British policy will not appear mysterious to the students of this volume.

There has been a welcome, though unacknowledged, change of editorial policy in this volume. Until now we have been denied the minutes of the foreign secretary. They would, it was claimed, take up too much space; and 'constitutional propriety' forbade the revelation of conflicts within the office or the government. Mr Butler has evidently revolted against this self-denying ordinance. This, like all revolts, is to be encouraged.

CHAPTER TWENTY-SIX

Documents

This essay was first published as a review of *Documents on British Foreign Policy 1919–1939*, Second Series, Vol. 4: *1932–3*, edited by E.L. Woodward and Rohan Butler (London, HMSO, 1950), in the *Manchester Guardian* (14 July 1950).

The latest addition to *Documents on British Foreign Policy 1919–1939*, edited by E.L. Woodward and Rohan Butler, is Volume IV in the Second Series. This second series began with the events of 1929 and was intended to run until the outbreak of war. Later a third series was started from the spring of 1938; and this has made the documents in the earlier series seem remote. Still, even the dullest period has to be covered in such a publication of documents. This present volume covers the latter half of 1932 and the first few months of 1933 from two angles. About a third of the book – some two hundred pages – gives the reports of the British Ambassador at Berlin on political developments in Germany. Though there are no revelations, it is interesting to read the account of a skilful observer on Hitler's rise to power. As to British policy concerning Hitler, there was none. The bulk of the volume deals with the Disarmament Conference and especially with the German demand for 'equality of rights'. It shows Great Britain as mediating between France and Germany and brings out clearly the salient point in British policy in this period – so long as there was no German navy, the British government assumed that they could be impartial, if not indifferent, in questions of German armament. Incidentally, the record of the discussions at Geneva shows MacDonald to have been an extremely competent negotiator – certainly an improvement on his foreign secretary.

CHAPTER TWENTY-SEVEN

The Morning After

This essay was first published as a review of *Documents on British Foreign Policy 1919–1939*, Third Series, Vol. 3: *1938–9*, edited by E.L. Woodward and Rohan Butler assisted by Margaret Lambert (London, HMSO, 1950), in the *New Statesmen and Nation*, 40, 1029 (25 November 1950). The essay ends with a characteristically colourful and memorable comment.

He also reviewed the volume in the *Manchester Guardian* (22 November 1950), under the title 'Failure of the Munich Policy' and reprinted it as 'From Munich to Prague: British Version' in his collection of essays, *Rumours of Wars* (London, Hamish Hamilton, 1952), and *Europe: Grandeur and Decline* (Harmondsworth, Penguin, 1967).

It was not to be expected that the British record of the months after Munich would contain anything startling or even interesting. Stale cigar-smoke and broken glasses dominate the scene; the diplomats tried to sweep up the mess, though they dared not open a window. Most of this volume is dreary, much of it discreditable. The achievements of Munich withered at once. It had been represented as a great victory that the Germans agreed to an International Commission to settle the new Czech frontier; in the outcome they got more than Hitler had demanded at Godesberg and broke the nerve of the Czechs into the bargain. It had also been represented as a great concession that the new Czechoslovakia would receive a British guarantee; this caused a headache when the men of Munich woke up. First they tried to persuade the French not to insist on the British guarantee; then they asked the Czechs to let them off; finally they flew into a temper with the Czechs for not making the dishonourable course easy. Munich and its discreditable consequences are usually blamed on Chamberlain; in this volume, at any rate, Lord Halifax is shown as directing a policy perhaps more adroit but equally discreditable. In fact the time is approaching when the polite silence concerning Lord Halifax's conduct of foreign policy will have to be broken. An essay on 'the foreign policy of Lord Halifax' will make a surprising study; this essay might even by comparison enhance the reputation of Sir John Simon.

Appeasement, the policy of Munich, failed as soon as it began to operate. By November 1938 it was obvious even to the British government that Hitler's appetite had merely increased. Chamberlain and Lord Halifax hesitated as to the remedy. Should they buy him off with more concessions, this time at the expense of Poland? If they did, Germany would become so strong that even the Western bloc of England and France might not hold. Yet Poland seemed an unsatisfactory ally, liable to disruption and unreliable into the bargain. Of course the British government regarded an eastern expansion by Germany as less unwelcome than a western expansion; this is very far from implying that they welcomed even this. Lord Halifax even wished to keep Russia rather vaguely in the European balance of power; and the British observers in Moscow rightly dismissed the possibility of an independent Ukraine which would fall within the German orbit. In fact, if the British rulers thought at all, they must have known that the German storm would shortly blow and that it would blow against them. Hence they needed allies; a search peculiarly difficult when Munich had just shown that the reward for being faithful to the Western powers was to be dismembered for Germany's benefit.

The real theme of this volume, so far as it has one, is therefore the problem – how to win over Italy without estranging France? This was a problem without solution. The more conscious the French were of their weakness, the more they jumped at the chance of a dispute with Italy, a foeman worthy of their inferior steel. Mussolini on his side, had fallen under the spell of German power: the British approach flattered his vanity, but it could have achieved nothing even if the British had been prepared to offer him the French colonial empire. Thus the volume is a record of futility and failure. Munich was at least a policy, though a mistaken one. When it miscarried, there remained only the pretence that nothing had happened. Most of this volume is concerned with matters so trivial that it will never be opened, let alone read. But the accounts of the meetings with the French ministers in November 1938 and with Mussolini in January 1939 recapture the atmosphere of that posthumous period in which the world of Versailles walked and talked half a year after its head had been cut off.

CHAPTER TWENTY-EIGHT

Franco's Friends

This essay was first published as a review of *Documents on German Foreign Policy*, Series D, Vol. 3: *The Spanish Civil War* (London, HMSO, 1951), in the *New Statesman and Nation* (14 April 1951). Alan Taylor also reviewed the volume in the *Manchester Guardian* (18 April 1951), an essay which was reprinted under the title 'Spain and the Axis' in his collection of essays, *Rumours of Wars*, (London, Hamish Hamilton, 1952) and *Europe: Grandeur and Decline* (Harmondsworth, Penguin, 1967). As well as his comments on Germany and Spain, this essay is also notable for his further thoughts on the value, or lack of value, of large, official collections of diplomatic documents.

There is not much to be learnt from the latest volume of documents from the German Foreign Ministry. The Spanish civil war never played an important part in German policy. The Germans had had no previous dealings with Franco; and when the rebellion started they merely gave it the casual patronage that they would give to any Fascist movement. But they took good care that it should never bring them within sight of a general war. The most serious advantage of the civil war for the Germans was that it continued and completed the estrangement of Italy from the Western powers which the Abyssinian affair had begun. Hence they were quite prepared to act as Italy's second. It is said that the Germans got valuable military experience in Spain; this does not, of course, appear from these purely diplomatic documents. They certainly enjoyed showing off their power by an occasional bombardment of the Spanish coast; and they welcomed the chance of reasserting their equality as a great power which was given to them by the non-intervention committee. But England and France could have secured the victory of the Spanish republic at any time, if they had had the courage and the will to do so. As it was, the Germans drew the lesson that if the democratic powers would not risk a war for the sake of the Western Mediterranean which was vital to them, they would certainly not risk one of the sake of Eastern Europe.

At the end of the war the Germans tried to collect a payment for their very limited assistance. They got economic concessions. These were nothing new; other things being equal, any Spanish government would prefer German to England or French economic penetration, simply because Germany was farther away and politically less dangerous. But their political gains were small – merely the prospect of Spanish neutrality which again could have been secured from any Spanish government.

Franco did not become a member of the Axis; and he gave no encouragement to German designs on Morocco – he did not even support their claim to a voice at Tangier. International Fascism got a victory of prestige; Germany reaped no material advantage as a great power.

These are elementary conclusions to be drawn from a volume of over a thousand pages; and it is difficult to resist asking the question – is this monstrous project of publishing the records of the German Foreign Ministry really worth while? Of course, a historian should never grudge the publication of evidence; but here there is so little evidence and so much verbiage. The enterprise employs eighteen editors; and there are eight former editors who have resigned. Series D, which opened with March 1938, is going to take seven volumes merely to get to the outbreak of war in 1939. Later there will be Series A, B and C to cover the period between 1918 and 1933. A few conscientious reviewers plough through each volume. How many other readers in the whole wide world? Not more than a hundred all told; the gigantic volumes on the best paper go to clutter up the shelves of public libraries. The original project seemed admirable. It was to prevent the Germans making a tendentious selection of documents as they did after the First World War and so to make plain their responsibility for the Second World War. Unfortunately the German Foreign Ministry was no longer the decisive authority on foreign policy as perhaps it had been before 1914. Of course, this is also true of the British Foreign Office and even of the State Department of the days of Roosevelt. In fact these publications butter up the shaken self-esteem of British and American professional diplomats: if the German diplomatic service was important, then perhaps the British and American were important too. But you certainly cannot prove German responsibility for the Second World War from the achieves of the German Foreign Ministry. It was not responsible for the war, because it was not responsible for anything. To judge German policy in the age of the Nazis, we need the military records which are locked up unpublished in Washington; and we need still more the non-existent records of Hitler's private conversations and decisions.

The problem of presenting and using the evidence is becoming increasingly baffling in contemporary history – and increasingly ignored. It seems to be forgotten that history – not only contemporary history, but all history – is not a game for scholars; it has a great social purpose, and it achieves this purpose only when it reaches a wide body of readers. These volumes cannot be widely read and therefore do not achieve the purpose of history; they are merely slabs of raw material, very expensively produced. I sometimes wonder whether it would not be better to make these German documents (and the British documents, too, for that matter) readily available to scholars on microfilm; and then to spend the money on subsidizing readable books by leading contemporary historians. But where are the readable historians whom any government would subsidize? The worst offence a professional historian can commit is to write books that sell. The few contemporary historians who write well, such as Mr Trevor-Roper or the great Namier, are condemned as provocative and controversial. The impartial, that is mealy-mouthed, historians are unreadable. The thing really is insoluble. At any rate if the paragon is ever found he will devote a very short chapter to German foreign policy in the Spanish civil war.

CHAPTER TWENTY-NINE

The Moment of Decision

This essay was first published as a review of E.L. Woodward and Rohan Butler (eds), assisted by Margaret Lambert, *Documents on British Foreign Policy 1919–1939*, Third Series, Vol. 4: *1939*, (London, HMSO, 1951), in the *New Statesman and Nation* (15 September 1951). Alan Taylor also reviewed this volume in the *Manchester Guardian* (16 August 1951), an essay subsequently reprinted as part of 'From Munich to Prague: British Version' in his collections of essays, *Rumours of Wars* (London, Hamish Hamilton, 1952) and *Europe: Grandeur and Decline* (Harmondsworth, Penguin, 1967).

This essay is notable not only for the argument that Hitler was 'defeated by the blunders of his opponents, not by their foresight' but also for his praise of the editors now printing Foreign Office minutes with the documents. He also raised in the essay the need for the publication of documents on the military advice given to the British government.

Foreign policy is usually a matter of compromises and expedients, not of clear-cut decisions. It was not so in the short period when Chamberlain was prime minister. Appeasement, including if necessary the sacrifice of Czechoslovakia, was a conscious policy, deliberately pursued, as earlier volumes of the Foreign Office documents have shown. The most recent volume, which runs from 20 January until 3 April 1939, tells a different story: the end of appeasement and the helter-skelter decision, taken overnight, to guarantee Poland – a decision which committed this country to European war on the most unfavourable terms. It is an admirable volume, excellently arranged (except for putting relations with Italy in a separate chapter), and with some uncovenanted blessings, such as Nevile Henderson's private letters and minutes by permanent officials, which the editors once intended to exclude. These minutes are much to the credit of the Foreign Office; it is the more regrettable that earlier minutes, perhaps less to their credit, were not published. There is one lamentable, though inevitable, omission. We still know nothing of the military advice given to the British government. Were the military advisers of the opinion that we could not fight a successful war against Germany with the aid of the Czechs in 1938? And were they of opinion that we could fight a successful war with the aid of Poland in 1939? Or were the two great decisions of appeasement and resistance taken for political reasons without consulting the military advisers? We have still no means of knowing. Yet, if the Foreign Office documents are to be published, why are military papers or the records of the cabinet to be treated as sacred?

By the end of January, 1939, the Foreign Office had lost all faith in Hitler's good intentions. They were prepared for the worst: a sudden attack on Holland, on Belgium, or even on the British Fleet. They pressed for, and apparently got, practical military discussions with the French. Their only scrap of policy was to try to win over Italy, or at any rate to secure her neutrality. But this had an awkward consequence. Italy could be appeased only at the expense of France; and when the French were asked not to take any steps against Italy without British permission, they objected to being treated as they and the British had treated the Czechs. British policy was at a dead end. France was essential to them; they could not buy Italy without offending France (naturally they never thought of buying Italy at their own expense); therefore they had to drift in the vague hope that Hitler would somehow frighten France or Italy or both. Instead Hitler frightened the British themselves.

It had always been foreseen by Nevile Henderson, and presumably by the British government, that Czechoslovakia would become a German protectorate. The alarming thing about Hitler's occupation of Prague on 15 March was its haste; it made the British think that Hitler was in a hurry to go farther. Of course the Prague *coup* had also a decisive effect on British public opinion; and the government would have had to protest in any case. But they would not have acted unless they had been convinced that Hitler meant to march straight on into Romania – probably with Hungarian assistance. The British could do nothing to help Romania; they did not suppose that Russia could do much; hence Poland seemed essential. Even when the immediate alarm blew over, the British continued to argue that Poland, and Poland alone, could provide the 'second front', by which Germany could be defeated. In the decisive fortnight between 15 March and 30 March Colonel Beck bluffed the British government into believing that he had freedom of choice – that Germany had no designs on Poland and that she could stay neutral in the coming war if she chose. Thus when the British guaranteed to help Poland on 30 March they thought that they had scored a great success and obtained a Polish guarantee to help them. The guarantee was supposed to commit Poland to war; the British thought that they themselves were committed already.

The guarantee to Poland was also decisive in regard to Russia; this was certainly not intended by the British government. They realized that Russia was withdrawing into isolation as the result of Munich; plenty of warnings from Moscow are printed in this volume. But they supposed that if they abandoned the policy of Munich and committed themselves to Europe, the Russians also would return to collective security. Moreover, they argued that, if they made an alliance with Russia, Poland would go over to Germany, whereas if they allied themselves with Poland, Russia might still join the anti-German front or, at the very least, remain neutral. This was, in fact, what happened. British and Soviet policy alike took Poland seriously as a great power. If the Russians had realized that Poland would collapse within a month, they would probably not have made the Nazi–Soviet pact; if the British had realized it, they would not have given their guarantee. In that case, Hitler would have overrun the whole of Europe without a war. He was defeated by the blunders of his opponents, not by their foresight.

The decision of 30 March led England to war, with Poland and without Russia. Yet it was not meant as a decision, except in the sense that a speculator on the Stock Exchange decides to cut his losses. Chamberlain meant to have another go at agreement with Germany and, more half-heartedly, at agreement with Russia. This will be the theme of the following volumes.

CHAPTER THIRTY

The Phoney War

This essay was first published as a review of *Documents on German Foreign Policy 1918–45*, Series D, Vol. 8: *September 4, 1939 to March 18, 1940* (London, HMSO, 1954), in the *New Statesman and Nation*, 49, 1243 (1 January 1955). In it he portrays an insane Hitler.

We are becoming jaded with volumes of diplomatic documents. Their bulk, their jargon, their insistence on forgotten issues combine to make them unreadable. The present volume, in particular, has had a poor press. The Stationery Office apparently omitted to send out review copies until late in the day; and the newspapers grabbed hurriedly at anything which would provide a headline. They found their sensation in gossip about the Duke of Windsor – gossip that would not have been worth publishing if it concerned any lesser mortal and which is obviously without foundation. If the journalists had had more time, they might have unearthed more curious items – no doubt also exaggerations, but this time with a more circumstantial air. For instance, in the autumn of 1939 the Germans received a good many hints that a group in the British government was ready to disavow Churchill and to make peace if some face-saving arrangement could be made in Poland. To take one example at random. In November 1939 Mr Butler (then under secretary of foreign affairs) is reported to have told the Italian ambassador 'that Churchill's speech (of 12 November) was in conflict with the Government's views not only in the present instance'. According to the same source, while Mr Butler wanted 'concrete guarantees that such attacks (i.e. as those against Poland) cannot be repeated in the future', he also 'denied in the most categorical manner that it was the intention of his Government to demand evacuation of Poland by German troops; the absurdity of such a demand, which Germany – or any other Great Power – could never accept, was obvious, he added'. It is also curious to read of Lord Halifax showing 'lively interest' for suggested peace terms which included 'an alliance between the belligerent countries, together with Italy and Spain, to guarantee the peace in Europe (Russia omitted!)'

Every statesman makes indiscretions or is falsely reported. There is a question of more serious import throughout this volume, a question which the documents go far to answer. Was there ever a chance of peace in the autumn of 1939? Or, to put it another way, would Hitler have welcomed a chance of breaking with Soviet Russia and going over to the side of the West? The answer is important for such as Mr Trevor-Roper, who believe that Hitler's heart was in war against Soviet Russia and in no other. It is important also for all who are now seeking to demonstrate German enthusiasm for the crusade against Bolshevism. There were such sincere crusaders – Goering, for example, a real advocate of European unity, who ought to have been acclaimed at Nuremberg instead of being sentenced to death! But Ribbentrop was an equally sincere enthusiast for the Nazi–Soviet pact – not from any profound understanding, but merely because he was its author.

It is a different matter when we come to Hitler. Here we discover with every new scrap of evidence a man truly beyond good or evil, unprincipled as no one has been except Napoleon. Hitler could really judge a situation as it existed at the moment without worrying about systems of geopolitics or what he said the day before. Of course he did not believe Ribbentrop's nonsense about Stalin's honesty and reliability; but he believed equally little in his mission to save Europe from Bolshevism. Every step in his policy was a prelude to something further. He was a man without aims – the greatest asset for success (or failure). The Nazi–Soviet pact prepared the way for victory in the West; and that in its turn was intended as preparation for victory in the East. If he had reached Moscow he would then have turned round and aimed at Washington in an indefinite process of achieving success on a greater and greater scale. This is, of course, insanity. And perhaps he was always mad. If he was ever sane, he certainly became mad in the six months covered by these documents. After the conquest of Poland, Hitler could have no stopping-place until he reached the bunker at Berlin.

CHAPTER THIRTY-ONE

Raw Meat

This essay was first published as a review of *Les Deliberations du Conseil des Quatre*, 2 vols (Paris, Centre national de la récherche scientifique, 1955), *Documents on British Foreign Policy 1919–1939*, Third Series, Vol. 8: *1938–9*, edited by E.L. Woodward and Rohan Butler (London, HMSO, 1955) and *Survey of International Affairs, 1939–1946. The Realignment of Europe*, edited by Arnold Toynbee and Veronica M. Toynbee (Oxford, Oxford University Press, 1955), in the *New Statesman and Nation*, 50, 1274 (6 August 1955).

Arnold Joseph Toynbee (1889–1975) was director of studies at the Royal Insitute of International Affairs (Chatham House), 1925–55, as well as research professor of international history in the University of London. He is best known for his twelve-volume opus *A Study of History* (Oxford, Oxford University Press, 1934–61), with its controversial 'challenge and response' interpretation of civilizations.

We are always being told that no records are left of the really important things in history; and the meetings of the Big Four at the Paris Peace Conference in 1919 are quoted to prove it. Lloyd George, Clemenceau, Wilson and Orlando met in private, and made their decisions without formality. We shall never know what really happened. But not at all. Full records have been there all the time. Sir Maurice (now Lord) Hankey acted as secretary of the Big Four for part of the time; and his papers were published by the Americans years ago. The British government also had a copy; but they apparently thought that it could not be published during the lifetime of Lloyd George. He has been dead ten years; British secrecy is still maintained. No matter. We now have something even better. Professor Paul Mantoux attended all the meetings as interpreter, and, with great foresight, recorded his notes for the benefit of the Quai d'Orsay every evening. They have now been published, and very good reading they make. The Big Four were talking with complete freedom, and Mantoux gives their talk just as it comes – vivid, rambling, convincing – a great improvement on Hankey's official rendering. We are a long way from Keynes's version of ignorant evil men. Instead we see high-minded statesmen, overwhelmed by their tasks but trying to do their best, trying above all to be fair.

They decided every disputed point in favour of Germany. The Saar; the left bank of the Rhine; Danzig; Silesia – in all these questions they devised settlements which, they believed, would lead to reconciliation. Lloyd George even said: 'France would go to war for Alsace tomorrow.

But should we go to war for Danzig?' Even on reparations they spent
their time cutting down the demands of their expert advisers. The
question which occupied them most was the Italian claim to Fiume,
and, though they failed to achieve a satisfactory settlement, their policy
compares favourably with the feeble shiftiness over Trieste of the peacemakers after the second war. There are endless fascinating details in
these volumes. The whole story of peacemaking in 1919 will have to be
re-written – a plum of a subject for some young historian of detached
gifts. But he must not expect any encouragement from the British government.

The latest volume of Foreign Office documents is small beer in comparison, not much more than a tidying-up operation. Volumes I to VII
in the third series covered relations with Germany from the annexation
of Austria to the outbreak of war in 1939. The two remaining volumes
(of which this is the first) cover more or less the same period in the Far
East. It is a story in a minor key. The British government had no forces
to spare. It balanced between provoking Japan on the one hand and
discouraging China on the other, and somehow scraped through without disaster. There is nothing here to confirm the excuse sometimes
peddled for the men of Munich that they were selling out in Europe in
order to have their hands free against Japan. Their policy, if anything,
was the reverse. But it would be truer to say that they had no policy one
way or the other except to hope that the storms would somehow blow
over. Here, too, a book will have to be written, digesting these documents and co-ordinating them with the information which the Americans
– of course! – published years ago. It will make a dreary story.

The latest volume in the Chatham House survey of the war years is
something between raw material and a digested narrative. Its theme is
what happened in the conquered countries of Europe when the Germans went away – a theme which began as liberation and ended as
partition, more or less disguised, between the two World Powers. Apart
from an opening chapter on the work of UNRRA [United Nations
Relief and Rehabilitation Administration, 1943–47], the book deals
with each country individually; the result is an encyclopaedia, not a
narrative that can be read with pleasure. It is also odd, though perhaps
inevitable, that Germany and Austria are left out, so that everything
revolves round an obscure, unmentioned vacuum. On the other hand
Professor Toynbee's introduction for once has some bearing on the
volume he is introducing: no cosmic ravings, no Biblical quotations,
instead a brilliant summing-up of the territorial and political changes
which followed the war. He asks again the well-worn question why the
Russians disrupted allied unity at the end of the war; thinks perhaps
that Poland was the explanation; but, like everyone else – including

perhaps the Russians? – confesses himself baffled. Mr Toynbee is a skilful commentator on the contemporary scene when he can bring himself to put off his prophet's robe.

CHAPTER THIRTY-TWO

After Versailles

This essay was first published as a review of *Documents on British Foreign Policy 1919–1939*, First Series, Vol. 6: *1919*, edited by Rohan Butler (London, HMSO, 1956), in the *New Statesman and Nation*, 52, 1341 (24 November 1956).

This unwieldy volume is the sixth and, fortunately, the last devoted to the record of British diplomacy in the second half of 1919 – that is, after the signature of the treaty of Versailles. The first part deals with Central Europe; the second with the Far East. It would have been more convenient to have the two parts in separate, and less expensive, volumes; but throughout the series the convenience of the reader has been little regarded. Indeed, the wisdom of publishing the documents on such a gigantic scale seems more and more doubtful. If everything is to be published, why not let students have a free run of the original archives? If some documents are still concealed, what happens to editorial integrity? The first part, in particular, is a brute to use. The Supreme Council in Paris was still dealing with many of the affairs of central Europe from Silesia to Hungary; and the present volume is only comprehensible if reference is constantly made to the earlier one which contains the proceedings of the Supreme Council.

There is much of great interest, often highly creditable to British policy. Its main concern was the economic restoration of central Europe, particularly of Vienna; and a good beginning was made here. In Hungary Sir George Clerk, acting on behalf of the Supreme Council, managed to restrain the Romanians and even arranged the one free election under universal suffrage which that sad country has ever enjoyed. He cannot be blamed for the later victory of Horthy and the White Terror. The information from British representatives in Germany is persistently sensible; that from Czechoslovakia already shows the lack of sympathy with Czech difficulties which was to mark British diplomacy throughout the interwar period.

The second part on the Far East has a different character. Here the Supreme Council had little concern. Curzon, the foreign secretary, knew little about Central Europe and cared less. He prided himself on being a Far Eastern expert; and there are some tremendous pieces here, recording the magisterial lectures which he delivered to the Japanese ambassador. The great dispute was over Shantung – the German concession which the Japanese had conquered and from which they now refused to withdraw. Concealed behind this was the yet greater problem – what course should British policy follow if Japan ran into serious conflict with the United States? The Foreign Office would have liked to have things both ways – to keep the Japanese alliance without offending the Americans. But it already foresaw that its hope was in vain: in the last resort Great Britain would have to go with America – regretfully, hesitantly, but inescapably all the same.

CHAPTER THIRTY-THREE

Collapse of Versailles:
The Moment of Crisis

This essay was first published as a review of *Documents on British Foreign Policy 1919–1939*, Second Series, Vol. 5: *1933*, edited by E.L. Woodward and Rohan Butler (London, HMSO, 1956), in the *Manchester Guardian* (10 December 1956).

The second series of documents from the Foreign Office was suspended in 1950 when the editor turned to the period immediately before the Second World War. Now it is resumed with a volume covering the six months from March to October, 1933. Its unwieldy bulk merits some excavation. This was the decisive moment when Europe set out on the road to catastrophe. Hitler announced his intention to break the shackles of Versailles. It would have been easy to arrest him. The former victors failed to do so; and the cost of opposing him grew higher on each subsequent occasion. Why did England and France let the favourable opportunity pass? Was it blindness, fear, or merely sloth? Something of all three, but perhaps most of all a reluctance to believe the evidence of their eyes. Time and again a statesman stated the problem plainly, drew the unwelcome conclusion, and then exclaimed that things could not really be as bad as that.

There is a good example here in a dispatch by Sir Eric Phipps from Berlin. This reports with unvarnished truth an interview with Hitler. Any reader must feel that nothing could stop Hitler's march to European supremacy short of a united resistance by the other powers. Phipps rubs this in. Then he draws back from the logic of his own argument and adds, still doubting, an optimistic conclusion:

> National socialism is a new faith composed of many ingredients. These include a certain idealism and sentimentality, and it may be that there are possibilities inherent in it which, if it survives, may ultimately prove of value in European politics. It must not be identified with the sterile German nationalism of 1914, from which Europe could expect nothing. With skilful handling Herr Hitler and his movement may be brought to contribute some new impulse to European development.

Baldwin expressed much the same hope that something would turn up when he made one of his rare utterances on foreign affairs:

He could not conceive that European countries were going to allow one country to convert Europe once again into a butcher's shop. If that situation arose, His Majesty's Government would have to consider it very seriously.

Disarmament

The British government were not ignorant of what was happening in Germany. On the contrary, they were persistently and accurately informed. But even the most critical reports also contained the hope that Hitler would come to his senses or that the moderate elements in Germany would reassert themselves.

In March, 1933, when the volume opens, the British government still regarded French obstinacy as the main stumbling-block in the way of disarmament. The Four-Power Pact which Italy initiated was welcome to them mainly as a device for exerting pressure on France; at the same time they hoped that Mussolini would win over Hitler to his own position as a tame elephant. Ramsay MacDonald was an enthusiast for Fascist achievement:

> France and Great Britain were old-fashioned. Unless they put new energy into their countries such as he had seen in Rome, they would be overwhelmed. Lenin, dead in the Kremlin, was keeping Russia awake, and Mussolini was reanimating Italy.

MacDonald wrote to Mussolini in his inimitable style:

> I am still as keen as ever I was that your efforts to stabilise the politics of Europe on the basis you contemplate should be crowned with success. There are difficulties, of course, and you, as a realist, no doubt see them clearly. But we have to take the world as we find it and then make the best of it. You and I have had to do this so often that it depresses neither of us to do it again.

The Four-Power Pact soon faded into oblivion. It was impossible to agree with Italy even over the defence of Austrian independence. There is a remarkable memorandum here of 28 August by Sir Robert Vansittart, in which he argues for a united front over Austria. But even this clear-sighted observer underrated the burden of resisting Hitler. The most that he advocates is an economic boycott; and the only difficulty he foresees is that Russia will not observe it. He adds cheerfully:

> This is an obstacle, but not a prohibitive objection. Some intertrading between two bankrupts would not long mask the defeat of Hitler.

Even this was too strong for the government. A telegram of 12 September sums up all the delays of these sad years:

> The Cabinet considered the whole question of Austro-German re-
> lations on September 5, and although no definite decisions were
> taken the general view was that if it were decided that we must
> take some initiative, we should not be drawn in the direction of
> referring the question to the League ... His Majesty's Government
> do not propose to take a decision on such an important and
> difficult question without considering it in all its aspects.

Squaring the circle

Again and again the British government tried to square the circle. They
sought in vain some formula which would seem to offer equality to
Germany without lessening the security of France. Such a solution did
not exist. In the end they devised the idea of a probationary period.
Germany had infringed the existing restrictions upon her. She was now
to be given a second chance for four years. If she kept her word, all
would be well; equality would follow. But if she did not, what then?
This vital question was discussed with the French ministers on 22
September. Daladier asked 'what guarantees there would be of the
observance of the Convention? He apologised for bringing up the question, but it was necessary to be quite clear'. Sir John Simon gave a firm
British answer:

> His Majesty's Government could not accept new responsibilities in
> the nature of sanctions under the new agreement. Public opinion in
> England would not tolerate it. His Majesty's Government could
> offer to co-operate, however, in making it quite clear that the
> second period could only come into force if the first were observed.
> The gravity of the situation then arising would affect His Majesty's
> Government as much as the French Government, and he did not
> suggest that they would disregard it or dissociate themselves from
> it, but he could not consider putting anything in the nature of new
> sanctions into the present document.

Baldwin endorsed this statement adding the characteristic remark: 'He
had not been in touch with His Majesty's Government as he had been
on holiday ... The subject in question had been on his mind during his
holiday.'

On 4 October Mr Eden took the same line to the French ambassador:

> I hoped that the French Government had not still any expectation
> of any new departure on our part as to sanctions. Not only His
> Majesty's Government but the British nation were unalterably op-
> posed to undertaking any new commitments on the continent of
> Europe ... If a new commitment was what the French Government
> really desired then clearly no form of words could bridge the gap.

By this time the British government had lost all faith in Hitler's word. They had no longer any sympathy with German grievances or any hope that she would settle down as a civilized state. But they clung desperately to their line of 'no new commitment'. Someone else must find a solution or pay the penalty. They could offer only endless procrastination. Their ambition was not that the Disarmament Conference should succeed but only that it should go on and on and on. They still hoped that the French by some new twist would 'reanimate' the discussions.

Instead Hitler kicked the bottom from under the conference. On 14 October he announced Germany's withdrawal from the Disarmament Conference and from the League of Nations. The long chase after phrases was over. Disarmament, security, peace became empty words overnight. Yet words were the only weapons in the armoury of the British government. They went on mouthing the old words and coining new ones. But Hitler had turned the decisive corner. The settlement of Versailles was in ruins. Post-war history ended; and pre-war history began. If we seek to pin down the moment of crisis, it was that September afternoon when Baldwin revealed the broodings which had occupied his holiday.

CHAPTER THIRTY-FOUR

How Hitler Went to War: The German Record

This essay was first published as a review of *Documents on German Foreign Policy 1918–1945*, Series D, Vol. 7: *The Last Days of Peace, August 9– September 3, 1939* (London, HMSO, 1957), in the *Manchester Guardian* (19 February 1957). In this essay Alan Taylor firmly states that 'the date for the outbreak of war (with Poland) had already been fixed', with Hitler 'relentlessly set on war with Poland'.

The German Foreign Ministry has now yielded all its secrets on the outbreak of the Second World War, so far as it had any. The latest volume, published by a joint team of British, American and French editors, opens on 8 August 1939, when Weizsäcker, the German secretary of state, made 'a serious oral communication' to the Polish chargé d'affaires. It ends on 3 September when Great Britain and France fulfilled their pledge to Poland, a little tardily, by declaring war on Germany. It would be unreasonable to expect sensational revelations. The most important documents have already been used at the Nuremberg trials and on other occasions. Nevertheless it is good to have them in their setting.

The volume makes a strange contrast with the similar collection on German diplomacy in July 1914. Then William II, the central figure, spattered the documents with emotional comments: and we can follow every wavering of his erratic mind. In 1939 Hitler was relentlessly set on war with Poland and ignored the diplomatic turmoil. He took no personal part in the intrigues at Danzig, which were handled by Ribbentrop. It is indeed puzzling why the Germans went through all the diplomatic palaver against Poland when the date for the outbreak of war had already been fixed. Were the Nazi leaders trying to set themselves right with history or satisfying their consciences? Did the Foreign Ministry perhaps hope until the last moment to give Hitler what he wanted without war? Or was it just the routine continuation of functions which had lost all purpose?

Sleepwalker

Probably the last. Hitler had bluffed before. It seems inconceivable that this time any peaceful triumph would have satisfied him. He advanced towards war, according to his own phrase, with the certainty of a sleepwalker, and was unaffected when some of his calculations went awry. On 12 August he was still 'absolutely convinced that the Western democracies would, in the last resort, recoil from unleashing a general war'. This conviction was not surprising when Roden Buxton was trailing offers of appeasement round Berlin on 16 August, or when Sir Nevile Henderson could say to Hitler, as late as 23 August: 'The hostile attitude to Germany did not represent the will of the British people. It was the work of Jews and enemies of the Nazis.' The British ratification of the alliance with Poland on 25 August perhaps made Hitler hesitate, but only for a moment. He merely shifted his ground. He had held that Great Britain and France would not go to war; and in this he was wrong. He now held that they would not wage war seriously: and in this he was right until June 1940.

Hitler's conviction that Russia would remain neutral was equally absolute, though for long without facts to justify it. On 14 August the 'most reliable source' in London which had given the Germans every detail of the Anglo-Soviet negotiations reported: 'The Soviet Government have given so many signs of their desire to conclude the agreement that there can no longer be any doubt that it will be definitely achieved.' And again on 17 August: 'The Anglo-French-Soviet Russian military negotiations are so far advanced that conversations with the Polish General Staff can be opened. Poland, who has hitherto shown reserve towards attempts to offer her Soviet assistance, now declares herself ready to open conversations.' These reports had no effect on Hitler. He had already decided that things would happen otherwise. On 12 August a telegram from Moscow was brought in during his conversation with Ciano: and Ciano was told: 'The Russians agreed to a German political negotiator being sent to Moscow.' Sir Lewis Namier long ago dismissed this telegram as a 'concoction'; and, though he was much criticized, the present volume confirms his suspicion. There was no telegram from Moscow; and Molotov agreed to a visit from Ribbentrop only on 19 August. The rational explanation would be that Hitler had some secret, intractable line of contact with Stalin: yet this is unlikely. Hitler simply guessed, and once again he guessed right.

The Nazi–Soviet pact gave the final push to war, but it was not as decisive as some writers have made out. Russia would have remained neutral, pact or no pact, and Hitler would have gone to war even without a firm promise of Russian neutrality. Indeed what was the value of the pact to either Hitler or Stalin, since both had shown time and again that their promises were worthless? The Germans really hoped to pull Soviet Russia into collaboration; and the Russians were equally determined not to be committed. On 28 August the German ambassador complained to Molotov about rumours that Soviet troops were being moved away from the Polish frontier. Molotov 'laughed heartily' and said 'So much nonsense was published in the press nowadays that one could not concern oneself with all of it'.

'Minsk'

There is, however, one little piece of evidence which indeed damns the Soviet government as collaborators. On 1 September the Luftwaffe asked that the Minsk Broadcasting Station should provide navigational aid by sending out agreed signals. The reply came from Moscow: 'The Minsk Broadcasting Station will introduce as often as possible the word "Minsk" during the course of its programme, which could be extended by two hours for this purpose ... The Soviet Government would prefer to omit the addition of a call-sign, so as to avoid attracting attention.' This was an infamous transaction.

The real effect of the Nazi–Soviet pact was on Hitler's allies, not on his opponents. The Japanese were so angry that they broke off negotiations for a military agreement and threatened to abandon the German side altogether. Mussolini also backed away, though from fear of war rather than from dislike of Soviet Russia. On 25 August his boastings faded into the admission that Italy would be ready for war only in 1942. Oddly enough, Mussolini's defection was the one bit of reality which made some impact on Hitler during these crazy weeks. It, and not the Anglo-Polish alliance, led him to call off the war, though only for twenty-four hours. He wrote to Mussolini two and three times a day and was tormented by the increasingly evasive answers. In the end, he resigned himself to the belief that neutral Italy would be as great a nuisance to Great Britain and France as if she were in the war – again, a correct conclusion. Yet the Axis somehow represented the one illusion which Hitler insisted on retaining in spite of repeated buffetings.

A minor amusement of these volumes is to come across the casual indiscretions of British statesmen. A report of 28 August gives a remark alleged to have been made by Sir Samuel Hoare before the Cabinet meeting: 'Although we cannot in the circumstances avoid declaring war, we can always fulfil the letter of a declaration of war without immediately going all out.' An appendix, sweeping up material missed in earlier volumes, gives a message allegedly sent to Hitler by Lord Halifax on 18 July 1938: 'I, as English Foreign Minister, aim to get so far in my lifetime that one day the Führer will be seen entering Buckingham Palace at the side of the King of England.'

CHAPTER THIRTY-FIVE

Feebler and Feebler

This essay was first published as a review of *Documents on British Foreign Policy 1919–1939*, Second Series, Vol. 6: *1933–4*, edited by E.L. Woodward and Rohan Butler (London, HMSO, 1957), in the *Manchester Guardian* (31 May 1957).

This volume of records from the Foreign Office covers one of the saddest periods in British policy. It begins on 1 November 1933, just after Germany had left the Disarmament Conference. It ends in August 1934 with the conference abandoned and nothing devised to take its place. The endless schemes for enticing Germany back to the conference are not worth cataloguing. They all have a single theme: demanding more concessions from the French. Yet Hitler clearly had no further interest in an agreement unless it gave him all he wanted. The Foreign Office imagined (No. 363) that Germany would still pay a price for having her armaments legalized. On the contrary, it was she who demanded a price, as Eden pointed out on one occasion: 'The only alternatives I can see are preventive war or unlimited and uncontrolled German rearmament. We cannot contemplate the former, and surely we do not want to contemplate the latter.' The British simply gave way to whichever party caused most trouble. For a long time it was Hitler. But when Barthou became French foreign minister and took a strong line, they gave in to him instead. Not only did they acquiesce in the negotiations for a Franco-Soviet pact. They themselves suggested that Soviet Russia should be invited to become a guarantor of Locarno, though refusing on their side to undertake any commitments in Eastern Europe. The next stage of British policy was being unconsciously drawn: an Anglo-French alliance in the West, but rejection of Russia as partner in a general security system. A private letter (No. 196) well expressed the British view of the league:

> We have never believed very strongly in the League as policeman. What we looked for in the League was rather the machinery which should enable the Governments of the world, by frank discussion, to devise before it was too late some peaceful means of settling every dispute in which in most cases there is a good deal of right on either side and in which in any case butchery settles nothing.

Yet the British government was kept accurately informed concerning the true nature of Nazi policy. On one such report, Sir John Simon commented helplessly: 'This is the most illuminating document – and terrifying.'

CHAPTER THIRTY-SIX

Out of the Diplomatic Bag

This essay was first published as a review of *Documents on German Foreign Policy 1918–1945*, Series C, Vol. 1: *The Third Reich: First Phase, January 30–October 14, 1933* (London, HMSO, 1958), and *Documents on British Foreign Policy 1919–1939*, First Series, Vol. 12: *1920*, edited by Rohan Butler and J.P.T. Bury (London, HMSO, 1958), in the *Manchester Guardian* (14 February 1958).

Constantin von Neurath (1873–1956) was an aristocratic diplomat, whose posts included ambassador in Londin, 1930–32. He was foreign minister under von Papen (1932–33) and under Hitler (1933–37). Ulrich von Hassell (1881–1944), another aristocratic diplomat, was ambassador in Rome (1932–38). He took part in the July 1944 bomb plot against Hitler and was hanged after its failure. Alexandre Millerand (1859–1943) succeeded Georges Clemenceau as prime minister (January–October 1920) and was then president (1920–24).

When the German archives fell into allied hands it was originally intended to publish a full selection from the end of the first war to the end of the second. The British, American, and French governments are now more modest. Covering the whole period would take too long and maybe cost too much. The Weimar period has been sliced off the beginning; the years after Pearl Harbor have been omitted at the end. These seem sensible decisions. The Weimar records will soon be available to students on microfilm: and the German Foreign Ministry counted for virtually nothing in the last years of the Reich. All that remains of the old scheme are the misleading dates in the general title; and the description, Series C, for what is in fact the beginning of the collection. Still, the principle is easy to grasp; and a little confusion is better than making us spend money on unnecessary volumes.

The present volume opens on the day Hitler took power and ends with the German withdrawal from the League of Nations and this Disarmament Conference. These were the months when Hitler was playing himself in; parading his respectability and learning how the machine of government worked. For anyone acclimatized by documents of later years, when policy was settled hugger-mugger by Hitler on impulse, it is a shock to find him presiding over formal cabinet meetings and summing up just like any democratic prime minister. Yet coming events cast their shadow before. Hitler reined himself in with difficulty; and it is already possible to detect his divergence from 'respectable' German foreign policy. The professional diplomatists – Neurath, the under-secretaries, and the ambassadors – certainly aimed at the overthrow

of the Versailles system. By this they meant equality of status in armaments and, on the territorial side, the destruction of the Polish Corridor.
Hassell for instance, wrote on 24 September: 'The most important goal
is rearmament ... The next aim is to do away with our mutilation in the
East.' These professionals feared isolation. Their policy rested on friendship with Italy and Soviet Russia, the other 'revisionist' powers: and
they hoped also gradually to detach England from France.

Hitler pretended to agree to all this, but he never lived up to his fine
words. Friendship with England? Certainly, but not at the price of
slowing down the anti-Semitic programme. He accepted the Four-Power
Pact and talked about the ideological ties with Italy. But when it came
to restraining the Austrian Nazis for Mussolini's sake he would not
yield an inch. Most interesting is his behaviour towards Russia. The
German Foreign Ministry and the German generals did their best to
maintain the old co-operation. The Russians, on their side, were suspicious and full of complaints. They were met by promises, never by
action. Finally, Bülow, secretary of state, took the question of Russian
relations to the cabinet. The ministers approved his sensible statement.
Hitler, however, waved it aside: 'The Russian Government will never
forgive Germany for our having smashed communism in Germany ... In
the relations with Russia the liabilities have always exceeded the profits.' With sublime self-confidence, Hitler did not fear isolation. Hence
the cool way in which he broke with the League of Nations. Oddly
enough, the grievance he felt least deeply was the Polish Corridor. The
war against Poland was from his point of view a mishap; the war
against Soviet Russia was the real thing.

Some readers study these volumes for scandal. There is not much
here: only a survey of British feeling towards Germany. The alleged
pro-Germans are such old friends as Lord Lloyd, Lord Rothermere,
and the Prince of Wales. Queen Mary is a new name on the list.
George V, on the other hand, 'has become more and more critical in
his attitude towards the German revolution'. There are other enjoy-
able judgements. Sympathy for Germany was stronger in the army
than the navy. The clergy, led by the Archbishop of Canterbury 'have
boundless admiration for the moral and ethical side of the National
Socialist programme, its clear-cut stand for religion and Christianity,
and its ethical principles, such as its fight against cruelty to animals,
vivisection, sexual offences, &c'. The intellectuals, however, were hope-
less: they showed 'a dull opposition to Fascism', 'a degree of obstinacy
that seems to me to offer little hope of an early change of feeling'. The
working class 'coincides here with the followers of Marxism and trade
unionism'. And then there is the usual rigmarole about cultural exchanges, sport fixtures, and so on. But it is drab, vague stuff: the kind

of nonsense that all ambassadors have to write in order to fill their waking hours.

In 1920 the victorious allies still felt themselves masters of the world, though their confidence waned from day to day. On 12 February the Conference of London took up the unfinished business left over from the great meeting at Paris the year before. It continued to meet until 10 April. The present volume of 'Documents on British Foreign Policy, 1919–39', gives the full record as kept by the British secretary. Most of it is new to the public eye, though Lloyd George (who never showed any respect for the Official Secrets Act) published some extracts in his later vindication. The main purpose was to draft peace terms for Turkey, but the conference ranged over every topic in the world. The record begins with a squabble over the meeting-place, with Lloyd George insisting that, while he had spent seven months in Paris to please Clemenceau, it was now time others settled in London to please him. Then there was the Anglo-French row over Mosul, the French repudiating the gentlemen's agreement of December 1918 (as the British had already repudiated that over the Rhineland). On the other hand, both powers wanted to keep others out of the oil fields and puzzled how this could be done without breaking the rules for mandates. Lloyd George put it clearly: 'Anything the Allies could do to prevent the United States entering these territories, with the support of possibly Germany and Russia, was greatly to be desired.' Another of his remarks shows the general irritation at American withdrawal from peace-making: 'The Americans appeared to assume responsibility for the sole guardianship of the Ten Commandments and for the Sermon on the Mount; yet, when it came to a practical question of assistance and responsibility, they absolutely refused to accept it'.

Most fascinating are the disputes between Lloyd George and Millerand over the policy to be adopted towards Soviet Russia. Millerand wanted a war of intervention, though others would have to fight it. Lloyd George pressed for recognition: 'was not afraid of Bolshevism as long as people had plenty of food'; and offended the French by drawing a parallel with the war of intervention against the Jacobins. There are many other topics of lasting interest: Fiume, the Kapp Putsch, the proposed trial of the ex-kaiser. The central theme of peace with Turkey, which takes up most of the book, is, however, uninteresting in the highest degree. The admirable resolve to print everything is carried to a pitch of absurdity when we are offered this mountainous documentation of a peace treaty that is not only dead but was stillborn. Even the most ingenious student will shrink from manufacturing a thesis on the Treaty of Sèvres.

CHAPTER THIRTY-SEVEN

Foreign Relations

This essay was first published as a review of *Documents on British Foreign Policy 1919–1939*, edited by E.L. Woodward and Rohan Butler, Second Series, Vol. 7: *1929–1934* (London, HMSO, 1958), in the *Manchester Guardian* (3 April 1958). Louis Barthou, who was foreign secretary and a right-wing figure in the national government, was killed when King Alexander of Yugoslavia was assassinated in Marseille in October 1934.

The great questions which occupied diplomacy a quarter of a century ago now seem dead indeed. German reparations; the Disarmament Conference; Hitler's intentions – these have some interest, perhaps, for the historian. But we do not read the records from the Foreign Office with excited surprise. The present volume is tedious in a different way. It presents the single theme of Anglo-Soviet relations from their renewal in 1929 until the entry of the Soviet Union into the League of Nations in 1934. The theme is oppressive from its actuality, not from its remoteness. The conversations might have taken place yesterday: the same reports are no doubt still coming from the British ambassador in Moscow. Studying Anglo-Soviet relations is a life-sentence on the treadmill: an endless round of incomprehension. There is little here of policy in the usual sense of the term. The Labour government of 1929 had no idea of bringing Soviet Russia back into the family of nations when it resumed relations in 1929, its only motive, apart from satisfying the Left-wing, was to make trading conditions easier. But at once the weary disputes of 1924 were renewed also: tsarist debts, Comintern propaganda. These things were wrangled over surely from obstinacy and routine. Even in the Foreign Office no one can have hoped for a settlement or a solution. It was pointless to ask the Russian rulers to stop being communists; and therefore pointless to demand the stopping of Communist propaganda. Litvinov – the most attractive character in the volume, by the way – remarked cheerfully of the Comintern: 'Why don't you take the thing? You are a free country. We do not want it here. Do arrange for it to hold its sessions in London.' This was not a helpful suggestion.

The bulkiest subject in the volume is the arrest and trial of the Metropolitan-Vickers engineers. The details add little to our existing knowledge; and the contemporary puzzle remains unsolved – why did the Soviet rulers do it? There can be no shadow of doubt that the engineers were altogether innocent of the charges made against them, otherwise the Soviet government would not have climbed down so readily. It rather looks as though the affair had been mistimed. Until January, 1933, Great Britain was the chief imperialist villain in Soviet eyes; and if discontent at home needed the diversion of foreign wreckers on trial Englishmen were the appropriate victims. But the arrests only took place in March; and by then Soviet apprehensions had switched against Hitler. Hence the half-hearted conduct of the trial and the shamefaced evasions when it was over. Of course the British embargo had its effect also, particularly when the Soviet government was trying to liquidate their German commitments with sterling. However, this is surmise. On paper the affair still seems senseless. The British spokesmen from Sir John Simon to Mr Strang come out of it very well. The story, however, leaves a regret that the foreign secretary and others had none of this admirable resolution left over when it came to dealing with Hitler.

The final chapter sounds a rather different note. French diplomacy under Barthou was trying to make Soviet Russia a real factor in European affairs; and the British government had to trail along behind – acquiescing in French plans, yet sceptical as to their value. In fact the events of 1934 were a foretaste of 1939. France would have liked to pull Great Britain and the Soviet Union closer together. Both resisted: and the French had no strength with which to pull. We are back once more on the old treadmill.

CHAPTER THIRTY-EIGHT

Lloyd George in Action

This essay was first published as a review of *Documents on British Foreign Policy 1919–39*, First Series, Vol. 8: *International Conferences on High Policy 1920*, edited by Rohan Butler (London, HMSO, 1959), in the *Manchester Guardian* (3 April 1959).

The new volume of documents from the British Foreign Office well illustrates the folly of the 'fifty-year' rule, which keeps the archives sealed until the life has departed from them. If these documents had been published some twenty years ago no damaging secrets would have been revealed or hard feelings caused. But they would still have had relevance to political issues. They might have helped towards a better understanding with Soviet Russia; they would have been a useful reminder of the underlying problems in relations between France and Germany; they would even have been a warning against distributing guarantees which could not be fulfilled. Now, who cares about German coal deliveries or the future of Smyrna or even about the Russo-Polish War? All that keeps these records alive is the personality of Lloyd George. They present a wonderful picture of Lloyd George in action, the statesman of infinite resource, able – as Tom Jones said – to charm a bird off a branch, but himself always unmoved. In 1920 Lloyd George was at the height of his power. He ran British foreign policy almost alone. Curzon, the foreign secretary, trailing after him like a humble Foreign Office clerk. He was the only European statesman who had held office all through the war and the only survivor of the Big Four who had made the peace settlement of 1919. He strove at one international gathering after another to produce reconciliation from his conjurer's hat. Sometimes he would threaten, sometimes cajole. He would denounce Germany as the arch-aggressor at one time; deplore the unnecessary misunderstandings with her at another. He was the man of order and a near-Bolshevik. One can understand why he insisted on a careful recording being taken at all these meetings. Otherwise he could never have remembered what he had said from one day to the next.

The Spa conference – the first which the Germans attended – is a wonderful example of his methods. He ran over with sympathy for French grievances and French demands; yet at the same time explained to the Germans how unreasonable the French were being. Almost to the last movement he gave the impression that he favoured an occupation of the Ruhr, thus flattering the French and frightening the Germans. Then, pulling out his watch, he more or less dictated an agreement with half an hour to go; and the contestants found it hard to decide which of them had been diddled. Another beautiful example is Armenia, where President Wilson was invited to determine the frontiers as mediator. When Wilson proposed generous lines, the very existence of the Armenia was shrugged aside, the fault quietly shifted from the allies to the United States.

The gravest problem covered in this volume was the Russo-Polish War. There are full records of Lloyd George's discussions with the Soviet representatives, Kamenev and Krassin, as well as with the French and other allied powers. Lloyd George was operating from weakness. He knew perfectly well that neither Great Britain nor any other ally could do anything effective to help the Poles. On the other hand he could not win over the Bolsheviks by a promise of allied recognition, owing to French insistence on the pre-revolution Russian debts. In the end he had a stroke of luck; the Poles won without assistance. Lloyd George could emerge both as the man who had saved Europe and the man who had saved the peace. It was a remarkable performance. Lloyd George once said that he would as soon go for a walk with a grasshopper as co-operate with Lord Northcliffe. But Northcliffe was not the only grasshopper on the political scene.

CHAPTER THIRTY-NINE

Some Awkward Questions

This essay was first published as a review of *Documents on Foreign Policy 1919–1939*, Second Series, Vol. 8: *Chinese Questions 1929–31*, edited by Rohan Butler and J.P.T. Bury, assisted by M.E. Lambert (London, HMSO, 1960), in the *Guardian* (19 February 1960).

Many volumes of the *Documents on British Foreign Policy 1919–1939* have been heavy going. The latest is perhaps the heaviest. It is by no means without interest, but on a remote and somewhat specialized subject. Its theme is 'Chinese Questions 1929–1931'. These fall under two headings. First there are long, and incredibly complicated, negotiations with the Chinese government, principally over the surrender of British extra-territorial rights. No conclusion was reached, in spite of goodwill on one side and subtlety on the other. The second question was more important. It was the problem raised by the Japanese action in Manchuria. The British government has been much blamed for its failure to assert the authority of the League of Nations over this. For the first time we have the materials for judging British policy more fairly. The British wished to strengthen the moral authority of the league. But how? Of course, it would be a fine thing if the Japanese were told to leave Manchuria and obeyed. But what if they did not? This was an awkward question: and had consequences which were more than awkward later on.

CHAPTER FORTY

Conflict at Versailles – and After

This essay was first published as a review of *Documents on British Foreign Policy 1919–1939*, First Series, Vol. 9: *Germany, 1920*, edited by Rohan Butler (London, HMSO, 1960), in the *Guardian* (6 May 1960).

The German problem has been with us for a long time. Forty years ago the victorious allies were already puzzled where to strike a balance between firmness and conciliation. A new volume of *Documents on British Foreign Policy 1919–1939* covers this problem in the early months of 1920, when the Treaty of Versailles first came into force. Though there are no startling revelations, the documents give a clear picture of the conflicting trends. The general staff, for instance, submitted a recommendation that the British Government should promote revision in order to assist the forces of moderation in Germany. On the other hand, Sir Henry Wilson, chief of the imperial general staff, believed that the Germans were already within sight of victory in a new war. Headlam-Morley, the historical adviser to the Foreign Office, was also in favour of relaxing the provisions of the treaty even before it had begun to work. The government was embarrassed by such recommendations – ready to find fault with the treaty, yet unable to repudiate what was in part its own handiwork.

The great insoluble question was already raised. The treaty of Versailles had been signed by the Germans. Its clauses over the demilitarization of the Rhineland and war criminals would work only if the Germans made them work. What were the allies to do if the Germans failed to carry out their promises? The French favoured coercing the Germans. But to what purpose? Only to secure the signing of another promise which would be disregarded in its turn. The British did not know what to do. They told the Germans to execute the treaty; but they also told the French that it was no good trying to enforce a treaty which the Germans did not respect. In April the Germans sent armed forces into the Ruhr to restore order after the Kapp putsch. This was a breach of the treaty. The French answered by extending their own occupation of the Rhineland. There was a fierce Anglo-French dispute, generously recorded here in Lord Curzon's most opulent prose.

One interesting point emerges: the workers of the Ruhr welcomed the French forces as protection against the German reactionaries. French intervention, far from weakening German democracy, helped to sustain it. This was overlooked by the British government, as it has been subsequently ignored by British writers. Instead the British tried to conciliate the Germans; and it is clear, in spite of laboured denials, that the British offers in Berlin were misleadingly sympathetic towards German military quarters.

The other great conflict was over the trial of war-criminals. The German government refused to surrender them. The French favoured trial in absentia; the British were prepared to leave the trials to the Germans themselves, and carried the day. This volume contains the masterly advocacy with which Lord Birkenhead put the British case – one of the greatest accomplishments even by that remarkable man. Finally, the volume gives the prolonged wrangle with the Dutch government over the extradition of the kaiser, so that he too could be tried. The Dutch, with some hesitation, took a brave line of independence and refused to surrender him. The British government aired all sorts of notions for coercing the Dutch – exclusion from the League of Nations, economic sanctions, blockade of the Dutch colonies. In the end the British merely expressed their displeasure. The kaiser remained at Doorn.

CHAPTER FORTY-ONE

Germany's Breakthrough

This essay was first published as a review of *Documents in German Foreign Policy 1918–1945*, Series C, Vol. 4: *The Third Reich: First Phase, April 1, 1935–March 4, 1936* (London, HMSO, 1962), in the *Observer* (30 December 1962). This essay, written after Alan Taylor's *The Origins of the Second World War* (London, Hamish Hamilton, 1961), echoes a theme in his book: 'Others provided the opportunity for Hitler: he duly took advantage of it.'

Diplomatic documents are an acquired taste, like Greek wine or frogs' legs. This volume is a mountain of dreary stuff: 600 documents occupying over 1,200 pages. Most of them are routine business. The professional diplomatists were still running things. Hitler was watching and waiting, until his dramatic decision to reoccupy the Rhineland at the end of the volume. There is one piece of light relief: the report by the Duke of Saxe-Coburg of his visit to England for the funeral of George V.

The Duke was a grandson of Queen Victoria. He claimed to have been at Eton with Duff Cooper, Eden and, surprisingly, with Neville Chamberlain. His conversations are entertaining, though trivial and probably imaginary. Thus he reported Edward VIII as saying:

> An alliance Germany–Britain is an urgent necessity and a guiding principle for British foreign policy ... The League of Nations was a farce ... Who is King here? Baldwin or I? I myself wish to talk to Hitler, and will do so here or in Germany.

Eden said: 'England was in no way anti-German or anti-Italian. England desired peace at all costs.' Duff Cooper: 'That Germany and England should collaborate, and that France should be drawn in, seemed to him the only possibility for maintaining peace ... The League of Nations was, in its present state, impossible.' 'Chaimberlain (*sic*) hates Russia.' Mr Astor, Editor of *The Times* (*sic*), 'abused Roosevelt, who, in his opinion, was establishing a new kind of Communism in America'.

On a more serious level, the volume treats of the vital year when Germany broke the ring which had seemed to be forming against her. In the early months of 1935, Germany was faced with the Stresa front of France, Great Britain and Italy. She was also restrained by the Franco-Soviet pact. Her first initiative was the naval agreement with Great Britain, by which the German navy, apart from submarines, was limited to 35 per cent of the British. This did not basically alter the diplomatic situation. Germany's position improved with the Abyssinian crisis.

Mussolini relaxed his guard over Austria. The British and French sought to involve Germany in sanctions.

The documents do much to explain British policy. The British government wanted to try out the League of Nations as a non-violent means of preventing war. If this succeeded, well and good; if it failed, as they thought it would, they would be free from the embarrassment caused by the Peace Ballot, and could pursue a more 'realistic' line. Hence their policy was 'all sanctions short of war', a policy endorsed by the general election. This meant in practice only such sanctions as Mussolini did not object to. As early as 26 September Hoare promised Mussolini that Great Britain would neither close the Suez Canal nor stop Italy's oil.

A deal was envisaged all along. On 8 November Vansittart told the German Ambassador that a compromise would be produced 'in the second half of December', when the Negus had been sufficiently tamed. This compromise was the Hoare–Laval plan – not a sudden aberration, but the logical development of British policy. Public opinion intervened; and the British government had to go on pretending to take the League of Nations seriously, much to their regret. Could they have done anything else? Only if they had given France a watertight guarantee to resist remilitarisation of the Rhineland; and this, they knew, would be repudiated by British opinion.

This was Hitler's opportunity. The British were angered at French hesitations against Italy; the French at British equivocations over the Rhineland. Mussolini was angered at the continuation of sanctions. Belgium, the remaining participant in Locarno, wanted to back out of the whole affair in order to get a German guarantee of Eupen and Malmedy.

On 12 February 1936 Hitler made up his mind. Hitherto he had intended to wait until 1937, when the German army would be stronger, and Russia perhaps distracted by a conflict with France. Now he proposed to use the French ratification of the Franco-Soviet pact as his pretext. But it was only an excuse. His real motive was the continuing dispute between Italy and her former friends: and particularly the fear that this dispute might be brought to an end, either by a fresh compromise or by an Italian conquest of Abyssinia.

Hitler later called the reoccupation of the Rhineland his greatest gamble. It was a gamble in which the cards had been stacked beforehand in his favour. The British had virtually told him to go ahead. Mussolini wanted to see France humiliated. It was obvious that the French would not fight alone. The consequences too, were obvious. France lost her influence in Eastern Europe. Mussolini had to go over to the German side, as the only means of obtaining security on the Brenner.

Others provided the opportunity for Hitler: he duly took advantage of it. The fate of Europe was shaped by Mussolini's absurd desire to build an empire in Africa, and by the equally absurd attempt of others to stop him.

Part IV

From the Prelude of the Second World War to Cold War

CHAPTER FORTY-TWO

American Foreign Policy

This essay was first published as a review of W.L. Langer and S.E. Gleason, *The Challenge to Isolation 1937–1940* (London, Royal Institute of International Affairs, 1952), in the *Manchester Guardian* (8 April 1952).

The people of a democratic community have a right to know the motives and methods of foreign policy, particularly when it lands them in a great war. But how to present them? This is one of the greatest problems for a contemporary historian. In this country we are still using the old-fashioned way of publishing the official records from the Foreign Office; a great deal of twaddling material has come out, at the taxpayer's expense, and the springs of policy are still largely obscure. The American Council on Foreign Relations has tried a different approach. It has engaged two distinguished historians to write the full record of American foreign policy from Roosevelt's first initiative in 1937 until the victory of 1945. They have used all the printed material and have had the free run of the papers in the State Department, Roosevelt's own papers, and the relevant material on the military side.

Of course the two writers would not have been given this free run had they not proved their political reliability; but no one can complain that they have hesitated to express their opinions. They have not pulled their punches. Where there was muddle they have shown the muddle; where there was illusion they have rubbed it in. They have not been content with the official record. They have tried to show the development of American public opinion as well as of policy. The result is incomparably the best account of international affairs at the opening of the Second World War. The English reader may complain that the authors have a soft spot for Vichy (Professor Langer once wrote a defence of America's 'Vichy policy'). Apart from this, he can only praise this brilliant analysis of the development of foreign policy in a democracy. The whole work will be four volumes of 800 pages each. They will be heavy going, but worth it. The authors could not have discharged their task in less.

The present volume works out as a vindication of Roosevelt, though of his character rather than of his vision. No more than anyone else did he foresee the full American commitment that would be finally involved; and his methods were fantastically casual. But he meant to keep the free world going somehow. We could say of him what Cromwell said of himself: 'He goes furthest who knows not whither he is going.' At the beginning he thought that Hitler could be restrained by moral pressure: 'We have put the bee on him.' He was offended and estranged by Chamberlain's scepticism at this moral approach. In one sense Chamberlain was right. Roosevelt could offer nothing; he could not move faster than the American people. But the essential thing was to bring the American people to move; and only Roosevelt could do it. As late as July 1940 he said: 'If we want to keep out of his war, the longer we keep the British going, that much longer we stay out of this war.' Curiously enough, this is exactly what Stalin said to Sir Stafford Cripps at just the same time.

Roosevelt sometimes had doubts whether the British would keep going; and these doubts were strengthened by Kennedy, his ambassador in London, and his appeasing friends. Indeed, Stalin had more faith in Great Britain than had Roosevelt or some of the British themselves. But Roosevelt's doubts had ended by August 1940 when he made the destroyers-for-bases deal. This was the great significance of Dunkirk and the Battle of Britain. It led America to make 'the great commitment'. Roosevelt moved slowly and had to have his mind made up by events; but no one can read this book without being clear at the end that he was a great man.

CHAPTER FORTY-THREE

Roosevelt and the War

This essay was first published as a review entitled 'A Devil's Advocate: Roosevelt and the War' of Charles Callan Tansill, *Back Door to War – Roosevelt's Foreign Policy 1933–41* (Chicago, Henry Regnery, 1952), in the *Manchester Guardian* (24 October 1952).

The Americans may have many faults, but they certainly take democracy seriously. If the people are really the rulers and the government their servant, then they are entitled to know everything that it does and who does it. There can be no place in a democracy for the 'mystery' of politics, which treats public records as secret so long as any of the participants are alive. A new American study of Roosevelt's foreign policy gives dramatic illustrations of this. Shortly after the war two distinguished scholars, Professors Langer and Gleason, were given a free run of the State Department archives and of all available private papers, in order to write a history of American foreign policy from 1937 to 1945; their first volume was noticed in these columns some months ago. But protests followed; it was alleged that their work would be a 'whitewash', and Charles A. Beard – a distinguished historian, though a notorious isolationist – wrote: 'Official archives must be open to all citizens on equal terms, with special privileges to none.' This principle was accepted, and Professor Tansill, another isolationist, was also given a free run of the archives. His book was not checked in any way by the State Department: it is a triumphant demonstration of free research.

American policy

The result is perhaps not worth all the fuss. Mr Tansill set out to show 'the President's policy of proclaiming pacifism while working for war'. Mr Tansill himself is clear what policy should have been followed. He is contemptuous of Chiang Kaishek's attempts to unite China, and holds that she was doomed to be dominated by either Russia or Japan; therefore the United States should have backed Japan, who was incidentally its best customer. Similarly in Europe there was only a choice between Germany and Russia; and the right course for all of us was 'welcoming war between these two enemies of democracy and sitting on the side lines with cheers for their mutual destruction'. Instead Roosevelt followed a conscious policy of opposing both Germany and Japan, and so made Russia the dominant power in Europe and Asia.

A similar thesis has been put forward by Mr Kennan in America and by Professor Butterfield and Mr Chester Wilmot in this country. It cannot, however, be sustained from the record. The choice never existed in this clear-cut form. Policy was shaped by events; it did not shape them. Mr Tansill is too conscientious an historian to tamper with the record; and his practical conclusions are not far removed from those of Messrs Langer and Gleason. Roosevelt was an opportunist, not a states-man with a long-term plan. He was at first an isolationist, then an appeaser; and even in 1940 he had no clear design except somehow to keep this country going. He said of the Munich settlement: 'I am not a bit upset over the final result.' Mr Tansill claims that he pushed Eng-land and France into war with Germany in 1939; but this is based on later second-hand gossip and there is no contemporary evidence for it. In fact, the real criticism of Roosevelt is not that he followed the wrong policy but that he had no policy at all; and the 'official' historians. Langer and Gleason, are more damning with their account of his im-provisation and drift than the 'revisionist' historian, Tansill, in his attempt to present Roosevelt as the leading war-criminal.

All the same, it was right that the attempt should be made. A demo-cratic foreign policy is possible only if its background and assumptions are constantly discussed. Even in the courts of Heaven there was a devil's advocate. Though the revisionist case in regard to the Second World War seems pretty good nonsense to our eyes, it is worth remem-bering that most English historians were revisionist after 1918. Lowes Dickinson and even Dr Gooch, in a more cautious way, found plenty to say in favour of Germany. Now we all seem emphatically in agreement that collective security ought to have been applied in Manchuria, in Abyssinia, in Czechoslovakia; and we have applied the principle with-out reserve in the post-war world. Mr Bassett has recently fired a first shot against this thesis in regard to Manchuria.

Again, authorities so various as Mr Churchill and Sir Lewis Namier have asserted that alliance with Russia was possible in 1939, and that it would have averted the war. Now we are more doubtful; and Sir Lewis Namier seems to have come round to the view that even if Russia had gone to the help of Czechoslovakia in 1938 it would only have been in order to grab the eastern territories of Poland for herself. If our authori-ties are wrong in thinking that alliance with Russia was possible in 1939, might they not possibly be wrong also in believing that she is incurably hostile in 1952? Books which support our current assump-tions are all very well; but we also need books which challenge them.

Official archives

Mr Tansill's book is a reminder how much we in this country have to depend on 'official' historians when we do not remain in ignorance altogether. The public does not appreciate the obstacles which face the independent researcher. The Foreign Office papers are closed after the end of 1902. The volumes edited by Gooch and Temperley do something to fill the gap until the outbreak of war in 1914, though they cannot be a full substitute for the original papers. But no one can study foreign policy during the First World War; and there is, no present project even of publishing a selection from the archives. The Documents on Foreign Policy between 1919 and 1939 have been under way for more than five years; at their present rate of progress it will be another fifteen years before they are complete. And, in any case, they publish only the telegrams and dispatches. No minutes are published; and it is almost impossible to deduce the motives behind the decisions that were made. Moreover, they are a strictly departmental record, showing only the activities of the Foreign Office.

But since 1916 there has been a cabinet secretariat not only keeping the minutes of the cabinet (no doubt a very jejune record) but accumulating papers on a vast scale. Why should we not see, for instance, the opinions of the chiefs of staff in regard to German rearmament or the fighting capacity of Poland or Russia? If they had no opinion so much the worse for them. Instead the cabinet secretariat regards it as its duty to push secrecy farther and farther back; even the jottings which Gladstone made for cabinet meetings have now been solemnly placed under official seal. Yet Mr Churchill can use documents of staggering intimacy – and very welcome they are. In truth, everything that happened before 1939, or even 1945, is now history. There is nothing, except the pomposity of a few officials, to prevent unrestricted access to the records by any reputable (or even disreputable) scholar. Probably nothing very sensational would emerge; Mr Tansill's book is itself evidence of it. But you cannot paint the full picture until you have the full record. Beard's law is incontestable in a democracy: 'Official archives must be open to all citizens on equal terms, with special privileges for none'. The Americans have done it; why cannot we do the same?

CHAPTER FORTY-FOUR

The Revision of Treaties:
1830 and 1938

This essay was first published in the *Manchester Guardian* (23 September 1938), with sub-headings 'Guarantees for Czechoslovakia' and 'Lesson from Belgium'.

The revision of the settlement of 1814–15 in regard to Belgium presents some interesting analogies with the present attempt to revise the settlement of 1918–19 concerning Czechoslovakia – and many important differences. During the revolutionary wars the Netherlands had been incorporated into France – the southern part in 1793, the northern in 1810; in the southern part a certain proportion of the inhabitants (later dignified as Belgians) was French-speaking and welcomed French rule. The area now known as Czechoslovakia had never been included in Germany; but a certain proportion of the inhabitants (later dignified as the Sudetens) was German-speaking, and of these some wished to join Germany in 1918. In 1814 the allies conquered the Netherlands and established the Kingdom of the United Netherlands as a barrier against France; this was a settlement imposed by the allies (particularly England), and the House of Orange could never have obtained it of its own strength. Czechoslovakia, on the other hand, was set up by the Czechs and Slovaks themselves, and the allies were only called upon to recognize an accomplished fact – though they certainly welcomed it as a barrier against Germany.

The Belgian revolt

After 1815 there was discontent against Dutch rule in the French-speaking areas, and this discontent was fostered by France. The French Revolution of July 1830 brought matters to a head; revolt in Brussels took the Dutch unawares, and their troops were expelled from all Belgium except Antwerp. (The Sudeten attempt to imitate this revolt has, however, been a failure.) The rebels rejected a tardy offer of Home Rule and declared the independence of all Belgium; but it was well known that many of them wished to be reunited with France, and the French Liberals, excited by their own successful revolution, had the same object in mind.

Of the allies of the Napoleonic Wars, Austria was fully occupied in Italy, but both Prussia and Russia were anxious to restore Dutch rule. England had drifted away from her late allies and was particularly unwilling, as at the present day, to co-operate with Russia; she sympathized strongly with the new constitutional regime in France, but on the other hand she was determined that France should not acquire any territory for herself. Louis Philippe, the new ruler of France, needed a show of success in order to satisfy public opinion, but he was an elderly civilian who sought every excuse to escape war. In the autumn of 1830 Russia was crippled by a revolt in Poland; Prussia dared not act alone; France, threatened with a complete breach with England, renounced her territorial ambitions, and England and France were then able to present the other powers with an agreed solution – Belgium was to be an independent state with an international guarantee.

Palmerston's success

The settlement remained to be enforced: the new state had no organized army, and in August 1831 the Dutch advanced up to the walls of Brussels. A French army was sent to the rescue and the Dutch withdrew; a general war now seemed imminent, for the French refused to leave Belgium until the fortresses – the first line of Belgian defence – had been demolished. The British foreign secretary, Palmerston, now issued an ultimatum – 'The French must go out of Belgium or we have a general war, and war in a given number of days' – and this ultimatum was successful; the French left Belgium unconditionally. The Dutch still refused to surrender Antwerp, but they received no aid from the Eastern powers and in 1833 they were expelled by a French army and a British fleet acting in co-operation. This was the end of the crisis, though the treaty of guarantee was not actually signed by the Great Powers until 1839.

Palmerston had averted war; but he did not believe that he had solved the Belgian problem. He wrote: 'Unfortunately, the History of the World abounds with instances to show that it is unwise for any State to rely entirely for its defence even upon the most solemn engagements of other Powers', and he gave Belgium only a generation of independent existence. He was very nearly right, for France was within an inch of absorbing Belgium in 1866. Only the folly of Napoleon III, the brilliance of Bismarck, and the defeat of France in 1870–71 gave Belgium another lease of life.

Conditions for existence

The factor which gave Belgium not one but three generations of undisturbed neutrality was not a diplomatic arrangement but the totally unforeseen shifting of the European balance consequent upon the economic and political growth of Prussia-Germany and the relative decline of France. Similarly, the only thing which can preserve the independence of Czechslovakia will be the decline of German strength relative to that of her neighbours.

But even to achieve the temporary success which was all that Palmerston hoped for in relation to Belgium four conditions are necessary: (1) that there exists in the German government a peace party which will seize any honourable excuse for avoiding war, and that the word of this government shall be at any rate as reliable as was that of Louis Philippe; (2) that no territory be directly acquired by Germany; (3) that the state guaranteed shall be at least as accessible to the guaranteeing powers (particularly England and France) as was Belgium to her guaranteeing powers (particularly England and Prussia); and (4) that there shall be as close an ideological bond between the governments of England and Germany as there was between the constitutional monarchies of England and France a century ago. Of these conditions only the last seems likely of fulfilment.

CHAPTER FORTY-FIVE

Munich Examined:
Mr Wheeler-Bennett's History

This essay was first published as a review of J.W. Wheeler-Bennett, *Munich: Prologue to Tragedy* (London, Macmillan, 1948), in the *Manchester Guardian* (15 May 1948). The review is notable for Alan Taylor's comment, 'If after 1936 there ever was a chance of stopping Hitler without war, Munich was the moment; but perhaps there was no such moment'.

Sir John Wheeler-Bennett (1902–75) was long associated with the Royal Institute of International Affairs (Chatham House), editing the annual *Documents on International Affairs*, 1929–36, and came to know most leading German politicians while living in Berlin in 1929–34. After the Second World War he lived at Garsington Manor, taught at New College, Oxford and was a founding fellow of St Antony's College, Oxford.

Munich was the most disputed event in British foreign policy between the wars. As Mr Wheeler-Bennett says 'Families were divided and friendships sundered. Social life became actually endangered, since no hostess could guarantee that any dinner party would not break up in passionate recrimination.' Yet all, or almost all, had been compromised at some moment or other: the *New Statesman* gave the signal for the partition of Czechoslovakia eleven days before the notorious leader of *The Times*, and Labour members too joined in the hysterical outburst of 28 September (according to Mr Wheeler-Bennett, only Mr Eden and Mr Harold Nicolson abstained: he omits Mr Gallacher). As a result, later, Munich became a subject better avoided and the biographer of Neville Chamberlain was commended for having directed attention to his subject's love of birds. Mr Wheeler-Bennett has broken this silence with a book that is at once a work of scholarship and of controversy, a reconstruction of the diplomatic details, and an advocacy of collective security.

Mr Wheeler-Bennett is a distinguished diplomatic historian as was shown in his brilliant book on Brest-Litovsk. Less lapidary and perfect than Professor Namier, he is also less relentless; and the reader is often entertained with character-sketches and with anecdotes drawn from personal experience. In Professor Namier's narrative of the origin of the war there was a sense of great historic forces moving towards a predestined tragedy: Mr Wheeler-Bennett makes more of the little men who made this tragedy possible. This is not to deprecate his scholarship: he has pieced together his narrative in a way that is likely to stand the test of time. Full use is made of the information on German military plans revealed at Nuremberg. Thus, it is now clear that German action was always fixed for 30 September: therefore Hitler was deceiving Chamberlain (not for the only time) when, at Berghtesgaden, he agreed to 'postpone' his attack on Czechoslovakia for a fortnight, and Chamberlain's claim to this achievement was an empty boast.

The German generals

Mr Wheeler-Bennett steers clear of some of the extreme versions of the opposition which the German generals are alleged to have prepared against Hitler: still, it is certain that they were doubtful of a successful outcome, and would have shrunk back in face of resolute opposition. On the other hand, it is also clear that Hitler was not bluffing, as is sometimes claimed: if England and France had stood firm nothing short of a generals' revolt would have averted war – and later events showed the danger of relying on the German generals. If after 1936 there ever was a chance of stopping Hitler without war Munich was the moment: but perhaps there was no such moment.

Mr Wheeler-Bennett dismisses, and explodes, the later versions according to which Munich was a last-minute improvisation, a surrender inevitable owing to British and French weakness. Appeasement, as he shows, was a deliberate policy, consistently pursued by Chamberlain as both wise and morally right. For Chamberlain, the Czechs were an obstacle to appeasement, the only stumbling-block in the way of a peaceful Europe. Hence they were cajoled and bullied from start to finish. Even on 27 September, when war seemed certain, the British government, after first placing the responsibility for war on the Czechs, warned them that Czechoslovakia 'could not be reconstituted in her frontiers, whatever the result of the conflict may be'.

Though impatient with Chamberlain's ignorance and short-sightedness, Mr Wheeler-Bennett yet sees something sturdy even in the record of blunders; his own contempt is reserved for the two former foreign secretaries (Sir John Simon and Sir Samuel Hoare) who were Chamberlain's principal advisers. This Munich triumvirate, with its self-righteous pacifism was indeed the last gesture of the Nonconformist conscience. Over against these three Mr Wheeler-Bennett sets the figure of Lord Halifax. He attributes to him the rejection of the Godesberg terms and the short period of Anglo-French preparation for war: and, writing of a later period, he ascribes Chamberlain's repudiation of appeasement in his speech at Birmingham on 17 March 1939, to an ultimatum from

Lord Halifax on the previous day. These revelations from a private source are as tantalizing as the information from Brüning which Mr Wheeler-Bennett drew on when writing his life of Hindenburg. More precise details would also be welcome, too, concerning the statement that, 'if not in the mind of Mr. Chamberlain himself at any rate in the minds of some of his advisers' there was a secret hope of provoking a war between Germany and Soviet Russia. Who were the 'advisers' – the inner cabinet or some less official persons? It is surely time that they were named.

Bonnet and Hodza

Less delicacy is shown in discussing the course, or rather the collapse of French foreign policy. The intrigues of Bonnet and the weakness of Daladier are treated almost too ruthlessly. Still, there can be no doubt that, whatever Chamberlain's hankering for appeasement, his visit to Berchtesgaden was undertaken only on an agonized appeal from Daladier after a majority of the French cabinet had determined to abandon Czechoslovakia. Bonnet has argued that on 20 September at any rate the Czechs – shrinking 'from a war' with Germany – asked to be abandoned. Mr Wheeler-Bennett sets against Bonnet's story the version of Hodza, the Czech prime minister: Hodza claims that he insisted only on an answer 'in the most explicit terms' whether France would help Czechoslovakia or not. But Mr Wheeler-Bennett admits that there is other evidence that Hodza and perhaps other members of the Agrarian Party, were intriguing behind Beneš's back to prevent a war in which Czechoslovakia would be the ally of Russia. General Syrovy told Mr Wheeler-Bennett: 'We shall fight the Germans either alone or with you and the French, but we don't want the Russians in here. We should never get them out.'

Russia remains the great enigma, as in most questions of international affairs. The effectiveness of Russian aid cannot be decided, though undoubtedly it was feared by the German generals. Russian aid was however, certainly offered. According to Mr Wheeler-Bennett, the Soviet minister in Prague declared on 21 September that 'the Soviet Government would come to the support of Czechoslovakia as soon as Moscow was informed that the League had been appraised of the case and would not wait for a decision to be reached at Geneva'. This offer was rejected by Hodza and the other Agrarian ministers. Indeed, Russia was persistently snubbed by all throughout the crisis (except for the anonymous Foreign Office announcement on 26 September). In 1938 and probably never thereafter, Russia could have been brought back into the system of European order. This lost chance, even more than the moral vapourings, was the ineffaceable sin, before their own people and before posterity, of 'the men of Munich'.

CHAPTER FORTY-SIX

Munich Again

This short essay was first published as a review of R.G.D. Laffan, *Survey of International Affairs, 1938*, Vol. 2: *The Crisis over Czechoslovakia, January to September 1938* (Oxford, Oxford University Press, 1951), in the *Manchester Guardian* (3 August 1951).

Chatham House is now trying to catch up the work that was interrupted by the war and has resumed its annual surveys of international affairs. The first volume on 1938 was published ten years ago; the second volume, devoted entirely to the Munich affair, is necessarily of a different character. It lacks immediacy; instead it attempts history. Earlier volumes were based on the events themselves and what was published contemporaneously; this one can use the secret documents that have recently been brought out.

The standpoint is what might be called 'British-respectable'. Munich was a mistake, but an honest mistake. Hitler was at fault; the Czechs were at fault; the French were at fault; no wonder that poor old Chamberlain found the world a bit too much for him. There is no mention of the discreditable items on the British side; nothing of Sir Nevile Henderson's activities; nothing of the way in which Sir Eric Phipps depreciated (*sic*) the French; nothing of the extraordinary way in which Lord Runciman was induced to write a report which bore no relation to his previous recommendations. The author clings firmly to the principle of writing nothing which might give offence to any member of Chatham House or to anyone likely to dine at the high table of any Cambridge or Oxford college. In short, though a good deal of material is summarized here, it brings us no nearer the book that will one day have to be written and which will be of decisive importance. This book will be called 'The Foreign Policy of Lord Halifax'.

The most curious part of the book is the half-concealed conflict between Mr Laffan, the author commissioned by Chatham House, and Professor Toynbee, the director of Chatham House, who writes the introduction. Mr Laffan ascribes Munich solely to British weakness in armaments – good Munichbeering stuff. Professor Toynbee will have none of this (no evidence for it, he suggests in a footnote): he goes deeper, though perhaps not farther. The reader may therefore take his choice. For a serious account of the Munich crisis he will probably still turn to the work of Mr Wheeler-Bennett.

CHAPTER FORTY-SEVEN

How the War Began:
An Essay in Diplomatic History

This essay was first published as a review of L.B. Namier, *Diplomatic Prelude 1938–9* (London, Macmillan, 1948), in the *Manchester Guardian* (10 January 1948). Alan Taylor was much influenced by Lewis Namier (1888–1960), who had been Professor of Modern History (1931–53) for all but his first year at Manchester University; not least by this book on the origins of the Second World War.

Diplomatic Prelude is a show-piece of the historian's art. It can stand comparison with Sorel's *Diplomatic History of the War of 1870*, published in 1873 and still the best book on its subject. Meticulous scholarship and deep insight go together, and a sentence often says as much as many pages by another writer.

The skeleton of the narrative is made from the 'coloured books' – the collections of documents published by the various governments at the outbreak of war. Professor Namier adds material not otherwise available in this country – reminiscences (in Polish) by the Polish ambassador in Paris, documents published in France during the rule of Vichy to discredit pre-war governments, and Daladier's defence of his policy in the National Assembly in July 1946. These sources, taken together, make it possible to give a coherent account of German, French, and Polish policy. The Soviet government cannot be expected to explain its policy either to its own people or to the rest of the world, but it is surely discreditable that the British government has published nothing except a meagre Blue-book on German–Polish relations. Until it does Professor Namier's book is likely to remain the most precise and accurate narrative in any language on how the war began.

New details are added in regard to Polish policy. This merits careful study for the two Polish decisions – to resist Hitler and not to cooperate with Russia – shaped the course of events. Namier describes the helter-skelter way in which the British guarantee to Poland was offered; he adds the agreeable detail that Beck decided to accept it 'between two flicks of the ash off his cigarette'. Beck held that the alliance with Great Britain did not imply an 'option' against Germany and believing this expected the Germans to believe it too. In any case, the Poles were convinced right to the end that the Germans were bluffing and made neither economic nor military preparations for imminent war. In Namier's words, 'so far from being rash, provocative, or bellicose, the Polish Government can much rather be accused of behaving like people who reacted to air raids by falling asleep'.

Sir Nevile Henderson

Hitler, on his side, often talked of war; but, as Namier shows, he was taken aback at the end when England and France actually put their threats into action (or at least into the words of a declaration of war). Hitler had some justification for his error in the constant sympathy with the German case shown by Sir Nevile Henderson. The British government attached great importance to making sure that, this time, the Germans should be adequately warned of the British determination to go to war; but how could the Germans take seriously warnings from an Ambassador who even at the end found the German claims 'not unreasonable', and who blamed the Poles (as previously he had blamed the Czechs) for not running quickly enough to Berlin.

Namier's best stroke against Henderson, perhaps, is his proof that whereas Henderson (in his book) condemns the Czechs for not taking his advice and coming to Berlin on 13 March 1939, the conversation on which Henderson bases his complaint only took place on 14 March. Even more discreditable is the record of the attempts made by Henderson to push the German terms unofficially on to the Poles, although these terms had not been communicated officially to him, still less to the Poles.

The story of the negotiations between the Western powers and Russia has to be written largely on the basis of contemporary newspaper reports. The British government negotiated with Russia to quieten public opinion rather than with any real hope of achieving an alliance. (Nevile Henderson expressed more than his own opinion when he said to Hitler on the news of the Nazi–Soviet pact: 'If an agreement had to be made with Moscow ... I had rather Germany made it than ourselves.') Therefore the government wished to make public the difficulties, while avoiding parliamentary pressure.

Russia and Poland

Namier adds further some interesting details from Daladier. The negotiations had been started by the British government for home consumption; as they proceeded the French government came to see in them the one hope of safety and perhaps even of peace – a reasonable view. By August the French were ready to pay any price for the Russian alliance. The Russians said that it was useless to go on talking unless it was agreed that Russian troops could cross Polish territory and that France, as the ally of Poland, must obtain this permission. Daladier claims that on 21 August he said to the Polish ambassador: 'If early in the afternoon, after having telephoned to Warsaw, you come to tell me that Poland maintains her previous attitude, I shall summon a Cabinet and put to them the problem of the Franco-Polish Alliance.' He adds that as the Poles made no answer he assumed their agreement and authorized the French representative in Moscow to agree to the Russian demand.

The Polish ambassador, however, asserts that this conversation never took place. In any case, Voroshilov at once destroyed the French answer by saying: 'We require an assurance that the Polish and Romanian Governments have agreed.' Even after the news of Ribbentrop's visit to Moscow, Daladier proposed to the French cabinet 'a threatening diplomatic démarche in Warsaw to force Poland into accepting the passage of the Russians'.

On the last stages, Namier shows, by abstract reasoning, that the negotiations between Germany and Russia cannot have been of long standing, and he has the satisfaction of having his argument confirmed from documents put in at Nuremberg. He clears up, too, the final problem of the delay of the British and French governments in declaring war. This delay led to a dramatic scene in the House of Commons and to charges of renewed appeasement against Chamberlain; for once the charges were false. The delay was entirely due to Bonnet's hope of Italian mediation; and this mediation was ended by the British insistence that, first, German troops must be withdrawn behind the German frontiers.

Namier prints the report by Corbin, the French ambassador, of his interview with Chamberlain when the prime minister insisted on action. Corbin adds a description of a stormy telephone conversation with Mr Churchill: 'Bursts of his voice made the telephone vibrate.' If Britain and France could not act together now said Mr Churchill, 'Britain will shut herself up in her island and will offer fierce resistance, but will not wish to be concerned any further in Continental affairs.' The French cabinet was reluctantly drawn in. According to De Monzie, a member of the cabinet said at this final meeting: 'It is regrettable that at the very outset there should be lack of synchronisation among the Allies.' De Monzie replied: 'If for once we are late as against England, we can well afford the luxury.' Thus the French men of Munich were already on their way to Vichy.

CHAPTER FORTY-EIGHT

Diplomatic Supplement

This essay was published as a review of L.B. Namier, *Europe in Decay: A Study in Disintegration, 1936–40* (London, Macmillan, 1950), in the *Manchester Guardian* (7 March 1950). It is unlikely that Lewis Namier would have received well the final paragraph, not least as Alan Taylor's own collection of essays included reviews of such memoirs and volumes of documents.

Professor Namier can best describe his new book himself. He writes in the preface:

> Two years have passed since I finished writing *Diplomatic Prelude 1938–1939*, and more than a year since it was published. During that time books bearing on its subject have been appearing at such a rate that my essays about them fill by now this new volume ... I propose to keep myself and my readers up to date by continuing a critical analysis of the most important new publications ... adding occasionally essays on particular subjects: and whenever there is enough to hand I will reprint them in book form.

The book is thus a collection of reprinted essays rather than a study, as claimed in the title; and these essays have been written as much for Professor Namier's use as for the reader's. They summarize, for the most part, evidence for pre-war diplomatic history which may one day modify Professor Namier's existing account; and they are sometimes difficult to follow unless that account is kept clearly in mind. Of course Mr Namier cannot keep out the trenchant generalization which has always distinguished his essays; but readers of his earlier collections will regret that there is so much of Bonnet, of Ciano, and even of Mr Churchill, and so little of Mr Namier himself. Where, as in the preliminary essay on memoirs born of defeat, he lets himself go, he repeats old themes: the decline of France and the illusory nature of French predominance after 1919 were established in essays which he published twelve years ago. Others can analyse memoirs and collections of documents; only Mr Namier can generalize and illuminate with that massive sweep, and it is impossible not to miss the titanic sentences of his earlier volumes.

The most considered essays here are those on the memoirs of French statesmen – Flandin, Bonnet, and Baudouin. As well as informing himself and his readers, Mr Namier seems to have had the further object of ensuring that none of these tattered figures shall ever restore his reputation. Certain collections of documents are analysed: the first volume of

British documents on Munich; the German documents published by the Russians; and the documents on Nazi–Soviet relations published by the Americans. This is all historical evidence in the first stage of digestion. The process is carried a step farther in an essay on the Anglo-French negotiations with Russia in 1939, which uses most of the evidence recently published in France. Finally Mr Namier prints some Czech documents on Czech–Polish relations which were supplied to him by Beneš. These are accompanied by the interesting statement that it was the Polish refusal to promise neutrality in 1938 'which provided me (Beneš) with the last and decisive reason for the fact that, in spite of the insistence of Moscow, I did not provoke war with Germany in 1938'. Beneš was always adroit at shifting his responsibility on to others.

It is of course highly desirable that Mr Namier should review these volumes as they appear, and it is convenient to have his summaries of foreign books brought together. It is more doubtful whether any reader of this volume needs a summary of Mr Churchill's history, particularly when it is made in an atmosphere of romantic praise. And however much we may admire Mr Namier as a journalist and contemporary historian, we cannot forget that these activities distract him from the great work on the history of eighteenth-century England which he alone is qualified to write. So long as his Ford Lectures of fifteen years ago remain unpublished we shall resent his preoccupation with Stalin and Hitler and such small fry.

CHAPTER FORTY-NINE

Old Tunes

This essay first appeared as a review of Martin Gilbert and Richard Gott, *The Appeasers* (London, Weidenfeld and Nicolson, 1963), in the *New Statesman*, 65, 1666, (15 February 1963). It is a notable plea for vigorous revisionism by Alan Taylor.

The British government made a fine mess of things before the war. They tried to buy Hitler off and failed. They brought upon themselves much moral discredit. They promoted the dismemberment of Czechoslovakia; guaranteed the remnant, and did not fulfil the guarantee; guaranteed Poland and, in practice, did not fulfil that guarantee either. They landed Great Britain in war with one inadequate ally, a war for which, it seemed, they had inadequately prepared. In May 1940 the government was driven from office amid general obloquy, an obloquy which has grown stronger with the years. Many distinguished historians condemned the appeasers at the time; and they repeated the condemnation more sharply as documentary evidence of British policy accumulated after the war. The folly and weakness of the appeasers has become the accepted version. This does not necessarily prove that it is wrong. All the same, I think that historians ought to regard, with some detachment, even events in which they were once themselves engaged. As a humble fighter against appeasement, I have now little interest in denouncing the appeasers. I am more interested in finding out why we, the opponents of appeasement, failed. I am even interested in finding out why the appeasers acted as they did, what they were trying to do, what were the motives of their policy. It depresses me that two young historians, neither of whom can remember the outbreak of war, should be content to play old tunes. They conclude their preface by saying: 'The story we have pieced together ought to be known.' Alas, it is known only too well – known by every undergraduate, repeated in every lecture and every textbook. I doubt whether it is understood.

This book is painstakingly put together from the diplomatic documents. The authors rely perhaps too much on the memoirs of Hore-Belisha, which, I suspect, exaggerate the resolute part which he claimed to play. Otherwise, the book is accurate and honest within its limits. These limits are narrow. This is a rigid diplomatic narrative, ignoring the climate of opinion at the time. There is no reference to contemporary newspapers and political literature; few references even to *Hansard*. The British government sought to avoid another great war. Their method may have been mistaken. Their aim was endorsed by the overwhelming majority of the British people. The National government, with their great majority in Parliament, no doubt bear the prime responsibility. Yet one cannot ignore the policy of the Labour Party, as it is ignored here. Until 1936, at least, the Labour Party sympathized with German grievances. Even Hugh Dalton applauded Hitler's reoccupation of the Rhineland; and thereafter Labour continued to have an uneasy feeling that German claims had some foundation, though maybe Hitler was not entitled to make them. Again, Labour opposed all measures of rearmament until 1937; and then their conversion had little reality.

Labour policy was, or seemed to be, collective security, without the arms to support it. Labour believed that security could be enforced by economic sanctions. They refused to recognize that collective security was a recipe for universal war, not for preserving peace. Other supporters of collective security also had their illusions. The authors quote a letter from Gilbert Murray on 29 October 1938: 'I believe that (the small nations of Europe) would still stand together to prevent German aggression if England and France would give them a lead; but of course they won't.' The record is quite other. All the small nations obstinately ducked until they were overwhelmed; and their resistance then was quite unavailing. Only great powers can resist a great power. Small nations are window-dressing.

The Great Powers are another grave omission from this book. There is throughout an unspoken impression that Hitler would have been stayed in his course if the British government had wagged their little finger. Where was the material for an effective coalition against Germany? Some of the critics, especially Churchill, had an exaggerated faith in the French army and, still more, in its willingness to fight. All the evidence points the other way. The French did not need much discouragement from the British. It was what they were resolved on all along, as they showed both at the time of Munich and on the outbreak of war. The British had no army of their own to use against the Germans. It was the French army or nothing; and the French were determined that it should be nothing.

Namier wrote immediately after Munich: 'The key to the situation is in the relations of the British Empire and France with the United States and Russia.' This was, I think, a correct diagnosis. There is now conclusive evidence that there was no chance in 1938 or 1939 of involving the United States in European affairs. Even in 1941 they entered the European war only because Hitler declared war against them. Alliance with Soviet Russia remains a dark speculation. I advocated it passionately as the cure for all our ills. I now recognize its doubts and difficulties.

Many good judges think that it was impossible of attainment or that it would have been ineffective, even if attained. In any case, there was a price to pay. The independent states of Eastern Europe could be kept going only if war were avoided. Once a general war came, there was a choice only between German and Russian domination, and it is not surprising that the British government shrank from that choice, or even preferred the Germans. I was always clear the other way, and still am. But it puzzles me when those who rejoiced at war against Germany now gird against the Russian domination which was the inevitable result of that war. The authors of this book think we did right to resist German claims on Poland. Do they also think that Great Britain and the United States were right to acquiesce in a greater dismemberment of Poland at Yalta? Lord Dunglass (now Lord Home) seems to me to have been more consistent. He was against Yalta, and therefore for Munich. No one can have everything in this world.

Great Britain could not impose her will on Germany. Resolute words were not enough. Vansittart's favourite remedy of getting the Italians to do the fighting for us was surely even more futile, though Vansittart gets his meed of praise in this book. British foreign policy cannot be judged in detachment from British armaments, a subject almost ignored by the present writers. The National government did better than is usually alleged. Indeed Chamberlain and his associates laid the foundations for British power throughout the Second World War. But armaments cannot be conjured up at once. There could be no British army of any size until 1941. Everyone was obsessed with the prospect of catastrophic destruction from the air on the outbreak of war. Half a million dead within the first fortnight was the accepted estimate of experts, not of timid amateurs. Everyone exaggerated German strength, the critics of appeasement most of all. Churchill and others played into Hitler's hands by their well-meant alarms. In fact, the Germans spent on arms about half what they were supposed to have spent; and Hitler made no preparations whatever for war against England. He had no strategic bombers, no landing craft, and very few ocean-going submarines.

The civilian ministers of the National government erred over this, but they erred along with nearly everyone else. It was not unreasonable for them to try to avoid war, if Great Britain were really as weak as the critics made out. Maybe the appeasers went wrong in being so bad at appeasement. They did not convince Hitler that they were really anxious to meet his reasonable claims, nor that they would oppose him if he were unreasonable. They hesitated over appeasement, and gave the impression that they were ashamed of what they were doing. It is an ironical conclusion, nicely brought out here, that in the end Sir John Simon forced Chamberlain into war and that Sir Kingsley Wood turned him out of the premiership. No one, it seems, genuinely believed in appeasement, except Sir Horace Wilson.

At any rate, morality triumphed. It was dishonourable to desert Czechoslovakia in 1938, honourable to stand by Poland in 1939. Others paid the price for this vindication of British conscience. Less than a hundred thousand Czechs were killed in the Second World War. Prague was undamaged. Czechoslovakia survived virtually intact. Seven million Poles were killed. Warsaw was razed to the ground. Poland was dismembered. Did we really do all that much better than the appeasers?

CHAPTER FIFTY

After Appeasement

This essay was first published as a review of Sidney Aster, *1939: The Making of the Second World War* (London, Deutsch, 1973), in the *Observer* (2 September 1973).

'The Second World War only became inevitable on 15 March 1939.' This is the key sentence of Mr Aster's book. On that day Chamberlain and his government decided that Hitler was not to be trusted. They resolved to resist him unless he showed signs of true repentance. 'Britain and France frantically prepared for war. Massive rearmament programmes speeded ahead.' Hitler failed to repent, and in September the Second World War duly started. The argument is sustained by 'the full archives of the Foreign Office, here used for the first time'. The dustcover informs us that 'this book is the definitive account of one of the most critical years of this century'.

These exaggerated claims are unkind to a book which presents a competent, though by no means novel, picture of British policy in the six months before the outbreak of war. The approach is narrow. Surely the British government did not 'make' the Second World War entirely unaided, as the title of the book seems to imply? Nothing is said about Hitler's policy except a couple of slapdash judgements from the Foreign Office at the end. 'Hitler wanted his pretext and he would have found it even if he had been dealing with the Archangel Gabriel. *Nothing* would have made any difference – except complete surrender to Herr Hitler's demands.' Maybe, but these dogmatic statements would have been the better for some scholarly support.

The text of the book does not sustain the argument so bravely presented in the introduction. Aster sometimes recognises this himself. Of the wholesale distribution of guarantees in April 1939 he writes:

> What was in the minds of the Allied Governments in this new policy has always remained a mystery. Were the guarantees a manifestation of suicidal tendencies in the capitals of western Europe? Had heroism and bravado replaced caution and appeasement?

Grudgingly he provides an answer. The guarantees were bluff. The chiefs of staff repeatedly reported that nothing could be done to implement them and that Poland, far from providing a second front, would be destroyed within a few weeks. The cabinet duly heard these warnings. It disregarded the further point made by the chiefs of staff that resistance to Hitler could be effective only if Soviet Russia were drawn in. Discussion of this is the most valuable part of Aster's book. Some revisions follow. Sir Samuel Hoare, for instance, was a persistent advocate of the Soviet alliance. Halifax acquiesced though with no great enthusiasm: 'If the negotiations should, after all, fail, this would not cause him very great anxiety. For whatever form an agreement finally took, he believed the Russians would ultimately act in their own interests' – presumably unlike the British. The stern, unrelenting opponent of the alliance was Chamberlain, and he imposed his will on a reluctant cabinet.

Aster summarizes Chamberlain's illusion which apparently he himself shares:

> British strategy was planned to defeat Germany by a defensive strategy at the outset on the western front, giving way later to the offensive and backed by the strangulating, though long term, effects of the allied blockade. This strategy eventually won the Second World War.

This is quite untrue. The British blockade had virtually no effect on Germany. The Russians defeated the German army, and the belated offensive on the western front only hastened victory. The choice – Russia or Germany? – was already clear in 1939. Chamberlain and his government failed to make it.

Or rather, they would have preferred to choose Germany if only Hitler had let them. Aster makes heavy weather with the attempts at appeasement in the summer of 1939. The conversations between Sir Horace Wilson and Wohltat, Goering's representative, are described solely from Wilson's point of view, though with the tantalising addition that the Foreign Office files relating to Wohltat's selection to attend the whaling conference (his excuse for coming to London) are still closed until the year 2015. This does not sound like innocence. Similarly Wilson's talks with Dirksen, the German ambassador, are written down, though Dirksen was a trained diplomatic reporter and Wilson was not. As to Dahlerus, the final intermediary, he hardly appears at all. No one would guess from this book that Chamberlain and Halifax were on their knees to Hitler for concession and compromise till the last moment.

However, there are many miscellaneous plums. Thus Sir Alexander Cadogan, admired permanent under-secretary at the Foreign Office: 'If the problem could be so implied as to be put in the form of a question – Italy or Russia? – I would unhesitatingly plump for the former.' And there is of course the alarm from Tilea, the Romanian minister, which started the Gadarene rush. Aster has had the benefit of information from Tilea, and the alarm becomes more tenuous than ever. Still Aster is unshaken: 'Written evidence of the German ultimatum (to Romania) never turned up in 1939, nor since, indeed, in any archive. Perhaps it may never come to light.' So perhaps it was a false alarm, a concoction, as Tilea himself virtually admitted? Aster will have none of this. Yet previously he has catalogued half a dozen false alarms peddled by the British intelligence service. He would do well to ask: what was the explanation of these false alarms? Was it the extreme incompetence of the intelligence services – a more than possible explanation? Or were high-placed Germans, perhaps opponents of Hitler's, deliberately planting false news in order to promote a compromise?

The actual outbreak of war is presented in terms favourable to Chamberlain with the version, now almost become gospel, that delays were the fault of the French. Let Georges Bonnet take the blame. I prefer Nicholas Bethell's judgement: 'Great Britain went to war in order to save the Chamberlain Government from falling.'

On a minor but tiresome point, Aster should read the contemporary newspapers instead of relying on later gossip. If he does, he will find that Leo Amery shouted to Arthur Greenwood: 'Speak for England.' All other cries are the product of a vivid imagination.

CHAPTER FIFTY-ONE

Munich Twenty Years After: Appeasement – with the Wrong Man

This essay was first published in the Manchester Guardian *on the twentieth anniversary of the Munich agreement (30 September 1958). Its conclusion was one of the many controversial points made in Alan Taylor's* The Origins of the Second World War *(London, Hamish Hamilton, 1961).*

On this morning twenty years ago the Munich conference was breaking up. In the early hours a yawning and impatient Chamberlain had told the Czechs their inexorable fate. Now it only remained to sign the agreement formally. At the last moment Chamberlain proposed to Hitler that they should renounce war between their two countries for ever. Hitler replied with an ecstatic 'Ja! Ja!' adding that he hated the thought of women and children being killed by gas-bombs. Then Chamberlain flew off, to proclaim Peace with Honour; Daladier more gloomily to receive an enthusiastic welcome which surprised and humiliated him.

Nothing now remains of this gathering where the Great Powers of Europe occupied the centre of the stage for the last time. Chamberlain lived long enough to see the ruin of his policy. Hitler and Mussolini perished miserably, their names a byword of infamy for ever. Only Daladier ploughs on with an ox's stubbornness, still upholding democracy, still unsuccessful. The Sudeten Germans have indeed gone 'home to the Reich', in a way most unwelcome to them. Czechoslovakia has again her pre-war frontiers. She has not recovered her independence. The rulers of Soviet Russia occupy the place left vacant by Hitler. The settlement of Munich was meant to bring peace to Europe. Instead it was the prelude to a fierce conflict which ended her centuries of world dominance.

Glittering affair

How does it seem to us twenty years afterwards – this glittering affair, so trumpeted at the time, so soon discarded? Was it simply a fraud – for Hitler merely a stage in his plan of world conquest, for the British a device to buy time while they completed their rearmament? None of these things. The leading actors at Munich were sincere – at any rate for the time being. They really thought that they had secured the peace of Europe, though, of course, their versions of this peace varied. Chamberlain supposed that Germany's last grievance was removed; Hitler that his mastery of East-Central Europe was recognized. Daladier and Mussolini only cared that their countries had escaped living up to their pretensions as great powers.

The Czech crisis was made in London, not in Berlin. Hitler had indeed visions of world conquest, but no defined plan. The seizure of Austria earlier in the year had been improvised at the last moment. Thereafter he was content to wait while the Spanish civil war continued to distract the Western powers. He began to push at the Czech door only when the British government insisted that it was already opening. The British had been caught napping over Austria. They were determined not to be caught again. They would anticipate Hitler's next grievance instead of acquiescing in it. It was the British, not Hitler, who wrung concessions from Beneš in a melancholy series; the British, in fact, who envisaged the conference at Munich from the beginning. Hence Chamberlain's jubilation at the end. In the most literal sense, he had beaten the gun.

Limitless confidence

Why did Chamberlain prefer concession to resistance? This is the central question of the Munich affair. Obviously, his temperament pulled him towards negotiation and away from war. More than this, war seemed ineffective for the purpose. Everyone exaggerated the strength of his defensive position – and of his opponent's. The French did not believe that they could break through the fortifications of the reoccupied Rhineland; yet themselves felt secure behind the Maginot Line. The British had virtually no expeditionary force, but limitless confidence in the navy. Alone the Western powers could not 'stop' Hitler, or so they supposed. What of alliance with Soviet Russia? Here the decisive obstacle was undoubtedly political – profound suspicion on both sides. Even in June, 1939, George VI recorded of his conversation with President Roosevelt: 'He was definitely anti-Russian. I told him so were we.' Yet alliance was unrewarding even on a military basis. How could the Russians help Czechoslovakia effectively while Poland remained neutral or even, as she was, anti-Czech? The idea of sending Soviet forces through Romania was futile, evidence only that the Russians had never contemplated the problem seriously.

But supposing that the Czechs had firmly rejected British promptings and stood to their defences? The Russians, we know, constantly urged them on this course. The Czech army was certainly strong enough to hold its own against the Germans. But there are factors on the other side. The Czech frontier with Austria was unfortified; and the Czechs would have been hard pressed if they had been attacked also, as seemed likely, by Hungary and Poland. These speculations are in any case unrewarding. Beneš never contemplated isolated resistance from first to last. He relied on treaties, not on armed strength, and could not change his nature at a moment's notice. Besides, in view of the Spanish war it was difficult to believe until June 1940, that the British would resist Hitler seriously: and Beneš shrank from fighting with only Soviet Russia as a doubtful ally. He played for time. Assuming rightly that Hitler would go on to new conquests, he hoped that Czechoslovakia would sit out the next round and thus survive unbroken, as in a sense she did.

There was another military factor of an opposite kind. While everyone exaggerated the strength of land defences, they also exaggerated the power of air bombardment. Munich was played out under the shadow of Guernica. Everyone supposed that London and Paris would be razed to the ground within the first few hours of war. The Russians even believed that their planes, operating from Czech airfields, would do the same for Berlin. In the event indiscriminate bombing turned out to be ineffective. I would even guess that it cost more in manpower and economic effort to the attacker than it did damage to the attacked. This has had a curious effect to the present day. Since bombing in the last war was a hundred times less effective than was expected, men now fail to realize that nuclear bombing in the next will be a hundred times more devastating than anyone can foresee.

Sanctity of treaties

Essentially, however, the Munich crisis was determined by moral considerations, not by calculations of war. On the one side was collective security, loyalty to allies, and the sanctity of treaties; on the other the sacred claim to self-determination. The Czechs defended an 'historic' frontier; the Bohemian Germans asserted their national character. How could Chamberlain refuse to these Germans what had been granted to Ulster? Partition along the national line is now the accepted rule, in the Indian subcontinent and in Cyprus; and even the Czechs agreed that nationalities could not live side by side when they expelled the Sudeten Germans after the war. Liberals and Labour could talk of defending democratic Czechoslovakia; it was difficult to forget the many years when they had denounced her as an imperialist creation of Versailles.

Has the story a moral? An obvious one: no deal with Hitler was ever possible. But he was a human phenomenon who occurs once in a thousand years. Appeasement was a sensible course, even though it was tried with the wrong man; and it remains the noblest word in the diplomatist's vocabulary.

CHAPTER FIFTY-TWO

Soviet Policy and Czechoslovakia

This essay was first published as a review of the Czechoslovak government's *New Documents on the History of Munich* (Prague, Orbis, 1958), in the *Manchester Guardian* (5 January 1959).

There was no chair for a Soviet delegate at the Munich conference. Did the Russians hang back, hoping to involve others without being involved themselves? Or did they offer the Czechs any serious support? Historians have answered according to their political taste or private whim. Solid evidence has been lacking. At last we have some. The Czechoslovak Government has recently published *New Documents on the History of Munich*, some from its own, some from the Soviet archives. Czechoslovakia and the Soviet Union were bound by a pact of mutual assistance; but it came into operation only if France acted first. The clause had been inserted by the Czechs so as not to find themselves alone with Bolshevik Russia. Instead it enabled the Russians to combine honour and inaction. Yet was this their intention? The record suggests that they were willing to act and that the weakness of France bewildered them as much as it ruined the Czechs.

Roundabout answer

On 15 March, immediately after Hitler's seizure of Austria, Fierlinger, the Czech representative in Moscow, 'exchanged opinions' with Potyomkin, deputy foreign commissar. Fierlinger was confident that France and Great Britain would stand by Czechoslovakia. Potyomkin was more doubtful. However, he concluded:

> If France did not evade, under some excuse or other, the fulfilment of her obligations as Czechoslovakia's ally ... Britain would, in the final analysis, be compelled to follow in her footsteps. As far as the Soviet Union was concerned, nobody had ever been able to reproach her with evasion of the international obligations she had undertaken.

On April 23 Fierlinger reported a meeting in the Kremlin of Stalin, Molotov, Voroshilov, Litvinov, and Kaganovich. They decided:

> If requested, the U.S.S.R. is prepared – in agreement with France and Czechoslovakia – to take all necessary measures relating to the

security of Czechoslovakia. She disposes of all necessary means for doing so. The state of the Army and Air Force allows of this. Voroshilov is very optimistic.

On 25 May Litvinov told Fierlinger of the talks he had had at Geneva. Bonnet had asked: 'What does the U.S.S.R. intend to do?' Litvinov answered that this should be discussed jointly by representatives of the French, Soviet, and Czechoslovak General Staffs. 'Bonnet sighed and said that Poland and Rumania are emphatically opposing the transit of our troops'. On 30 May Krofta, the Czechoslovak foreign minister, gave a roundabout answer to these hints:

> Czechoslovakia cannot be the initiator, cannot speak before France. If France remains silent then, formally Czechoslovakia will have to be silent.

A long period of silence followed. On 1 September the French chargé d'affaires came to the Kremlin. Bonnet, he stated, had tried to get the unhindered passage of Soviet troops through Poland and Romania. 'The attempts had not brought positive results. Poland had been particularly categorical in her objections.' Bonnet therefore asked: 'On what aid from the Soviet Union could Czechoslovakia count if the difficulties placed in the way by Poland and Rumania were taken into consideration?' Litvinov replied the following day:

> France was under an obligation to assist Czechoslovakia irrespective of our help, while our help is conditional on that of France ... We are determined to fulfil all our obligations under the Soviet-Czechoslovak Pact ... Although Poland and Rumania are now putting obstacles in the way, their behaviour, especially that of Rumania, may be different if the League of Nations takes a decision on aggression ... Even a decision of a majority would have a great moral effect, especially if Rumania herself were to come to agree with the majority.
>   As far as a definition of concrete help is concerned, we consider that for this it would be necessary to call a conference of representatives of the Soviet, French, and Czechoslovak armies.

Britain, France, and the Soviet Union should also meet in conference 'to adopt a common declaration that would no doubt receive the moral support of Roosevelt'. Litvinov repeated to Fierlinger the answer that he had given to the French; 'if the British Ambassador had applied to me, I should have deemed it advisable to tell him of these talks, too'.

Mutual distrust

On 10 September Coulondre, the French ambassador, returned from Paris. He told Fierlinger that Bonnet had understood Litvinov's answer to mean 'that the U.S.S.R. was only demanding the use of all diplomatic means'. Coulondre, a sincere advocate of Franco-Soviet co-operation, had contradicted this interpretation. Fierlinger replied: 'The misunderstanding is characteristic of the mutual distrust which should finally be put an end to.' On 11 September Coulondre saw Potyomkin. He declared: 'In the final count the determination of the French Government to render assistance to Czechoslovakia remains unshaken.' He again asked what the Soviet Union would do. Potyomkin repeated Litvinov's four points: (1) appeal to the League of Nations under Article XI; (2) a conference of the USSR, France, and Britain; (3) consultations between representatives of the Soviet, Czechoslovak, and French general staffs; (4) the USSR would carry out all its obligations under the Soviet-Czechoslovak pact, 'using all ways accessible to us for this'. The statement was repeated to Prague 'in order to support the Czechoslovak Government in their most trying hour'.

There it caused embarrassment, not encouragement. On 15 September (according to the Czech archives) Beneš sent a message to Chamberlain through Runciman: 'Czechoslovakia has no special agreements with Russia even for the event of war, and she has not done, and will not do, anything without France.' On 19 September Britain and France presented Hitler's terms to Beneš with the demand that they be accepted. Beneš at first refused. He asked the Soviet representative: (1) Will the USSR render immediate effective assistance if France remains true and also renders assistance? (2) Will the USSR help as a member of the League of Nations on the basis of Articles 16 and 17? He also saw Gottwald, the Czech Communist leader, and asked his opinion 'about the course of action of the U.S.S.R.'. Gottwald replied:

> It is not my business to answer for the U.S.S.R. but nobody has any grounds to doubt that the U.S.S.R. will meet its obligations. If it is a question of something over and above the obligations then Beneš should formulate exactly what and put an inquiry to the Government of the U.S.S.R.

On 20 September the Soviet government replied to Beneš's first question: 'Yes, instantly and effectively'; to the second: 'Yes, in every respect.' This was all in vain. On 21 September the Anglo-French ultimatum compelled Czechoslovakia to accept Hitler's terms. On 22 September Potyomkin asked Fierlinger 'why our Government had never raised the question of unconditional aid by the Soviet Union'. Fierlinger replied: 'It was difficult to consider this in view of the geographical situation.'

Raised terms

All was not yet over. At Godesberg Hitler raised his terms. War seemed likely. On 24 September Gamelin, French chief-of-staff, told the Soviet air attaché in Paris that there were 30 (or perhaps 38) German divisions on the Czechoslovak frontier and that the French were placing fifteen divisions in the Maginot Line. On 25 September the Soviet commissariat of defence replied to Paris: 'Thirty completely alerted divisions have been drawn up in the areas in the immediate vicinity of the Western frontiers'; aviation and tank units were also in full readiness; general mobilization 'would enable the Soviet Union to put a large new army into the field, for equipment and the appropriate war industry allow of this'. Fierlinger added the optimistic footnote: 'According to my information there exists in Government circles here a much greater determination to extend considerable efforts in the event of a world conflict than outward appearances might suggest.'

It was again in vain. On 29 September Chamberlain and Daladier went off to Munich and settled the fate of Czechoslovakia over her head. Beneš made a last splutter of resistance. At 9.30 a.m. on 30 September he telephoned to the Soviet representative: 'Czechoslovakia is confronted with the choice either of beginning war with Germany, having against her Britain and France ... or capitulating to the aggressor ... Beneš wants to know the attitude of the U.S.S.R. to these two possibilities, that is, of further struggle or capitulation.' The telegram reporting this began coming over the wire in Moscow only at 5 p.m. It was followed at 5.45 p.m. by a second message:

> Beneš no longer insists on an answer to his last question because the Government has already passed a decision to accept all the conditions.

It may still be uncertain precisely what aid the Soviet Union would have given to Czechoslovakia. But one thing is quite certain: the French and Czechoslovak governments were determined that this aid should not be given.

CHAPTER FIFTY-THREE

The Myths of Munich

This essay was first published in Purnell's *History of the Twentieth Century*, published in magazine-size parts (1968–70). Alan Taylor's essay was part of a section 'Understanding Munich', the other four contributions being by Czech, German, French and Russian historians.

The international conference at Munich on 29 September 1938 had a practical task: to 'solve' the problem of the three million German-speakers in Czechoslovakia and so to prevent a European war. Apparently it succeeded in this task. The Czechoslovak territory inhabited by the three million Germans was transferred to Germany; the Germans were satisfied; there was no war. The controversy which has raged over the conference from before it met until the present day sprang more from what it symbolized than from what it actually did. Those who welcomed the Munich conference and its outcome represented it as a victory for reason and conciliation in international affairs – appeasement as it was called at the time, 'jaw, not war', as Winston Churchill said of a later occasion. The opponents of Munich saw in it an abdication by the two democratic powers, France and Great Britain; a surrender to fear; or a sinister conspiracy to prepare for a Nazi war of conquest against Soviet Russia. Munich was all these things.

The problem of the German-speakers in Czechoslovakia was real. They had been privileged people in the old Habsburg monarchy. They were a tolerated minority in Czechoslovakia. They were discontented and grew more so with the resurgence of national pride in Germany. No doubt Hitler encouraged their discontent, but he did not create it. Those in the West who called out, 'Stand by the Czechs', never explained what they would do with the Czechoslovak Germans. Partition seemed the obvious solution. In fact, as later events proved, Bohemia was the one area in Europe where partition would not work. Czechs and Germans were so intermingled that one or other had to dominate. Once Czech prestige was shattered, a German protectorate inevitably followed six months later, to the ruin of the Munich settlement. The Czechs themselves recognized that there was no room in Bohemia for both nationalities. When independent Czechoslovakia was restored at the end of the war, the Germans were expelled – a solution which is likely to prove final.

The timing of the Czech crisis was not determined by the Czechoslovak Germans or by Hitler. It was determined by the British government, and especially by Neville Chamberlain, the British prime minister. He wanted to restore tranquillity in Europe and believed that this could be done only if German grievances were met. Moreover they must be met willingly. Concessions must be offered to Germany, not extracted under threat of war. Until 1938 Hitler had been destroying one bit of the 1919 settlement after another, to the accompaniment of protests from the Western powers. This time Chamberlain meant to get in ahead of him. Hitler was to be satisfied almost before he had time to formulate grievances.

Fear, not reason

Chamberlain set himself two tasks. First, the French must be induced not to support their ally, Czechoslovakia. Second, the Czech government must be persuaded or compelled to yield to the German demands. He succeeded in both tasks, but not in the way that he intended. He had meant to use the argument of morality: that German grievances were justified and therefore must be re-dressed. Instead, as the months passed, he came to rely on practical arguments of force and fear. The French were driven to admit, with a reluctance which grew ever weaker, that they were unable to support Czechoslovakia. The Czechs were threatened with the horrors of war unless they gave way. When Chamberlain flew to Munich on his first visit to Hitler, it was not as the emissary of even-handed justice. He came in a desperate effort to avert a war which the Western powers dreaded. Thereafter fear, not reason, was his main argument, and the principal moral which the British drew from Munich was not that conciliation had triumphed, but that they must push on faster with rearmament.

At the Munich conference there was certainly an abdication by the Western powers. France especially had been the dominant power in Eastern Europe since the end of the First World War. Germany was disarmed; Soviet Russia was boycotted; all the new states of Eastern Europe were France's allies. She regarded these alliances as a source of strength. As soon as her allies made demands on her, she turned against them. France had been bled white in the first war, and Frenchmen were determined not to repeat the experience. They believed that they were secure behind their fortified frontier, the Maginot Line. Hence they did not care what happened beyond it. As to the British, they had always insisted that their interests stopped at the Rhine. Austen Chamberlain had said that no British grenadier would ever die for Danzig – or for anywhere else in Eastern Europe. The British recognized that German predominance would take the place of French. But this did not trouble them. Eastern Europe and the Balkans were no great prize economically. If they absorbed German energies and ambitions, it was all the more likely that Germany would leave Western Europe and the British Empire alone.

Fear of war was also a dominant motive at the Munich conference, but for the Western powers it was war that was feared rather than defeat. The French had confidence in their army, the British in their navy. But while they did not expect the Germans to defeat them, they doubted whether they could defeat Germany – except at a terrible price. There was no way in which the Western powers could give limited aid to the Czechs, as they might have done to the Spanish Republic. The facts of geography stood in the way. It was war on the largest scale or nothing. In those days, everyone believed that aerial bombardment would reduce the cities of Europe to ruin within a few weeks. European civilization would come to an end. This was the peril which Chamberlain sought to avert.

The Czechs themselves shared this fear of war. President Beneš believed that Hitler was bluffing and would give way if faced with a firm united opposition. When Hitler did not give way, even Beneš in the last resort preferred surrender to war. The Czechs, Beneš held, were a small people, who must preserve their lives for a better future. Their country had been occupied before and they had survived. They would survive again. In a sense, his arguments were justified by events. The Czechs were abandoned by the Western powers. Their country fell under German tyranny for six years. But only one or perhaps two hundred thousand of them lost their lives. Prague, their capital was the only great city of Central Europe to remain undamaged in the Second World War, and Czechoslovakia re-emerged with unbroken spirit at the end. In contrast, Poland was guaranteed by the Western powers, who went to war for her sake. As a result, six million Poles were killed. Warsaw was reduced to a heap of ruins, and Poland, though restored, lost much of her territory and of her independence.

Was Munich a conspiracy?

Did more lie behind? Was the Munich conference not merely a surrender, an abandonment, or even a betrayal of Czechoslovakia? Was it also part of a deliberate attempt to promote a German hegemony and to clear the way for a German attack on Soviet Russia? This is a view strongly held by Soviet and other Communist-inclined historians. The Munich conference was certainly an assertion that Europe could settle its own affairs. Only the purely European powers – France, Germany,

Great Britain, and Italy – were represented. The two world powers, Soviet Russia and the United States, were absent. The United States had persistently refused to be involved in European conflicts ever since the end of the First World War. It is likely, too, that the Western powers welcomed the absence of any American representative. If one had attended the conference, he would have preached morality to others without being prepared to act on it himself. Great Britain and France looked forward to a time when there might be a great war and they would need American aid. Even with this in mind, they preferred not to be exposed to American reproaches before the time came for action.

Soviet Russia was a different matter. The Western powers never counted on Soviet aid. They did not believe, and quite rightly, that even if Soviet Russia entered a war against Germany she would be fighting either for Democracy as they understood it or for the sanctity of treaties. After all, the settlement of 1919 had been made quite as much against Soviet Russia as against Germany, and the Russians would aim to take Germany's place in Eastern Europe, not to defend the independence of the small states. As well, the Western powers doubted whether Soviet Russia intended to fight Germany seriously or whether she was capable to doing so. They distrusted Soviet Russia quite as much as she distrusted them. Each side suspected the other of pushing it into the front line. Moreover, this was the period of Stalin's great purges. Nearly all the marshals and generals of the Red Army had been murdered or imprisoned. Under such circumstances, it was hard to believe that Soviet Russia could conduct a successful offensive. Geography stood in Russia's way even more than in theirs. Soviet Russia could not strike at Germany without crossing the territory of either Poland or Romania. Both countries refused to allow the passage of Soviet troops – the Poles more vigorously than the Romanians. The Western powers were supposed to be defending the rights of small nations and could hardly begin their campaign by trampling on the rights of Poland and Romania.

On paper, the Soviet government had a position of impregnable righteousness. According to the Czech–Soviet treaty, Soviet Russia was committed to supporting Czechoslovakia only if France did so first. The Soviet rulers surmised correctly that France would not honour her word. Therefore they were quite safe in declaring that they would honour theirs. Soviet leaders went further. They often hinted that they would be prepared to aid Czechoslovakia even if France did not act. But they would do this only if President Beneš and the Czechoslovak government asked them to do so. Here again the Soviet government was quite safe. The Czechoslovak government was predominantly right-wing, and President Beneš, though less on the right, was determined not to fight with Soviet Russia as sole ally. This, he thought, would invite the fate of Republican Spain, and he was not far wrong. Hence we cannot tell what the Soviet government really intended to do. They could promise great things in the secure confidence that they would never be called on to fulfil their promises. Similarly, we do not know whether the Soviet government made any serious preparations for war. Most Western observers reported at the time that the Red Army had taken no measures of mobilization. Nowadays the Soviet spokesmen claim that the Red Army had mobilized thirty divisions. This, even if true, was a derisory force to use against Germany, and suggests that the Soviet government were intending only to seize some Polish territory. But as the Soviet government refuses to release evidence, all statements about its policy are guesswork.

We may dismiss one guess the other way round. Soviet writers then and later alleged that the Western powers aimed to switch German aggression eastwards, against Soviet Russia. Many Soviet writers even allege that the Western powers dreamed of joining in this aggression themselves. There is virtually no foundation for their theory. The Communists imagined that everyone in the capitalist world was afraid of them and therefore wanted to destroy 'the workers' state'. In fact, Communism had lost its appeal. Soviet Russia was the best propaganda against Communism – it offered tyranny, starvation, inefficiency. No one in Western Europe feared Soviet Russia any more. Indeed, sensible English people regretted that Soviet Russia was so weak. In the end, German aggression was indeed switched. But it was switched from east to west by the Nazi–Soviet pact. It was not switched from west to east by the conference at Munich.

CHAPTER FIFTY-FOUR

Europe, 1939:
The Negotiations with Russia

This essay was first published as a review of Gregoire Gafencu, *Derniers Jours de l'Europe* (Paris, LUF, 1947), in the *Manchester Guardian* (2 September 1947). Emil Hácha succeeded Beneš as Czech President (1938–45). Josef Tiso was President of Slovakia (1939–45) under Hitler.

Mr Gafencu, former foreign minister of Romania, had a deserved success with his 'Prelude to the Russian Campaign', a first-rate analysis of the relations between Russia and Germany from the signing of the Nazi–Soviet Pact to the outbreak of war in June, 1941. He has drawn again on his experiences in an attempt to repeat his success with an account of the capitals of Europe on the eve of war. As foreign minister, Mr Gafencu toured Europe in April and May, 1939, in an effort to discover what policy Romania should follow. He returned no wiser than he set out. He found Beck in Warsaw, still convinced of the wisdom of his policy of balancing between Germany and Russia; and Beck told him frankly that his object in making the alliance with England was to prevent any entente between England and Russia, an object fully achieved. There are the usual pictures of the gangster crowd in Berlin, posing and ranting. A typical card-sharper's trick was to invite Mr. Gafencu to join the guests of honour at a review; the other guests were Hácha and Tiso, and Mr Gafencu escaped the embarrassing association only by simulating illness.

British hesitations

In London he found bewilderment, but determination; in Paris clearer vision, but fear. There was divergence in the British and French approaches towards Russia. The British wished to bring in a little Russian weight to redress the balance, certainly not to tip the balance on to the Russian side; the French politicians, terrified of war, sought full Russian support and, in Munich spirit, would pay any price for it. Here Mr Gafencu's book makes real revelations and becomes an invaluable source. Immediately after the breakdown of negotiations with Russia the British government was reluctant to reveal its hesitations: later, in the spring of 1940, the French government was reluctant to reveal its eagerness. The official documents were therefore never published as a Blue Book, and we shall have to wait some years until the Woodward and Butler series reaches this point. Mr Gafencu was shown the early correspondence during his visit to Paris in May 1939: and a fellow-exile in Geneva, whose identity is easy to guess, has shown him the rest. These selections have little to do with his journey of April 1939; still, this does not matter – however irrelevant, they provide the fullest documentary account of the abortive negotiations which by their failure precipitated the second German war.

The first stage, in April, 1939, was the search for a formula of entente. The British asked of Russia a unilateral promise to assist her neighbours if attacked: the French proposed a pact of mutual assistance in case any of the three Great Powers was involved in war with Germany. Mr Gafencu reproduces a British Note of 29 April revealing the British doubts and lack of enthusiasm:

> The policy which H.M.G. follows, in its contacts with the Soviet Government, has to aim to try to reconcile the following considerations: (a) not to neglect the chance of receiving aid from the Soviet Government in case of war; (b) not to compromise the common front by overriding the susceptibility of Poland and Rumania; (c) not to alienate the sympathy of the whole world by giving a pretext for the anti-Comintern propaganda of Germany; (d) not to compromise the cause of peace by provoking any violent action on the part of Germany (Retranslated from the French).

What hope was there for an alliance inaugurated with such reserves? The anxiety about Romania was, in any case, fraudulent: Mr Gafencu agreed with M. Bonnet that the hesitation of Romania would disappear once there was a real accord between Russia and the West. The objection concerning Poland was real; till the very end Beck succeeded in his policy of preventing an Anglo-Russian alliance. The alliance with Poland, made without conditions, was the supreme blunder of British pre-war policy – all the worse for the penalty of the blunder falling in the end most heavily on the Poles themselves.

French urgency finally imposed the principle of mutual assistance on the British, agreement to agree on this was reached on 2 June. June was taken up with the problem of what states the proposed allies should assist. This was, in essence, the problem of the Baltic States; in these the Russians saw, rightly, a German route of aggression; the Western powers, also rightly, feared for their independence. M. Bonnet tried to escape the problem by assuring the Russians of British and French good faith; after Munich this had little value in Russian eyes – and who can blame them? They asked for something more solid, and, after endless wrangles, got it: they were to be allowed to assist the Baltic States and what is more, the Western powers agreed to a definition of indirect aggression in Russian terms. Still, these concessions were without effect: they were all wrung out of the British government, and each fresh contortion convinced the Russians that they were being pushed ahead to bear the brunt of a German attack. This was not true: the British hoped that apprehension of a Triple Alliance would keep Germany from war, without involving any real increase in Russia's strength; the French, driven on by justified fear, staked everything on Russia's military support. England genuinely wanted to save the *status quo* created in 1919 and therefore could not genuinely desire Russia as an equal partner; France genuinely desired Russia as a full ally and was therefore insincere about the *status quo*.

Poland's position

The final blow came when the Russians demanded military conversations. This demand too was justified, in view of the Russian experience of the Franco-Soviet pact, which without military conversations had proved worthless. Military conversations, however, led to the inevitable questions. On 14 August Marshal Voroshilov asked: 'Would the Soviet troops be authorised, in case of an aggression directed against France and England, to penetrate into Polish territory across the corridor of Vilna and Galicia and also into Romanian territory?' It is possible that in presenting this question the Russians deliberately provoked a rupture; it seems more likely that to the very last moment they would have agreed to an alliance if the British and French had accepted them as the paramount great power in Eastern Europe (which in any case, as the result of victory against Germany, they were bound to become). At any rate the question put Poland in control of Europe's destinies, and the Poles were justified in blaming France, their ally, for having started a negotiation which was bound to lead to this question. French diplomacy reached its nadir; though still bound to Poland as an ally the French government decided to ignore the Polish refusal, and on 21 August Daladier authorized the French military representative to sign the military agreement 'on the best conditions possible'. Mr Gafencu does not reveal the British answer to Marshal Voroshilov's embarrassing question. Probably none was made in time: on 21 August it was announced that Ribbentrop was leaving for Moscow. This was the end of the Europe of 1919, the Europe which tried to ignore both Russia and Germany as great powers. Henceforth who fears the one must go with the other.

CHAPTER FIFTY-FIVE

The False Alliance

This essay was first published in Purnell's *History of the Twentieth Century*, published in magazine-size parts (1968–70).

Nearly two years elapsed between the signing of the Nazi–Soviet Pact and Hitler's invasion of Russia. It was a time of opportunism in foreign policy: Stalin hoped to make gains without effort and to involve others in war without being involved himself. Instead Soviet Russia was thrown into the most terrible war ever fought by a civilized power.

The Nazi–Soviet Pact of 23 August 1939 gave the signal for the Second World War. This may not have been the intention of its authors. Both Hitler and Stalin may have thought that the Western powers would abandon Poland once there was no chance of a Soviet alliance, and the Soviet promise of neutrality was at once made public in order to produce this effect. Stalin was not content with a similar German promise of neutrality in return. He demanded what he thought were concrete measures of security, and secret clauses drew a firm limit to German gains in Poland. What had once been called the Curzon Line was to be roughly the boundary between Soviet and German 'spheres of influence'.

The pact did not shake the nerve of the Poles nor, in appearance, that of the Western powers. On 1 September German armies therefore invaded Poland. On 3 September Great Britain and France declared war on Germany. At first the Russians pretended to be genuinely neutral and even talked of supplying Poland with raw materials and armaments. Soon they grew alarmed at the speed of German victories. They wanted to collect their share of Poland before the Germans forestalled them. But how were they to justify their move in the eyes of the world? Molotov, the Soviet foreign commissar, proposed to announce that the Red Army had entered Poland in order to protect the Ukrainians and White Russians 'threatened' by Germany. Ribbentrop did not like this at all. The Russians had a further worry. There were rumours that an armistice might be signed between Germany and Poland. In that case, Germany would gain her share of the plunder, and Soviet Russia would not. Thus the Soviet government was pulled in opposite directions: anxious to keep up an appearance of neutrality and at the same time to be in on the kill.

Practical considerations decided Soviet action. The Red Army could not be ready until 17 September, and by then the Polish forces had been largely destroyed. Even so the Red Army saw some fighting. Seven hundred Soviet troops were killed, and Stalin was able to declare that Soviet–German friendship had been 'sealed in blood'. Soviet intervention did not cause the defeat of Poland, but by carrying off some 200,000 Polish soldiers as prisoners-of-war it greatly hindered the creation of a new Polish army in the West.

On 27 September Ribbentrop went to Moscow again. This time he was received as an old friend with flamboyant honours. The original pact had left open the question whether any Polish state should be allowed to survive. Now Stalin was determined that Poland should cease to exist, and for a very obvious reason: a rump Poland would be within the German sphere and its grievances could easily be turned into a German spearhead against Soviet Russia. With the Western powers still at war, Ribbentrop needed Soviet friendship and accepted Stalin's terms. Soviet Russia renounced its small share of ethnic Polish territory and received in exchange undisputed control of Lithuania. There was a further clause: 'Both parties will tolerate in their territories no Polish agitation which affects the territories of the other party.' Since there were few Poles in the territory acquired by Soviet Russia, this was a one-sided promise by Germany to suppress Polish national claims – a promise which Hitler had no reluctance to keep. Everyone was happy. Ribbentrop attended a great dinner at the Kremlin and reported that he felt as if he were among 'old Party comrades'. The Bolsheviks were elevated to the rank of honorary Nazis.

Both Hitler and Stalin believed that the accord would last a long time. Hitler always thought in ideological terms, though of course believing that only his ideas were valid. He easily persuaded himself that Stalin had ceased to be a Communist and had become a purely nationalist leader, in which he was not far wrong. He was even ready to profess a personal admiration for Stalin as his only equal among statesmen. He said: 'Stalin and I are the only people who have considered the future.' At the same time he attributed to Stalin his own lack of scruple, in which also he was not far wrong.

Stalin claimed to judge politics in harsher terms. Yet he too had an illusion, constantly shown by Soviet statesmen. Though themselves dismissing good faith as 'bourgeois morality', they expected good faith from others, even from the most unscrupulous, and expressed great indignation when they were cheated. Now Stalin believed that the Nazi–Soviet Pact was worth more than the paper it was written on – an agreement which Hitler would keep even if he himself did not. He had more practical grounds for confidence. Germany and Soviet Russia had a long experience of co-operation during the partnership of the Rapallo Treaty, and this partnership was apparently restored. Soviet Russia would supply Germany with raw materials, and Germany would supply Russia with machinery. Not that Stalin expected the partnership to last for ever. Soviet policy was always dominated by the fear of an anti-Soviet alliance among the 'capitalist' powers and was now haunted by the spectre that Great Britain and France might switch the war by joining Germany against Soviet Russia. It would suit Stalin best if the war came to an end, and he therefore instructed the Communist parties of Western Europe to launch a peace campaign against the 'imperialist war'. Great Britain and France, once numbered among the anti-fascist and peace-loving powers, were transformed into imperialists, anxious only to crush their German rival. From the autumn of 1939 until 22 June 1941 Communist parties everywhere used what influence they had to oppose the war, and the Comintern became implicitly Nazi Germany's ally.

At the same time, Stalin took precautions against Germany by establishing Soviet control of the Baltic. This seemed the one gap in Soviet Russia's defences. The Red Army was supposed to be strong enough to hold the land frontier. But the German navy could dominate the Baltic, if its big ships were moved there, and German troops could be landed behind the Russian lines. The Soviet government forced the three Baltic states – Lithuania, Estonia, and Latvia – to accept defensive alliances and Soviet garrisons. It made the same demand of Finland. The Finns refused, and Soviet Russia began the Winter War. The Soviet generals had misjudged Finnish strength and began the war without careful preparation. The Finns resisted and were at first victorious.

The Soviet attack on Finland was solely directed against Germany. Nevertheless, Hitler needed Soviet friendship and paid with benevolent neutrality in return. Fascist Italy was prevented from sending aeroplanes to Finland, and other Fascist states were prevented from sending volunteers. The Western powers, on the other hand, succumbed to collective madness and talked of aiding Finland, though they had no means of doing so. Influential Frenchmen imagined that bombing the Russian oil wells would be the most effective means of striking against Germany. Some even aspired to 'switch' the war by joining Germany against Russia. Western statesmen had denounced the Nazi–Soviet Pact. Now they did everything they could to force Stalin into Hitler's arms. Their mad plans went further on paper. Their forces could not reach Finland without crossing Sweden and Norway, and the two Scandinavian countries refused to allow this. The Western powers then proposed to force their way through, despite Norwegian and Swedish resistance. This plan, apart from being unworkable, would have turned the two Scandinavian countries also into Germany's allies. Fortunately, before Great Britain and France could commit this act of supreme folly, the reinforced Soviet army defeated the Finns, and peace was signed on 12 March 1940. Stalin had made Soviet Russia secure against Germany, or so he imagined. However, he claimed that his acts had no anti-German purpose. Russia was merely recovering the position she had lost after the First World War, much as Hitler was doing for Germany in Central Europe.

The honeymoon of Nazi–Soviet friendship

The winter of 1939–40 therefore saw the honeymoon of Nazi–Soviet friendship. Soviet Russia sent great quantities of raw materials and allowed supplies from Japan and other Asiatic countries to cross her territories, thus defeating the British blockade of Germany. The Comintern used such influence as it had in Germany's favour. Czech Communists sabotaged attempts at national resistance; French Communists appealed to the war-weariness of the bored French soldiers. In return Germany sent electrical and other machinery to Soviet Russia. The German generals, old associates of the Russians, would have sent tanks and aeroplanes also. Hitler forbade it. His faith in Stalin was not as complete as he professed, and Germany ran up a heavy bill on Soviet account.

Stalin did not worry at the German failure to supply him with armaments. He believed that he had plenty of time, and the Red Army showed no urgency in preparing the 'Stalin Line'. Like many other authorities, including Winston Churchill, Stalin greatly overrated the strength of the French army, which on paper was indeed superior to the German. Stalin believed that, if Germany launched an offensive in the West, trench warfare would last for years, at it had done during the First World War. Germany would be weakened and would become increasingly dependent on Soviet supplies. The Western powers would be weakened also. Ultimately Soviet Russia would dictate terms to all Europe. Perhaps Communism would triumph – of course under Soviet control. At any rate, Soviet Russia would be secure. Thus, while the Comintern preached peace, Stalin did what he could to lure Hitler into taking the offensive in the West. When Germany overran Denmark and invaded Norway, Molotov wished the aggressor 'complete success', and the Soviet press explained, not altogether unjustly, that the German intervention had been provoked by British and French actions.

Hitler knew that he was secure on his eastern frontier. Only seven German divisions were left in the east when Germany attacked Belgium, Holland and France, and two of these were moved west as the campaign proceeded. Here was Stalin's crowning blunder. He had meant to hold the balance between Germany and the Western powers. He was in no position to do so. As the German armies rolled towards total victory in France, there was consternation in the Kremlin. Marshal Shaposhnikov, chief of staff of the Red Army, urged that Soviet Russia should mobilize and intervene in the name of peace. This was impossible. By the time the Red Army had mobilized, it would be too late, if indeed it were capable to taking the offensive at all. There was nothing for it but to display continued confidence in German good faith. Molotov expressed 'warmest congratulations on the splendid success of the German armed forces' and announced in public on 31 July that 'the friendly relations between Germany and the U.S.S.R. were based on the fundamental interests of the two countries'.

Soviet acts belied these words. The three Baltic States, already bound by treaties of mutual assistance, were occupied in mid-June and soon incorporated in the Soviet Union. A fortnight later, Bessarabia was taken from Romania. Soviet factories were put on a war footing. In July Stalin told Sir Stafford Cripps, the newly-arrived British ambassador, that he expected an attack by Germany at some time and meant to postpone it as long as possible. Really he went on hoping that it might not occur at all, as often happens in such cases. If he grovelled enough in words, if he maintained his supply of raw materials, if he kept his fingers crossed, perhaps the storm would blow over. At any rate, he would do nothing to provoke Germany by closer relations with Great Britain.

Hitler was certain that Soviet Russia would not attack him, in which he was right. This did not mean that he was willing to leave Russia alone. The Soviet move into Bessarabia seemed to threaten the oil supplies from Romania on which the German armies depended. Beyond this loomed the prospect that Soviet Russia would soon claim the predominance in the Balkans which Imperial Russia had once enjoyed or asserted. The Balkans were not essential to Germany's economic position, and Hitler never contemplated advancing through the Balkans in order to strike at British forces in the Near East. He would have been content if the Balkans had remained a no man's land, but such wishes are rarely granted in time of war. Once the Russians stirred his suspicions in the Balkans, Hitler had to respond with precautions which stirred their suspicions. Thus tension mounted on both sides.

Hitler's plans against Soviet Russia did not stop at security in the Balkans. As early as July 1940 he gave the first orders for the destruction of Soviet Russia as a great power. This had nothing to do with his ideological dislike of Communism, as is sometimes alleged. It had nothing to do with his vague aspirations of Lebensraum (living space), nor with his need to exploit Russia's economic resources, which the Soviet government was doing for him already in an eminently satisfactory way. Hitler's plans for attacking Russia were simply an offshoot of his conflict with Great Britain. Even in July 1940 Hitler doubted whether a direct invasion of Great Britain would succeed. He doubted whether aerial bombardment would bring her to surrender. On the other hand, it never crossed his mind that the British might have any hope of winning the war unaided. They would go on only if they looked forward to the active help of the two neutral great powers, Soviet Russia and the United States. Therefore, according to Hitler, the British would give up once they realized that such hopes were futile. With America, Hitler counted on isolationist sentiment and for more than a year tolerated many unneutral acts by the United States so as to keep them out of the war. With Russia, Hitler's method was more direct. He would knock her out by yet another Blitzkrieg. Then surely the British would make peace and Hitler's domination of Europe would be beyond challenge.

Hitler's first measures against Soviet Russia were a mixture of precaution and preparations for an aggressive war. If the Russians had renounced the Balkans, he might have tried peaceful co-operation with them. But the Russians, with equal suspicion, expostulated at each step in the Balkans which Hitler took. In August, Ribbentrop and Ciano carried out a partition of Transylvania, hitherto Romanian, in Hungary's favour. In return, they guaranteed the rest of Romania – obviously, only against Russia. Molotov complained that this was a breach of the Nazi–Soviet Pact. In the autumn, Mussolini, restless under Hitler's control, played for an entente with the Soviet government. Hitler forbade this, and the Russians were more suspicious than ever. The Germans took another provocative step. They concluded a three-power pact with Japan and Italy. Was this solely directed against Great Britain? Or did the Germans mean to turn it against Soviet Russia as well? Ribbentrop assured the Russians that there was plenty of room for them to expand in Asia if only they would forget about the Balkans.

In November Molotov came to Berlin. This was the decisive moment. Hitler spread before him the delights of joining the Tripartite Pact. Soviet Russia could expand into Persia and reach the 'warm seas' of the Indian Ocean. Molotov agreed that this was an attractive prospect, but there were more immediate problems to settle first. Germany was supporting Finland – this must stop. Germany had guaranteed Romania – this must not operate against Soviet Russia. Bulgaria must become a Soviet sphere of influence. The Russians must be given bases at the Dardanelles. More than this, Soviet Russia could not tolerate any German interference with Yugoslavia; she must share in determining the future of Poland; she could not allow any interference with Sweden. Ribbentrop boasted that the British Empire was already finished. As this conversation took place in an air-raid shelter, with British bombers overhead, Molotov was not impressed. He asked: 'If the British Empire is finished, why are we here?' When he departed, he promised to think over the Tripartite Pact. His answer soon arrived. Soviet Russia would join the pact, but only on condition that she controlled Bulgaria and that Germany withdrew her troops from Finland.

Hitler did not reply. Further Soviet requests for an answer were ignored. Any real negotiations between Germany and Soviet Russia ended in November 1940. The rest was only a matter of time, Hitler made up his mind. He would destroy Soviet Russia in the course of the coming year. Though the final breach was caused by Soviet claims in the Balkans, these were merely a symbol, not the real cause. Soviet Russia had to be eliminated one way or another as an independent power, so that Great Britain would be driven to make peace. When Stalin refused to become a gullible and subservient associate of Hitler as Mussolini had done, the destruction of Soviet power in war seemed the only answer. Hitler judged that 1941 was a favourable year in which to undertake this. The expansion of British armed strength was only be- ginning, and Great Britain would not be in a position to act seriously against Germany until 1942. Meanwhile Hitler had a large army doing nothing. He moved against Russia much as Great Britain and the United States launched their North African offensive in 1942 – for want of anything better to do. Hitler did not regard the invasion of Soviet Russia as a formidable operation. He despised the Red Army and, intoxicated by his earlier successes, was confident that he would defeat it without any great effort. Indeed, German armament production was run down steadily before the attack on Russia and even after it had begun.

Hitler's formal decision to attack Russia was made on 18 December 1940 when he issued the directive for Operation Barbarossa. The attack was to begin on 15 May 1941, and Soviet Russia was to be pushed back beyond a line running from Archangel to the Volga. There would be a swift decisive campaign. All would be over before the autumn. Plans for dealing with the occupied Russian territories were drawn up in haste: plans for exterminating the Jews and political commissars; plans for exploiting Russian economic resources; plans for destroying them; plans for co-operating with the non-Russian nationalities; plans for reducing them to slavery. This was all hugger-mugger, and the plans were the result of Hitler's decision to attack Soviet Russia, not its cause.

The Soviet government appreciated that there was an estrangement, but not its extent. It went on with diplomatic protests – over Romania, over Hungary, most of all over Bulgaria. Its protests were ignored. The pact of mutual assistance between Soviet Russia and Bulgaria was never achieved. Instead German troops entered Bulgaria on 1 March. Hitler had a preliminary task before he invaded Soviet Russia – to rescue Mussolini from his difficulties in Greece. German troops would have to go through Yugoslavia. The Yugoslav government agreed and was then overthrown by the patriotic rebellion on 27 March. Stalin imagined that Yugoslavia would be a formidable barrier against Germany – an illusion which the British government shared. On 6 April he signed a pact of friendship and non-aggression with Yugoslavia. On the same day German troops invaded Yugoslavia and destroyed her armies within ten days. A fortnight later the Germans entered Athens. In May they took Crete. Germany's Balkan flank was thus secure. It is true that the Balkan campaign compelled a postponement of Barbarossa from 15 May to 22 June, but Hitler did not worry. He still thought he had time in hand.

Stalin was repeatedly warned of the coming storm – by the American government, by the British government, and by Richard Sorge, the Soviet intelligence agent in Tokyo. He refused to believe that the attack would come so soon. The Soviet armies were massed on the frontiers, their defences unprepared, their organization not designed for war. In this brief period, Stalin was the last of the appeasers, striving to conciliate Hitler by empty gestures. In April Matsuoka, the Japanese foreign minister, came to Moscow and signed a pact of neutrality on German instructions. Hitler was confident that he could beat Soviet Russia on his own and wanted the Japanese to turn all their strength against the British in Singapore and the Americans in the Pacific. When Matsuoka left Moscow, Stalin came to see him off and embraced the German military attaché on the railway platform, saying: 'We will remain friends with you, whatever happens.'

On 6 May Stalin became chairman of the Council of People's Commissars – official head of the Soviet government – for the first time. In gestures he was craven. To please Hitler, he broke off relations with the exiled governments of Yugoslavia, Belgium, Norway, and Greece. Though German deliveries of machinery were much in arrears, Soviet supplies to Germany were speeded up. Two hundred thousand tons of grain were delivered in April, and five million promised for the coming year – far more than the Germans extracted later from conquered Russia. Rubber from the Far East was rushed through Soviet Russia by special trains until the very day war broke out. On 13 June Stalin himself drafted a public statement, denouncing the rumours of German troop concentrations on the Soviet frontiers as 'a clumsy propaganda manoeuvre of forces hostile to the U.S.S.R. and Germany and interested in spreading the war'.

In the early hours of 22 June German troops crossed the Soviet frontiers. German bombers destroyed most of the Soviet air force while it was still on the ground. The German ambassador pulled Molotov out of bed and delivered a declaration of war. Molotov gasped: 'Do you think we have deserved this?' Stalin remained silent until 3 July when he spoke on the Soviet radio for the first time. In slow, toneless Russian with a Georgian accent, he complained: 'Fascist Germany treacherously and without warning violated the non-aggression pact. The war has been forced on us.'

So ended two years of *Realpolitik*. Stalin had hoped to make gains without effort and to involve others in war without being involved himself. Instead Soviet Russia was thrown into the most terrible war ever fought by a civilized power. She was saved more by the heroism of her people than by the ability of her rulers. Hitler had hoped to crown his career of victory with a success easier than any previous one. Instead the German forces were ground to pieces. The war which Hitler began so lightheartedly ended with Germany in ruins and he himself a charred corpse in the garden of the Chancellery at Berlin. Stalin had not intended to destroy German Fascism. The Russians destroyed it all the same.

CHAPTER FIFTY-SIX

The Outbreak of War

This essay was first published in Purnell's *History of the Twentieth Century*, published in magazine-size parts (1968–70).

On 1 September 1939 Poland, the ally of Great Britain and France, was attacked by German forces. Hitler wanted Danzig and the Polish Corridor. The British government was almost prepared to let him have his way ... .

The war crisis of 1939 began on 21 August, with the announcement that Ribbentrop, German foreign minister, had been invited to Moscow by the Soviet government. Though the Nazi–Soviet Pact was not formally concluded until 23 August, it was obvious that Ribbentrop would not go to Moscow unless agreement had already been reached in principle. Hence it was certain that the negotiations for an alliance between France, Great Britain, and Soviet Russia had broken down. This is what Hitler wished to establish. Soviet neutrality in itself was not enough for him. What he needed was public news of this neutrality so that he could shake the nerves of the British and French governments. Stalin, the Soviet dictator, exacted his price in return. Though he, too, like Hitler, probably expected British and French resolution to collapse, he wanted to keep the Germans far from the Soviet frontier if war occurred after all. Hence the Nazi–Soviet Pact drew a barrier in Eastern Europe which the Germans were not to cross.

The pact was neither an alliance nor a partition agreement. The Soviet government merely promised to stay neutral which is what the Poles had always asked them to do, and in addition they set a limit to German expansion. However, the immediate effect was certainly discouraging for the Western powers. Until the last moment they had gone on dreaming either that Hitler would be frightened by the Soviet bogeyman or that Soviet Russia would do their fighting for them. Now they had to decide for themselves, and Hitler was convinced that they would run away. On 22 August he delivered to his generals a wild oration: 'Close your hearts to pity. Act brutally.' He boasted: 'I have got Poland where I wanted her', and added cheerfully: 'The probability is great that the West will not intervene.' Hitler was play-acting in order to impress the German generals. He guessed that some of them would leak to the British, and sure enough some did. Almost at once the British embassy received an exaggerated version of Hitler's speech and was correspondingly alarmed.

On 23 August Hitler went a step further. He moved forward the attack on Poland, fixed for 1 September, to 4.40 a.m. on 26 August. This, too, was play-acting. The German preparations could not be complete before 1 September. Attack on Poland before then was possible only if she had already surrendered. Thus Hitler counted confidently on the collapse of the Western powers.

The French almost came up to his expectations. Georges Bonnet, the foreign minister, had always wanted to desert the Poles. He accepted the German case over Danzig. He had no faith in the Polish army. On 23 August Daladier, the Premier, summoned the Committee of National Defence at Bonnet's request. Bonnet asked: should they push Poland into a compromise and postpone the war until they were stronger? Gamelin, the French commander-in-chief, would not admit the weakness of his army. He asserted that the Poles could hold out until the spring. By then, France would be 'impregnable'. There was no suggestion that France could aid Poland in any way. Nor did the French attempt to discuss the situation with the British. There were no Anglo-French meetings of ministers such as had marked the Czech crisis. Ideally, the French would have liked the British to force surrender on them. But they would not take the lead in abdication themselves. There was a choice between abandoning Poland and fighting a great war in which France would carry most of the burden. The French refused to choose. They sat helplessly by throughout the week when others decided the fate of Europe and of France.

British obstinacy

The British government were apparently more resolute. On 22 August they issued a statement that the coming Nazi–Soviet Pact 'would in no way affect their obligation to Poland'. There was nothing else to do. The British ministers were proud and obstinate. They were not going to have the Opposition crowing that their policy was in ruins. Besides, they feared to be swept away in a storm of public opinion if they showed weakness. Conservative back-benchers had disliked the negotiations with Soviet Russia. But many of them had fought in the First World War. They could not imagine that Great Britain was unable to impose her will on Germany if she determined to do so. As for the Opposition, they had championed the Soviet alliance. Now they were resolved to show that, unlike Stalin, they stuck to their principles.

In secret the British ministers wanted to give way. Chamberlain told Kennedy, the American ambassador: 'The futility of it all is frightful; we cannot save the Poles; we can only carry on a war of revenge that will mean the destruction of all Europe.' Chamberlain said he could not put pressure on Poland himself. Would President Roosevelt do it for him? Roosevelt refused. The only hope was to warn Hitler, or rather to plead with him. On 23 August Nevile Henderson flew to Berchtesgaden. He delivered a warning that Great Britain would stand by Poland. But he also asserted that Hitler could get Danzig peacefully, and he spread out the delights of an Anglo-German alliance. Hitler appeared to be unimpressed. He stormed and ranted. When Henderson left, Hitler slapped his thigh and exclaimed: 'Chamberlain will not survive that conversation. His government will fall tonight.' Back in Berlin, Henderson told Lipski, the Polish ambassador, that the only chance was for Poland to start negotiations immediately. Lipski took no notice.

On 24 August the British Parliament met. It unanimously applauded what it supposed to be the government's firm stand. Hitler began to doubt whether the British government had yet reached the point of surrender. He flew to Berlin and held a conference with Ribbentrop and his leading generals. He asked: should they stick to 26 August as the date for the attack on Poland? He decided that he would make a further attempt to detach the Western powers from their alliance with Poland. This took the form of a 'last offer' which Hitler made to Henderson soon after midday on 25 August. He declared that the problems of Danzig and the Corridor must be 'solved' – though he did not say how. Once this was done, he would guarantee the British Empire, accept an agreed limitation of armaments, and renew his assurance that Germany's western frontier was fixed for ever. Henderson was impressed as usual and thought that Hitler spoke 'with apparent sincerity'. Henderson promised to take Hitler's offer to London the next morning. Hitler approved. What was he up to? By the time Henderson left Berlin the German attack on Poland would presumably have begun. Did Hitler think that the British would abandon the Polish alliance on sight of his offer? Had he forgotten his own time-table? Or was advancing the date of attack to 26 August a bluff all along?

The last seems the most probable explanation. All afternoon on 25 August Hitler raged round the Chancellery. At 3 p.m. he ordered the attack to proceed. Three hours later Attolico, the Italian ambassador, brought the news that Italy could not enter the war unless she received vast quantities of raw materials which Germany was in no position to supply. Immediately afterwards Ribbentrop reported that the Anglo-Polish treaty had been formally signed in London. Hitler pulled back. He summoned Keitel, the chief-of-staff, and said: 'Stop everything at once. I need time for negotiations'. The attack on Poland was called off at the last moment.

The British government seemed to have committed themselves for good when they signed the alliance with Poland, particularly as it included a guarantee of Danzig. Their real attitude was quite different: they were still eager to sell out. The Foreign Office drafted terms for an offer to Hitler which stated that Danzig should have 'the right to determine its political allegiance', and Halifax, the foreign secretary, told the Polish ambassador that the Polish government would make a great mistake if they ruled out 'peaceful modifications of the status of Danzig'. Hitler and the British government thus agreed how negotiations should end – with a Polish surrender. The problem was how to get negotiations started. The two sides circled round each other like wrestlers before a clinch. The British offered to arrange direct negotiations between Germany and Poland if Hitler promised to behave peacefully. Hitler answered that there would be no war if he got his way over Danzig.

Goering, who did not want war, now called in an unofficial intermediary, a Swedish businessman called Dahlerus. Dahlerus flew to London on 25 August and back to Berlin on 26 August; to London and back on 27 August; and the same again on 30 August. In Berlin he saw Goering and sometimes Hitler. In London he saw Chamberlain and Halifax. Each side got the impression that the other was weakening. Both wanted another Munich, but on favourable terms, and neither side knew how to push the Poles over the brink.

On 28 August Henderson delivered the British reply to Hitler's last offer. The British government urged that there should be direct negotiations between Germany and Poland. If these reached agreement, the way would be open for 'a wider and more complete agreement between Germany and Great Britain'. Hitler had repeatedly declared that, as his offers to Poland had been rejected in the spring, he would never negotiate directly with the Poles again. On the other hand, Henderson made no objection when Hitler said that negotiations must involve a Polish surrender over Danzig and the corridor. Thus Hitler thought he would succeed either way. If the Poles yielded, he would get Danzig and the corridor. If they refused, the British government would repudiate them. He decided to accept direct negotiations, but to do it in such a way that Germany would still seem to be dictating to both Great Britain and Poland.

On 29 August Hitler saw Henderson again and delivered his answer. He agreed to direct negotiations, but a Polish representative, with full powers, must arrive in Berlin within the next twenty-four hours. Henderson objected that this was an ultimatum. Hitler and Ribbentrop answered, with typical German pedantry, that the word 'ultimatum' nowhere appeared in the German note. Ultimatum or not, Henderson was eager to accept it. Hitler's offer, he telegraphed to London, was 'the sole chance of preventing war'. Henderson urged acceptance on everybody – on his own government, on the French, on the Poles. He hurried round to Lipski and urged immediate acceptance. Lipski was unmoved and did not even report Hitler's offer to Warsaw. The French were as resolute in the opposite direction. Bonnet telegraphed to Beck that he should go to Berlin at once.

Decision rested with the British government. Here was the proposal they had always wanted: direct negotiations between Germany and Poland. Hitler had agreed. Now they could not deliver the Poles. Chamberlain told Kennedy that he was 'more worried about getting the Poles to be reasonable than the Germans'. And with reason. Beck replied firmly: 'If invited to Berlin of course he would not go, as he had no intention of being treated like President Hácha.' (President Emil Hácha of Czechoslovakia had, five months before on 15 March, been forced by Hitler, Goering, and Ribbentrop to sign away his country's independence.) The British government had to make a temporizing reply, which Henderson delivered only twenty-five minutes after midnight on 30 August, that is after the German 'ultimatum' had run out. The British welcomed Hitler's proposal, but they asked him to wait a bit – they could not produce a Polish representative at such short notice.)

Hitler meanwhile had prepared terms which he would present to the Poles. They were for him moderate: immediate return of Danzig and a plebiscite in the corridor. Henderson thought that these terms were 'not unreasonable'. Back at the British embassy, he summoned Lipski and urged him to seek an interview with Ribbentrop at once. Lipski refused and went back to bed. The next morning Goering sent Dahlerus to Henderson with the German terms in writing. Henderson again summoned Lipski, and when he refused to come, sent Dahlerus round to him. Lipski was still obstinate. He declared that 'German morale was weakening and that the present regime would soon crack'. Dahlerus reported his failure to London and added that the German terms were 'extremely reasonable'. The British agreed. Henderson telegraphed to London that 'on German offer war should be completely unjustifiable', and Halifax telegraphed to Warsaw: 'I do not see why Polish government should feel difficulty about authorising Polish Ambassador to accept a document from the German government.'

Hitler's manoeuvre was succeeding. A breach was opening between Poland and her Western allies. But Hitler was trapped by his own timetable. He had repeatedly declared to his generals that he would either produce a Polish surrender by 1 September or go to war. He dared not face their contempt if he confessed failure. Besides, military action could not be improvised at a moment's notice. If the attack planned for

1 September were called off, it would have to be postponed for many weeks or even months. All the British messages had been intercepted, and Hitler knew how anxious the British government were to surrender. He had to gamble that they would surrender even if war against Poland had started. In this tight situation he had no choice if he were to maintain his prestige. Maybe, too, he liked gambling. As he told Gœring: 'I always call *va banque*. It is the only call I know.' At 12.40 p.m. on 31 August he ordered that the attack on Poland should proceed.

At 1 p.m. Lipski asked to see Ribbentrop. He was asked whether he was coming as a plenipotentiary. He replied: 'No, as ambassador.' This was enough for Hitler. The Poles were still obstinate. At 4 p.m. Hitler confirmed the order for war. At 6.30 p.m. Lipski at last saw Ribbentrop. Lipski said that the Poles were 'favourably considering' the idea of direct negotiations. Ribbentrop again asked whether he was a plenipotentiary. Lipski again said no. Ribbentrop did not communicate the German terms. If he had tried to do so, Lipski would have refused to receive them. The Poles had kept their nerve unbroken to the last moment. At 4.45 a.m. on 1 September the German forces attacked Poland without warning or pretext. At 6 a.m. German aeroplanes bombed Warsaw.

Trapped into war

The ally of Great Britain and France had been wantonly attacked. It only remained for them to declare war on the aggressor. They did nothing of the kind. The two governments merely 'warned' Hitler that they might have to go to war unless he desisted. Meanwhile they hoped that Mussolini would save them as he had done during the Czech crisis, and he duly did his best. He proposed a European conference to survey all causes of conflict, with the condition that Danzig should return to Germany at once. Hitler replied that he would answer on 3 September. The British and French governments were therefore desperate to post-pone any action until that day. But they, too, were trapped – by the indignation of British opinion. The French remained supine. The British were in an uproar. At the very least, German troops must be withdrawn from Poland before the proposal for a conference was accepted. Mus-solini knew that this was hopeless and dropped his proposal. The British and French governments went on hoping for a conference which was already dead.

On the evening of 2 September Chamberlain addressed the House of Commons. MPs expected to hear that war had been declared. Instead Chamberlain said that, if the German government would agree to withdraw their troops from Poland (not actually to withdraw them), the British government would forget everything that had happened, and diplomacy could start again. Chamberlain sat down in dead silence. Greenwood, rising to speak for Labour, was greeted with a shout from Amery: 'Speak for England, Arthur.' Afterwards Greenwood warned Chamberlain that there would be no holding the House if war were not declared. The cabinet met late at night and resolved that an ultimatum should be sent to Germany at once. Halifax, who regretted this decision, put off the ultimatum until the next morning.

The British ultimatum was delivered in Berlin at 9 a.m. on 3 September. The German government made no reply, and the ultimatum expired at 11 a.m. The French trailed after their ally and declared war at 5 p.m. The Second World War had begun. It is possible that Hitler intended to conquer Europe at some time. It is also possible, though less likely, that the British government intended at some time to resist him. Neither of these intentions caused the actual outbreak of war. Then Hitler merely wanted Danzig and the corridor, and the British government wanted to give them to him. These plans were wrecked first by Polish obstinacy and then by the indignation of Conservative backbenchers. The very men who had applauded Munich now insisted on war.

There was much talk later about a crusade against Fascism. In fact most countries were pushed into war. The Poles had no choice. The French were dragged along by the British. Russians and Americans, mighty boasters both, waited supinely until Hitler chose to attack them. Only the British people and their dominions went to war of their own free will. They were not concerned about Fascism. They did not even save Poland. They went to war out of national pride and for the sake of national honour. Ultimately they brought Hitler down, and this was something to be proud of.

CHAPTER FIFTY-SEVEN

1939 Revisited

This was given as the 1981 Annual Lecture at the German Historical Institute, London, and was published as a 20-page pamphlet by the Institute. It is doubtful if Stanley Morison (1889–1967) departed from the editorship of the *Times Literary Supplement* over the ill-feeling engendered by Alan Taylor's review of the first volume of the interwar British foreign policy documents.

It is just twenty years since I published *The Origins of the Second World War*[1] and of course in many ways it is out of date. I welcome this opportunity of considering how it ought to be revised. Perhaps I can make my position clear by telling how it came into being at all. It was certainly not designed as a provocative book; indeed, I can say hand on heart that I have never written a book which was designed to be provocative. If other people choose to be provoked that is not my doing. *The Troublemaker*, which is my favourite brainchild, has something provocative in it, though not deliberately; my other books contain just what I discovered by looking at the sources.

The Origins of the Second World War has two origins itself. One is that I had written a large work, *The Struggle for Mastery in Europe 1848–1918*[2] which went virtually up to the end of the First World War and I was interested in what happened thereafter. More than this, I had, since soon after the second war, read and reviewed the documents both of British and German foreign policy as they came out. In those days the editor of the *Manchester Guardian*, as it then was, was acutely interested in history, which is unusual for editors, and he gave me a whole page on each volume so that I really accumulated, quite by accident, a good deal of historical awareness. I had done a lot on the documents as they had come out. Now I could make a presentation of them. There was another reason, I was really engaged in another major project – my volume in *The Oxford History of England, English History 1914–45*[3] – and then just at this time I became Vice-President of Magdalen College, which is usually not a very onerous task, but this happened to be the quincentenary of the college and I had to run the whole thing. It was quite clear to me that for at least a year, and possibly two years, I should not have much time for research, so why not write a book where I had done the research already?

The Origins of the Second World War was a fill-up book. It would be wrong to say that it was not meant to be a serious contribution, but it was not meant to be an enormously long contribution. I wrote it pretty fast and a good deal of it simply derives from my earlier generalizations and knowledge adding to this the sources as they had come out. And it seemed to me it came out as a reasonable picture.

Now that I look back at it I could tell you some of the defects. The major defect was that the sources which I used were grossly inadequate. Of the two great series, the German one was proceeding with some sort of organization, but the British one was absolutely chaotic and grossly inadequate for a scientific publication.[4] For instance, it did not until much later in the day print any of the Minutes which are extremely valuable for the understanding of foreign affairs and had been a striking feature of the documents before 1914. Moreover, as we now know, it was steadily and consistently rigged in favour particularly of the then foreign secretary, I mean before the war, Lord Halifax. Curiously enough I did not get into trouble myself over this, but I landed someone else in trouble. When the first volume of the documents on British foreign policy came out I wrote a long review on the encouragement of the editor of the *Times Literary Supplement* [TLS], pointing out that they had not included the statement which Gooch and Temperley included in every volume, that they would feel themselves compelled to resign if there was any attempt to interfere with them.[5] It just had not occurred to the then editor that such a stance was required of an editor of diplomatic documents. I pointed out the absence of Minutes and in general concluded that it was an extremely inadequate volume. I then went away on holiday, to Yugoslavia as a matter of fact, where I could not be got hold of, and it was not possible for me to produce any defence or explanation. As a result Stanley Morison, the then editor of the *Times Literary Supplement*, was so harassed by complaints, both from the editor, Woodward, himself and from the Foreign Office, that he decided to resign his post and that is how he ceased to be editor of the *TLS*. I have often brought great misfortunes on my editors and have escaped them myself. But certainly there was no intention on my part of making a provocation then; now, I think, everyone is agreed that the earlier volumes of the documents on British foreign policy are highly inadequate and every detailed researcher now working in the archives finds flagrant suppressions and concealments.

Apart from that – some British documents, some German documents – I had nothing. The Italians, I think, had begun and done a couple of volumes on 1918, but they were of no significance.[6] The French had produced nothing at all and I had to make up a great deal from unreliable memoirs, or even from reliable memoirs; but there was certainly a great shortage. When I consider some of the things that have appeared later, not only in the diplomatic documents, but elsewhere, I appreciate how inevitable, no doubt, but unfortunate it was, that my book was so superficial and could have been reinforced.

I will give you a couple of examples, both in relation to British foreign policy. At this time, and until comparatively recently, our information came almost entirely from documents produced in the Foreign Office and this at a time when the Foreign Office had, I do not say nothing, but comparatively little to do with the great decisions in foreign affairs. It is only quite recently, about eight years, that we have learned anything extensively of the proceedings of either the Chiefs of Staff Committee or the Committee of Imperial Defence and here, for instance, we find, and it made me smile, the report of the Chiefs of Staff Committee each year, beginning from 1934, that of course the object of British defence policy must be to prepare for war with Germany.[7] When the scholars first discovered in German records that they had actually put it down, or Hitler had put it down, that they must prepare for a war against England and France, what a howl there was. but I have never heard a howl at the suggestion that the British chiefs of staff actually set it as their aim to prepare for war with Germany, because they called it defence; when other people do it, I have forgotten the word you call it, but it is not such a kind word as defence. But we knew absolutely nothing of this fifteen to twenty years ago, at least I did not. The other thing which, I think, is more important and still leaves enormous gaps in our knowledge is the foreign policy pursued not by the Foreign Office, but by the Bank of England, the Board of Trade and other economic organizations. We have only that splendid volume of Bernd-Jürgen Wendt which, unfortunately, he had to finish for all practical purposes in 1938, because the documents were not then available for 1939.[8] And here again, there is an entirely different story; just as the defence chiefs admitted preparing for a war against Germany, what one might call the economic branches of the British government were steadily pursuing a policy not of appeasement, but of collaboration with Nazi Germany. This was to continue, as we know, though we do not know all the details, not only until March 1939 when the mission had to be called off, but was still being pursued in July 1939 and this may help to explain why Hitler, until very late in the day, did not take the British warnings seriously.

The whole pattern of British policy in the earlier 1930s was a strange contradiction: on the one side arguing that if Germany became really powerful an Anglo-German war was bound to take place and on the other side, seeking to build up an economic alliance, possibly just to develop the resources of Europe in combination. It was an earlier, though no doubt less reputable, version of the Common Market and in those days Germany was the only country worth joining. The others were all shaky and broken down and the French, in any case, would not join. We know very little about it, but it is surely clear that it had its effect on Hitler's outlook, on the outlook of others in Germany and, what is more, it helps to explain the hesitations and oscillations of the British government.

I did not have any of this and there again if I was to write my book again I would bring it in much more strongly. When I started I accepted all the then assumptions; for instance, one you will recognize now as pure myth, the overwhelming advance in armaments which Germany had accomplished, not only by 1939, but apparently as early as 1936. Living through that period influenced me, I suppose, quite as much as the post-war documents. And the impression that we had from 1936, or indeed earlier, was that Germany was fully equipped for war, that Great Britain was not equipped at all and that France was equipped only for a defensive war. There was a period, just when my book was being completed, when there was a dispute over this and one lot of economic pundits announced that Germany was not so advanced, others announced that Germany was even more advanced. My impression of this controversy, as it ran then and has since concluded, is that German armaments, if not a false alarm, were at any rate an exaggerated alarm. Moreover, we exaggerated the deliberation in Hitler's policy.

I have quite a long background in dealing with German, or Anglo-German affairs; I am not saying for a moment that my views were correct, obviously not all of them could have been, but it offended me very much and still offends me, when I read the critics of my book, who implied that I had been blind about the German danger before 1939 or that my only concern in 1960–61 was to write a book apologizing for German policies, that I was the worst kind of collaborator and appeaser.[9] My reply was twofold. My reply to English critics: I was making speeches about the German danger and how we must rearm from 1936 onwards, when all they were doing was sitting in the Common Room at All Souls College gossiping about politics after dinner; I never was joined by any of my colleagues in agitating for greater armament and urging the Labour Party, of which I was and amazingly still am a member, that we must rearm. Right up to 1936 I was against rearmament in the sense of putting arms into the hands of the then, as it was ludicrously called, 'National' government, because I believed and, to judge by the later behaviour of British governments, not altogether wrongly, that the 'National' government if it got great armaments in its hands would use them to support Germany against Russia. By 1936, I do not say that I had decided this was an illusion, but I certainly thought that the situation was so serious that we had no option but to prepare for a war and abandon every other consideration. At any rate that was my view. I must be one of the very few people who actually addressed public meetings outside London against the Munich Settlement while it was being negotiated, and they were very tough meetings. They are the only meetings where I have had to sit down before the end, because people were shouting so indignantly: 'you mean war', 'you want war', 'we don't want war', 'the Germans are right' – they were terrifying meetings. Not many people that I know of undertook meetings of this kind and I was offended and still am offended by people who imagine that I was interested in appeasing Hitler. I believed, among other things, that a stronger line would not only have been virtuous, to which I do not attach much importance, but that it would have arrested Hitler. It seems to me that all the evidence, and there is more and more, indicates that Hitler had quite clearly decided his policy in 1938, when he was pushed into the Czech affair and the policy, as he said himself, was that he would not go to war unless he was absolutely sure that France and England were going to keep out themselves. My reply to Americans is different; it is that it ill becomes citizens of a state which had to be kicked into war first by Japan and then by Germany, to criticize those who took a different line and were already at war. It never seems to have any effect. The one time when I felt my views really had been somewhat exaggerated was a splendid pamphlet by Harry Elmer Barnes, inventor of one of the greatest of modern political phrases, when he described the League of Nations and all the schemes for collective security as 'Perpetual war for the sake of perpetual peace', an outlook which I have always believed in. But in other ways I think he went a bit far in praising my books as 'blasting the historical blackout'.[10]

Now when I look back and reflect on the background of the outbreak of war in 1939 I see immediately one or two things I missed. It was when I was once more reading over the foolish argument about the blueprint that Hitler was supposed to have made of his plans; this we owe, incidentally, to the editors of the British documents. They discovered a very questionable document, so questionably indeed that it was not seriously used in the Nuremberg tribunal, a document which we now know had been manufactured for the Nuremberg tribunal, and described it in a solemn footnote as Hitler's blueprint for the coming war.[11] And as I reflected on this provocative phrase it occurred to me that, of course, I ought to have written that Hitler had a clear blueprint, a blueprint which was provided by history and that was to overturn the peace settlement of 1919 and demolish its conditions one after another. I know that Hitler said quite early that merely to undo the Treaty of Versailles was a feeble, a petty ambition and that his ambitions were much greater. But I think it gave him a schedule. Hitler continued to follow the line which Stresemann had charted and which Brüning had followed. It was a great disappointment for him that reparations had already been ended. He went on to disarmament and so worked through the clauses of the treaty up to the reoccupation of the Rhineland. It is very characteristic of Hitler's methods that his original intention was to reoccupy the Rhineland sometime in the spring of 1937. Then he saw a wonderful opportunity with the confusion arising over the Abyssinian question and speeded it all up in such a chaos that his generals, as we know, were greatly alarmed. I remember at the time, I was sure that immediately after the reoccupation of the Rhineland Hitler would move into Austria. On the contrary, he not only delayed this, but, in my opinion, was pushed into Austria before he was anxious to act. But still, the schedule is there and in this sense the last of of what one might call his revisionist actions was, of course, the outbreak of war in September 1939 which arose, people sometimes say as a mere excuse, from the question of Danzig. I think one can see a pattern, that he was operating within the framework of revisionism, at any rate until 1939 and was then caught up in a situation where, for some time at any rate, he was prepared to make peace.

Looking back on this record how have my views changed? Primarily, as I have suggested, the attempts by the British to secure Anglo-German economic co-operation and then the way in which defence preparations became more and more the determining factor; we know this in regard to Hitler who often talked as though he would not be adequately prepared for war until 1943 and then felt that the other side would catch up on him. He was paying them a great compliment in doing so. The greatest flaw in my book, I can see as I look at it now. British policy was never able to concentrate on Germany in the way that German policy could concentrate on the East or the West. Indeed, if you judge British policy from defence papers instead of Foreign Office papers (and to do either exclusively is a mistake) the Far East and the Japanese question were for the British a greater obsession and anxiety than Germany. British policy hoped somehow to push the German problem aside. It was to a great extent a dispute between the different services. There was not much mileage, or so the Admiralty thought, in Anglo-German naval conflict. The Admiralty before 1939 had a curious idea that they had solved the submarine menace. Whereas Japan represented an entirely new and ripening threat. One of the great misfortunes of recent historical studies is that Arthur Marder only completed the first half of his study of Japanese–British naval rivalry before his death.[12] He intended to carry it to the end of the war and only reached the battle in the Malaya Sea. Here is a remarkable reminder that it was possible for the most distinguished naval historian of his day to write a book which was largely about British naval policy from 1936 to 1941 and hardly mention Germany at all. It was so secondary.

But when we look at the other services, particularly the Royal Air Force, then there is a different problem again. For the Royal Air Force British policy was a straightforward, simple competition in bomber planes, with the curious idea that the one that got ahead in bomber planes would decisively win the war. As to the army, it had two virulent rivals in this country, one called the Admiralty and the other called the Air Ministry. It was not in a position, at any rate before 1940, to contemplate a serious enemy at all. British defence policy did not wish to concentrate on Germany, but very often did so.[13]

When I come to 1939, I think we are still very short of material in some ways, and particularly for the Polish guarantee and all that followed from it. There has recently appeared a new book by Simon Newman on the guarantee to Poland which is a great deal more reliable in its presentation of British sources than mine was, though I think he carries his view too far.[14] I remember that when *The Origins* came out, about the same time, there appeared a large book by a man called Hoggan, so denounced that although written in English, or at any rate in American, it never managed to find an English publisher.[15] I, glancing at it, felt that it was superficial and trivial and that it would be embarrassing to be linked with it, but now Newman has managed to do this. The new version presents us with a picture of Halifax as the man who organized the war and that it was Halifax who urged the guarantee to Poland, who did so in order to provoke a war. And, there are certainly many things which Halifax said which sound like it: 'If I have to choose between a compromise with Hitler and a war, I would rather have war.' I would put the explanation another way: Halifax was a trimmer, in other words, he always tried to dress the boat. When the boat was on the side of opposition to Hitler, he moved over the other way. When the boat was on the side of compromise, concession he moved the other way again. That is the only explanation I can give to you, but in any case it is delightful to think that an accepted picture in regard to the guarantee to Poland has been very much shaken.

Here is another confession, I think we are so short of material in regard to the attempts at an alliance between Soviet Russia and the Western powers that I am not sure whether one should write anything about it at all. Most of my historical colleagues are so corrupted and blinded by their obsession with the Cold War that it is quite impossible for them to see clearly or to speak honestly about Soviet policies. It is fair to say that Soviet historians are also so blinded by the Cold War that one can make the same criticism of them.

We have more material from the British side than we had, but it is still baffling. For instance, the chiefs of staff unanimously reported that Great Britain would be much better off with a Soviet alliance than a Polish alliance and this opinion, repeatedly stated to the cabinet, to the prime minister, to the foreign secretary, carried no weight whatsoever.[16] I do not attempt to understand this. Cold War is perhaps too strong a word, but if I put it as anti-Russian and still more anti-Bolshevik prejudice I think my criticism is correct. At any rate, alas, there is one source which I must confess we shall not know in my lifetime and it may not even exist; we shall never know the pattern and the springs in Soviet policy. This makes things difficult, but it makes things more difficult if you start off with a prejudice against Soviet Russia.

There are two things that I missed out. I will be able to talk about one, but not the other. The only good point that Hugh Trevor-Roper made in his somewhat foolish criticism of my book was this. After the German occupation of Prague on 15 March 1939 the British government, as we know, at first made complacent, cover-up remarks, principally provided naturally by Sir John Simon, but echoed by Neville Chamberlain with Halifax, as I said before, trimming the boat by taking a rather different line.[17] But what followed therefrom was a totally unexpected explosion of British public opinion. In 1938 over Munich British public opinion, especially the opinion of the House of Commons, was passionately, wildly, hysterically in favour of appeasement and regarded Chamberlain as one of the greatest statesmen of all time. Six months later the same public opinion, perhaps upset at its own enthusiasm for appeasement, turned with equally hysterical violence against the logical consequences of Munich. Anyone who was aware of the situation knew that sometime after Munich, not necessarily in six months, Czechoslovakia would lose its independence. I assumed in the autumn of 1938 that the unity of Czechoslovakia would be dissolved and that the Slovaks would use their position to get the autonomy or independence that they had wanted ever since 1918. I ought to have made more of the outcry.

Perhaps because I have taken part in explosions of public opinion, I find it very difficult to analyse them. You can record the reactions of individuals here and there, you can record something that is profoundly unreliable and yet inevitable as a source and that is the reactions of the House of Commons. I think it is carrying enthusiasm for democracy too far to imply that the House of Commons normally and naturally represents the majority feeling in the country. It may be that there is no majority feeling, it may be that when we talk about public opinion it means simply some editors and journalists plus the members of the House of Commons, but certainly there was an explosion of public opinion in March 1939 and I ought to have gone into it more. I ought to have emphasized the difficulty that the British government worked under when it was trying to accomplish a new stroke of appeasement, because of the reaction of public opinion in March. I will add further, the explosion of opinion after the Nazi–Soviet pact in this country. The feeling that Great Britain should take a firm line was stronger in the House of Commons than elsewhere, but certainly I ought to have developed it.

I do not know how to handle public opinion; what historians have done in the past is to take the public opinion of a tiny group and call it British public opinion which was deeply stirred or not deeply stirred. Until the twentieth century that was the best you could so, because the majority of people were unaware of what was happening. How many Anglo-Saxons do you suppose were deeply stirred by the Battle of Hastings, most of them did not hear about it for months afterwards and this applies to all our history until the twentieth century with some modifications. To discover the sentiments of a nation was a very difficult thing to do, until recently. Now we know the sentiments of a nation, you turn on a knob, noise comes out and that is the sentiment of the nation, at least we are told that it is.

At any rate, these are some of the things which led me to an extraordinary ending of *The Origins*. English people assume that the Second World War started on 3 September and I thought that was when my book had ended, but it had not, it ends with the Germans going into Danzig. Curtain. Now I think that is absolutely wrong, you cannot say that you have told the whole story with the German attack on Danzig and Poland in general. Surely you must explain how the others got in and so quite a number of books tend to go on to 3 September. I am sure when I told the same story in *English History 1914–1945*[18] I carried on the story to 3 September.

But the more I reflected on this, the more I realize that I had given my book quite the wrong name. The Second World War did not begin on 1 September or even on 3 September. There was a small European war which involved only a decision over Poland and then a war which came to an end in June 1940. From June 1940 until June 1941 there was virtually no war in Europe. One can even go further and say that Europe was united for the only time in its history. Hitler's empire had been achieved with far less trouble than Napoleon's empire and was far more complete. There is an interesting subject which indeed people have worked on: the transformation of an European war into a world war.[19] Incidentally, I do not think we will be able to handle this theme in our lifetime, but I may be wrong. I may have got a bit too sensitive and too much aware of official interferences, but there is a theme called the abortive Anglo-German peace negotiations beginning in October 1939 and going on until when, I wonder, perhaps July 1940. If there was a change in British policy it came with the Battle of Britain, and victory in the Battle of Britain, which meant that Great Britain could go on with the war as long as she did not go on with it. I mean by that, as long as she kept out of Europe, which Great Britain successfully did until 1944. Whether there is material for this, the subject sometimes comes to the surface and maybe records will tell us – there is enough to make a story, but not enough to make a book, or not enough to arrive at conclusions. The most you can say is that the possibility of a negotiated peace with Germany was seriously contemplated by the War Cabinet in late May 1940 and continued to be pursued by some branches of the Foreign Office until July. Whether it completely faded thereafter who shall say; I would guess, yes.

But if we are going to tell the story of the origins of the Second World War there are two themes which I left out, one out of carelessness, coupled with ignorance and the other because I was perfectly aware of it, but saw the difficulties of presenting it. The Second World War had preliminaries of small wars, which started in 1931 and continued until June 1940, then there was virtually a period of peace. There was a little colonial war between England and Italy, but it was not of significance for the great course of the war. Two steps led to world war. The first was the German invasion of Russia. We know exactly why it took place, though people invent extraordinary ideas that Hitler was short of raw materials and apprehensive of the Russian danger. Hitler, like so many others, had been deceived by success. His argument to the German generals was that it would be much easier to defeat Russia than it had been to defeat France. 'I have got a big army hanging around, they are getting bored, they must be used and it will clear up the European situation if we knock Russia out.' Here again, there came a first murmur of the negotiated peace idea: with Russia out of the war Great Britain, who could not do anything against Germany, would be ready for a negotiated peace. We have good material on this. I think it needs to be amalgamated into the general story of the war and there is this great significance in it. The Russian war was without the slightest doubt the solitary decision of Hitler. The earlier decisions developed from the general situation in which Hitler was only one of the contributing factors.

The second war, of course, which has been worked on much more by American scholars than by Europeans was the war in the Far East which, having contributed difficulties to British foreign policy ever since 1939, flared up in 1941.[20] But the last point which I have to make is the reminder that the war in the Far East, Pearl Harbor and so on, although it brought the United States into a war, did not bring the United States into the European war and, in other words, did not round out the war into a world war. This, too, was a decision of Hitler. Of all Hitler's decisions it is, I think, the only one which has no rational explanation. The other decisions may have been wicked, they may have been miscalculated, they may have been aggressive, they may have been tyrannical, but it is perfectly possible (that is what people do not like about my book) to explain Hitler's wicked ways by reason and not by hysterics. I do not think he was mad at all, except in so far as anyone pursuing foreign or world policy is mad. There was a time when you could judge a man mad who prepared anything so appalling as the Second World War, but now when you contemplate the activities of American statesmen and Soviet statesmen conceiving wickedness far beyond anything ever thought of by earlier statesmen of any century it is very difficult to get worked up about the wickedness of the Second World War. The fascinating thing is that you can explain everything, except Hitler's declaration of war on the United States, and Hitler obviously found it puzzling himself, since he commented, on occasion, that Germany ought to be fighting on the side of the Anglo-Saxon powers, but that providence had imposed upon her this world historical mistake.[21] That is a good way to describe the outbreak of a world war.

Addendum: Small wars, great wars, world wars

When delivering this lecture it occurred to me that it might help historical understanding to discriminate more precisely between types of war by size and character. We cannot draw a precise line of size but the distinction is clear enough. The Schleswig-Holstein war of 1864 was obviously a small war. The Napoleonic Wars were obviously a great war and indeed were the first to be known as such. Even so, it is worth remembering that all the principal powers of Europe were not engaged simultaneously against Napoleon until 1813. Until then Napoleon was the only factor tying the wars together.

The other most usual distinction is of place. The campaigns of King Henry V are known in English history as the French Wars. I do not know what the French call them. The first great war of the twentieth century was to all intents and purposes an exclusively European war. The little colonial campaigns in Africa or the British campaign against the Ottoman Empire hardly count. At the end of the Great War, as contemporaries called it, the British Colonel Repington invented the title of world war 'to prevent the millennial folk', he said, 'from forgetting that the history of the world is the history of war'. Quite clearly the Great War of the early twentieth century was not a world war, but thanks to the diarist Colonel Repington we are stuck with it.

When another large-scale war or perhaps rather an assembly of different wars broke out at some date between 1932 and 1943 we were stuck with the name world war and mistakenly adopted it for this miscellaneous collection of wars. I have amused myself and I hope my readers by attempting a periodization of wars which occurred in the years usually allotted to the Second World War and allotting them to a specific class. No doubt I have left some out:

China and Japan, 1931–33, renewed rather feebly 1937 and after
    small war

Italy and Abyssinnia, 1935–36
    small war

Germany and Poland, September 1939
    small war

Germany and France, May–June 1940
    expected to be a great war, turned out to be a small one

Germany and Great Britain, June–September 1940, thereafter a deadlock and no serious military engagements until 1944
    small war

Italy and Great Britain, war in Africa, autumn 1940–May 1943
    small war

Italy and Greece, November 1940–April 1941
    small war

Germany and Yugoslavia, April 1941
    small war

Germany and Soviet Union, June 1941
    expected to be a small war (Hitler thought it would be over sooner than the French campaign), turned out to be a great war in a limited sphere, July 1941–May 1945

Japan and United States, December 1941–September 1945
    a great war in a limited sphere

Japan and Great Britain, December 1941–September 1945
    a great war at outset, then a small war until summer 1945

Germany and United States, December 1941–May 1945

small war, indeed a purely theoretical war until June 1944, then a
great war

Anglo-American campaign in Italy, September 1943–May 1945
aspired to be a great war, became in fact a small one of little significance

Japan and Soviet Union, last week of August 1945
small war.

Conclusion

At least two great wars are required to make a world war. The two
great wars – Pacific and European – occurred together from 6 June
1944 until 8 May 1945. Those eleven months alone deserve the title of
Second World War.

Notes

1. *The Origins of the Second World War*, first edn (London, Hamish Hamilton, 1961); new edn (with foreword 'Second Thoughts') (London, Hamish
   Hamilton, 1963; repr. 1965, 1971, 1972, 1973–76).
2. (Oxford, Clarendon Press, 1954; repr. London, 1971).
3. *The Oxford History of England*, Vols 15 (Oxford, Clarendon Press,
   1965; repr. 1979).
4. I am referring here to the then published *Documents on German Foreign
   Policy 1918–1945*, Series C, Vols I–III (30 January 1933–31 March 1935),
   Series D, Vols I–VII (September 1937–3 September 1939), (London,
   HMSO, 1948 *et seq.*). *Documents on British Foreign Policy 1919–1939*,
   First Series, Vols I–IX (1 July 1919–1920), Second Series, Vols I–VIII (23
   May 1929–1934), Third Series, Vols I–IX (9 March 1939–September
   1939), (London, HMSO, 1946 *et seq.*).
5. G.P. Gooch and H.W.V. Temperley (eds), *British Documents on the Origin of the War 1898–1914* (London, HMSO, 1926–38).
6. *I documenti diplomatici italiani*, Sixth Series, Vol. I (4 November 1918–
   17 January 1919), Seventh Series, Vols I–III (11 October 1922–14 May
   1925), Eighth Series, Vols XII–XIII (23 May to 3 September 1939), 1952.
7. See the recent book by B. Bond, *British Military Policy between the Two
   World Wars* (Oxford, Clarendon Press, 1980), esp. pp. 93–7, 193–4,
   211–12.
8. *Economic Appeasement. Handel and Finanz in der britischen Deutschland-
   politik 1933–1939* (Dusseldorf, Berkelsmann Universitätsverlag, 1971).
9. For a discussion of the various critics see W.R. Louis (ed.), *The Origins of
   the Second World War: A.J.P. Taylor and his Critics* (New York, John
   Wiley, 1972); C.R. Cole, 'Critics of the Taylor View of History', *Wiener
   Library Bulletin*, Vol. XXII, 3, New Series 12, (1968), pp. 29–35.

10. H.E. Barnes, *Blasting the Historical Blackout: Professor A.J.P. Taylor's The Origins of the Second World War: Its Nature, Reliability, Shortcomings and Implication* (a pamphlet published privately in the USA in May 1963).
11. Memorandum by Hossbach, 10 November 1937, *German Foreign Policy*, Series D, Vol. 1, No. 19. See the discussion of this document in 'Second Thoughts', a supplementary preface to *The Origins of the Second World War* (note 1).
12. A.J. Marder, *Old Friends, New Enemies: Royal Navy and the Imperial Japanese Navy. Strategic Illusion 1936–41* (Oxford, Clarendon Press, 1981).
13. Cf. Bond, *British Military Policy*; also R.P. Shay jr, *British Rearmament in the Thirties. Politics and Profits* (Princeton, NJ, Clarendon Press 1977).
14. S. Newman, *March 1939: The British Guarantee to Poland. A Study in the Continuity of British Foreign Policy* (Oxford, Clarendon Press, 1976).
15. D.L. Hoggan, *Der erzwungene Krieg. Die Ursachen und Urheber des 2. Weltkriegs* (Tübingen, 1964).
16. Cf. Newman, *March 1939*, pp. 119–21; Bond, *British Military Policy*, pp. 318–19.
17. H.R. Trevor Roper, 'A.J.P. Taylor, Hitler and the War', *Encounter*, 19 (July 1961), pp. 88–96.
18. See note 3.
19. See among others J. Lukacs, *The Last European War, September 1939–December 1941* (London, 1977); H. Michel, *La Seconde Guerre Mondiale* (Paris, 1968); A. Hillgruber, *Hitlers Strategie, Politik und Kriegsführung 1940–1941* (Frankfurt a.M., 1965).
20. See L. Allen, *Singapore, 1941–1942* (London, 1977); C. Thorne, *Allies of a Kind. The United States, Britain and the War against Japan, 1941–1945* (London, Hamish Hamilton, 1978).
21. Cf. D. Irving, *Hitler's War* (London, 1977), p. 354; see also F. Genoud (ed.), *The Testament of Adolf Hitler. The Hitler–Bormann Documents*, intro. by H.R. Trevor-Roper (London, 1960), p. 98.

CHAPTER FIFTY-EIGHT

Old Foreign Office Tie

This essay first appeared as a review of Llewellyn Woodward, *British Foreign Policy in the Second World War* (London, HMSO, 1962) in the *New Statesman*, 63, 1618 (16 March 1962). Woodward had taken great offence at Alan Taylor's review of the early volumes he had co-edited of *Documents on British Foreign Policy 1919–39* and had threatened legal action if Taylor's acknowledgement and thanks to Woodward were not removed from *The Struggle for Mastery in Europe* (Oxford, Clarendon Press, 1965), even though he had commented on an early version of part of the book. This review can hardly have been balm on raw wounds.

During the First World War a number of cavalry divisions were kept behind the lines in France, waiting for the breakthrough which never came. Imagine that one of the cavalry officers was commissioned to write a history of the war, and used only his divisional records. He would describe the months of waiting; go carefully into the problems of forage and remounts; even reach occasional excitement when swords were sharpened. To keep the story in focus, he would remark now and then that infantry were being killed in tens of thousands. Being a generous and broad-minded man, he would mention aeroplanes in one footnote and tanks in another. The result, though no doubt scholarly, would be an odd book.

This is exactly how Sir Lewellyn Woodward has treated his subject. British foreign policy during the Second World War was shaped by a number of authorities. The prime minister determined some of it himself, particularly in important questions. The War Cabinet confirmed the larger decisions, and sometimes initiated them. Other bodies contributed: the Ministry of Economic Warfare, the Special Operations Executive, the Political Warfare Executive. Occasionally policy was imposed on Great Britain by the American State Department or by President Roosevelt himself. All this is clearly explained by Sir Llewellyn Woodward in his admirable introduction. But the introduction leaves virtually no mark on the body of the book. This is, in Sir Llewellyn's words, a large-scale *précis* work; compiled from British archives; and by the archives he means solely the archives of the Foreign Office. Apart from these, the only references are to the six volumes by Sir Winston Churchill. The result is an account of what the Foreign Office thought or tried to do, not of British foreign policy. Perhaps this book, particularly in its original larger form from which the published work has been abridged, had some use for office reference. But it is now offered to the general reader. And for him it has very little use.

Here are two examples taken at random. On 16 June 1940, at the moment of French defeat, the British government made a dramatic proposal for Anglo-French union. No doubt this was a proposal without a morrow. But it illuminates the spirit of the time, and it had an important, though unfavourable, effect on French policy. The proposal did not, however, originate in the Foreign Office. It is therefore mentioned here only by implication. A reader, relying solely on this book, could not discover what it was. Again, there were a number of German offers, mostly unofficial, for a compromise peace. We know that the offers were ignored or rejected. It would be interesting to know why. Presumably they were discussed by the War Cabinet. The Foreign Office was little involved. Hence the offers are dismissed here in a footnote. The truth is that British foreign policy can no longer be described solely from the records of the Foreign Office. We need to see the records of the cabinet – not so much for its deliberations as for the papers on which it reached a decision. The Cabinet Office, however, is peculiarly secretive; and so encourages a smoke-screen of departmental studies.

Sir Llewellyn Woodward knows this. He recognizes that he is describing a subject of marginal importance. But, whether deliberately or not, the result is to recover for the Foreign Office an imaginary independence. Moreover the 'Office' becomes a personality in itself. Even the foreign secretary disappears except as an exalted clerk. The change, for instance, from Halifax to Eden is mentioned only in a footnote. The 'Office' is all. It 'thinks', 'proposes', 'disagrees'. Sir Llewellyn adds: 'Such terms may not stand up to exact analysis, but everyone knows what they mean.' To me they mean only that a particular under-secretary or clerk thought this or that at a certain time. 'Information in the possession of the Foreign Office' sounds impressive. In my limited experience, gossip from right-wing, respectable sources counts in the Foreign Office as 'information'; from left-wing sources not even as gossip. It is dangerous for any institution to forget that it is composed of men, whether the institution be a church or a government department. The Foreign Office has become a tribal god; and Sir Llewellyn Woodward is numbered among the god's worshippers.

The book represents a wider illusion which goes back to Ranke. This is devotion to 'the fact'. Never mind if the facts are trivial, partial, obscure. Merely accumulate, and wisdom will follow. Maybe the fault is in me. Sir Keith Hancock, the general editor of the History of the Second World War in which this book appears, is a historian of great discrimination. No one needs to be reminded what Sir Llewellyn Woodward has contributed to the study of recent history. His book on *Great*

Britain and the German Navy, for example, is an almost flawless masterpiece. These distinguished scholars must have known what they were doing when one authorized and the other wrote this book. I find it exasperating that a great historian should have spent time and energy in this penitential labour of misguided devotion.

CHAPTER FIFTY-NINE

How Germany Lost the War

This essay was first published, with the subtitle 'A German General on Hitler', as a review essay of Franz Halder, *Hitler als Feldherr* (Munich, Münchener Dom-Verlag, 1949), in the *Manchester Guardian* (6 September 1949).

The tradition of the German generals was 'to keep the army out of politics'. Politics, however, in the shape of Hitler, came to them. Halder, chief of the German General Staff from 1938 to 1942, has learnt his lesson, and his pamphlet on Hitler as war leader has been a best-seller in Germany, a successful stroke of politics as well as of literature. No more hostile picture of 'the greatest war leader of all times' has yet been painted: though this version is not new, it has not been given before by one who writes with such authority.

Hitler, according to Halder, had no understanding of the conduct of war. At one moment he would sketch the vague strategy of a distant future; at another busy himself with technical details of a trivial kind. Thus he brushed aside the military doubts as to the value of the 'Atlantic Wall'; what interested him was the exact composition of the cement to be used in it. He did not allow for awkward facts; he denied them. His method in face of difficulties was to increase his harshness and brutality. He really believed that if he demanded the impossible of the fighting forces he would always get it. At first this brought him unexpected successes; later he ran into the truly impossible and so came to disaster.

Mistrust

Hitler never trusted the generals; even when he had made himself commander-in-chief, he used to boast that 'he had had to force success on them'. He endorsed Goering's insistence on creating special divisions for the men transferred from the Luftwaffe in 1942. Goering said to Hitler: 'I am not going to give them to the army, where it may occur to a general to send my young National Socialists to church.' Again out of jealousy for the army leaders, he stopped rocket research when he learnt of it in 1939; his revival of it in 1942 was too late to alter the course of the war.

In the actual conduct of war Hitler showed a mixture of obstinacy and irresolution. After the defeat of Poland the General Staff wished to

STRUGGLES FOR SUPREMACY

stand on the defensive and thus compel the allies to violate the neutrality of the Low Countries. Hitler's nerves could not face the strain. The General Staff then devised the strategy of an advance though the Ardennes; Hitler nearly ruined this stroke by the purposeless strengthening of the right wing which was to invade Holland. Halder blames Hitler for allowing the British army to escape at Dunkirk. In one passage he attributes this to Hitler's refusal to risk his tanks in the marshy land round Dunkirk; in another he alleges that Goering persuaded Hitler to leave the destruction of the British to the Luftwaffe so that the generals should not get too much credit in Germany. This story has been disputed by others; and it has even been suggested that the German army had outrun its supplies. It serves, at any rate, as an illustration of Halder's method. Halder next insists that an invasion of England was impossible so long as Russia remained powerful:

> This problem could not be solved by military means. The political leader had to solve it, and could have solved it, with the west against the east or with the east against the west. Each of these solutions would have demanded a high political price, which it was beyond the capacity of the dictator to pay.

There followed the futile waste of the strength of the Luftwaffe in the attacks on England.

The Russian campaign brought the real conflict between Hitler's strategy and that of the General Staff. The generals, according to Halder, thought they could defeat the Russian army and could hold most of the Ukraine and the Baltic provinces 'as pledges for peace negotiations'. Hitler, however, aimed at eliminating Russia as a great power and at turning most of European Russia into a zone of German colonisation. The generals wished to concentrate on an attack against Moscow, where the bulk of Russia's armed strength was; Hitler insisted on switching the attack against Leningrad and Stalingrad, 'these breeding-places of Bolshevism'. 'If these were once destroyed by powerful armies in north and south, then Bolshevism would be dead, and that was the essential point'. But when he was on the point of taking Leningrad (still according to Halder) he called off the attack: 'He couldn't think what to do with a million inhabitants.' All the stronger was his insistence on transferring forces to the southern wing. In Halder's words, 'the task of destroying the Russian army was subordinated to the effort of occupying an industrial area and advancing towards the Russian sources of oil'. The Battle of Kiev, though it ended in victory, exhausted the German armed forces; as a result they were defeated before Moscow, the decisive battle of the war.

Brauchitsch now resigned and Hitler took over his position. He said to Halder: 'Anyone can do that bit of directing operations. The real job of the commander-in-chief is to make the Army National Socialist; and I know no general who could do that.' The 'bit of directing operations' was the campaign of Stalingrad, a campaign based on Hitler's dogma – 'The Russian is dead'. Halder claims that Stalingrad could have been taken, if Hitler had concentrated on it; but he diverted forces to the Caucasus and even sent armed forces to the west when Churchill spoke publicly of 'the second front' (a bluff which evidently worked, after all).

Stalingrad

The failure at Stalingrad did not need to be a disaster. It was almost a matter of routine strategy to order the Sixth Army to fight its way westwards:

> Hitler's answer was an obstinate No. The man who had so often spoken contemptuously of the pointlessness of the consideration of prestige in political and military leadership now felt himself at the turning-point of his self-awarded fame as a war leader. The magic of the name of Stalingrad made him grasp at the straw offered by Goering that the Luftwaffe could supply the encircled army for a year.

Hitler refused to learn the lesson of Stalingrad. Instead of devising a flexible defence. Hitler drew on his recollections of the first German war and made every position a Stalingrad in miniature: to satisfy his prejudices millions of Germans were taken prisoner by the Russians. By 1943, Halder asserts, the war was lost. The possibility of defending the Atlantic coast was 'a fairy tale'; and Hitler's 'fame' ended in the manoeuvring of imaginary armies in 1945. Hitler ought to have admitted that the war was lost; 'but Hitler lacked even this quality of leadership'.

Halder's pamphlet ought to end the Hitler legend. Millions of Germans have excused the concentration camps and the pogroms on the ground of Hitler's military gifts; this excuse is now taken from them. Will Halder's pamphlet substitute a legend of the German General Staff? Hardly. Hitler was right that he had forced the generals to succeed. Without him they would never have organized Germany for war, nor would they have taken the risks which brought success between 1936 and 1940. Besides, even the Germans are likely to reflect that these generals who now expose Hitler's mad strategy and disregard of German lives served Hitler without complaint or resistance. A few of them tried too late to overthrow him, and even then bungled it. Most, like Halder, waited for the allies to do their work for them. After all,

the General Staff on Halder's own showing knew that Hitler was leading Germany to disaster. In condemning Hitler, Halder condemns himself
still more.

CHAPTER SIXTY

Potsdam: The Seeds of Cold War

This essay was first published as a review of Herbert Feis, *Between War and Peace: The Potsdam Conference* (Princeton University Press, 1961), in the *Guardian* (12 January 1961).

On 17 July 1945, the victors in the Second World War met in conference at Potsdam. Stalin, Truman, Churchill – these three seemed to hold in their hands the destinies of mankind. Churchill, with his gift for words, had chosen the name for the conference. It was to be 'Terminal' – the end of the line; all out from the harsh carriages of war to enjoy life for ever afterwards. Instead Potsdam turned out to be a mere change of trains: the end maybe of the old fighting war (though technically not even of that), but the start of a new cold war, which has by now become almost a law of nature.

Everything that happened before 1945 has sunk into the past; matters simply for historical curiosity. At Potsdam the present begins. The arguments, the topics of dispute, might all be going on now instead of sixteen years ago. We feel ourselves involved. We itch to remake the record and to make it differently. Why did everything go wrong? Who blundered or sinned? Need it all have happened as it did? Perhaps the story will itself provide the answers if told in sufficient detail. This is what Dr Herbert Feis has set out to do in his new book.

Dr Feis has a distinguished reputation. His books on American policy in the Far East and on the wartime relations of the Big Three are highly esteemed. His style is drab and aloof, leaving the story to speak for itself. There is little attempt at creating characters or drama: the record can provide the excitement without literary aid. Most of the evidence comes from printed sources – the memoirs of Truman and Harry Hopkins, Churchill's final volume, and other books which the experienced reader will recognize. Dr Feis has also had access to some new American sources, particularly to the papers on the Potsdam conference which are being prepared for early publication. Though these do not change the broad outline, they sometimes add vivid details.

The most striking is the report on the first successful explosion of the atomic bomb, which reached Truman just after the conference opened. As the scientists waited for the explosion: 'It can be safely said that most of those present – Christian, Jew, and atheist – were praying and praying harder than they had ever prayed before.' (They were praying for success, not for forgiveness.) When the explosion rocked the hut, 'Dr. Oppenheimer's face relaxed into an expression of tremendous relief ... Dr. Kistiakowsky threw his arms round Dr. Oppenheimer and embraced him with shouts of glee. Others were equally enthusiastic ... All seemed to sense immediately that the explosion had far exceeded the most optimistic expectations and wildest hopes of the scientists.'

Possession of the atomic bomb played some part in deciding the Americans that they need no longer conciliate the Russians. Stimson, the secretary for war, thought it 'a master card in our hand'. He proposed that the Russians should be told the secret on condition that they instituted a democratic Constitution and free speech. But the bomb was not the only cause of American firmness. Soviet Russia was assumed to have been devastated during the war; and the abrupt termination of lend–lease ensured that she would not be reconstructed with American aid. Most of all, the Americans believed that the Russians were behaving badly on a variety of issues, each of which Dr Feis explores in detail. They are well known: conflict over the political situation in Poland and over the frontier between Poland and Germany; conflict over the reparations to be exacted from Germany and over her political future; minor conflicts ranging from Tangier to the Black Sea Straits. Dr Feis returns a seemingly impartial verdict: there was suspicion and misunderstanding on both sides. He writes:

> In the West fear of broken Germany was overcast by fear of Soviet Communist domination of Europe. In the Soviet Union brief trust in the true goodwill of the West was giving way to the belief that the West was bent on depriving the Soviet Union of the benefits of its victory.

He concludes his book by warning the great nations that they 'must one and all live and act more maturely and more trustfully than they did during the months that followed the end of the war against Germany'.

This even-handed justice is not, however, sustained in the detailed narrative. An unwary reader would receive from this the impression that, while the Americans behaved foolishly, the Russians behaved wickedly; and his impression would not be redressed by the few sentences of general rebuke at the end. Even the most complaisant congregation like to be told that they also are miserable sinners. Dr Feis's book, in spite of its air of impartiality, is not a truly detached survey of what happened at the end of the Second World War; it is a State Department brief, translated into terms of historical scholarship.

To some extent this springs inevitably from the nature of the evidence on which the book rests. The State Department, and individual American statesmen, have been lavish in opening their records; the Russians have revealed nothing. When American policy is being discussed we can follow the puzzled working of Truman's mind: we recognize that here was a man of goodwill, fumbling towards a peaceful settlement, though often making mistakes. Soviet policy can only be guessed at from outside: and the historian who starts guessing (as he often must) always tends to stress the element of deliberate intent. Again, the Russians have brought it on themselves. They claim that they always know what they are doing; and would probably be offended at being told that their policy moved from one blunder to another, much like anyone else's.

But the bias goes deeper. Would an Indian or a Swedish historian have returned Dr Feis's verdict, even given the evidence in its present form? The question answers itself. For that matter a Soviet historian could turn the present evidence on its head and arrive at a precisely opposite conclusion – simple, innocent Stalin cheated by a designing, aggressive Truman. One conclusion would be as much dogma as the other. Dr Feis's conclusions are not derived from the evidence; they were assumed, as self-evident, before the book was begun.

There was a time when historians shook off their national commitments and wrote as though observing from another planet. Indeed, when American historians wrote on the origins of the First World War they leaned over backwards so far that they became partial on the German side. In the Cold War, apparently, even the world of scholarship knows no detachment. The academic historians of the West may assert their scholarly independence, even when they are employed by a government department; but they are as much 'engaged' as though they wore the handsome uniform designed for German professors by Dr Goebbels. What good purpose do they serve? A book such as this will not lead the Russians to confess their wickedness; it provides little guidance about how to do things better in future. Is it a form of whistling in the dark in order to still the gnawing doubt whether the Cold War be as sensible an enterprise as everyone supposes?

CHAPTER SIXTY-ONE

Trieste

This essay first appeared as a pamphlet published in 1945 by the Yugoslav Information Officer. It was reprinted with the 1949 postscript in A.J.P. Taylor's first collection of essays, *From Napoleon to Stalin: Comments on European History* (London, Hamish Hamilton, 1950).

Alan Taylor was the most prominent non-Yugoslav supporter of the case that Trieste should go to Yugoslavia at the end of the Second World War, rather than to Italy or be a free city. In the *New Statesman and Nation*, 28, 720 (9 December 1944) he argued the case for Istria and Trieste more rationally belonging to Yugoslavia and observed, 'we can be more confident of the future of the Anglo-Soviet alliance when we have learnt to think of Trieste as Trst'. After the publication of the pamphlet government figures complained to the BBC about his talk on Trieste, part of a BBC radio Home Service programme on the subject of 'Russia's return as a Great Power'.

In 1920, after the first German war, a frontier was established between Italy and Yugoslavia which offended against both national principles and economic sense.

British memories are short: a frontier which has existed for twenty years appears to us to have existed from time immemorial. It has long been forgotten that the frontier of 1920 had no other justification than that the Italians possessed superior force.

The territory in dispute is the area between the Italian frontier of 1914 and the Italian frontier of 1920, or roughly between the River Isonzo and the Julian Alps. Nowadays it is often described as Istria, though the former Austrian province of that name made up less than half of it.

The frontier of 1914 was also the old frontier between the Republic of Venice and the Holy Roman Empire, a frontier therefore of very long standing. It had been as well the national frontier between Italians and Slovenes, except for a handful of Slovenes (now about 50,000) west of the Isonzo, who were for centuries under Venetian, and since 1866 under Italian, rule.

The frontier marked, that is, the point at which Slav incomers were arrested in the seventh century as they tried to come out on to the Italian plain; and it had thus remained a clear national frontier for over a thousand years.

The Slovenes are a distinct Slav people, not 2,000,000 all told, who have been settled for 1,500 years on both sides of the Julian Alps – the most western fragment of the southern Slavs. Not only was their territory without Italian inhabitants: it never had political connection with any Italian state. It was subdued from the north by German rulers and early in the sixteenth century became part of the family possessions of the House of Habsburg.

The Slovenes were once the people of the country. With the growth of towns they became the people of the countryside, in common with all other Slav peoples of Europe except the Poles.

The Germans and the Italians had a consolidated national territory for many centuries before they established a national state; even when the upper classes spoke French they did not cease to regard themselves as Germans or Italians. Beyond the German and Italian national boundaries events took a different course, though less completely with the Poles and Magyars than elsewhere.

Here, the national differences of today are the class differences of yesterday. The towns did not grow out of the country: they were the creation of foreign conquerors and of foreign merchants, German or Italian 'islands' in a Slav sea. The peasants remained Slav; the trader, the shopkeeper, the artisan, in time the administrator and the professional man, spoke the language of the town and, whatever his racial origin, became German or Italian, Pole or Magyar. The prosperous lawyer would in this period no more continue to use the Slav tongue of his parents than he would continue to sleep over the stove.

Not a town in Eastern Europe but bears witness to this rule. In 1815 two-thirds of the 60,000 inhabitants of Prague called themselves German. A century later, when the population had increased tenfold, only 20,000 Germans were counted.

Until 1880 the city council of Budapest transacted its business in German, since it was the body of the city merchants.

Riga was German; the towns of Transylvania were German; even the trading quarters of Constantinople had a German character.

Farther east the Poles played both parts in turn: in western Poland there were German towns in a Polish countryside, in eastern Poland there were Polish towns in a Ukrainian or Lithuanian countryside – Lvov the great example of the first, Vilna the great example of the second.

The territory of the Slovenes had two 'colonizers'. On the eastern side of the Julian Alps were the Germans, creating towns with a German character at Ljubljana, Klagenfurt and Maribor. On the Adriatic coast were the Italians. Two centuries ago every fishing village and to outward view every port from Venice to the southern tip of Greece appeared Italian. These towns and villages were not inhabited by Italians; but Italian was the language of administration and trade, especially the language of maritime trade. Every seaman spoke Italian as the uniform of his profession.

The peasants remained Slovene, as they had always been. But until the beginning of the nineteenth century peasants had no political existence; their nationality counted no more than the nationality of their cattle. Even the French revolutionaries reckoned only with the educated and propertied classes, reckoned, that is, with the towns. Hence, in 1815, Istria seemed to be Italian, so far as it seemed to be anything at all, as Dalmatia (where the Italians were not 5 per cent of the population) seemed to be Italian, as Bohemia seemed to be German, or as the Ukraine seemed to be Polish.

The great political event of the nineteenth century, which is shaping the destinies of Central and Eastern Europe to the present day, was the awakening of the peasant peoples. Towns grew no longer slowly, but at breathless speed. Peasants crowded in from the countryside too rapidly to be absorbed into the urban nations. Their peasant dialects revived as literary languages, and every peasant nation found intellectual leaders.

This great process created, or re-created, the Czechs, the Croats, the Slovaks, the Ukrainians – and the Slovenes.

In much of the area 'colonized' by the Germans the Slovenes asserted themselves without difficulty, and before the end of the nineteenth century everybody recognized that Carniola, the Slovene territory beyond the Julian Alps, was inhabited almost exclusively by Slovenes.

It was the great misfortune of the Slovenes that, just before their national awakening, there was created, on their national territory, a great Mediterranean port, the greatest port in southern Europe after Marseilles and Genoa, and that this port was, quite without design, given an Italian character. Even without Trieste the Italians would no doubt have striven to maintain their superiority over the Slovenes, just as other 'historic nations' – the Germans, the Poles, the Magyars – resisted national emancipation elsewhere and resist it to the present day. Without Trieste the Italian claims would have lacked plausibility and substance. Even Italian patriotism could not have been inflamed for the 20,000 Italians of Gorica, the westernmost part of this territory.

Trieste was an 'artificial' town, a creation of the railway age and of German plans for European domination. Until the 1840s it had been but an obscure fishing port of no trading importance. Its creator was Baron Bruck, a German from the Rhineland, and the first great advocate of the project which later became known as 'Mitteleuropa' – the plan for bringing all Europe east of the Rhine under a single economic and political administration.

Bruck chose as the framework and trade name of this plan the Austrian Empire and the House of Habsburg. Only this mistake distinguished his aims from those of William II or Hitler.

Bruck built the first docks in Trieste and founded the first shipping lines. In 1848 he became Austrian minister of commerce and then made the Austrian Empire a single-tariff area with Trieste as the principal imperial outlet to the world.

These great schemes could never have been achieved before the age of railways, which freed Central Europe from dependence on waterways and ended the monopoly of the Rhine, the Elbe and the Danube. So far as foreign trade was concerned, the Austrian railways were made to centre on Trieste. By the beginning of the twentieth century there was a double-track line to Salzburg and so to southern Germany; a double-track line to Vienna and so to Bohemia; a single-track line through the Julian Alps to the Slovene districts and Styria; a double-track line to Ljubljana which gave another route to Vienna and which, after the first German war, was extended to Zagreb and so tapped Croatia and western Hungary. But all this time no line of importance connected Trieste with Italy. Nor was this surprising – there was no real connection between Trieste and Italy.

Trieste fulfilled all Bruck's expectations. It became (to use the twentieth-century state names) the port of Austria, of Bavaria, of Hungary, of northern Yugoslavia and, to a considerable extent, of Czechoslovakia. Its trade range reached to western Romania and to the Ukraine.

At the same time it would be a mistake to exaggerate the importance of the share of central European countries and to minimize the share of the territories which later became Yugoslav. One of the more subtle arguments of Italian apologists is to suggest that Trieste is the port of central Europe, not of Yugoslavia. The trade figures of 1913 do not bear this out. Of the total railway traffic of 2,800,000 (metric) tons more than a quarter (800,000) came from the lands inhabited by Slovenes: German-Austria and the Czech lands came next with about 600,000 tons each.

Austria and Czechoslovakia had also other outlets through the German North Sea ports. The Slovenes had only Trieste and when, after 1920, they were cut off from Trieste by the Italian frontier, they were ruined.

Two countries hardly figure in the statistics of 1913. One is Croatia. Croatia was severed from Trieste by the railway policy of the Hungarian government (which controlled Croatia), designed to prevent any contact between Croatia and the Austrian part of the Austro-Hungarian Empire. Once a railway was built between Ljubljana and Zagreb, the capital of Croatia, as it was immediately after 1919, Croatia would have become a great user of Trieste, had not the Italian frontier barred the way. Then the Yugoslav share of the total traffic would have reached at least 1,000,000 tons.

The other country which did not use Trieste was Italy. The Italian traffic with Trieste in 1913 was 85,000 tons, not 3 per cent of the total. The great port of Venice was more than adequate for Italian needs; and the Italians desired Trieste, not to use it themselves but to ruin it for the benefit of Venice, the merchants of which largely financed the political campaigns for its annexation and to prevent its use by others.

The trade statistics of 1913 can be thus summarized: Trieste was essential for the foreign trade of the Slovenes and of northern Croatia; it was useful for the foreign trade of Austria and Czechoslovakia; it played no part whatsoever in the foreign trade of Italy. Thus, on economic grounds, Yugoslavia had the decisive claim to Trieste after the dissolution of the Habsburg monarchy.

The great port traffic naturally brought with it industrial developments: not only shipbuilding but oil refineries, food industries and a great banking organization.

Trieste, not surprisingly, became the most important insurance centre in Central Europe. It became, too, a cultural centre.

Just before 1914 it was inhabited by at least two writers of European importance, Svevo and James Joyce. It would be fanciful to find much of Trieste in *Ulysses*, though it must have been through Trieste that Bloom reached Dublin.

The writings of Svevo contain the full spirit of Trieste. Though written in Italian (by no means the purest Tuscan), they have nothing in common with Italian literature, but are manifestly the work of a fellow-countryman of Schnitzler. In other words they are works of 'Austrian' literature, which merely happen to be written in Italian, as Schnitzler's happen to be written in German. Both writers felt as 'Austrians' and, like many who felt so, both writers were Jews.

Trieste thus grew, *par excellence*, as an 'Austrian' town, created for an Austrian imperial purpose. It owed nothing to Italian effort. Like the Austrian Empire, it had no national character. It certainly did not serve, could never serve, any Italian economic need. So far as it served a national purpose, that purpose, again like the Austrian Empire, was German, not Italian.

But, for convenience and certainly not by national design, Italian was the maritime language of the Austrian Empire, a language inherited from the Republic of Venice, and this at a time when the Slovenes of the surrounding countryside were still a 'submerged people'. Therefore, when Trieste started on its career of greatness, it started as an Italian-speaking city, and remained predominantly so at the beginning of the twentieth century.

Thus its Italian language by no means meant that its inhabitants were predominantly Italian by descent. The few thousand Italians who had made up its total population at the beginning of the century were soon swamped by a flood of immigrants from the neighbouring countryside, from the German lands farther north, and from the Levant. An Austrian inquiry of 1915 ascertained that more than half the population of Trieste was of Slovene descent, though two-thirds of the population considered themselves Italian.

A further element was of Croat descent. Add Germans and Jews (the most loyal of all Austrians) and there was little enough left of Italian blood. The majority of the population certainly called themselves Italian. But they did this rather as a mark of class distinction than out of Italian patriotism. The 'Italian' lawyer, clerk, or merchant was asserting his distinction from the unskilled labourers who still admitted to being Slovenes; not in the least was he demanding separation from the Austrian Empire and inclusion in Italy. That would have been, and eventually was, his economic ruin.

The 'Italians' voted together. But they did this rather as a party of middle-class interests, not on grounds of nationality. Even so, despite the majority who returned themselves as Italians (i.e. Italian-speakers) in the census, the Italian political party never won a majority of votes. The inhabitants of Trieste simply were not Italians. They were at that time Austrians, meaning by that controversial word subjects of the non-national Habsburg Empire, who spoke Italian only because they had to speak something. Through the traditions of Venetia and Mediterranean trade, at that time Italian seemed the obvious tongue.

The high-water mark of Italian preponderance in Trieste was reached about 1880, when Trieste had become a great port, and before the Slovenes began to recover their national consciousness. In 1880 only 22 per cent of the population was returned as Slovene.

Thereafter the tide turned. The 'Italians' maintained a monopoly of commercial life, and practically a monopoly of schools and newspapers, the two weapons without which it is difficult to develop a national consciousness. Nevertheless Slovene nationalism asserted itself. At the last Austrian census, in 1910, 29 per cent of the population was returned as Slovene.

This increase owed something to further Slovene immigration from the countryside, but more to 'conversion' of many who had previously been ashamed of their lower-class nationality. To be Slovene was at last becoming respectable, and since the majority of the population was indisputably Slovene or Croat by origin it was only a matter of time – had no outside force checked this development – before the majority of the population of Trieste would have reverted to its original nationality.

Austrian rule did not hold the balance perfectly even between South Slav and Italian. Like all imperial bureaucrats, the Austrian officials sympathized (perhaps unconsciously) with the wealthier upper-class Italianizers. Still, even so, had the Austrian Empire lasted for another generation, Trieste would have had a South Slav majority. Twenty-five years of Italian rule did not reduce the Slovene proportion to less than it was in 1910. The Italians, in fact, had to exhaust every weapon of national oppression merely to keep their numbers from declining.

The Austrian census of 1910 was the last free census, and also the last to take account of national character. It is therefore the only reliable basis on which to judge the national composition of these disputed areas.

It is not without faults. The census in the towns was taken by the municipal authorities, and these were still predominantly Italian.

The first count in Trieste found only 36,000 Slovenes; a revision made by the imperial authorities brought the number up to 56,000. In the other towns the figures were not revised. Further, the figures could give only the national balances as it existed in 1910; they could not allow for the process of Slovene awakening which was going on at an ever faster rate.

Grouping together all the Yugoslav territory acquired by Italy in 1920, and adding the 50,000 Slovenes already in Italy before 1914, there were altogether 638,331 Yugoslavs (Slovenes and Croats) and 354,000 Italians. A third of these Italians lived in the two towns of Trieste and Gorica. The southern half of the Istrian peninsula was inhabited not by Slovenes but predominantly by Croats, kindred Yugoslavs who were passing through the same process of national awakening. Here, too, the Italians lived in the coastal towns, above all in Pola, a great harbour important not as a commercial port but as the base and the construction centre of the Austrian navy.

These figures give an unmistakable picture. The countryside was solidly Croat or Slovene. The towns were Italian 'islands', which were gradually being submerged by the rising tide of the awakening peasant nation. As Prague and Brno became Czech; Bratislava, Slovak; Riga, Latvian; Posen, Polish; and Lvov, Ukrainian; so it seemed certain that Trieste would become Slovene.

The Slovenes had every quality of the other awakening people. Their only fault was to be overtaken, while still half-submerged, by the war of 1914–18.

Trieste was not a traditional object of Italian ambition. It was a recent creation and therefore counted for nothing in Italian tradition, unlike Venice – or even such Dalmatian towns as Split (Spalato). It had no economic significance for Italy. Moreover, the leaders of the Risorgimento, especially after 1848, saw that their success depended on preventing the Habsburg Empire from receiving German support.

Anxious not to offend German sentiment (as against Austro-Hungarian), they consistently halted their ambitions at the frontier of the German world, and recognized that Trieste served German, not Italian needs. Even Mazzini, a man not usually influenced by practical considerations, declared the River Isonzo to be the natural frontier of Italy.

When the rising Kingdom of Italy acquired the province of Venetia from Austria in 1866 and occupied Rome (the papal territory) in 1870, she had achieved full national unity. She could no longer live on an enthusiasm for national emancipation. The Italians had been promised great things from unification. Yet, in fact, Italy lacked all the qualities of a great power – except ambition.

Her politicians had exhausted themselves in achieving unification. None of the younger men now possessed those practical gifts in the international field which had distinguished Cavour. Thus, in the 1870s, when Italy was torn by popular discontent, by resistance to taxation and by anarchist outbreaks, her rulers could think of no other solution than artificially to return to the days of the Risorgimento and to divert Italian feeling against the former Italian bogy – Austrian rule.

The programme of this substitute-risorgimento, a very inferior edition of the original, was a mixture of nationalist claims and assertion of natural frontiers – the line of the Alps and the emancipation of Italians still in Austria were demanded together, though the two did not by any means coincide.

In fact the 'natural frontier' involved the inclusion of 300,000 Germans and 500,000 South Slavs in Italy. Still, this hardly mattered. The demand was not put forward as a matter of serious politics. It was a safety valve for internal discontent. Trieste was the only place of any size in these coveted areas.

Therefore Trieste became the symbol of the programme as a whole, and for more than a generation the Trieste question was kept alive so that riotous mobs should throw their stones through the windows of the Austro-Hungarian embassy instead of through the windows of the Italian Home Office.

The agitation for Trieste did not prevent Italy being for more than thirty years (from 1882 to 1915) the ally of Austria-Hungary in the Triple Alliance; just as membership of the Triple Alliance did not prevent Italian politicians continuing to proclaim the grievance of Trieste.

Italy would never have gone to war for the sake of Trieste, yet when she went to war in 1915 Trieste inevitably provided the excuse. Italy wished to take part in the first German war in order to prove herself a great power, and she was anxious to sell herself to the highest bidder. The Germans were ready to bribe Italy with Habsburg territory, but they could not agree to their own exclusion from the Adriatic: they offered south Tyrol, but not Trieste.

England and France had no such hesitation. They believed that the unbreakable German front in France could be turned by an attack through Italy, and they were willing to pay almost any price, in terms of Habsburg territory, for Italy's entry into the war. They accepted Italy's claim to the 'natural frontiers' of the Alps, and, knowing little or nothing of the national circumstances, hardly realized that they were agreeing to an act of national injustice. Even if they had, they would have argued that this was an inevitable sacrifice, worth making for the sake of a speedy victory.

Besides, the dissolution of Austria-Hungary was at this time no part of their programme. They supposed that the Habsburg Empire would continue to exist, even though in diminished form; and since the Habsburgs were now the agents of Germany, it was reasonable to transfer Trieste and Pola to Italy in order to cut Germany off from the Adriatic.

England and France made, no doubt, a bad bargain; still, they acted with fairness according to their lights. The Italians had demanded the whole of the Dalmation coast; but the Western allies were loyal to Serbia and insisted that she should have her share in southern Dalmatia. Their fault was to fail to foresee the emergence of a state comprising all the South Slavs, though this was a fault shared by many of the South Slavs themselves.

At any rate, the Treaty of London paid to Italy an acceptable price and Italy entered the war with her claims to Trieste internationally recognized. The Treaty of London is the only legal basis for Italian rule in Trieste; and anyone who wishes to maintain this rule is, inescapably, an advocate of the Treaty of London. He is asserting not merely that Italy performed valuable services in the first German war, but that by these services (and despite her subsequent acts) she earned a reward which must be immutably preserved, whatever the injustices to others.

The Italians had called the war of 1859 'the war for Lombardy' and the war of 1866 'the war for Venice'; so in their attempt to recapture the glamorous days of the Risorgimento they called the first German war *'the war for Trieste'*. But when the end of the war came in 1918 it was in circumstances very different from those envisaged in 1915. The Habsburg Empire dissolved and a state of the South Slavs sprang up overnight.

But the Italians refused to abandon anything of their treaty rights. Italy was a nation of over 40,000,000 with a powerful army, ineffectual indeed against Germany or Austria-Hungary, but well-equipped by England and the United States; and England and France were bound to support her claims. Yugoslavia was newly created, without friends, her only force the Serb army which had paid a terrible price in the fighting against Austria-Hungary. Her first leaders, too, were Serbs who cared too little for the destinies of Slovenes and Croats in the remote north-west.

The Yugoslav cause was defended in the peace negotiations by President Wilson; he achieved nothing, except to destroy his popularity in Italy. The Great Powers would not coerce Italy, but shrank from themselves committing an act of national injustice. Therefore they passed by on the other side and left Italy and Yugoslavia to settle their frontier between themselves.

Yugoslavia was helpless and had to accept the Italian terms. The outcome was the Treaty of Rapallo of November 1920, which gave Italy all her demands except the coast of Dalmatia. This imperialistic treaty was not the work of Fascists. It was concluded when Italy was still a liberal parliamentary country, and her foreign minister responsible for the Treaty was Count Sforza, a man of Liberal reputation.

This was not all. By the Treaty of Rapallo, Fiume was to become a Free City. Hardly had the treaty been signed, when an Italian adventurer, financed with Italian money and equipped with Italian arms, seized the city under the protection of the Italian navy. Once more the Yugoslavs could do nothing and in 1924 they acquiesced in the incorporation of Fiume by Italy.

The fate of the Free City of Fiume is worth meditating by those who welcome that Trieste has become a Free City in its turn; and it is also worth meditating that the 'legionaries' who seized Fiume became thereafter the most violent and successful agents of the Fascist *coup d'état*. Italy paid for the enslavement of Fiume by being herself enslaved.

Thus Italy brought under her rule more than 600,000 Slovenes and Croats. The Italians rejected as an insult to their national honour a proposal to give these South Slavs the protection of the minorities treaty, though they were fulsome in their assurances that their nationality would be respected.

Italy did not wait until the coming of Fascism to break these assurances: they were never fulfilled even in the days of constitutionalism. The guilt for the ill-treatment of the Slovenes and Croats cannot be placed solely on Fascism: it must be shared by Bonomi, by Count Sforza and by every liberal parliamentarian.

Even were the future of Italian liberalism secure, it would be small consolation to the Slovenes and Croats to return to the days of 1920. Italian rule over these South Slavs had no parallel in Europe until the worst days of the Nazi dictatorship. The South Slavs were deprived of their schools; they were deprived of their newspapers and books; they were not allowed to use their language in public meetings or in the law courts; the Slovene-speaking bishops and clergy were expelled, with the connivance of the Vatican; even Slovene-speaking doctors were forbidden. When it was urged on an Italian doctor that his patients could no longer explain their symptoms to him, he replied: 'nor can the cow explain its symptoms to the veterinary surgeon'.

Such was the Italian estimate of these peaceful, educated, civilized Slav peasants. No Italian ever protested; no attempt at improvement was ever made. Italians of all parties agreed in the aim of exterminating the nationality of the Slovenes and Croats under Italian rule.

This aim was not achieved. A people proves its right to live by asserting its will to live; and no people has proved its right better than the Slovenes west of the Julian Alps. The Italians were driven to ever-more terroristic methods and to great treason trials, one in 1930 an even more brutal one in 1941.

The British public is fond of plebiscites. Here was a plebiscite continuing over more than twenty years, a permanent popular vote of which the result cannot be doubted. The Slovenes as a people refused to die; they refused to accept Italian rule.

Their opportunity came in 1940 when Italy entered the war on the side of Germany. At last the Slovenes could have allies. They then became, before the war had reached Yugoslavia proper, the allies of Great Britain when she had few others. They served as a rallying point for resistance thoughout south-eastern Europe; and they became in time one of the strongest elements in the National Liberation Movement which grew up in Yugoslavia under Marshal Tito.

Thus the Slovenes do not ask to be liberated from Italy. They have liberated themselves. All they ask is not to be put forcibly back under Italian rule.

The Italians paid a heavy price for the possession of Trieste. Many of those who burnt trade union buildings and beat or murdered liberal Italian politicians had learnt their trade in Trieste, burning the head-quarters of the Slovene national club and murdering Slovene spokesmen – with the approval of liberal Italians. Still worse, the possession of Trieste compelled Italy to a foreign policy of imperialism, led her to revisionism and ultimately brought her to all the disasters of 1940 and the years that followed.

For Trieste was not, and never could be, an Italian port: it had neither trade connections with nor economic meaning for Italy. Under whatever national sovereignty, it remained the port of Central Europe; it was inextricably bound up with its hinterland, as far north as Prague and as far east as Budapest. Formerly it had been the means by which German Imperialism advanced to the Adriatic; now it became the means by which Italian Imperialism tried to thrust itself into Central Europe. Italian governments, even before Mussolini, manipulated the tariff charges of Trieste in order to compel the states of Central Europe to become Italian satellites. Yugoslavia and Czechoslovakia would not degrade themselves in this way and so were driven to use the ports of northern Germany, until – too late – they discovered that they had given themselves an even worse master.

So grossly did the Italians abuse their control of Trieste that goods produced five miles over the Yugoslav frontier were exported by way of Hamburg. In Austria and Hungary, however, there were reactionary Fascist parties, which rejected the settlement of 1919; and Italy held out the promise of preferential treatment at Trieste as a means of helping them to power. Horthy in Hungary, Dollfuss and Schuschnigg in Austria, were Italian dependents; each destroyed democracy, each preached revisionism, each opened the way to a new German aggression. And the Italian control of Trieste was the origin of their power.

Such are the facts about Trieste, and they are beyond dispute. In the area as a whole the Yugoslavs are in an unchallengeable majority, and even in Trieste the majority is not Italian by origin. Trieste has no historical significance for Italy. It has always been exploited by Italy for imperialistic purposes and Italy has proved herself unqualified to rule over peoples of other nationalities.

There were four proposals before the negotiation of peace:

(i)   The frontier could be left unchanged on condition that Italy gave guarantees of good treatment of the Slovenes;
(ii)   The territory could be partitioned, giving the country districts to Yugoslavia and leaving Trieste in Italian hands;
(iii) The country districts could be given to Yugoslavia and Trieste could be made a Free City; or
(iv)   All the territory east of the Isonzo could be given to Yugoslavia.

The principal argument in favour of the first course was that the frontier established by the Treaty of Rapallo existed. For the Yugoslavs to demand Trieste seemed somehow grasping, in a way that it did not appear grasping of the Italians to desire to retain it.

This was not a very serious argument. It was more to the purpose to argue that the new democratic regime in Italy would start life under an impossible handicap if it were compelled to renounce territory for which Italy fought a great war and which a generation of Italians had been taught to regard as an integral part of Italy.

A plausible argument – though it would have applied with even more force to Alsace or Posen in 1919. Germany, too, had fought a great war for Alsace and this had been German for more than forty years, whereas Trieste has been Italian for only twenty-five. Yet the victorious allies, of whom Italy was one, were unanimous in inflicting this handicap on the democratic German republic. Posen had been in German hands for more than a century and was universally regarded in Germany as German; yet the allies were unanimous in restoring it to Poland.

The argument would appear equally fraudulent in the case of Trieste, were it not that Poland and France are historic countries, and the Slovenes are not – therefore it was possible to advocate national injustice at their expense in a way that would not be possible with the French or Poles. In any case, was it so certain that Italian national feeling was really so deeply bound up with the fate of Trieste? Certainly those elements which in essence had remained Fascist deplored the loss of Trieste, since this marked the end of Italy's imperialist plans in Central Europe; but it is difficult to suppose that these elements carry much weight with democratic opinion.

Or rather they would not carry much weight if the present leaders of Italy genuinely set their faces against them. Italian feeling about Trieste is deliberately provoked by the new 'democratic' journalists and politicians, as it was deliberately provoked by the liberal politicians of a previous generation. The purpose is the same: it is to unite Italy in some foreign quarrel and so distract attention from the terrible, and perhaps, insoluble domestic problems. Once it was the Austro-Hungarian embassy, now it is the Yugoslav mission, which provides the safety-valve for Italian political feeling.

Trieste is not the only object of Italian ambition which is endangered. Italy fought a war, with a great deal of patriotic enthusiasm, for Libya, which has been Italian for thirty years; and she fought a war, with quite unparalleled patriotic outbursts, for Abyssinia, which has been a principal element in Italian policy ever since 1889. If the Italian masses felt deeply about any foreign issue – and there is no evidence that they do – they would feel more deeply about Abyssinia, or even Libya, than about Trieste. Yet we are not told that the loss of Libya and Abyssinia will discredit the new democratic Italy beyond redemption.

And for a very simple reason: the Italian leaders know that in the present circumstances, their outcry will be ineffective where British interests are concerned. But they hope that the freedom of 500,000 Yugoslavs and the economic co-operation of Central Europe is not a British interest.

One Italian argument in favour of retaining the 1920 frontier was, however, well founded, though it was no longer an argument which the Italians cared to use. When in 1919 the Italians pressed their claims to Trieste, they were repeatedly asked by President Wilson whether they would not be content with the possession of the city, allowing the country districts to go to Yugoslavia. The Italians always replied that he who possesses Trieste must possess its hinterland as far as the line of the Alps; and they were right.

To draw the frontier five miles behind the coast would create an impossible strategic position. It would condemn Trieste to starvation, since the city draws its food supplies from the whole of the hinterland.

The experience of a city without hinterland was tried on a small scale at Zadar (Zara), a town on the Dalmatian coast which was allotted to Italy. This experiment was the ruin of Zadar: the inhabitants had to get their food supplies by sea from Italy; they could not even go for a country walk; and no peasants could come into the town to use the ships. Yet Zadar is little more than a village, Trieste a city of 250,000 inhabitants.

Such a frontier, ruinous to the inhabitants of the city, is also ruinous to the peasants of the hinterland. They lose the natural market for their products; they lack the enormous convenience of a great city at their doorstep; there are no secondary schools to which they can send their children; they have to put up with the very inferior amenities of petty village life.

Imagine what it would be like to live at St Albans and be unable to visit London, or to live at Bury and be unable to visit Manchester. Yet St Albans and Bury are sizeable towns: the Yugoslavs of Istria have none such. This argument was very well put by the Italians in 1919; it has now disappeared from their repertoire.

The argument of the last paragraph has anticipated the consideration of the second solution: solution by partition. This solution has a misleading appearance of fairness, attractive to the British public. The countryside is Slovene and Croat (Yugoslav), Trieste is – as to a majority – Italian, and is perhaps linked by an Italian-speaking coastal strip with Italy proper. This last is not an important consideration, since Trieste in practice is linked to Italy not by land but by sea.

Nevertheless, why not draw the frontier along the national line? This proposal was for more than twenty years violently rejected by all Italian writers, even the most enlightened, and it was repudiated by Count Sforza as late as the summer of 1944. But now the more skilful Italian propagandists realize that they must yield something, though they seek to yield as little as possible.

Salvemini, a man with a distinguished Liberal record, devised a most ingenious solution. He admitted that if the area be taken as a whole the Yugoslavs were in a considerable majority. Therefore, he said, let us not take it as a whole! Let us take the areas most distant from Trieste, the least valuable districts and the most backward; let us peel them off, as it were, until we have reduced the Yugoslavs from 600,000 to 300,000. Then the Italians would be in a majority and entitled to retain not only Trieste, but also territory inhabited by more than 250,000 Yugoslavs.

By a similar selection of certain wards of Glasgow or Liverpool, it could be proved that Glasgow and Liverpool ought to be ceded to Eire. Yet no one doubts that Glasgow is Scottish and Liverpool English.

And for a very simple reason: all over Europe, except in Istria, it has become an indisputable rule that the population of a territory must be taken as a whole and that a language 'island' must follow the nationality of the surrounding countryside. Lvov, isolated from its countryside, has beyond dispute a Polish majority; yet with general approval it has become Ukrainian. The heart of Prague had, until recently, a German majority; yet it became Czech, with the approval of all but the Germans. In fact, as the historical analysis of the earlier part of this pamphlet showed, every town in Eastern Europe was a foreign 'island' in a peasant sea; but every 'island' has had to accept the way of life imposed by the sea about it. Only the Slovenes are denied the advantage of this rule.

To leave Trieste, and no more, to Italy, has every conceivable disadvantage. It is economically ruinous. The Italians claim that by partition a national division has taken place and that they are therefore free from any obligations to the Slovene minority which remains.

For, while it was possible to partition this disputed area so as to leave no Italians under Yugoslav rule, it is not possible to partition so as to leave no Slovenes under Italian rule; and, despite the silence of the Italian census figures, there are at least 60,000 Slovenes in Trieste alone.

Every friend of Italy hopes that Italian liberalism will have a rebirth, and in this hope keeps charitably silent about Italy's record during the twenty years between the wars. For this reason I have deliberately spent only a brief paragraph on the story of Italian terrorism and misrule over the Slovenes, though it is a story which could fill a book. But when Italians write as though it were unthinkable that Italians should ever be under Yugoslav rule, but reasonable that Slovenes should be under Italian rule, it is impossible not to recall the record of those twenty years. On that record there can be only one verdict: Italy, whether liberal or Fascist, cannot be entrusted with rule over non-Italian peoples.

Perhaps it is harsh to make too much of the historical record; but it would be dishonest to pass it over. These things happened. They may be excused – though I can think of no excuse. But they cannot be ignored. Italian rule over the Slovenes (and over the Germans of the Tyrol) had no parallel in Europe, until the worst days of Hitler.

Let us, with the Italian propagandists, question the good faith of the new Yugoslav rulers; let us suppose that in a little while Yugoslavia will revert to the worst days of the dictatorship of King Alexander. Even in those days the 10,000 Italians of Dalmatia under Yugoslav rule had their own newspapers, and more schools than all the 600,000 Yugoslavs in Italy. Thus, the record of Yugoslavia at its worst is better than that of Italy at its best.

But even were we to turn our backs altogether on the past and to suppose that Signor Bonomi, Count Sforza and their liberal colleagues would behave in 1946 or 1947 in a totally different way from the way that Signor Bonomi, Count Sforza and their liberal colleagues behaved in 1920, the economic arguments against partition remain. The British and American public are not much concerned with these political disputes. For the sake of peace they are prepared to acquiesce in national injustice. But they desire that Trieste shall recover its old greatness and become again the port of Central Europe.

For the sake of argument we may pretend that Italy will give up her imperialist plans in Central Europe. But Trieste has no economic meaning for Italy except as an instrument for these economic plans; a truly pacific Italy will therefore inevitably neglect Trieste. Trieste is a great port; its docks and harbours cost money and need constant care. But Italy is a poor country and is likely to remain so. For very many years the Italian minister of transport will have a limited budget; and he would have in his charge four great ports – Naples, Genoa, Venice and Trieste.

The first three of these serve Italian needs and every penny spent on them will benefit Italy. Trieste does not serve Italy, and money spent on it would be merely a charitable contribution for the benefit of the states of Central Europe. Will an impoverished Italy be anxious to make these gifts of charity? It is indeed reasonable to expect her to do so? To leave Trieste in Italian hands is to condemn Trieste to decay, to fetter the economic development of Yugoslavia, and to compel both Austria and Czechoslovakia to depend on the North Sea ports of Germany.

Thus, the proposal to leave Trieste in Italian hands is condemned on every ground. The third solution is to attempt to devise some method of taking Trieste away from Italy without giving it to Yugoslavia. This seems a strange ambition; but the reason for it, though not consciously appreciated by its authors, is easy to appreciate. It springs from the belief that the Italians are civilized and that the Yugoslavs are not, and that therefore Italians should not be put under Yugoslav rule. In the popular mind, the Italians are still the heirs of Dante and of the Renaisssance; and the Yugoslavs are, as Bismarck called them, 'sheep stealers'. No one can hold this view who has ever been to Ljubljana or has lived among the Slovenes. But few English people visit Ljubljana and many visit Rome; and, when they visit Rome, they conveniently forget that they are visiting the city of Mussolini.

If we pass the sponge of oblivion over the Italian record of the last twenty years, we must also pass the sponge over the record of the preceding centuries, which the Italians themselves have found it easy to forget. To talk as though the Italians belong to Western civilization and the Slovenes and Croats do not is indeed to remain faithful to the spirit of the British prime minister who supported German claims against another 'far-away people of whom we know nothing'.

The only serious proposal which would keep the Yugoslavs out of Trieste was to make Trieste a Free City. This is a very different thing from making Trieste a free port, a proposal that is not in dispute. A free port merely implies that goods passing to or from Czechoslovakia, Austria, Hungary or other countries beyond Yugoslavia would not have to pay Yugoslav customs dues; apart from any international obligations that were imposed, this would be imposed by Yugoslav self-interest, since it would promote the prosperity of Trieste.

Since even if Trieste does not go to Yugoslavia, Yugoslav territory will intervene between Trieste and these countries; exemption from Yugoslav customs dues will have to be arranged in any case.

A Free City is much more than a free port; it is an independent state, governing itself; perhaps under some international supervision. To make Trieste a Free City has certainly ensured that its Italian character will be preserved, since the Italians have a majority on the city council. It may ensure that Trieste will play its part as the outlet for Central Europe.

But, since neither Italy nor Yugoslavia are willing to provide the money for its upkeep, it has to be subsidized by the Great Powers who imposed the solution. Does this also ensure the Slovene minority in the city their full national rights or that the Slovenes of the hinterland can develop their national culture in Trieste?

The answer is easy. If the city council is unchecked, there is no national equality. The immediate majority are Italians – the very men who took the lead in all the worst activities of Fascism. They are perfectly aware that, with fair play, the Slovenes will eventually acquire a majority, as they were already on the way to do before 1914. The Italians can hold their own only by forbidding Slovene schools, Slovene newspapers, and the use of Slovene in the law courts and public offices.

The international commission will, therefore, have constantly to intervene. If it insists on fair treatment for the Slovenes, there will be Italian riots in Trieste, and all over Italy as well; if it fails to insist, there will be Slovene riots in Trieste, and a violent outburst of feeling all over Yugoslavia.

Ultimately, the international commission, inadequately provided with armed support – or, probably, not provided with it at all – will despair, and Trieste will relapse into Italian hands. The Yugoslavs are the smaller state and will have to acquiesce, as Poland had to acquiesce in the German advance at Danzig.

But, no, Poland did not acquiesce. At the last moment she found backers among the Great Powers and resisted German demands. Is it likely that Yugoslavia will be without a backer among the Great Powers?

After all, we have a certain experience in how Free Cities work. History may not be a good guide, but it is all we have; and in regard to Free Cities the experience of history is decisive. Two Free Cities were created after the first German war – Fiume and Danzig.

The severance of Fiume from Italy was not imposed upon Italy by the Great Powers, as the severance of Trieste from Italy was imposed by the Great Powers. It was proposed by the Italians themselves and contained in the Treaty of Rapallo, which Italy voluntarily signed with Yugoslavia. Yet, as soon as the treaty had been signed, Italian filibusters seized Fiume, with the support of Italian warships; and the Italian government threatened the Yugoslavs with war when they attempted to restore the settlement according to the treaty which Italy herself had proposed.

In 1924, four years after the Treaty of Rapallo, Italy compelled Yugoslavia to tear up the Treaty and to agree to the Italian annexation of Fiume. Is it surprising that the position of Trieste as a Free City is regarded without enthusiasm by the Yugoslavs? They believe, and not without good grounds, that it is a method of keeping the door open for Italian claims until Italy is strong enough to enforce them.

But it may be said that the cases of Fiume and Trieste are not analogous: Fiume became a Free City by a voluntary act and its freedom depended solely on Italy's good faith, never a strong element in Italian policy. Trieste has been made a Free City by the Great Powers and its freedom will be maintained by them.

We have also had experience of this type of Free City. In fact, the friends of Italy in 1945 need simply to take out of the second-hand cupboard the arguments which were used against the Polish claims to Danzig in 1919. Danzig was said to be inhabited solely by Germans. This was true, a good deal truer than that Trieste is inhabited solely by Italians. Of Danzig's 360,000 inhabitants, less than 10,000 were Poles; within the city limits of Trieste there are at least 60,00 Slovenes, a third of the population, and since the Free City has been extended to include some of the immediate hinterland this proportion has been at least doubled.

It was said that German sentiment would be offended if Germans were put under Polish rule, in fact, that it was impossible to put civilized Germans under the rule of the barbarous Poles. A great deal was made of Danzig's historic significance for Germany and of the cultural importance of Danzig for Germany; just as some now talk of the importance of Trieste for Italian culture and Italian history.

In both cases, this importance is imaginary, though in the case of Danzig there was perhaps a little excuse for it. It was asserted that Polish economic needs would be perfectly met by the creation of a Free City. And, finally, it was emphasized that the Free City would be under the guarantee of the League of Nations and that the Great Powers could be relied upon to defend it from either Polish or German encroachments.

Every schoolboy knows how these expectations were falsified. Danzig did not serve Polish economic needs. The Poles were compelled at enormous expense to build a harbour of their own. German sentiment was not satisfied with the position of Danzig as a Free City; rather it regarded this position as a standing invitation to agitate for the return of Danzig to Germany.

After all, if the Great Powers had refused to give Danzig to Poland in 1919 when Germany was prostrate, they would surely not refuse it to Germany when she was again powerful. The League of Nations proved impotent to protect the rights either of Poland or of the democratic German minority in Danzig.

The Great Powers made feeble attempts not to intervene but to mediate. Soon they wearied even of this and left Poland to negotiate directly with Germany – as Yugoslavia was left to negotiate directly with Italy in 1920. Danzig's final gift to mankind was to provide an excuse for the most destructive war in history, in which both the Soviet Union and the British Empire only just escaped total defeat. And this is the experiment which the friends of Italy have repeated at Trieste!

The experiment will have the same results. Italian sentiment will not be satisfied with the status of a Free City; it will accept the invitation to agitate for the return of Trieste to Italy. The city council, with its Italian majority, will not seek to promote Yugoslav commerce. Still more – a cause of quarrel which did not exist at Danzig – it will neglect the Slovene schools, or, more probably, attempt to close them.

To make Trieste a Free City has no other purpose than to hold the door open for the reassertion of Italian claims at a time when Italy will be better equipped to enforce them than she is now. The Free City idea is a post-dated cheque with which to buy off the Yugoslavs; but when, in a few years' time, they present it to the World Security Organization, it will be returned marked 'refer to drawer'. And where then will be the drawers, the unpractical idealists of England and America?

They will be explaining away, or ignoring, the Italian treatment of the Slovenes, declaring that, after all, civilized Italians cannot be put under the rule of barbarous Slavs, and denouncing, as harsh and unjust, the very peace settlement which, it was claimed, would satisfy Italian opinion!

Thus, by a process of elimination, we are left with the fourth solution: of applying in this disputed territory the rule which has been accepted everywhere else in Europe and determining its destiny *according to the predominant nationality of the whole*. The frontier should be drawn where the Slovene countryside ends and the Italian countryside begins, a national frontier which has not changed for a thousand years; and the towns should share the destiny of the countryside.

This would undoubtedly be the best economic solution. Trieste would be the only great port in Yugoslav hands, and the Yugoslav minister of transport would make it his principal concern. Fiume, its only rival, has only a single-track line with a very steep gradient to the main trunk line through Zagreb and, owing to natural obstacles, can never be a port of the same scale; it would never have been created at all, except for the Hungarian desire to have a port not under the control of Vienna.

Moreover, co-operation with the other states of Central Europe must be an essential element in Yugoslav policy; therefore, as a matter of Yugoslav interest, everything will be done to make Trieste the major port of Czechoslovakia, Hungary and Austria. This would have a profound political effect, and one which it is a British interest to promote.

When Trieste was in Italian hands, it was used as a political weapon to divide Central Europe and to compel Austria and Hungary to follow a policy hostile to Czechoslovakia and Hungary. If Trieste were in Yugoslav hands, it would also be used as a political weapon, but to compel Austria and Hungary to co-operate with Czechoslovakia and Yugoslavia.

This would be regretted only by the friends of Archduke Otto of Habsburg and of Admiral Horthy, and it is difficult to believe that they are deserving of sympathy.

There remains the national question. Would not the Yugoslavs inflict on the Italian inhabitants of Trieste all the injustices which the Italians have inflicted on the Slovenes and Croats? There are strong grounds for believing that they would not.

In the first place, Yugoslavia is not, as Italy is, a national state. It is a federal state, containing at least five distinct nationalities and comprising six federative units. The present Yugoslavia has far more in common with the old non-national Habsburg Empire than with a national state such as Italy; and though there are likely to be national disputes in the future – as there should be in any healthy country – no one nationality will predominate. Besides, the Slovenes are less than 2,000,000, of a total Yugoslav population of 16,000,000, so even the idea of a Slovene domination is out of the question.

There is a second, and more decisive, argument. The Italian majority in Trieste is artificial. It can be maintained only by denying to the Slovenes their national rights, and when in the old days of the Habsburg Empire the Slovenes enjoyed something like fair play, the Italian majority was dwindling rapidly. The Italians had to close the Slovene schools in order to keep their position. The Slovenes will only have to open their schools in order to start catching up again. It will not be necessary for them to close the Italian schools.

Once the Slovenes are allowed to use their own language in the law courts and public offices, once they can send their children to Slovene schools, once Slovene books and newspapers can circulate freely, thousands who have called themselves Italians will revert to their nationality of origin. Moreover, when Trieste again becomes a great port – which it can never be under Italy – there will be a great demand for labour, and Slovenes will crowd in from the neighbouring countryside.

The Slovenes will become a majority, probably within a generation; but they will become the majority by a natural process. To do so they will not need to employ the weapon of national persecution. This process has taken place, or is taking place, in every town of Eastern Europe; it can take place just as easily in Trieste.

The reader will observe that I have conducted this argument on the most cynical basis. I have not attempted to make out that the Italians are, by nature, intolerant and chauvinistic or that the Slovenes are, by nature, tolerant and pacific. Though I think that the evidence would justify such an attempt, we must apply the same measure to both sides. Either we assume (as Italy propagandists do) that the Yugoslavs will remain bellicose and intolerant – in which case we must assume the same of the Italians. Or we assume, as Italian propagandists do, that the new Italy will behave in an entirely different way from the old – in which case we must assume the same of the Yugoslavs.

But it is an outrageous assumption to suppose that the Yugoslavs, who have been our allies, will possess all the vices of the old Italy; and that the Italians, who have been our enemies, will possess more virtues than any people has ever shown.

If both nations remain in the future what they have been in the past, then Trieste should be Yugoslav, for the Italians have shown themselves unfit to rule over Slovenes, whereas the Yugoslavs are likely to treat the Italian minority considerately, if only as a matter of self-interest.

If both nations live up to the fine promises of the present, then Trieste should be Yugoslav; since an Italy which had genuinely abandoned imperialist ambitions would not desire to retain Trieste, and the Italians in Trieste would be more prosperous under Yugoslav rule than if they remained in Italy.

If the Italians live up to all their fine promises and the Yugoslavs to none of theirs – then and then only, Trieste should indeed be Italian – but Malta, Tobruk and Addis Ababa should be Italian as well!

The liberal Press in England was shocked that the Yugoslavs insisted on liberating Istria themselves, instead of waiting for the decision of a peace conference; from this the worst conclusions were drawn.

Memories, especially British memories, are short. But the Yugoslavs had not forgotten that they awaited the decision of a peace conference in 1919. In 1919 they went to Paris with clean hands and their claims were supported by the President of the United States; they came away from Paris with their hands empty.

Italian rule in Trieste rested on the same right as German rule in Prague, in Warsaw, in Paris, or in the Channel Isles – the right of conquest; the only difference is that the Yugoslavs were compelled to agree to their temporary defeat by the Treaty of Rapallo.

Thus, too, the Soviet Union was compelled to acknowledge the loss of the western Ukraine and of western White Russia to the Poles by the Treaty of Riga in 1921. But that did not prevent the Russians liberating these territories – with the approval of Great Britain and the United States.

What sanction and authority does the Treaty of Rapallo possess which the Treaty of Riga did not possess? What claim has the Ukraine to Lvov which Yugoslavia does not possess to Trieste? The Yugoslavs have not attempted to seize any territory which is either ethnically or historically Italian. They have simply claimed territory in which there is an indisputable Yugoslav majority and of which they were robbed by violence in 1920.

They did no more than the Czechs did in liberating all Czechoslovakia to the pre-Munich frontiers, without waiting for the verdict of an international conference. Yet the Munich settlement was an international arrangement, agreed to by England and France, while the Treaty of Rapallo was imposed upon Yugoslavia by Italy without the consent of any third party.

It was strange political mathematics to suppose that it is right in 1945 to repudiate an agreement imposed by force in 1938, but wrong to repudiate an agreement imposed by force in 1924. Fourteen years was indeed a short period in which to turn wrong into right.

Postscript – (1949)

This essay was written as a pamphlet in 1945 at the request of the Yugoslav government. It originally ended with the plea that to recognize

Slovene claims to Trieste would strengthen good relations between East and West. This ending was removed at Yugoslav suggestion; it was not for them, they said, to advise on the relations of the Great Powers. At the time I supposed this to be an exaggerated demonstration of Yugoslav independence. Now I know better. The only chance for the Yugoslavs was to base their claim on historic and national justice; Soviet backing, far from being a help to them, drove the other great powers into uncompromising opposition. The question of Trieste and of Istria was conducted purely as a trial of strength. The Russians backed Yugoslavia solely in order to show that they could protect their satellites; the others opposed Yugoslav claims in order to weaken the Communists in Italy and in order 'to keep Russia off the Adriatic'. A glance at the map would have shown that, if Russia and Yugoslavia were indeed the same (which has proved to be far from being the case), then Russia was on the Adriatic already – at Rijeka (Fiume) and Pola, to say nothing of Split and the bay of Kotor. In these circumstances, though the Slovenes were robbed of their historic city and Yugoslavia of her natural outlet, it was a great victory to have secured even the establishment of Trieste as a Free City.

The policy of the Western powers was calculated to force Yugoslavia even more firmly into the arms of Russia; only the fantastic pride of the Yugoslavs defeated this outcome. Though I thought poorly of Western policy, I confess that it never occurred to me that, within two years of signing the treaty of peace, the Western powers would propose to hand over the Free City to Italy. A strange argument: since Trieste cut off from its hinterland proved unworkable, a way out was to be found by cutting it off still more completely. And since Fascism is reviving in Italy, it should be countered by granting the demands which the Fascists make. In my naive view the wisest course for a great power, even in its own interest, is to follow the path of right and justice; this view does not seem to be held by others. The Western powers, far from welcoming Yugoslav independence from Russia, seek only to demonstrate Yugoslav dependence on themselves; and now demand that Yugoslavia should abandon Trieste even as a Free City. Those who did not shrink from the roars of Marshal Stalin are not likely to be overawed by Mr Bevin; and the Yugoslavs will disappoint the Western powers as much as, previously, they disappointed the Kremlin.

CHAPTER SIXTY-TWO

Czechoslovakia Today (July 1946)

These three reports written by Alan Taylor in Prague were published in the *Manchester Guardian* (24, 25 and 29 July 1946). They were written in the 'People's democracies' period before the Iron Curtain came down across Eastern Europe. Alan Taylor's essays were written when he was still optimistic that the wartime alliance with the Soviet Union could continue into the post-war period. They also follow on from *The Course of German History* (London, Hamish Hamilton, 1945), in dwelling on 'The German problem'.

I The situation in the Czech lands

In Czechoslovakia life is normal. This does not seem so surprising if you go from London to Prague by air, travelling more easily and more quickly than from London to Edinburgh. It is incredible and bewildering if you come to Prague overland through the chaos and starvation of any of the surrounding countries.

There are plenty of scars: scars of material destruction, scars from the German Terror, scars from the Communist effervescence of the last twelve months which has only just died down. In fact, most Czechs of liberal mind are still rather dazed to discover that they, and liberty, have survived both conquest by the Germans and liberation by the Russians. For there can be no doubt that liberty has survived. The Russians, maybe, regard Czechoslovakia as a show-piece, a model dominion, but it is more likely that they are simply relieved to have one responsibility the less.

Democratic freedoms

At any rate, there is not a scrap of Russian interference; there is nothing in the nature of a secret police; there are no restrictions on freedom of movement or of discussion. There is complete religious freedom, a freedom where both Protestant and Roman Catholic leaders take an active part in political life. On John Hus Day I heard the Protestant minister of a little hill town speaking in the open, declare that the defeat of the Nazis was worth nothing unless they conquered the Nazis in themselves and that the moving of peoples on racial grounds was not in accord with the principles of Masaryk.

There is, too, complete academic freedom. The University of Prague is now the only academic institution of indisputably first rank east of the Rhine. Other English visitors have commented on the Czech desire for cultural contacts with Britain, and culture does not mean here simply literature and the arts. In Moscow, too, everyone listens to Shakespeare and reads Dickens. In Prague they want also our 'political' culture.

The Czech people had, no doubt, a democratic tradition: but the man who preserved that tradition and restored liberty was Dr Beneš. He has obviously had a hard time standing up to both the Russians and the Czech Communists; but he has stood up to them successfully. He is that rare thing – a man of principle who is also adroit, even wily, in his tactics. His hand has, of course, been immensely strengthened by having the ideas of Masaryk behind him.

In most European countries liberalism was pulled down by *laissez-faire* and finally degenerated into 'collaborationism'. Now, the competing political philosophies are both totalitarian: they look to the Vatican or the Kremlin. In Czechoslovakia alone it is possible to be a Socialist without being a Marxist; a liberal without believing in Capitalism; and religious without being a Roman Catholic.

There is also a more mundane explanation of Czech democracy. Tolerance and liberty flourish with economic prosperity, and the Czech lands never ceased to be prosperous. The Germans murdered over a quarter of a million people in a deliberate campaign to destroy the Czech nation. Therefore they murdered selectively, killing exclusively intellectuals – teachers, administrators, trade union officials, lawyers, writers. The Czech workers had good wages and steady employment; the peasants had high prices and secure markets. Czech industry was little damaged except in the very last weeks of war, and most of the damage, even the damage to railways and bridges, has been restored. The Republic took over from the Germans a going concern.

The Kosice system

The political freedom has, of course, clear limits. It is freedom within the programme drawn up at Kosice before the liberation, freedom on the agreed principles of a nation-state and the nationalization of industry.

In the Czech lands (Bohemia and Moravia) only four parties are allowed to run candidates and to publish newspapers – the Communists, the Social Democrats, the National Socialists (who are collectivist liberals), and the Progressive Catholics. All four parties are represented in the coalition government, and this gives to the proceedings of Parliament a certain artificiality, or at least dullness. The real debates are within the Council of Ministers (which, having twenty-six members, is itself a debating assembly) and in the party meetings. Parliament records formal decisions and applauds agreements already made. It will face its real test if the coalition breaks up.

Mr Gottwald, the Communist prime minister, told me that democracy is secure 'so long as the other parties remain progressive', by which he meant so long as they were willing to co-operate with the Communists. The other parties are likely to remain progressive so long as the Communists remain democratic.

In the meantime each group is surprised how well it gets on with the others and how sensibly each behaves. The victory of the Communists, who won 40 per cent of the votes in the Czech lands, has given Czechoslovakia the first Communist prime minister in Europe to reach his position by democratic methods, and the Communists are as pleased with this as with a new toy. Mr Gottwald is a man of great ability and strong personality who is not afraid to say hard things to his followers. In fact he is already treating them as Mr Attlee and Mr Morrison treat the 'wild men' of the Labour Party.

The parties will not differ on the principle of the nation-state. All Czechs dislike the expulsion of the Germans; but all know that it is inevitable. The alternative would be worse: it would be the compulsory turning of Germans into Czechs, a policy only possible (if then) by Nazi methods. All the same, it is a strange historic moment which ends for ever the seven centuries of Czech–German conflict and co-operation in Bohemia.

Nor will the parties differ on the nationalisation of industry. For all practical purposes the controversy between capitalism and Socialism was settled by the Germans. They took over most important industries and ran them for their own purposes. Now it is impossible to 'unscramble' what the Germans have done. Instead the Czechoslovak people have become the residuary legatees of the German oppressors. Socialism has come, as in Great Britain, by legal means, though the German occupation was, no doubt, a very unpleasant way of accelerating it.

The present problems are strictly practical: to find efficient managers in the nationalized industries, to raise the level of productivity, and so on. The main responsibility in economic matters rests with the Communists, who now have to oppose further nationalization and to exhort the workers to work harder. Since the Communists are the leaders of industry, the peasants now vote for them as they used to vote for the misnamed 'Agrarian' party, the party of the banks and big business. For the Communists are the banks and big business.

In Czechoslovakia, as nowhere else east of the Rhine, there is at present both Socialism and democracy. Many Czechs ask, 'Can we have nationalisation without totalitarian rule?' The answer depends partly on the willingness of the Communists to be satisfied with economic gains without pushing Marxism down everyone's throat. It depends much more on the resolution with which the non-Communist parties defend their liberal morality and philosophy without slipping into a defence of capitalism. And most of all it depends on factors not under Czech control: a satisfactory relation with the Slovaks, a stable European order, and the revival of Czech foreign trade.

II   The position of the Slovaks

The Slovak question was troublesome in the first Republic; it threatens to be insoluble, but less troublesome, in the second. A settlement which would satisfy all parties is impossible in this generation. But there is every prospect of endless negotiations and compromises to satisfy the Slovak sense of importance.

The events of the last seven years have completed the process of making two distinct nations. There are now two languages, two cultural traditions, and – to crown all – two memories of the years of war. While the Czechs were oppressed and deprived of political rights, the Slovaks enjoyed a romantic quasi-independence.

The administration was in Slovak hands. There was a sort of parliament and a variety of newspapers, even Communist journals of a cultural nature. The University of Bratislava was open until the autumn of 1944, though some professors were dismissed or degraded for Czechoslovak sympathies. It is a somewhat curious experience to be sincerely welcomed with the phrases which a year or two ago greeted visiting German professors. The Slovaks talk of Slovakia and Switzerland as the two neutral states of the continent.

The Slovak rising in the later summer of 1944 gave the Slovak intellectuals a winter of partisan life and enabled the quisling state to transform itself into an ally. Still, had it not been for the Czech connection and the recognition of the authority of Dr Benes Slovakia would now be a defeated country in the same plight as Hungary or Austria. Realization of this makes all but the most romantic Slovaks acquiesce at least temporarily in the idea of Czechoslovakia.

Communist miscalculations

The political situation in Slovakia remains, however, different from that in the Czech lands. The Czech Right wing discredited itself by collaborating with the Germans. Now all Czech parties are of the Left. In Slovakia the Democratic party, which to everyone's surprise – including its own – won two-thirds of the Slovak vote, owes its success to Right-wing support, even though some of its leaders incline to the centre. Its followers are capitalist, clericalist, and anti-Semitic in outlook. (One of the show-pieces I was not supposed to see was the synagogues burned out by the Slovak 'Hlinka Guard').

The Communists thought that by the partisan rising and by the union which they achieved of Communists and Social Democrats they had secured control of Slovakia. They were therefore advocates of Slovak rights, threatening to secede to join the Soviet Union if they did not get their way. And, since they did not anticipate the sweeping Communist victory in the Czech lands, they insisted on giving the Slovak deputies an equal voice in constitutional issues.

The elections went quite contrary to the expectations of the Communists. The Russian occupation of Slovakia lost them Slovakia; the American occupation of Western Bohemia helped to give them Bohemia. Now the Communists have shifted their emphasis: they insist that Czechoslovakia is a unitary state, with merely administrative devolution for Slovakia.

But the Slovak Democrats are now also advocates of the unitary state. Alarmed lest the reactionary outlook of some at least of their followers may give the Communists a handle against them, they too insist on their loyalty to Prague and look to the Communist-led government there to protect them against both local reaction and the local Communists. They even talk of bringing to trial the leaders of the former quisling state. The trial of Monsignor Tiso for high treason, if it ever comes off, should prove singular.

A new nationalism

It would be a great mistake, and one which the Czechs do not make, to take Slovak politics too seriously. The Slovak people have only just begun to live after centuries of Hungarian oppression, and they have certainly not attained a level-headed political maturity.

Slovak nationalism is still in its first stages: that is, it is still almost the monopoly of intellectuals. These devise fine schemes in which Slovakia is to possess the decisive position in a new dualist state which Hungary had in Austria-Hungary. They would like to ape their former rulers. But the Hungarians had a strong political tradition and a united ruling class, while Austria had a background of absolutism and was torn with national conflicts. The Slovaks are not the Hungarians and the Czechs are not the Austrians, though they possess something of their political resourcefulness.

In the first Republic the Czechs tried to turn the awakening Slovaks into Czechoslovakia by filling their schools and universities with Czech

STRUGGLES FOR SUPREMACY

teachers. They are now resigned to the rise of a distinct Slovak nationalism. But they know from their own nineteenth-century experience that the national struggle is, for all practical purposes, a struggle for employment in the service of the State, and they have therefore made generous provision for the aspiring Slovak bureaucrats. The offices of the central government in Prague are required to have a certain proportion of Slovak employees at every grade. In addition there is a subordinate Slovak administration at Bratislava with the establishment and airs – though not the powers – of a government, staffed entirely by Slovaks.

In fact, the Slovaks are Slovaks, but the Czechs are Czechoslovakia; and they will have to pay for this privilege until industrialism has brought the two halves of the Republic more into line.

Meanwhile Slovakia gives Czechoslovakia a special problem in foreign politics. The Slovaks escaped German oppression and are hardly aware of the German problem. But their claim is to have had an oppressor of their own, and present the Hungarian minority in Slovakia as a problem comparable with that of the Sudeten Germans. Given the philosophy of the nation-state which is, after all, the starting-point for the Czechs as well, the expulsion of the Hungarians is logically inescapable. But it is difficult to take their presence seriously as a matter of life and death for the Republic.

The Slovaks, with their eyes focused solely on the Danube, cannot see that Hungary, in spite of her intransigent revisionism, can never be a serious danger without German support. On the other hand, having launched this proposal, they are now realizing that they are likely to lose a quarter of a million hard-working farmers and they are therefore trying to undo the effects of their own proposal by offering Slovak nationality to any Hungarian of remote Slovak descent or even of Slovak goodwill. The outcome will be to reduce the number of those transferred but to reap the full harvest in Hungarian resentment. Still, this resentment would exist in any case short of frontier revision on a large scale in Hungary's favour, and the need for support against Hungary makes the Slovaks resigned to the existence of Czechoslovakia.

Slovakia was exceedingly prosperous during the war, and there is now something like inflation in Bratislava, an economic condition quite different from that in Prague. Once the war profits at present saved or concealed in Switzerland have been spent the Slovaks will need the backing of Bohemian industry and, if they are sensible, will welcome a process by which the Czech and Slovak lands become more similar in character. But whether this can obscure the effects of traditions so different is a doubtful matter. Still, the Slovak question will never become acute so long as the international position of Czechoslovakia is secure. In the future, as in the past, the fate of Czechoslovakia will be determined by events in the great world.

III   Questions of foreign policy and trade

Czechoslovakia, democratic and prosperous, is surrounded by political and economic confusion. This exceptional situation cannot last. For Czechoslovakia, more than for any other part of Central Europe, the restoration of a peaceful order is essential.

If this were all, Czech and British policy would coincide. But for the Czechs there is something even more important than peace and prosperity, and that is to avert the recovery of a powerful Germany. Where we talk of someone as 'fallen in the wars' or of a house as 'destroyed in the war' the Czechs speak of their dead as 'killed by the Germans' and say a house was 'destroyed by the Germans' – even when the actual destruction was caused by American bombs or Russian shells.

Whatever the merits of the present British policy towards Germany, the effect on Czech public opinion has been disastrous. The shadow of Munich has again risen above the horizon. Even Dr Benes, a resolute Westerner, said to me, 'Can we rely on the Western Powers to act this time against Germany?'

Fear of Germany

The Czechs believe that Germany still possesses almost intact the resources of heavy industry which enable her to conquer Europe. They do not believe that anything short of the physical destruction of these resources will lessen the German danger. This fear of Germany may be exaggerated. But there are ten million Czechoslovaks and seventy million Germans. The Czechs had six years of German occupation, in the course of which a quarter of a million Czechs were murdered. The Czechs will pay any price to escape another six years of German occupation.

In the years between the wars the Czechs relied on the French alliance. During the war Czechs in exile talked of being 'between East and West'. Now Dr Benes says, 'We are not between East and West; we are between Germany and Russia'. The Czechs will never play the balancing game which brought Poland to disaster in 1939. Mr Gottwald said in his declaration of policy: 'The Soviet alliance is for us not merely a question of safety but even of existence.'

In foreign policy (and for that matter, in military policy) Czechoslovakia stands in the same relation to the Soviet Union as the Dominions stand to great Britain. The alliance does not preclude independent relations with other countries any more than the Commonwealth precludes independent Canadian or Australian relations with the United States. But it means that in the event of any deep breach between Russia and the Western powers Czechoslovakia would go with Russia, whatever the price politically and economically. Anyone who has seen the marks of German terror would find it difficult to condemn this decision.

All the same, the Czechs are discovering that the Soviet alliance is not the answer to every difficulty. The Soviet government, secure in Czech goodwill and satisfied, too, that it has discharged its duty by recognizing the pre-Munich frontiers, does not give Czechoslovakia much support in day-to-day affairs. Similarly, Britain and America are content to have restored Czechoslovak independence.

Return to France

But the Czechs sometimes need active support. They would like the district of Glatz, which is at present in Polish hands. They want to be free to expel the Hungarian minority from Slovakia. They want to be quite secure (though I believe they are) from any Polish claims at Teschen. Therefore the Czechs are going back to their old ally, France. They are coming to recognize that, since Great Britain will not try to maintain the balance between Russia and America, the best hope for the independent states of Europe is the restoration of France as a great power.

So far as the peace conference goes, this development of policy has probably come too late; but if France recovers it is surely the line of the future. A coalition of national states led by France, being resolutely anti-German, could rest on Russian support and yet allow the Russians to withdraw (as they wish to do) from immediate responsibility for European politics.

With the immense popularity which we gained during the war, enhanced by our Socialist home policy, we might once have taken this lead. But our sympathy with Germany and Italy, coupled with our attempt to restore a *laissez-faire* world market has now lost us this chance – at least that it my impression – in Czechoslovakia. It was surprising, for instance, how shocked the Czechs were at the British advocacy of Italian claims in Trieste.

The Czechs would like to restore the Little Entente, but with whom? 'Slav solidarity' is an attractive slogan. In practice it comes down to an alliance and a trade agreement with Yugoslavia, and many Czechs are doubtful about the stability of the present Yugoslav regime. Oddly enough, Mr Gottwold singled out for mention their desire to be on friendly terms with 'a democratic Austria'. It is puzzling to know whether this is a serious declaration of policy or simply a hint that the present regime in Austria is not democratic.

The immediate practical need of the Czechs is to find a substitute for the German market, to which they were geared during the war. Here, too, the Western powers push them into the arms of Russia. It is not enough to offer the Czechs the free world market. Someone must take the place of Dr Schacht. The Russians are ready to take a good deal of capital equipment, and even some semi-luxury goods. To make Czechoslovakia an economic dependency or Russia is neither a Russian nor a Czech interest. But if the Americans insist on applying their present view of the world market, by which the weaker must be crushed, the Czechs will seek protection within the Russian economic system.

Like most travellers, I have brought back conclusions with which I started out. First, this country can draw on an immense fund of goodwill, to be used in favour of democracy and political liberty, once it is clear that we shall never again falter in depriving Germany of power and that our influence will not be used in favour of discarded social forms. (Here I must add a word in praise of the British embassy in Prague: its members, from the ambassador down, actually like the country in which they are stationed and do not keep company with the defeated classes – something unique in British representatives in Central and Eastern Europe!)

Secondly, the democratic Socialism (that is, a combination of political liberty and economic planning) is the desire of most people in Europe, but if it is to work it must extend to international trade. If our principles mean anything we must not merely befriend democratic Socialist states, such as Czechoslovakia, we must have with them a planned foreign trade. If our international economic policy is negative we shall drive all Central Europe (and most of Western Europe too) into the arms of the Communists.

CHAPTER SIXTY-THREE

German Riddles

This essay was first published as a review of Edmund Vermeil, *The German Scene* (London, Harvey, 1956), in the *New Statesman and Nation*, 52, 1334 (6 October 1956). The essay marks Alan Taylor's continuing suspicion concerning Germany even in its post-war divided state. In it he observes of Hitler and his actions, that 'we have almost got to the point of admitting that it was all our fault for not standing up to him in March 1936'. The politician in his eighties was Konrad Adenauer (1876–1967), Chancellor of West Germany (1949–63).

The shutters are up on 'the German question'. Though more people live in western Germany alone than in either France or England, Germany counts for nothing as a great power. The political news from Bonn reads like gossip from a small provincial town; and we turn impatiently to another page. Nobody cares what the Germans are doing, not even the Germans themselves. They work hard, go about their daily business, and give no thought to the morrow. To use Professor Vermeil's favourite word, they have been 'atomized' out of politics. We can still work up some interest for what is happening in Japan or Tibet or Bulgaria. We follow enthralled the details of every school dispute in the United States and of every literary wrangle in the Soviet Union. Nor do we weary in the endlessly subtle manoeuvres between Nenni and Saraget. But Germany ... ? Heaven preserve us from such dead stuff. We have had too big a dose of German affairs, and we cannot swallow any more. We have been reading books about Germany for the last forty years: the kaiser's Germany, Weimar Germany, Hitler's Germany, bad Germany, good Germany, revolutionary Germany, Fascist Germany; how to save her, how to ruin her. Now it is all over. We do not need to open any more books about Germany, at any rate not until some new shift in the world constellation.

It is unfashionable, but also rather fun, to have a look at 'the German problem' when there is nothing to be gained by it. What did we miss in those detestable, exciting years when the books came tumbling out too fast? What can we see now in the perspective of comparative indifference? German historians are not much use to us. Instead of studying the past, they have merely retreated into it as historians often do; and they seem anxious to show that nothing has happened so far as they are concerned in techniques, in understanding, or even in literary style, since the fall of Bismarck. They are intellectual teddy-boys, conscientiously reviving the outlook of 1900. English writers are not much better. We are all rather ashamed of having told the truth about German behaviour. We like to pretend now that it did not happen; and we try to treat the German past as much like the past of any other country. We agree with the Germans that Hitler was a bit of bad luck that might have happened to anyone; and we have almost got to the point of admitting that it was all our fault for not standing up to him in March 1936. At least that seems to be the view of those two assiduous students of history, Sir Anthony Eden and Sir Robert Boothby.

Perhaps a Frenchman can give us more help. Professor Vermeil has been an outstanding authority on Germany for the last thirty years. An earlier book of his on *Germany's Three Reichs* brought a flood of enlightenment to English readers. His new book[1] is also enlightening, though very tough going. He has not been well served by his English publisher and translator. The French original on *Contemporary Germany* had two volumes: the first from the fall of Germany to the establishment of the Republic; the second from 1918 to the present day. In English the first volume has been squeezed into an introduction of just over twenty pages. Sense and pattern have been destroyed; we are launched in mid-stream without knowing how we got there. As a minor, but substantial, criticism the dates are persistently misprinted; a reader who took them seriously would end in the madhouse. A return to sanity is not helped by Professor Vermeil's style and method of presentation. He has studied the Germans so long that he writes like one. The sentences are long and involved; the thought obscure. And when one sees a sentence in italics shining like a beacon-light ahead, it turns out on arrival to be either irrelevant or a commonplace. The Germans have imposed many sufferings on us; among them, having to read Professor Vermeil's books.

Yet read them we must, if we are to get any nearer to understanding the German past. What distinguishes Professor Vermeil is the attempt, not always successful, to treat German problems as a unity – not economic or social or political or literary, but the single 'crisis' of a civilization. The trouble with the Germans is that they are always being pulled together and always being torn apart. Set up any proposition about them, and it is at once knocked down by its opposite. For instance, Germany is an unmistakably Protestant country and yet profoundly Catholic. The two creeds do not compromise, do not modify each other, do not even cancel out; they remain in permanent antagonism. Again, Germany has been the most avowedly national community in Europe; yet local loyalties are stronger than anywhere else. It is of no great importance in France to be a Norman or in England to be a Yorkshireman (I have been mistaken for one); but every German is as much a Bavarian or a Rhinelander as he is a German. In fact there are no Germans pure and simple, not even the refugees. It is just the same in politics. You think you have got something straight, and then it turns upside down. Marx thought that the German working class would be the most independent in Europe and that German Social Democracy would lead the International. So it did, but only to nowhere. The Social Democratic party grew to such a size that its leaders, and perhaps its followers, became terrified of doing anything. The only thing they ever did was to stop the revolution of 1918. If the party had been smaller, poorer, worse organized, the revolution might well have succeeded. The contradiction worked for Hitler also. Hitlerism did not succeed because the Germans were uneducated or uncivilized. It succeeded because they were highly educated, literate, politically conscious.

In fact the trouble with the Germans is that they can all read and that they take their reading seriously. They are for ever acting a part that they have read somewhere in print. Look, for instance, at Heinrich Mann's novel, *Der Untertan*, which describes a German businessman trailing around Europe simply in order to strengthen his imperial devotion by staring at William II. It was impossible to talk to a German after 1919 without discovering an aggrieved man. He might be prosperous, healthy, happy in his private life; but he could not sleep at nights for thinking of the Polish Corridor. Professor Vermeil emphasizes again and again the ruin which the Romantic movement caused to the Germans. They have never recovered from it. What is Romanticism in art, literature or politics? Simply a form of dressing-up. The wonderful photographs which Julia Cameron took of Victorian writers brings this out very well. Each one of them – Tennyson, Ruskin, Sir Henry Taylor – was a character-actor, imprisoned in his role. The Germans have prolonged this Romanticism into the twentieth century. People talk nonsense in every country, but only the Germans take it seriously. Anti-Semitism, for example, was not a German invention. The French started it as a modern political device; Chesterton and Belloc carried it on here. It needed the Germans to send five million Jews to the gas-chambers. Hitler, of course, was the supreme example. His so-called ideas are merely the disjointed ramblings of talk in a public-house; but Hitler put them in print, took them seriously, and counted on the Germans doing the same.

The Germans have had a rough time of it in the past – hence their escape to the world of literary fantasy. There are no settled periods in their history except those of exhaustion after defeat in war. Is there any time which one could look back to, if a German, and say: 'It would have been nice to live them?' Perhaps the twenty years when Bismarck was chancellor; and these were only a pause between two crises. Hence Hitler's 'Thousand-year Reich' – an absurd longing for an endless, imaginary stability. Now the Germans have attained this stability in an unexpected way. They have got nothing; and this is a form of contentment. There are no interesting books, no exciting ideas. They have the best-equipped theatres in Europe, and no plays to put on, except the Expressionist works of Brecht which are a generation out of date. They have no capital city; no statesmen but an old gentleman in his eighties; no army; nothing to boast of and, therefore, nothing to be sorry for. It often seemed during the war that the only solution for 'the German problem' was that the Germans should cease to exist. And so they have. They are still there as 'atomized' private persons, leading a quiet life, well-fed, prosperous, hard-working. But they are no worry to themselves or to anyone else. The best advice for everybody, including the Germans, is simply: don't give the Germans a thought, pretend that they don't exist. Maybe one day they will astonish us all. They may shake off the terrible legacy of Romantic ideas and come to their senses. We have failed to re-educate the Germans; but time may do it for us. Then 'the German century' will appear as a bad dream, which, indeed, it always was.

Note

1.   E. Vermeil, *The German Scene*, London, Harvey, 1956.

CHAPTER SIXTY-FOUR

Heartland

This essay was first published as a review of Henry Cord Meyer, *Mitteleuropa in German Thought and Action, 1815–1945* (London, Batsford, 1956) in the *Manchester Guardian* (13 January 1956). Tomas Masaryk (1850–1939) was a professor of philosophy and Czech nationalist, becoming President of Czechoslovakia, 1918–35. Karl von Bruck, the Austrian minister of commerce (1848–60), drafted in 1850 a proposal for a customs union between the Habsburg monarchy and the German Zollverein. Friedrich List was a German economist and publicist of nationalist causes.

This is a first-rate contribution to historical understanding, one of the most original and valuable books on international affairs published for many years. Everyone knows the word 'Mitteleuropa'; and it has long been used as an explanation for German policy. Masaryk, for instance, based his whole case on it during the First World War. But what did it amount to in practice? Mr Meyer, having read countless memoranda, articles, and books, answers surprisingly yet convincingly: not much.

There was a preliminary stir in the days before the unification of Germany when such men as List and Bruck aspired to a united Central Europe under German leadership. All this vanished with Bismarck's triumph. His Reich was a North Sea power, indifferent to the Balkans and even to the German Austrians, and concerned with the world market. Even the Baghdad Railway was secondary; and in any case it was for Germany an overseas enterprise. Mitteleuropa did not cause the First World War. Quite the reverse: the war, and especially the blockade, first made Germans interested in Mitteleuropa. Even now it was all talk. There was no effective economic co-ordination with Austria-Hungary, let alone with Bulgaria; and the Turks never accepted the position of honorary Prussians which was assigned to them. The German Austrians welcomed the idea as a device by which Germany would prop up their domination over the Slavs: the Reich Germans showed little interest in it. With the defeat of Russia Mitteleuropa went into eclipse. The Ukraine was a far more tempting object than the Balkans or Asia Minor for German ambition. Nor can Mr Meyer find much trace of it between the wars. If Germany was to march out to conquest, it would be against Russia or France: east-central Europe was not worth the trouble.

There are many strands to the story. Sometimes the basis for Mitteleuropa was German cultural supremacy: sometimes it was the desire for a great Free Trade area. But always it was the product of professors and dreamers, not of politicians or businessmen. Mr Meyer might have given us more trade statistics to reinforce his argument that the idea had no practical importance. It would have been particularly useful to have had an analysis of German investment. But he has proved his case. Everyone who writes about German policy will have to revise his outlook in the light of Mr Meyer's book before he writes again.

CHAPTER SIXTY-FIVE

No Sanctity of Contract between Nations?

This essay first appeared in *The Chelwood Review*, 9 (January 1981), and is one of the later of Alan Taylor's essays, written before the collapse of the Soviet Union. It takes Soviet Russia as a key player in international relations in the future. It also repeats his frequent warnings of the likelihood of a third world war. It was also the theme of his last prestigious public lecture, the Romanes lecture that he delivered in March 1982 at Oxford University entitled 'War In Our Time'.

The sanctity of contracts between individuals depends, as we all know, on two things: first, the willing recognition by most sensible people that the observance of contracts is to everyone's advantage and, second, the existence of an authority strong enough to enforce any contract that has been unfairly broken. Indeed Thomas Hobbes argued in the seventeenth century that the existence of a powerful state, Leviathan as he called it, was the essential thing: life without such a state would be 'nasty, brutish and short'. Later thinkers have modified this insistence and have asserted that co-operation between the state and its people was also essential in order to make 'the social contract' work smoothly. The emphasis can be moved one way or the other. But all political thinkers agree that the satisfactory working of society requires a general willingness to agree and an authority to enforce agreements when they have been made. This sounds obvious enough though perhaps it is not as easy to apply as it appears.

Similarities are often found in the relations between individuals and those between states. Such similarities exist. International treaties often take the form of contracts. There are international authorities and have been for a long time. But there is one vital difference which makes all the parallels inapplicable. Every state is 'sovereign'. There is no power above it except God and He is not likely to intervene. Of course there are states – colonies or satellites – that really depend on the will of a second state. But these are not true independent states and can be disregarded. Thus there have never been in international relations the 'sanctions', moral or legal, which reinforce contracts between individuals – or have not been until recently. A treaty, for instance, may look like a contract. But if one of the parties disregards or infringes the treaty there is no way it can be enforced except by war or a modified version of the same such as a blockade. This is the second vital difference between individual and international agreements. The only appeal court in international affairs is to the God of War. It is true that some states at some times have agreed to submit their disputes to an international tribunal. But this agreement has been purely voluntary. No international court has any force except public opinion behind its judgements.

This seems a grim outlook and has seemed so on and off for a very long time. Men have been seeking to escape the consequences of the sovereign state for as long as there has been human history. The first answer was to eliminate all states except one. Ancient history records a series of 'universal empires', all of which broke down in the end. The Roman Empire was among the most successful of these universal states. For some four centuries it imposed a Roman peace on the then known world. The Chinese Empire did even better with a universal state lasting for 2,000 years except for the occasional incursion of barbarians.

Europe has pursued the prospect of union for as long as sovereign states have existed there. In the Middle Ages the popes tried to give a vague unity to Christendom as when they inspired the Crusades. Charles the Fifth, Holy Roman Emperor, King of Spain and ruler of the Netherlands, was supposed to be on the point of uniting Europe in the sixteenth century, as Louis XIV of France was supposed to be in the seventeenth. Napoleon I may have projected a French Empire that should have dominated all Europe. The Imperial Germany of William II was accused of seeking to dominate Europe during the First World War, perhaps unjustly. Hitler certainly brought the entire continent under his sway for a short time during the Second World War – from 1940 to 1942.

All these attempts broke against resistance by the other European states and even more because of intervention from outside the continent. Opposition to any state seeking to dominate Europe was the key principle of British foreign power from the sixteenth to the twentieth century. Russia followed the same line in the nineteenth and twentieth centuries and the United States entered both world wars primarily for the same purpose. It is hardly too much to say that Europe, since Roman times, has never had unity imposed upon her by force because her conquerors could not isolate Europe from the rest of the world.

We now live in a period when the conquest of the world by a single power is seriously envisaged or seriously apprehended. American statesmen have sometimes talked in these terms. During the Second World War President Roosevelt proposed that after the war every power in the world should be disarmed with the exception of the United States, which would perhaps acknowledge the United Kingdom as a satellite. With the entry of Soviet Russia into the war Roosevelt forgot this idea and swung to the opposite extreme, announcing that American forces would withdraw from Europe as soon as the war was over. Perhaps both ideas were no more than passing whims, which often happened with Roosevelt. But there remains a tendency for Americans to talk as though their way of life were the only acceptable one.

At the present time there are two World powers, the United States and Soviet Russia, each accusing the other of seeking to dominate the world. In practice this is simply a new form of the rivalry between powerful states which has shaped much of man's history. The prospect of a single power dominating the world seems as remote as it has ever been. It does not follow from this that the establishment of peace throughout the world is impossible. There has always been an alternative way which men have explored for centuries past and particularly in recent times. This is the way of peace by agreement or compact. The sovereign states concerned put aside the idea of war in the hope that the habit of peaceful co-operation will become established. The Olympic Games were established in Ancient Greece for this very purpose: the city-states accepted a period of peace for the duration of the Games in the hope that this period would be gradually prolonged. The hope was not fulfilled. It needed conquest by Rome to impose peace on the Greek city-states and the price was the loss of their independence.

Nevertheless the history of Europe in modern times shows repeated and persistent attempts to lessen the likelihood of international war or at the very least to make the conduct of war less destructive. International diplomacy was specifically a European invention. Diplomacy implies the recognition of one sovereign state by another and therefore a restriction, however temporary, of sovereignty. This was particularly true in the days of kings and emperors. One monarch can recognize another as an equal more easily than an elected government can. Diplomacy demands certain common standards. In its great days it was virtually confined to the Christian states of Europe and almost confined to monarchies. For instance, after the French revolutionaries executed Louis XIV, it was thought no offence against diplomatic principles to murder two French envoys on their way home from an international conference in Germany. Attempts to extend diplomacy outside Europe usually ended in disaster. It was a normal expectation in the eighteenth century that an ambassador to Turkey would be executed as a spy or at the very least spend some years in prison before meeting the sultan.

Great wars have often provoked projects for preserving the future peace. After the Napoleonic Wars the rulers of Europe made a vague pact, sometimes called the Holy Alliance, to enforce peace throughout Europe. This was as much a pact against radicalism as it was against war and broke down largely for that reason. The national movements in Germany and Italy were not prepared to accept the political system imposed by the Congress of Vienna. As time passed these national movements were supported even by two of the Great Powers, France and Great Britain. The story of the Holy Alliance and its failure demonstrates that attempts to equate peace with the political *status quo* will end by destroying both the *status quo* and peace.

The nineteenth century was, however, memorable in a more modest way. It saw the development of many international institutions which in a sense abrogated the national sovereignty of the contracting parties for practical reasons. Thus the Red Cross secured the acceptance of rules that limited the barbarism of war. The international Postal Union ensured that the mails ran even across hostile frontiers. Similarly international trains traversed the European continent on the basis of rules, voluntarily accepted. Perhaps the most remarkable and certainly the most useful international conference of the age was the one which persuaded practically every country in the world to accept the meridian of Greenwich as the universal base-line for their time – an astonishing infringement of national sovereignty.

In the twentieth century men made more ambitious attempts to establish some international authority. The International Court of Justice at The Hague has functioned with some success though there is no obligation, other than a moral one, for parties to accept its decisions. The First World War produced the League of Nations; the second produced the United Nations Organisation [UNO]. For some people these bodies were conceived as preparing the way for a Parliament of the World. This aim has not been achieved. Both have been fair-weather systems, assisting states to resolve their differences when they already wished to do so. The League of Nations once attempted to restrain a member by economic sanctions against Italy. The attempt ruined the League without restraining Italy. UNO authorized the Korean War of 1950–53, but in fact the war was plainly conducted by the United States as a sovereign power. In any case these bodies can provide no security against war if they represent in practice the policy of 'perpetual war for the sake of perpetual peace'.

The United States preserved its sovereignty intact by refusing to join the League of Nations. After the Second World War the three great victors, Britain, Soviet Russia and the United States, asserted their sovereignty by adding France and China to their number and then giving the five Great Powers a veto over the proceedings of the Security Council, a veto that has often been used. UNO, like the League of Nations before it, has remained a voluntary association which can exercise no more than moral suasion unless one of the five Great Powers, and most specifically the United States, places its armed forces at the disposal of the United Nations – and that is not likely to happen.

Every member of UNO no doubt wishes to avoid a world war but not at the cost of what it regards as a vital interest of its own.

There is a further obstacle against any world institution for preserving peace. When such schemes were first propounded 'the world' really meant only the 'white' (really dirty pink) Christian states of Europe and America. No one in the nineteenth century imagined that the rules of warfare applied to the 'lesser' states outside Europe. Great Britain and France, for instance, did not observe the rules of war when they looted the summer palace at Pekin in 1861. The British did not observe the rules of war when they blew sepoys from the mouths of guns after the Indian Mutiny. Nor did the European powers consider the claims or even the existence of the native inhabitants when they partitioned the continent between themselves during the 'scramble for Africa'.

The period of European supremacy of even monopoly is now over. 'White' peoples make up less than a quarter of the populations composing the United Nations. Many of the others – yellow, brown or black – do not differ from the Europeans only in colour. They may not share the Christian ethic. They have no heritage of parliamentary government or the rule of law. They have never learnt that economic security is possible only if there is general agreement on the sanctity of contract. Diplomacy is for them a European idea imposed from outside. It is not surprising that diplomats are harassed in most 'developing' countries and illegally imprisoned in some, as witness Iran. On the contrary it is quite an achievement that Western diplomats have been tolerated in the 'developing' countries at all. At present these countries are not developing. They are reverting to the standards that existed before European intervention.

This need not be a reason for total despair. Keynes once said, 'All business is a bet'. For our grandfathers in the stable world of Queen Victoria and Edward VII the risks were less than they are now and the rewards were proportionately less also. This was a gilt-edged age with 2½ per cent Consols remaining roughly at par for half a century. That age has gone for good. In the words of Trotsky, 'Whoever wants a quiet life has chosen the wrong time to be born'. In most civilizations and at most times trade has been a risky business. One of the medieval companies was known as the Society of Merchant Adventurers. Many of the ships that left British ports in the eighteenth century for America or the Indies were lost. But those which returned showed a high rate of profit.

It is also true that most habits are catching, good habits as well as bad ones. The 'developing' countries seem violent and lawless in comparison with European ideals. They are, however, far less violent and lawless than they used to be.

We always tend to exaggerate our own troubles. For instance civilized standards are said to be breaking down in Britain. And so in a sense they are. On the other hand Britain is a far more peaceful and secure country that it was a century and a half ago. In those days women dared not go out in the streets alone. Police constables always walked in pairs and there were parts of London where no police ever entered. Highwaymen operated in Hyde Park as late as the reign of George IV. The recent riots in Bristol created some stir and some apprehension. Yet they were nothing to the Bristol riots of 1831 which preceded the passing of the great Reform Bill. It is likely that more and more of the world will be open to international trade. It is also likely that the conditions under which this trade is conducted will get more difficult. On a wider scale two tendencies, already in operation, will be carried further: too many people and too little energy. No one can tell which will win.

There remains the most urgent of questions: whether the world is moving towards another great war or away from it. No one is less qualified than an historian to foretell the future. The best he can do is to prolong past lines into the future. Sometimes this makes him a good prophet. Sometime his prophecies are not fulfilled. For instance most observers in the latter half of the nineteenth century expected an Asiatic war between Russia and Great Britain. This did not take place despite repeated alarms and even mobilizations. In the 1930s the one war universally expected by all good judges was a war in the Far East between Soviet Russia and Japan. This war did not break out until a week before the end of the Second World War and, despite Soviet boasting, was little more than formal. On the other hand, at the end of a great war men have often prophesied that there will never be another. It was said after the fall of Napoleon. It was widely said and believed after the end of the First World War, when young Germans marched through the streets of Berlin shouting 'No more war'. Most of these young Germans later became Nazis. After the Second World War a third was said to be 'impossible'. Now the two world powers are proceeding on the assumption that the impossible will occur.

Both Soviet Russia and the United States claim that they are preparing for a nuclear war in order to ensure that it does not happen. So far they have maintained a balance of power or rather a balance of terror. So far the deterrent has worked.

In the past there have been long periods of peace resting on the balance of power and enforced by the deterrent. There have been crises. Statesmen have shrunk from war. The crises have been resolved. In the end the balance of power has not been effective; the deterrent has failed to deter. There has been a war, culminating in the two world wars of the twentieth century.

Will history repeat itself? No one can tell. I venture only one prophecy and that with much hesitation. If men, and particularly statesmen,

behave in the future as they have done in the past, there will be a third
world war, a war more destructive than any previous war and one
which may shatter the structure of world civilization. But men have
sometimes learnt lessons from the past and behaved differently. Common sense occasionally prevails in human affairs, though not often. It
must be our hope that it will prevail now. Either mankind must end
war. Or war will end mankind.

As I have said, historians are not qualified to foretell the future or
even to lay down what should be the wisest course. If I now venture to
lay down what I think would be the wisest policy, this is as an ordinary,
though well-informed citizen, not as a pundit. First, Soviet Russia which
many people see as the greatest danger in the world. I do not share that
view. In my opinion, the prime motive of Soviet policy is anxiety: fear of
the other world power, the United States; apprehension regarding their
massive economic difficulties and above all a desire to be recognized as
equals, not as outsiders. The right course in my opinion is to show
understanding and endless patience. World Communism is a bogy even
if the Russians believe in it themselves. Shortly after the Second World
War, Stalin himself said that it would not be easy to find a basis for
close relations in the future. He added: 'But Christ said, "Seek and ye
shall find".' That is the only remedy I have in international relations.

CHAPTER SIXTY-SIX

How Near is World War III?
Dangers of a Power Balance

This essay was first published in the *Manchester Guardian* (28 August 1959), some two months before Harold Macmillan's victory in the October 1959 general election.

We all suppose that the laws of probability will be suspended in our favour. It is possible to foretell how many people will be killed on the roads each day. But no man, getting his car out of the garage, ever says to himself: 'To-day it will be me.' A similar feeling makes it hard to take a detached view about the probabilities of a third world war. To the very last moment we shall go on hoping that it will not happen. Nothing did the Beaverbrook press more good with its readers than the heading, repeated daily: 'There will be no war in 1939.' So now we are told there will be no war in 1959, no war next year, no war in the conceivable future. Yet preparations for war are being made on a more gigantic scale than ever before; and in the past preparations for war have nearly always led to war. Not always. There are exceptions to every rule. The naval race between England and France in the closing years of the nineteenth century did not lead to war; the French got entangled in domestic troubles, such as the Dreyfus affair, and dropped out of the race. But usually if two great powers, or groups of powers, arm against each other war will follow. Two great power blocks are certainly arming against each other now. What grounds are there for hoping that we shall not be run over?

War by calculation

We are told that there are no profound causes of conflict between the two great powers. This is true. Neither covets vital territory possessed by the other. Neither is particularly discontented or resentful. Even the differences of political system cause little conflict. There is no Communist peril in the West; and, so far as one can tell, no 'democratic' peril in the East. If profound causes for conflict were all that mattered, Soviet Russia and the United States could go on existing together in the world for centuries, like the empires of Rome and China long ago. Unfortunately profound conflicts are not the same things as reasons for war. The great conflicts over the division of Africa, for instance, were all settled without war. On the other hand, there was no special cause of conflict in 1914 – quite the contrary, most of the disputes were settled, or very nearly. The actual decisions for war springs from calculation not from conflict – the calculation: 'I can win if I fight now: I shall lose if I fight later.'

Every war of recent times has started as a preventive war, with the possible exception of the war of 1939. A power has felt itself slipping and has tried to get its blow in before it is too late. So Austria in 1859 tried to 'prevent' the danger from Sardinia: so Austria in 1866 and France in 1869 tried to 'prevent' the danger from Prussia; so Austria-Hungary in 1914 tried to 'prevent' the danger from Serbia and Germany the danger from Russia. In none of these cases was there a profound conflict: merely an overmastering apprehension. Perhaps Hitler launched an aggressive war in 1939. But it seems more likely that he was trying to 'prevent' the consolidation of the Grand Alliance against him; and there is no doubt that he extended the war for preventive reasons in 1941.

Declining strength

This may seem to run counter to the old faith, now revived, in the balance of power. A balance between two power-blocks is supposed to preserve peace. This is quite wrong historically. Metternich and Bismarck were the two greatest practitioners of the balance of power. What they meant by this was that there must be an overwhelming balance of power on their side. This is the only secure way to maintain peace; one side must be much stronger than the other. After 1815 the four powers who had been allies against Napoleon were much stronger than France; and peace was preserved. War broke out as soon as their unity was dissolved. In Bismarck's time Germany and her allies were much stronger than either France or Russia or even than both combined; and after this time peace was still preserved as long as Germany was markedly the greatest military power in Europe. War broke out in 1914 because of the national revival in France and the armament plans in Russia which were due to mature in 1917. Germany decided on war not because she was stronger than ever but because she thought she would not be strong much longer. A balance against one power and in favour of the other secures peace. A more or less equal balance between them leads to war.

Broadly speaking an equal balance of this kind exists now. For some years after the war there was an overwhelming balance of nuclear power on the American side. The American experts despised Russian science and assumed that this preponderance would last. Some people, more clear-sighted, warned them to undertake a preventive war in 1948. The opportunity was missed. The Americans were taken by surprise. The Russians caught up with them before preventive action could be taken. At the moment there is probably a more or less exact balance. But it will not last. One side or another will achieve a temporary advantage and then use it for fear of being outdistanced again. It looks at present as though the Russians will pull ahead with a large supply of intercontinental missiles. In this case they ought to bombard the United States some time in 1961. But my guess is that the Russians will repeat the American mistake: they will underrate the opposing scientists in their turn and will believe that they are ahead for good. Of course they may prove right, in which case there will be no World War III. But it is more likely, from past experience, that the Americans will catch up and actually go ahead. They will not only equal the Russians in intercontinental missiles; they will surpass the Russians in anti-missile missiles. This seems the most probable moment for World War III. It should come about 1965.

No restraint?

As a final ray of hope, we are told that modern weapons have made war impossible: they are so destructive that they will never be used. This hope is thin. Men, particularly men in power, soon get used to what seems inconceivable. Who would have supposed that outstanding British Liberals, to say nothing of Lord Robert Cecil, would cheerfully starve German women and children in the First World War, or that we should all applaud the random destruction of Hamburg and Cologne in the Second World War? Anyone in favour of retaining nuclear weapons must be ready to use them in some last resort. If the leaders of the Labour Party – and the *Guardian* – are in this position, we can be sure that Soviet and American generals are much less reticent. In fact, military experts in both countries (and here too) are already speculating how war can be carried on after the first phase of heavy nuclear warfare is over. We are never entitled to assume that men will continue to behave in the future as they have behaved in the past. But if men continue to behave as they have behaved, we should reach World War III within the next six or eight years, unless, of course, one Power manages (with or without war) to dominate the world.

CHAPTER SIXTY-SEVEN

War and Peace

This essay was first published as a review of Geoffrey Best, *Humanity in Warfare: The Modern History of the International Law of Armed Conflict* (London, Weidenfeld, 1980), and Martin Ceadel, *Pacifism in Britain 1914–1945: The Defining of a Faith* (Oxford, Oxford University Press, 1980), in *London Review of Books* (2 October 1980).

War has been throughout history the curse and inspiration of mankind. The sufferings and destruction that accompany it rival those caused by famine, plague and natural catastrophes. Yet in nearly every civilization war has been the noblest of professions, and among the heroes of every age those distinguished in war have always ranked first, as a visit to St Paul's Cathedral will bear witness. In many civilizations, war has been a once-and-for-all affair: the conquest of neighbouring territory or the repulse of an invader. In some, however, war between contending states has gone on for generations – the Time of Troubles, in Toynbee's phrase. Ancient Greece experienced such a Time, and there followed one of the first attempts to limit the sufferings of war, as the Olympic Games indicate. But the Greek wars were not ended by moderation and wise agreement. They were ended by the Roman conquest, which provided one solution to the problem of war: the establishment of a single dominant power that subdued or eliminated all other contenders.

Europe, too, has known attempts at a single universal state from the early days of the Holy Roman Empire to the brief domination of Hitler's Nazi Germany. But broadly speaking European history has been a continual Time of Troubles, interrupted by occasional periods of armed peace. The realization that war was here to stay produced a unique development in European thought: attempts to eliminate war altogether, or, if these failed, to lessen its horrific consequences. The first type of attempt lay behind the medieval pursuit of 'the just war', a pursuit as elusive as that of the Holy Grail. For it is almost universally true that in war each side thinks itself in the right, and there is no arbiter except victory to decide between them. Until recently, most historians have endorsed this verdict by applauding the victory or blessing the cause of their own state. Thus English historians saw little to question in the plundering raids of Henry V or even of William the Conqueror. French historians saw little to question in the Empire of Napoleon. The *jus ad bellum* has proved a will o' the wisp, though still actively pursued by some. The lesser attempt to moderate or even to civilize war has been more rewarding. This *jus in bello* is the topic of Geoffrey Best's fascinating book, a volume replete with scholarship and brilliant presentation.

Moderate or civilized wars can only operate within certain limitations. They are almost impossible when there is a conflict of creeds as well as of state power. The wars of religion or the crusade against the Albigensians were as savage as the wars of ancient Rome. Even the most civilized powers observe the rules only when at war with another civilized power. The British did not observe the rules when they blew Indian mutineers from the mouths of cannon. The Americans did not observe the rules when at war with the Red Indians, and of course the Red Indians also did not observe them. In fact, the laws of war were until recently confined to Europe, though Best ends by chronicling the present-day attempts to extend them more widely.

In more precise terms, the laws of war began when the European states contended over their respective ambitions, not over their fundamental beliefs, religious or political. Vattel was their acknowledged father. He sought for laws that the antagonists could accept without forfeiting their chance of victory. Ideally, wars should be conducted between professional armies without injury or disturbance to the civil population. Rousseau carried this view to extremes when he wrote: 'War, then, is not a relationship between man and man, but between State and State, in which private persons are only enemies accidentally.' Most theorists were more moderate and recognized that the laws of war must sometimes bow to 'necessity'. Indeed, far from necessity knowing no law, it became itself part of the law. Thus the soldier should not loot or plunder but he cannot be required to respect hen roosts when he is hungry. The bombardment of a town is deplorable but may be necessary in order to enforce its surrender, though only the necessary minimum should be used. Despite these exceptions, the Enlightened eighteenth century did pretty well with the laws of war. Armies carried their commissariat train with them instead of living off the countryside. Destruction was not operated for its own sake. There was little attempt to shake the morale of the civilian population. Combatants wore recognized uniforms and did not prolong a hopeless resistance.

There was one curious flaw which exasperated continental Europeans. This was the problem of how far the rules of war applied at sea. The continentals held that they should be applied unchanged. The British argued that the differing maritime circumstances fundamentally affected the laws of war. For instance, bombardments of towns were to be deplored but how else could the Royal Navy employ its strength against a land power?

Still graver was the problem of blockade. Continentals were clear as to the answer: neutral ships and neutral goods must be respected unless they were 'absolute' contraband. The British did not share this view. For them, blockade was a weapon with which to strangle an enemy and the rights of neutrals were of little account. This rigorous attitude weakened a little when Great Britain was faced with a powerful league of Armed Neutrality. But it was a hint of greater difficulties that were to arise in the future.

The French Revolution signalled the breakdown of enlightenment in the laws of war as in other matters, though its original intention was the precise opposite. The early revolutionaries certainly aspired to spread their example abroad, but they imagined that the instruments of liberation would be Jacobin chants and floral wreaths rather than muskets and cannon. Even when forced to fight they insisted that their antagonists were few: 'war to the castles, peace to the cottages'. But who were to pay the liberators? Revolutionary France could not do so with its finances in chaos. The liberated peoples must pay. Soon the revolutionary armies were expected to work at a profit. Add to this the revolutionary strategy of speed, carried to its highest point by Napoleon. There was no time to waste on commissariat trains. The French armies lived off the country and often did very well out of it.

These revolutionary wars lessened and in time almost obliterated the distinction between soldiers and civilians. The Jacobins proclaimed 'the nation in arms'. How then could the civilian claim immunity? Things grew still more troublesome when civilians in the shape of partisans or guerrillas took up arms themselves. In Spain, for instance, the French attempted to treat all partisans as criminals, an action they repeated in Russia. The British took the same attitude in 1798 when they accorded to the French invaders of Ireland the honours of war and massacred the Irish rebels whom the French had come to liberate. Even those such as the British in Spain who were in alliance with partisans agreed afterwards that this was an episode better forgotten.

Neutrals came off as badly as civilians. Nelson's assault on Copenhagen in 1801 brought him almost as much honour as the Battle of Trafalgar. Two years after his death the Danes had their fleet ruthlessly snatched away from them. During the French wars the British blockade gradually eroded the securities for neutral trade established during the eighteenth century. This culminated in the Anglo-American War of 1812–14, a war fought, ironically enough, after the British had conceded the main point at issue. Once more the British appealed to necessity: relying on maritime power, it was necessary for them to do things which land powers did not need to do – though Napoleon also disregarded neutral rights and imposed a fictitious blockade. By the end of the Napoleonic Wars neutral rights had almost ceased to exist.

More fundamentally, the revolutionary and Napoleonic wars demonstrated that the laws of war demanded some basis of common principles if they were to operate successfully. The Jacobins despised their enemies as tyrants. The tyrants responded by treating the Jacobins as subverters of civilization. Napoleon was given a half-hearted welcome as the restorer of law and order. But the victorious powers showed their true opinion of Napoleon when they proclaimed him the enemy of mankind. Even so, it is surprising how much of the law of war survived the impact of the French Revolution. Prisioners-of-war were still taken and were interned, usually under tolerable conditions. Flags of truce were generally respected and it was thought immoral to use them deceptively as a stratagem of war. The laws of blockade continued to provide matter for argument even if the British preferred maritime power to high principles. Enlightenment and revolution produced conflicting impacts – a legacy that Geoffrey Best has analysed with admirable clarity and frankness.

For forty years after the Napoleonic Wars the laws of war did not advance. Their renewal came with the Congress of Paris in 1856, perhaps because the congress had nothing better to do. The congress celebrated the end of a war predominantly on land by wrestling with the laws of war at sea, a topic where even the British representatives proved for once slightly conciliatory. From the Congress of Paris stemmed further international discussions culminating in the two peace conferences at The Hague. Despite this accumulation of pointless oratory and ingenious drafting, the greatest advance in the laws of war ever made was the achievement of one man, Henri Dunant, seconded by that impractical dreamer, Napoleon III. The Red Cross began with individual initiative and was continued by it. Great powers did not sponsor the Red Cross: they succumbed to it until it became as acceptable an element of international society as war itself. Further, the Red Cross did not grow out of the existing laws of war: it imposed itself upon them.

What was the cause of this universal acceptance? Did each power see advantage for itself in the Red Cross? Did the principles of humanity and civilization for once triumph? There is no easy answer. Certainly the triumph was not repeated elsewhere. Geoffrey Best again shows his powers of exposition as he traces the advance in the laws of war during the nineteenth century. Certainly there was a more conscious and official application to the subject than there had been earlier. During the Enlightenment, aloof philosophers enunciated general principles which each state and each soldier, almost, was expected to work out in practice for himself. The nineteenth century saw the arrival of the international lawyer, of whom the Russian Martens was the chief. Martens would have liked to formulate laws of war which should be at once wise and acceptable. In practice, this meant discovering laws that should have at least some humanity in them and that would despite this be tolerated by the military. The intellectual agility required to produce this was confined almost to Martens alone. The various conferences laboured productively. But there was always the shadow of 'necessity', sharply raised whenever the military saw some encroachment on their powers.

Broadly, the laws of war improved most in their application to actual fighting on land, which took on almost the medieval character of armed combat under chivalrous conditions. There was less advance over the problems that had arisen during the Napoleonic Wars: requisitions, reprisals, partisans and the treatment of civilians. The practices of the Royal Navy suffered further encroachments, even though Fisher dismissed them as 'nonsense' which would be 'ditched' if war came. The European legalists averted their eyes from bombardment as practised by the British at Alexandria, and still more from the Union operations in the American Civil War, particularly Sherman's demonstration to the inhabitants of the South that War was Hell.

The laws of war improved more in appearance than in reality. For, as Geoffrey Best points out, there were two flourishing movements during the nineteenth century: the Peace Movement, which everyone noticed and commended, and the War Movement, which many people ignored and which yet proved more powerful. Best has found a wonderful quotation from Joseph Conrad, who described the Hague Tribunal as 'a solemnly official recognition of the Earth as a House of Strife'. Conrad continued: 'War has made peace altogether in its own image; a martial, overbearing, war-lord sort of peace ... eloquent with allusions to glorious feats of arms.'

The nineteenth century formulated the laws of war; the twentieth century was expected to apply them. Geoffrey Best discusses in his powerful concluding chapter how far this has proved true. The answers, drawn from both world wars, are contradictory. The laws have been best observed in fighting between regular land forces, particularly on the Western Front and in such 'professional' areas as North Africa. It seems that soldiers have higher standards when they are not being criticized and provoked by civilians. On the Eastern front Soviet Russia observed the laws of war more nearly than did Nazi Germany, despite allegations to the contrary. The laws of war came off less happily at sea and in the air. This sprang partly from the British reversion to the ruthless application of blockade which she had developed in earlier wars. The deeper cause was the development of weapons of war which could not be covered by the existing laws.

The first of these, already effective in the First World War, was the submarine, which, as the Germans showed, had to sink its victims without warning if it were to operate successfully. The Germans pleaded that they were retaliating to the British blockade. The true situation was that the submarine had been projected as an additional naval weapon and that its role as a commerce-destroyer had not been foreseen. This was even truer of the Zeppelin, which first set the practice, however ineffectual, of indiscriminate bombardment. This problem was exacerbated with the arrival of bombing aircraft. Best makes two striking remarks about air experiences in the First World War. The first is that Trenchard enunciated the doctrine of indiscriminate bombardment, quite without practical experience. The second is that the Royal Naval Air Service developed precision bombing during its short life. This achievement was subsequently ignored, partly as impractical and partly as being not aggressive or terrifying enough.

Best continues the problems of air warfare when he reaches the Second World War. Here the Trenchard legacy came to fruition. It is often not appreciated that indiscriminate or area bombing was a British speciality. The American Air Force disliked it; the German Luftwaffe operated it sceptically and reluctantly. British obsession with area bombing was an extension of British reliance on blockade – the weapon of a power reluctant to develop a great army. Best traces Sir Arthur Harris's persistent and unjustified defence of area bombardment, which culminated in the unnecessary attack on Dresden in 1945 – not that this attack was any more reprehensible than earlier attacks except that it came towards the end of the war. Air warfare as practised during the Second World War, and particularly with its last achievements at Hiroshima and Nagasaki, left two profound holes in the restraining laws of war: the first that indiscriminate destruction, however horrible, was a legitimate means of war; the second that with 'the nation at war' there was no longer any distinction between the military and the civilians and that therefore civilians were legitimate targets. The same moral was drawn from the extension of partisan warfare, which led to the conclusion that every civilian who was not a collaborator of the invaders was a concealed or potential partisan, a moral the partisan forces applied the other way round. The logical consequence was that every inhabitant of a conquered country should be massacred or at the very least dispatched to slave labour, as the Germans demonstrated.

And so Best arrives at the present day. There have been even more conferences and regulations. The profession of international lawyer is more active than ever. There are two black clouds. The first is air warfare, which with the development of nuclear weapons transgresses all the laws of war ever known. The second is the attempt to extend the laws of war to cover colonial revolts or social revolutions, an attempt further confused by the Marxist insistence that Marxist acts of violence are always right and resistance to these acts always wrong. Despite these portents, Best remains mildly optimistic. He welcomes the persistent discussion of the laws of war as evidence that there is some desire to limit and restrain armed conflicts. He even brings a hope that this desire may be fulfilled. To my mind, the experiences of the past eighty years are not encouraging. Fortunately, the past is not always a guide to the future.

The experts in the laws of war claimed to be practical men, resigned to the fact that war, somewhat humanized, would go on for a long time, if not for ever. The search for an end to war has been of more recent origin, becoming almost confined to Great Britain during the last hundred years, with some echoes in the United States. Martin Ceadel approaches this search with a sharp distinction between pacificism (a word which he claims to have borrowed from me and which I gladly lend him) and pacifism. Pacificists are those who favour peaceful foreign policies and who seek to develop international institutions for the promotion of peace. Pacifism in its pure form is a total rejection of war as an instrument of policy.

The distinction is clear to Ceadel and will be clear to his readers. It has been less clear in the historical record. Pacifism is the older, in that there have always been a few men who refused to take part in war, but this was an individual gesture of abstention and not a contribution to solving the problem of war. The early Christians refused to serve in the Roman armies, but this sprang from their refusal to accord divine honours to the emperor. Once they could serve under the sign of the Cross the Christians fought vigorously enough, not only against pagans and barbarians, but against each other.

Modern pacificism was part of the humanitarian outlook which characterized the philanthropists of the nineteenth century: peaceful aims went along with anti-slavery and prison reform. Quakers tended to take up a pacifist position, but this did not prevent their becoming advocates of a peaceful policy. A Quaker delegation visited Nicholas I at St Petersburg in an attempt to prevent the Crimean War. John Bright opposed that war in his greatest speeches, but he was clearly not a pacifist: he supported the armed suppression of the Indian Mutiny and applauded the Union victory in the American Civil War. With Great Britain not involved in a European war for nearly a century, the question for humanitarians was not, 'What do we do in the event of war?' but: 'How do we discourage or prevent war elsewhere?'

There was a further obstacle to the development of a clear-cut pacifism in Great Britain: even when at war, as in the Anglo-Boer War of 1899–1902, Great Britain fought with professional volunteer forces. The potential pacifist did not have to resolve what he would do if called upon to fight. On the contrary, his difficulty was to find outlets for his humanitarianism either by providing medical services or by conducting political agitation against the policy and operations of war. The pro-Boers were often stigmatized as pacifists, but it is clear that they were nothing of the kind, and Lloyd George, one of the most assertive pro-Boers, became later an outstanding war minister. Ceadel is therefore right in taking the outbreak of war in August 1914 as the starting-point for his theme: pacifism in Britain. Even so, the emergence of pacifism remained obscure.

Ceadel is pretty firm in dealing with those who opposed the First World War as being a mistaken policy or even as fought against the wrong enemy. The Union of Democratic Control was clearly not pacifist. But what about the Fellowship of Reconciliation, which Ceadel specifies as 'quietist'? Even the No-Conscription Fellowship began as a political movement to oppose the legislative introduction of conscription, and continued on a practical basis after conscription operated. Conscription certainly made some people ask themselves whether they were pacifists or merely high-minded. There were few clear responses. Only 16,500 of those called up pleaded conscientious objection; only 6,000 of these refused to accept the tribunal's verdict, and only 1,298 of those resisted 'absolutely'. Nor were even the absolutists all of a kind. Some were religious pacifists; some were humanitarian pacifists. But a number were solely against the Great War which was raging: some as socialists, some as critics of British foreign policy, some as defenders of individual liberty. The experiences of war strengthened the confusion: conscientious objectors did not inquire into the theoretical basis on which the conviction of their comrades rested. All could be numbered as opponents of war, from the pure pacifist to the Marxist champion of war on the barricades.

The confusion which had developed during the Great War increased when the war was over. Many who had been combatants now regarded the war as mistaken in either its aims or its conduct or perhaps both together. Ceadel analyses this confusion with admirable clarity. Perhaps he is a little too rigorous. The man who defines his convictions with absolute accuracy is very rare and rarest of all in the world of politics. Ceadel tends to imply that all such confusions are foolish, and that pacifists and near-pacifists are peculiarly prone to them. Indeed, there is even a hint that those who reject the methods and arguments of pacifism are eminently sane – a strange view. How are we to describe the rulers of great states and their technical advisers who propose to defend civilization by blowing the peoples and cities of the world to pieces? 'Sane' is not a word that would occur to me.

The 1920s were the heyday of pacificism and pacifism in a tangle. The former absolutists did not reproach those who had served in the war, and these latter for the most part did not reproach the absolutists. Many who had preached and even practised individual rejection felt that this was too self-centered and co-operated with others in the search for means of preventing war. The former conscientious objector might join the No More War Movement, but he recognized no contradiction in joining the League of Nations Union as well. Yet the basis of the League of Nations as 'collective security', which implied in the last resort military sanctions, or, as the American historian Harry Elmer Barnes expressed it, 'perpetual war for the sake of perpetual peace'. This was not a problem of any practical relevance when the prospect of another great war seemed remote.

The hard core of Ceadel's book concerns the great transformation which began in the early 1930s with the realization that perpetual peace would not come of itself or perhaps was not on offer at all. Some of the one-time pacifists decided that with the rapid approach of social revolution they were not pacifists after all. Since social revolution failed to arrive, this conversion had little practical application except to remove a rather disruptive element from the pacifist movement. Fascism, or, to be more precise, the appearance of Hitler, was a different matter. Comparatively few recognized Hitler's threat from the first. On the contrary, pacifists like nearly everyone else argued that the wisest as well as the most moral course was the redress of German grievances. It is curious to read of a time when former conscientious objectors applauded Neville Chamberlain.

The final years before the Second World War saw the rise of a pacifist movement that was political rather than ethical: the Peace Pledge Union. The union was virtually the creation of one man, Canon Dick Sheppard, and a very erratic shepherd he proved. The origins of the union went back, I think, to the spate of anti-war literature that characterized the end of the 1920s. Not surprisingly, the union was an assembly of prima donnas, as Ceadel entertainingly demonstrates. Perhaps there is nothing more absurd than gifted writers earnestly believing in some cause. Quite a number were members of the League of Nations as well as the Peace Pledge Union; many moved from one union to the other and back again. Ceadel does not fail to add that many were vegetarians while some had a high track record in plurality of wives. The Peace Pledge Union enlisted an impressive total of pledges against war. Comparatively few of these pledges were honoured when war actually arrived. Though there were many more conscientious objectors than in the First World War – 60,000 against 16,000 – their impact was much less. Instead of being persecuted, they were tolerated or even admired. Some 5,000 were sent to prison, more in sorrow than in anger: most of these took up some form of humanitarian work before the war was over.

Only Christians – 'Christadelphians, Plymouth Brethren, Elimites, Particular People' – stuck to their belief. Ceadel concludes that pacifism has been reduced to a religious belief, rather than a solution to the problems of war.

Though never a pacifist, I had more patience with the pacifists of that age than he has now. In my view, they were, though often foolish, a good deal more sensible than their opponents. Martin Ceadel has a great future before him as a historian, particularly when he becomes more tolerant of human follies.

Index

Aachen 135
Abd-el-Aziz 97
Abyssinia 246
   occupation by Italy 238–9, 336
Adenauer, Konrad 356
Adler, Viktor 55, 61
Aehrenthal, Count Alois von 61, 62, 63, 64
Afghanistan 82–3
Africa, and the great powers 82, 106
Agadir Crisis (1911) 107, 121–3
Albert, Prince Consort 38, 47, 48
Albrecht, Archduke 25
Alexander II, Tsar 126
   assassination 79
Alexander III, Tsar 126
Alexander of Hesse, Prince 34, 35, 47
Alexander of Yugoslavia, King 230, 339
Alexandria 91, 124
Algeciras Conference (1906) 120
Algeria 95
Allen, L., *Singapore, 1941–1942* 313
Alsace and Lorraine 68, 69, 81, 86, 87, 91, 114, 143, 145, 146, 213, 335–6
Ambassadors, Conference of (1920) 174
America
   Blue Books 162
   and Czechoslovakia 189
   pre-WW II, foreign policy 245–7
   and WW II 244
American Council on Foreign Relations 243
Amery, Leo 267, 299
Andrássy, Count Gyula 71, 72, 73
Apponyi, Albert 30, 31, 34, 37, 38, 39, 41, 43, 44, 45, 46, 47, 48, 49–50
Armenia, massacres 87, 168
Ashley, E. 47
Asquith, Herbert Henry 125, 137, 138
Aster, Sidney, *1939: The Making of the Second World War* 265–7

Austria
   and France
      armistice 32
      war (1859) 23
   and Germany
      alliance 78–9
      annexation by 181–3, 187
   and nationalism 53–4
   and Prussia 23–4, 25–6, 54
Austria-Hungary
   and Bosnia and Herzegovina 61, 74
   and Croats 62
   and Russia 68, 70, 73, 133, 138
   and Serbia 62, 65, 122, 132–3
   and Southern Slavs 61–2, 65
   and WW I 143, 144
Azerbaidjan 176

Bach, Alexander 58
Bad Godesberg 195, 203, 275
Badeni, Count Casimir 58, 59
Baernreither, Joseph 62, 64, 67
Balabanoff, Angelica 156
balance of power
   in the late 19th century 68, 87
   in the 20th century 364, 367–8, 369–71
   and Bismarck 81, 84–5
   and Britain 104, 109
   and the Crimean War 21
   nature of 104
Baldwin, Stanley 218–19, 220, 221
Balfour, Arthur 111, 145, 170, 174, 176
Balkans, The
   revolt against the Turks 70–72, 122
   war of 1912 75
   see also Eastern Question
Baltic States, and Russia 198–9, 282–3, 286, 288
Barbarossa, Operation (1941) 290
Barnes, Harry Elmer 304, 380
   Blasting the Historical Blackout 313
Barraclough, Geoffrey, *From Agadir to Armageddon* 121, 122

Barthou, Louis 225, 230, 231
Battenberg, Prince Louis of 124
Batum 74
Beard, Charles A. 245, 247
Beck, Col. Jozef 196, 209, 256, 281, 282, 297
Belcredi, Richard 54, 57, 60
Belgian Congo, and Germany 121
Belgium
  formation 248–9
  and Germany, attack by 287
  neutrality 132, 137–8, 142, 145, 250
Belgrade 132, 133
Benedek, Count Ludwig August 53
Benedict XV, Pope 145
Beneš, Eduard 192, 253, 260, 269, 270, 274, 275, 278, 279, 281, 348
Bennett, Arnold 113
Beran, Rudolf 192
Berchtesgaden 295
Berchtold, Count Leopold von 132
Berlin Act (1884) 82
Berlin, Congress of (1878) 73, 74, 77, 78, 132
  consequences 75
Berlin Memorandum (1876) 71
Berlin–Baghdad railway 89, 122
Bernstorff, Count Albert 27, 29, 46
Berthelot, Marcel 175, 177, 178
Bessarabia 288
Best, Geoffrey, Humanity in Warfare, reviewed 372–81
Bethell, Nicholas 267
Bethmann Hollweg, Theobald von 132, 133, 135, 138, 141, 142, 145
Birkenhead, Lord 236
Bismarck, Prince Otto 24, 46, 52, 57
  and Austro-German alliance 78–9
  and the balance of power 81, 84–5, 360
  and the Balkans 76
  and the Bosnian revolt 71
  and France 70
  and League of the Three Emperors 70, 78
  and Lord Salisbury 84
  and overseas expansion 89–90
  and public opinion 162, 164

  and Russia 72
  and the Triple Alliance 80
Black Sea, The 69, 75, 76
Blomberg, General Werner von 186
Bloomfield, Lord 36, 45, 47, 48
Blue Books
  America 162
  Great Britain 162, 166
Blum, Léon 187
Boer Wars (1899–1902) 91, 93, 103, 108, 109, 378–9
Bohemia 197, 276
Bolsheviks 147–8, 151, 152–3, 199
  and public opinion 162–3
Bond, B., British Military Policy Between the Two World Wars 312, 313
Bonnet, Georges 189, 190, 193, 195, 253, 258, 259, 267, 273, 274, 282, 294, 297
Bonomi, Ivanoe 333, 339
Boothby, Sir Robert 357
Bosnia 71, 75
Bosnia and Herzegovina, and Austro-Hungarian Empire 61, 74
Boulanger, General Georges Ernest 84
Boxer Rising (1900) 92, 108
Bradshaw, Prof. Sidney 163
Brandenberg, Prof. Erich 163
Brauchitsch, Heinrich von 318
Brest-Litovsk, Treaty of (1918) 148, 154, 155, 156
Briand, Aristide 145, 172
Bright, John 22, 378
Britain, Battle of (1940) 309
British Empire, The, extent 103–4
Bruck, Baron, founder of Trieste 326–7
Bruck, Karl von 360
Brüning, Heinrich 171, 172
Budapest 325
Bulgaria 74, 75, 83
  and Germany, attack by 291
  and Turks, revolt against 71, 72
Bülow, Bernhard Heinrich von 120, 228
Buol, Count Karl 25, 43, 44, 45, 64
Bury, J.P.T. 227
Butler, R.A. 181, 194, 211
Butler, Rohan 161, 177, 198, 201,

202, 203, 208, 213, 218, 225, 230
Documents on British Foreign Policy, 1919–1939
  1919, reviewed 216–17, 227
  Germany, 1920, reviewed 235–6
  1920, reviewed 232–3
  1929–31, reviewed 234
Butterfield, Prof. Herbert 246
Buxton, Roden 223

Cadogan, Sir Alexander 266
Caillaux, Joseph 121, 145, 147, 148
Cambon, Jules 174
Cameron, Julia 358
Canning, George 41, 162
Caporetto, Battle of (1917) 147
Castlereagh, Robert Stewart, Viscount 17, 18, 19
Cavour, Camillo Benso, Conte di 26, 46, 47, 48, 128
Ceadel, Martin, *Pacifism in Britain 1914–1945*, reviewed 378–81
Cecil, Lord Robert 371
Chamberlain, Austen 277
Chamberlain, Joseph 103, 107
  and the Boer Wars 111
  as Colonial Secretary 111
  origins 110
  reputation 111–12
  and W.E. Gladstone 110–11
Chamberlain, Neville
  and appeasement of Hitler 181, 182, 183, 189, 194, 195, 208, 252, 266, 268, 269–70, 294–5, 298–9
  and the Munich crisis 188, 203, 251, 274, 275, 277
Chartists, and the Crimean War 21
Chiang Kai-shek 245
China
  and Britain 90, 108–9, 234
  and Germany 92, 179
  and Russia 90
Churchill, Winston 211, 246, 247, 258, 259, 262, 314
Ciano, Galeazzo 196, 223, 259, 289
Clemenceau, Georges 147, 148, 168, 169, 170, 174, 175, 227
  and Lloyd George 176
Clerk, Sir George 216

Cobden, Richard 22
Cold War, The 306
Cole, C.R. 312
Comintern 156, 286, 287
Committee of Imperial Defence 166, 302
communism 154–6
Compromise,The, Habsburg Monarchy 54, 55
Conrad, Joseph 376
Corbin, Charles 258
Corti, Count Egon 47
Coulondre, Robert 274
Cowley, Lord 24, 28, 29, 32, 35, 36, 42, 46, 47, 48, 49, 50
Crampton, A.A.E. 46
Crankshaw, Edward, *The Fall of the House of Habsburg*, reviewed 128–30
Crimean War 77
  and the balance of power 21, 30
  and the Chartists 21
  and German unification 21–2
  and Italian unification 21–2
  origins 20
  and public opinion 21
Cripps, Sir Stafford 244, 288
Croatia 327
Croats
  and Austro-Hungarian Empire 62
  and Hungarians 62–3
Cromer, Lord 115, 117
Crowe, Sir Eyre 166, 174
Curragh Mutiny (1914) 125
Curzon, Lord 175–6, 177, 199, 200, 216, 232, 235
Cyprus 74, 79
Czechoslovakia
  and America 189
  and democracy 347–8
  and France 253, 354
  and Germany
    annexation by 188, 189–90, 191–4, 250, 269–70
    fear of 353–4
  and Hitler 193–4, 203–4, 277
  and Munich 272–5, 276–80
  party system 348–50
  and Russia 253, 272–5, 354
  and Slovaks 350–53
  and WW II 208–10

post-WW II 347–55
Czechs, in Austro-Hungarian Empire
58

Daladier, Édouard 190, 220, 253,
257, 258, 268, 275, 283, 294
Dalmatia 56
Dalton, Hugh 262
Danzig 175, 214, 222, 293, 294,
295, 296, 308
as a free city 341–2
D'Azeglio, Massimo 39, 44, 47, 48
Delcassé, Théophile 114, 117, 118,
119, 120
Denikin, Anton Ivanovich 175, 199
Dickinson, Lowes 246
Dirksen, Herbert von 194, 266
Disraeli, Benjamin 24
documents
on British foreign policy,
availability 161–7, 247
on Italian foreign policy 312
Documents on German Foreign
Policy 1918–1945
30 Jan. 1933–31 March 1935 312
The Third Reich, First Phase, Jan.
30–Oct. 14, 1933, reviewed
227–9
The Third Reich, First Phase, April
1, 1935–March 4, 1936,
reviewed 237–9
The Spanish Civil War, reviewed
205–7
Sept. 1937–Sept. 1939 312
criticized 180
reviewed 179–84, 185–7
Nov. 1937–Sept. 1938, reviewed
191–7
August 9–Sept. 3, 1939, reviewed
222–4
Sept. 4, 1939–March 18, 1940,
reviewed 211–12
Dollfuss, Engelbert 335
Dreadnought battleship 124–5
Dunant, Henri 375
Dunglass, Lord 263

Eastern Question
and Bulgaria 83
significance 75–6
see also Balkans, The

Eden, Anthony 220, 225, 251, 357
Edward VII, King 116, 117, 125
Egypt 72
and Anglo-French rivalry 80–81,
117, 118
and British foreign policy 82, 105
as British protectorate 81
Eisenlohr, German minister 191–2
Elizabeth of Austria, Empress 129
empires, longevity of 363
Entente Cordiale (1904) 119
Erzberger, Matthias 144–5
Esterhazy, Prince Paul 26, 29, 41, 47,
49, 57, 60, 64
Euan-Smith, Sir Charles 96
Europe, and Morocco 94–7
Europe, Concert of 17, 19, 22, 71,
72, 76, 79, 82

Fashoda Crisis (1898) 91, 97, 107,
114
Feis, Herbert, Between War and
Peace: The Potsdam Conference,
reviewed 321–3
Ferdinand of Coburg, Prince 83
Fez 95
Ficquelmont, Count Karl Ludwig de
62
Fierlinger, Zdeněk 272, 273, 274, 275
Finland, and Russia 286–7
Fisher, John Arbuthnot
life 124
literary style 124
Royal Navy reforms 124–5
Fiume 343
becomes free city 333
Italian claim to 214, 229, 341
Flandin, Pierre 259
foreign policy, documents, availability 161–7, 247, 301–2, 315
The Foreign Policy of the European
Cabinets, 1871–1914 163
France
army, strength of 287
and Austria
armistice 32
war (1859) 23
and Bismarck 70
and Britain 22, 113–20, 169–70,
176–8, 184
and Czechoslovakia 253, 354

and Egypt 80–81, 113, 117, 118
foreign policy, documents 164
and Germany 68, 106, 136, 180
and Morocco 95, 96, 97, 117, 121, 122
and Poland 294
and Prussia 28, 68
Republic proclaimed 68
Revolution (1830) 248
and Russia, alliance 86–7, 106, 114, 258
and Tunis 80
and WW I, discontent 146–7
Francis I, Emperor 53
Francis II, Emperor 63
Francis Joseph I, Emperor 32, 43, 46, 48, 128, 129
and decline of Austro-Hungarian Empire 63, 130
and Emperor Napoleon III 33–4, 35, 40–41, 42, 44, 47, 49, 50
and parliamentary government 57–8
Franco, Francisco and Hitler 196
Franco-Prussian War (1870–71) 68–70, 104, 162
Frank, K.H. 192
Frankfurt, Treaty of (1871) 69, 70, 88
Franz Ferdinand of Austria, Archduke 129
assassination 132
free cities 341
French Revolution, The 18
and war 374
Friedjung, Heinrich 47, 66
The Age of Imperialism 52
and anti-Serbo-Croat forged documents 63–4
Austria from 1848 to 1860 52
and Austrian Social Democratic party 55, 56
Benedek's Literary Remains 52
The Crimean War and Austrian Policy 52
The Emperor Charles IV 52
Historical Essays 52, 65
political activities 54–5
The Struggle for Supremacy in Germany 1859–1866 51, 52–3, 56–7, 59–60, 64, 67

Fritsch, Werner von 186, 187

Gafencu, Gregoire, Derniers Jours de l'Europe, reviewed 281–3
Galicia 56, 151, 200, 283
Gamelin, Maurice Gustave 275, 294
Genoud, F., The Testament of Adolf Hitler 313
George V, King 125, 228
George VI, King 269
Georgia 176
Germans, character 357–9
Germany
Alsace and Lorraine, demand for 68
and Austria
alliance 78–9
annexation of 181–3, 187
and Belgian Congo 121
and Belgium, attack on 287
and Britain 106–7, 109, 115–16
appeasement by 179–84, 261–4, 295–8, 307–8
and Bulgaria, attack on 291
and China 92, 179
and Czechoslovakia, annexation of 188, 189–90, 191–4, 250, 269–70
foreign policy, documents 163, 164, 179–84, 185–7
and France 68, 106, 136, 180
and Japan 179
and League of Nations 180, 221, 227, 228
and Morocco 95, 120, 163
naval plans 106
and Poland, invasion of 284, 293–4, 298
and Romania 266–7, 289
and Russia 135–6, 154, 163, 180, 223–4, 284–90
attack on 290–92, 318–19
and Spanish Civil War 205–6
unification 52–3
and the Vatican 180, 185
WW I
economy 171–2
mobilization 135
peace overtures 144–5
and Yugoslavia, attack on 291
Gibraltar 117, 118

Gilbert, Martin, *The Appeasers,*
reviewed 261–4
Gladstone, William Ewart 30, 72, 76
and Concert of Europe 79
and the Franco-Prussian War 69
and Joseph Chamberlain 110–11
Gleason, S.E. 243, 245, 246
Glorious Revolution, The (1688) 104
Goebbels, Paul 172
Goering, Hermann 172, 179, 212,
296, 297, 317, 318
gold standard, and Great Britain 171
Goltz, Baron Kolmar von der 198
Gooch, G.P. 47, 165, 246, 247
*British Documents on the Origin
of the War 1898–1914* 312
Gorchakov, Prince 28, 46, 71, 72, 73
Gott, Richard 261
Gottwald, Klement 274, 349, 354
Grandi, Dino 173
Granville, Lord 30, 37, 38, 39, 41,
44, 47, 48, 49
Great Britain
and balance of power 104, 109
Blue Books 162
and capitalism 102–3
and China 90, 108–9, 234
and Egypt 81, 82, 105, 113
foreign policy, documents 163–4
and France 22, 113–20, 169–70,
176–7, 177–8, 184
and Germany 106–7, 109, 115–16
appeasement 179–84, 261–4,
295–8, 307–8
and the gold standard 171
and India 103–4
industry 102
isolation in late 19th century 87,
89
and Japan 109
and Morocco 115, 116
Royal Navy, supremacy 104, 105–
6, 107, 108
and Russia 71, 82–3, 90–91, 120,
198–201, 230–31
and the Sudan 91
and WW II, military preparation
305–6
Great Exhibition (1851) 102
Green, Sir William Kirby 96
Greenwich, time measurement 101

Greenwood, Arthur 267, 299
Grey, Sir Edward 132, 135, 136–7,
166

Habsburg monarchy, fall 128–30
Hácha, Emil 281, 297
Hague Court, creation 89
Halder, Franz, *Hitler als Feldherr,*
reviewed 317–20
Halifax, Lord 266
and appeasement of Hitler 181,
182, 183, 189, 190, 194, 203,
204, 211, 224, 252–3, 266,
296, 299
Hancock, Sir Keith 315
Hankey, Sir Maurice 213
Hassell, Ulrich von 227, 228
Hay, Sir John Drummond 96
Henderson, Arthur 173
Henderson, Sir Nevile 181, 188, 189,
193, 195, 196, 208, 209, 223,
255, 295, 296–7
criticism of 257
Henlein, Konrad 192, 194
Heron, George 149
Hillgruber, A., *Hitlers Strategie,
Politik und Kriegsführung 1940–
1941* 313
Hindenburg Line 141
Hinsley, F.H. 68
Hiroshima 377
Hitler, Adolf
and Czechoslovakia 193–4, 203–4,
277
and Franco 196
as military leader 317–20
and Mussolini 196, 204, 219, 224
Rhineland, reoccupation of 237–9
rise to power 218–19, 227–8
and Russia 211–12, 228
and Stalin 284, 285
Hoare, R.H. 199
Hoare, Sir Samuel 224, 252, 266
Hoare–Laval Treaty (1935) 238
Hobbes, Thomas 17, 362
Hodza, Milan 192, 253
Hoggan, D.L., *Der erzwungene Krieg*
313
Holy Alliance (1815) 70, 364–5
Hoover, President Herbert 172
Hopkins, Harry 321

Horthy, Miklós 216, 335, 343
Hossbach Memorandum (1937) 186, 313
Humbert I, King 80
Hungarians, and Croats 62–3
Hungary
  and Italian independence 33
  post-WW I 169

Imredy, Béla 196
India, and Britain 103–4
Inskip, Sir Thomas 181
Irving, D., *Hitler's War* 313
Italy
  and Abyssinia 336
  claim to Fiume 214
  independence, and Hungary 33
  and Libya 122, 336
  and Morocco 95
  and South Slavs 333–4
  and South Tyrol and Trieste 143, 329, 331–2
  and Tunis 80
  and the Vatican, occupation of 70

James I, King 161
Jameson Raid (1895–96) 88, 112
Japan
  and Britain 109
  and Germany 179
  and Manchuria 234
  and Russia 119
Jones, Tom 232
Joseph II, Emperor 59, 63
Joyce, James, and Trieste 328

Kagonovich, Lazar 272
Kamenev, Lev Borisovich 233
Kaplan, Dora 155
Kapp Putsch (1920) 229, 235
Karl, Emperor of Austria-Hungary 143
Keitel, Wilhelm 295
Kempen, Police Minister, Austria 41, 45
Kennan, George 246
Kennedy, Joseph 244, 294, 297
Kerensky, Aleksandr 153
Keynes, John Maynard 213, 366
Kiao-Chow seizure (1897) 90
Kiderlen-Wächter, Alfred von 121

Kirkpatrick, Sir I. 193
Kissinger, Prof. Henry 18
Kitchener, Lord 107
Kolchak, Aleksandr 175
Koller, Baron Alexander de 36, 48
Königgrätz, Battle of (1866) 41
Kosice 348
Kossuth, Lajos 21, 33
Krassin, L.B. 233
Kremsier Constitution (1849) 53
Krofta, Kamil 273
Kruger, President Paul 88
Krupps, arms sales to Morocco 96
Krupskaya 151
Kühlmann, Richard von 145, 146, 149
Kun, Béla 169

La Gorce, Pierre de 32, 47
Labour Party, and WW II 262
Laffan, R.G.D., *Survey of International Affairs, 1938*, reviewed 255
Lambert, Margaret 203, 208, 234
Langer, W.L., *The Challenge to Isolation 1937–1940* 243, 245, 246
Lansdowne, Lord 117, 148
Laval, Pierre 171
law, and war 373–81
Laxenburg Manifesto (1859) 43
League of Nations 174, 365
  and Germany 180, 221, 227, 228
League of the Three Emperors 70, 71, 78, 83, 84, 88
  purpose 79–80
Lenin, V.I. 147
  death 158
  in Finland 153
  health 157
  home life 155
  Imperialism, The Highest Stage of Capitalism 151
  in power 154–8
  return to Russia 152
  The State and Revolution 153
  in Switzerland 151–2
Libya, and Italy 122, 336
Linz programme 55–6, 65
Lipski, Jozef 295, 297
List, Friedrich 360

Lithuania 285
Litvinov, Maksim 197, 200, 230, 272, 273, 274
Lloyd George, David 137, 141, 143, 146, 148, 168, 169, 170, 174, 175
  and Alexandre Millerand 229
  and Georges Clemenceau 176
  and Paris Peace Conference 213–14
  and Poland 200–201
  post-WW I activities 232–3
Loftus, Lord 25, 26, 31, 45, 47, 48, 50
Lombardy 28, 29, 34, 40, 41, 42, 43, 49, 62
London, Conference of (1920) 229
London, Treaty of (1913) 332
Londonderry, Lord 187
Loubet, President Émile François 116–17
Louis Philippe, King 249
Louis, W.R., *The Origins of the Second World War: A.J.P. Taylor and his Critics* 312
Ludendorff, General Erich 140, 141, 149, 150
Lukacs, J., *The Last European War, September 1939–December 1941* 313
Lvov (Lviv) 330, 338, 345

MacDonald, Ramsay 171, 173, 202
  and Mussolini 219
Mackinder, Sir H. 199
Macmillan, Harold 369
Magenta, Battle of (1859) 25, 44
Maginot Line 269, 275, 277
Makhno, Nestor 177
Malmesbury, third earl of 24, 31, 33, 37, 40, 44, 45, 47, 48, 49
Malta 74
Manchuria 246
  and Japan 234
Mann, Heinrich, *Der Untertan* 358
Mannesman Brothers company 122
Mantoux, Prof. Paul 213
Marchand, J.B. 91
Marder, Arthur 124, 305–6
  Old Friends, New Enemies 313
Maria Theresa, Empress 63
Martens, J.B. de 375–6

Martin, Sir T. 48
Marx, Karl 70, 122
Mary, Queen 228
Masaryk, Tomas 360
Meeting of the Princes, Frankfurt (1863) 54
Memel 175
Mensdorff, Count Alexander von 64, 144
Metropolitan-Vickers affair 230–31
Metternich, Prince Klemens 17, 18, 19, 24, 25, 60, 89
  and German unification 53
Metternich, Richard 47
Meyer, Henry Cord, *Mitteleuropa in German Thought and Action, 1815–1945*, reviewed 360–61
Michaelis, George 145
Michel, H., *La Seconde Guerre Mondiale* 313
Millerand, Alexandre 227
  and Lloyd George 228
Milner, Lord 149
Mittel-Europa, concept 64–5
Modena 34
Molotov, V.M. 223, 224, 272, 284, 287, 288, 289, 290, 292
Moltke, Helmuth von 57, 135
Montebello, French ambassador to Russia 28, 46
Moore, George 113
Morison, Stanley 301
Morocco
  and Britain 115, 116, 118
  diplomatic activity 96, 108
  and Europe 94–7
  and France 95, 96, 97, 115, 117, 118, 121, 122
  and Germany 95, 120, 163
  and Italy 95
  and Spain 95, 97, 117, 118
  trade 95
Morocco City 95
Mosul 229
Moustier, Marquis Lionel de 26, 32, 35, 36, 45, 48
Mulai Hassan 95, 96
Munich crisis (1938) 188–90, 203–4, 251–4, 255, 268–71
  and Czechoslovakia 272–5, 276–80

and Neville Chamberlain 188, 203,
    251, 274, 275, 277
and Russia 279–80
Murray, Gilbert 262
Mussolini, Benito 173, 184
    Abyssinia, occupation 238–9
    and Hitler 196, 204, 219, 224
    and Ramsay MacDonald 219

Nagasaki 377
Namier, Sir Lewis 51, 189, 207, 223,
    246, 251, 262
    Diplomatic Prelude 1938–9 256–8
    Europe in Decay: A Study in
        Disintegration, 1936–40 259–
        60
Napoleon I, Emperor 69
Napoleon III, Emperor 20, 22, 29,
    32–3, 37, 43, 46, 68, 113
    and Emperor Francis Joseph I 33–
        4, 35, 40–41, 42, 44, 47, 49,
        50
Napoleon, Prince 42, 46
Nazi Party, rise 172
Nazi–Soviet Pact 223–4, 284–92, 293
Neurath, Constantin von 179, 180,
    182, 183, 185, 186, 187, 227
New Documents on the History of
    Munich (Czech Government)
    272
New Guinea 106
Newman, Simon 306
    March 1939: The British Guaran-
        tee to Poland 313
Nice 22
Nicholas I, Tsar 20, 21, 89, 378
Nicholas II, Tsar 126, 134, 140
    abdication 143
Nicholson, Sir Arthur 166
Nicolson, Harold 251
Nigra, Costantino 32, 46, 47
Nivelle, General Robert 146
Nuremberg Trials 222

Omdurman, Battle of (1898) 91, 107
organizations, international 365
Ottoman Empire 20

pacifism, and war 379–80
Paderewski, Ignace Jan 200
Palmerston, Lord 25, 27, 29–30, 31–

2, 36, 37, 38, 39, 44, 47, 48,
    162, 167
and Belgium 249
Papen, Franz von 181, 183
Paris, Congress of (1856) 22, 69, 375
Paris Peace Conference (1919) 213
Parsons, F.V., The Origins of the
    Morocco Question 1880–1900
    94, 97
Peace Pledge Union 380
Pendjeh 82, 83
Persigny, Duc de 29, 30, 31, 34, 35,
    37, 39, 40, 45, 46, 47, 48, 49
Pétain, General Henri-Philippe 147
Petrograd 152, 175
Phipps, Sir Eric 218, 255
Phoney War, The 211–12
Pilsudski, Jósef Klemens 201
Plevna (Pleven), Battle of (1877) 73
Poincaré, President Raymond 143,
    147
Poland
    claims to Ukraine 200–201, 204
    and France 294
    and Germany, invasion by 284,
        293–4, 298
    and Russia 284–5
    and WW I 140
    post-WW I 176, 228, 233
    pre-WW II 283
    and WW II 208–10, 211, 222, 223,
        256–7, 258, 278
Port Arthur 90, 91, 119
Posen (Posnán) 90, 91, 119, 335, 336
Potemkin, Vladimir 197, 272, 274
Potsdam Conference (1945) 321–3
Pribram, Alfred F. 51, 52
Prussia
    and Austria 23–4, 25–6, 54
    and France 28
    and Russia 28
public opinion
    and Bismarck 162
    and the Bolsheviks 162–3
    and foreign policy 161–4
    problems of discovering 307÷8

Quadrilateral, The 40, 42

Rapallo, Treaty of (1920) 333, 335,
    341, 345

Rechberg, Johann Bernard von 25, 26, 33, 34, 37, 41, 43, 44, 45, 46, 47, 48, 49, 57, 59, 64
Rechenberg, Baron von 180
Red Cross, formation 375
Redlich, Prof. Joseph 45, 49, 50, 61, 130
Reichstadt (Zakupy) 71
Reinsurance Treaty (1887) 84–5
Ribbentrop, Joachim von 179, 181, 182, 183, 184, 186, 187, 192, 193, 194, 195, 212, 222, 223, 258, 283, 284, 285, 289, 293, 295, 296, 297
Ribot, Alexandre 143
Riga 325
  Treaty of (1921) 156, 345
Rights of Man, Declaration of (1789) 113
Roberts, J.M. 110, 131, 139
Romania 22, 73
  and Germany 266–7, 289
  pre-WW II 281–3
Roosevelt, Franklin D. 269, 295, 363–4
  foreign policy 243–4, 246
Roosevelt, Theodore 63
Rothermere, Lord 228
Rousseau, Jean Jacques 373
Rudolf of Austria, Crown Prince 129
Runciman, Lord 194, 255, 274
Russell, Lord John 27, 29, 30–31, 34, 36, 37, 38, 39, 41, 43, 45, 46, 47, 48, 50
Russia
  and Afghanistan 82–3
  and Austria-Hungary 68, 70, 73, 133, 138
  and the Baltic States 198–9, 282–3, 286, 288
  and Britain 71, 82–3, 90–91, 120, 198–201, 230–31
  and China 90
  civil war 156
  Crimean War, influence after 21
  and Czechoslovakia 253, 272–5, 354
  and Finland 286–7
  and France, alliance with 86–7, 106, 114, 258

and Germany 135–6, 154, 163, 180, 223–4, 284–90
  attack by 290–92, 318–19
  and Hitler 211–12, 228
  and Japan 119
  and Munich 279–80
  and Poland 284–5
  and Prussia 28
  Revolutions (1917) 143, 147, 153–4
  and Serbia 133
  Tsars 126–7
  Turks, war with 21, 73–4
  WW I
    mobilization 134
    peace efforts 144, 146, 147–8
    post-war condition 198–201, 229, 233
  WW II, neutrality 223
  and Yugoslavia 346
Russo-Japanese War (1904–05) 81, 119, 132

Saar, The 213
Salisbury, Lord 74, 76, 79, 84, 87, 102, 111
  approach to foreign policy 95, 166
  and Bismarck 84
  and Egypt 107, 108
Salvemini, Gaetano 337–8
San Stefano, Treaty of (1878) 74
Sardinia 22, 25, 32, 40, 46
Savoy 22
Saxe-Coburg, Duke of 237
Saxony 41
Sazanov, Sergei 132, 133, 134, 135
Schacht, Dr Hjalmar 355
Schleinitz, Alexander von 24, 26, 27, 28, 35, 36, 40, 43, 45, 46, 48, 49, 50
Schleswig 71
Schleswig-Holstein war (1864) 310
Schlieffen, Count von 135, 136
Schmerling, Anton von 54, 60
Schneider-Creusot company 121–2
Schnitzler, Arthur 328
Schönerer, Georg von 52, 55, 58, 60–61
Schuschnigg, Kurt von 183, 187, 335
Schwarzenberg, Prince Felix zu 25, 43, 49, 59

Sebastopol 21
Sedan, Battle of (1870) 68, 69, 70, 81
Serbia
    and Austro-Hungarian Empire 62,
        65, 122, 132-3
    and Russia 133
Seton-Watson, Hugh, *The Decline of
    Imperial Russia*, reviewed 126-7
Sevres, Treaty of (1920) 229
Sforza, Count Carlo 333, 337, 339
Shantung (Shandong) 217
Shaposhnikov, Marshal 288
Shay, R.P., *British Rearmament in the
    Thirties* 313
Sheppard, Canon Dick 380
Siam 114
Silesia 213, 216
Simon, Sir John 190, 203, 220, 225-
    6, 231, 252, 263, 307
Sinope, 'massacre' of 21
Sixte of Bourbon-Parma, Prince 143
Skierniewice 82
Slavs, South 333-4
    in Austro-Hungarian Empire 61-2,
        65
Slovaks, in Czechoslovakia 350-53
Slovenes 324-6, 343
    in Trieste 329-30, 344
Smuts, General Jan Christiaan 144
Snowden, P. 171
Social Democratic party, Austria
    foundation 55
    programme 55-6, 65
socialist parties, and WW I 144-6
Solferino, Battle of (1859) 26, 32, 33,
    35
Somme, Battle of the (1916) 141
Sonnino, Baron Giorgio 143-4
Sorel, Georges, *Diplomatic History
    of the War of 1870* 256
Sorge, Richard 291
Spain
    Civil War, and Germany 205-6
    and Morocco 95, 97, 117, 118
Stalin, Joseph 151, 152, 155, 212,
    244, 272
    and Hitler 284, 285
Stalingrad, Battle of (1942-43) 319
Stephenson, Robert 101
Stimson, Henry L. 171, 172, 322
Strang, William 231

Stresa Conference (1935) 237
Stresemann, Gustav 180, 305
Stuart, Sir Campbell 194
Sudan, and Britain 91
Sudetens 189, 192, 248, 268, 270,
    276
Suez Canal 105, 113
Supreme Council, The 168-70, 174,
    216
Svevo, Italo, and Trieste 328
Sybel, Heinrich von 162

Taaffe, Count Eduard 54, 57
Tangier 95, 96, 97, 120
Tansill, Charles Callan, *Back Door to
    War – Roosevelt's Foreign Policy
    1933-41*, reviewed 245-7
Taylor, A.J.P.
    A.J.P. Taylor, A Personal History
        51, 121, 151
    The Course of German History
        347
    English History, 1914-45 300, 312
    Europe: Grandeur and Decline
        188, 203, 205, 208
    From Napoleon to Stalin 324
    *Germany's First Bid for Colonies
        1884-5* 51
    *The Habsburg Monarchy 1809-
        1918* 51
    *The Habsburg Monarchy 1815-
        1918* 51
    influences on 51
    *The Origins of the Second World
        War* 185, 237, 268, 300, 312
        criticism of 312-13
        update 300-312
    Rumours of Wars 188, 203, 205,
        208
    *The Struggle for Mastery in
        Europe, 1848-1918* 161, 300-
        301, 314
    *War by Time-Table: How the First
        World War Began* 131
Temperley, Harold 165, 247, 312
Tennyson, Alfred 21
Thiers, Adolphe 69, 70
Thimme, Friedrich 163, 164-5, 185
Thorne, C., *Allies of a Kind* 313
Tiso, Josef 281, 351
Tito, Marshal 334

Tocqueville, Alexis de 126
Toynbee, Arnold 127, 255
  A *Study of History* 213
  Survey of International Affairs,
    1939–1946 213, 214, 215
Toynbee, Veronica M. 213
Transcaucasia 175
Transylvania, partition 289
treaties, enforcement of 362–3
Trevor-Roper, Hugh 207, 212, 313
Trieste 214
  creation 326–7
  as cultural centre 328
  as a Free City 340–41, 342, 346
  and Italo Svevo 328
  and Italy
    claimed by 332–3
    influence of 329, 331–2, 345
  and James Joyce 328
  population mix 328–30
  proposals for future 335–45
  Slovene influence 329–30, 344
  trading centre 327–8, 334–5
Tripartite Pact (1940) 289, 290
Triple Alliance (1882) 84, 85, 86,
    105
  purpose 80
Tripoli 118
Trotsky, Leon 148, 153, 154, 155,
    157, 366
Truman, President Harry S. 321
Tunis
  as French protectorate 80
  and Italy 80
Turkey
  post-WW I 229
  reforms 72
  revolt in Balkans 70–72, 122
  Russia, war with 21, 73–4
Tuscany 34
Tyrrell, Lord 172

Ukraine, Polish claims to 200, 204
United Nations Organization 365–6
United Nations Relief and Rehabilita-
    tion Administration (UNRRA)
    214
Utrecht, Treaty of (1713) 119

Vansittart, Sir Robert 219–20, 238,
    263

Vatican, The
  and Germany 180, 185
  occupation by Italy 70
Vattel, Emmerich de 373
Venice 40, 49
Verdun, Battle of (1916) 140
Vermeil, Edmund
  The German Scene, reviewed 356–
    9
  Germany's Three Reichs 357
Versailles, Treaty of (1919) 163, 174
  collapse 218–21
  enforcement problems 235–6
Victor Emmanuel I, King 32
Victoria, Queen 38–9, 48, 101
  Diamond Jubilee 103, 107
Vienna, Congress of (1814–15) 17,
    18–19, 78, 189
Villafranca, Agreement of (1859) 23,
    33, 38, 40, 43
Vilna 283
Viviani, René 136
Voroshilov, Kliment 272, 283

Waldersee, Field Marshall 92
Wales, Prince of 228
Walewski, Alexandre Colonna 28,
    29, 32, 35, 36, 37, 42, 45, 46,
    47, 48, 49
Walpole, Sir Robert 113
war
  categories of 310–12
  and conscientious objectors 379
  and French Revolution, The 374
  and law 373–81
    in 20th century 377–81
    at sea 373–4, 376
  nature of 372–3
  and neutrals 374
  and pacifism 379–80
  probability of 369–70
Ward, John 125
Weizsäcker, Richard von 180, 192,
    193, 194–5, 222
Wellesley, F.A. 49
Wellesley, H.R. 49
Werther, Baron Karl von 27, 45, 46,
    49, 50
Wheeler-Bennett, J.W., *Munich:*
    Prologue to Tragedy, reviewed
    251–4, 255

White Russians 198–200
Wilhelm II, Kaiser 96, 133, 135, 136, 164, 222
William I, Prince Regent of Prussia 26
Wilmot, Chester 246
Wilson, President Woodrow
  and Trieste 333, 336–7
  and WW I 139–40, 141–2, 150
Wilson, Sir Henry 124, 235
Wilson, Sir Horace 181, 194, 195–6, 264, 266
Windischgrätz, Prince Alfred 26, 27, 33, 36, 46, 48
Wood, Sir Kingsley 263
Woodward, E.L.
  Documents on British Foreign Policy, 1919–1939
    criticized 165–7, 170, 177–8, 314–16
    reviewed 161–7
    1919, criticized 177–8
      reviewed 168–70, 174–8, 198–201
    1919–20 312
    1929–1934 230, 312
    1931, reviewed 171–3
    1932–3, reviewed 202
    1933 218
    1933–4, reviewed 225–6
    1938, reviewed 188–90
    1938–9, reviewed 203–4, 213–15

1939, reviewed 208–10
  9 March 1939–Sept. 1939 312
  Great Britain and the German Navy 315–16
World War I
  alliances 136–7
  and Austria-Hungary 143, 144
  mobilization plans 131–6
  peace
    obstacles 142
    overtures 140–41, 144–6
  and Poland 140
  social unrest 142–4, 146–7
  and socialist parties 144–6
World War II
  beginning 256–8
  origins 309–10

Yalta Conference (1945) 263
Yellow Sea 90
Yudenich, General Nikolay 175
Yugoslavia
  creation of 333
  and Germany, attack by 291
  and Russia 346

Zadar (Zara) 337
Zakupy (Reichstadt) 71
Zanzibar 96
Zimmerwald 151
Zinovyev, Grigory 156